"Sandy"

"Bruce"

RAISING THE RUINS

Love
Babe
+

Mary

RAISING THE RUINS

The fight to revive the legacy of
HERBERT W. ARMSTRONG

STEPHEN FLURRY

Distributed by Midpoint Trade Books, Inc., New York, NY

Scriptures in this publication are quoted from the
King James Version, unless otherwise noted.

ISBN 978-0-9745507-1-8

Library of Congress Control Number: 2006931940

PRINTED IN THE UNITED STATES OF AMERICA

FIRST PRINTING, October 2006, 15,000 copies
SECOND PRINTING, December 2006, 50,000 copies

Jacket design by Joel Hilliker

I dedicate this book to the memory of Herbert W. Armstrong—and to all those who supported his lifelong labor of love.

CONTENTS

PART TWO | OUR CHRISTIAN DUTY

FOREWORD

"Facts are stubborn things; and whatever may be our wishes, our inclinations, or the dictums of our passions, they cannot alter the state of facts and evidence."

U.S. PRESIDENT JOHN ADAMS
December 1770

MILLIONS of people around the world are familiar with the expansive humanitarian and evangelistic work of Herbert W. Armstrong, even though he died more than 20 years ago.

Tens of thousands—mostly people affiliated with the Worldwide Church of God, which Mr. Armstrong founded—are aware of what happened to that organization after he died, when Joseph W. Tkach rejected his predecessor's teachings, deserted his worldwide mission and reduced the church to a small, mainstream Christian denomination with practically no work.

Very few, however, know what really happened behind the scenes during the Tkach transformation. *And there is a scandalous reason for that.*

Of course, no one in the church would have suspected the new pastor general of any maliciousness. The reality of the betrayal and how it came about was so stunning that most members of the Worldwide Church of God refused to believe it was even happening.

But the *real reason* most people are so fuzzy on what happened was the sinister fact that the new administration CONCEALED its intentions from church members *for as long as possible.*

As Joseph Tkach, with the prodding of his staff, set about the business of converting the church and transforming the work that Herbert W. Armstrong had entrusted to him, these men spun an unthinkably elaborate and increasingly convoluted web of deceit. Events detailed in the first half of this book in particular will have a sickening ring of familiarity to anyone who experienced these events with their eyes half open. Under cover of "Changes? What changes?" the new leadership systematically dismantled the church's body of beliefs plank by plank. They destroyed doctrines and deceitfully forced new ones onto unwitting and unwilling members. They changed the church's commission and gutted its faith. They demoted, deported and replaced the old guard. Those who continued to believe and live the way they always had, the new leaders lied to, abused, intimidated, or—as in the case of my father—excommunicated. They shattered thousands of lives.

And in the process, they presided over the WORST SPIRITUAL SHIP-WRECK SINCE THE FIRST-CENTURY CHURCH SPLINTERED ON THE ROCKS OF APOSTASY.

But the spiritual Head of the church didn't go down with that ship. Beginning in 1989, the same God who raised up His church under Mr. Armstrong went to work raising the ruins. By 1997, the scattered remains of those who held to their original faith had grown in number to support an exciting new phase of God's work: reprinting and sending Mr. Armstrong's literature—particularly his masterwork, *Mystery of the Ages*—to the largest audience possible.

Immediately, the same leadership that cut down Mr. Armstrong came gunning for this resurrected work, promising to bury the facts again, saying it was their "Christian duty to keep this book out of print."[1]

A grueling, life-and-death, six-year copyright battle ensued in which the Worldwide Church of God and the Philadelphia Church of God went head to head over the beliefs outlined in *Mystery of the Ages.* The history of that amazing case and its wondrous outcome shines a stark light on what really happened inside the Worldwide Church of God.

Relying on a wealth of official wcg documents and depositions submitted in federal courts, this book reveals the truth behind the shipwreck of the Worldwide Church of God. Wcg officials *pleaded* in court for many of these documents to be kept confidential and ultimately destroyed after the litigation ended. Why? Because, as their former in-house attorney contended in a declaration at the conclusion of the case, "such documents constitute the private, confidential and internal discussion of underlying religious decisions regarding the changes in church doctrine," as well as "the discussion and decisions regarding the publication or non-publication of church doctrine."[2]

After years of obscuring their actions, denying their motivations and covering their tracks, that, as it turns out, was their final, desperate attempt to bury the facts about how they went about transforming the church. In this book, we exhume those facts and expose them to the furious light of day, as they should have been all along, for your scrutiny.

PART ONE
BETRAYAL

ONE
ABSOLUTE POWER

"Ironically, the same authoritarian governmental structure that created the heretical environment in the first place was necessary to correct it."

— MICHAEL FEAZELL
The Liberation of the Worldwide Church of God

THE Worldwide Church of God has not been transformed by truth over the past 20 years, as Joseph Tkach Jr. suggested in his 1997 book. The church has been transformed—no doubt about that. But *not* by truth. Rather, it was one of the most deceitful, treacherous and abusive transformations in the history of religion.

To understand the magnitude of the spiritual earthquake that has rocked this church, consider what it looked like before.

When Herbert W. Armstrong died on January 16, 1986, he left behind a church with 725 congregations in 57 countries[1] around the globe and a powerful work going out to the world. It had a weekly worldwide attendance of 120,000 people,[2] and another 210,000 outside the church donated money regularly.[3] Serving these many members, prospective members and contributors were more than 1,200 ministers worldwide.[4]

The church's annual revenue was $163.7 million,[5] a budget bigger than Jerry Falwell's and Billy Graham's organizations *combined.*[6] Religious writer Richard N. Ostling wrote a story for

Time just weeks after Mr. Armstrong died in which he analyzed the growing popularity of televangelists during the mid-1980s. NONE of the preachers spotlighted, however—not Jimmy Swaggart, Oral Roberts, Jim Bakker, Jerry Falwell or Robert Schuller—generated as much revenue as Herbert W. Armstrong.[7]

At the top of Ostling's list of televangelists was Jimmy Swaggart's weekly TV show, which could be viewed in 197 markets as of early 1986. It was followed by Oral Roberts, airing in 192. Jerry Falwell could be seen in 172 markets, while Schuller's "Hour of Power" aired in 169 cities. These programs were all dwarfed by Herbert W. Armstrong's *World Tomorrow,* which could be seen on 382 television stations—far more markets than *any other religious program in America*[8]—as well as 36 radio outlets around the world.[9]

HERBERT W. ARMSTRONG WAS ONE OF THE BEST-KNOWN, MOST PROMINENT RELIGIOUS LEADERS IN THE 20TH CENTURY. In fact, when you consider how tiny his work was at the beginning, in 1933, and how its far-reaching influence encompassed the Earth by the time of his death in 1986, one could justifiably argue that Herbert W. Armstrong was the most significant theologian *in American history.*

By 1985, Mr. Armstrong's flagship magazine, the *Plain Truth,* was being produced in seven languages and worldwide circulation had peaked at 8.4 million.[10] *Time* magazine's circulation that year was 5.9 million.[11] With world population then at 4.9 billion, that meant 1 out of every 583 human beings on Earth received the *Plain Truth.* In the United States, the ratio was even better than that—1 in 48;[12] in Canada it was 1 in 27.

Besides the *Plain Truth,* a newsmagazine that concentrated on current events and the fulfillment of Bible prophecy, Mr. Armstrong also produced the *Good News,* a monthly Christian living magazine. Its circulation was 828,000 when Mr. Armstrong died.[13] That means the circulation of Mr. Armstrong's two most popular magazines, when combined, actually exceeded the *combined* circulations of America's most popular newsmagazines in 1985—*Time* and *Newsweek.*[14]

For teenagers, Mr. Armstrong offered *Youth '85,* distributed into 138 countries and territories just before Mr. Armstrong died.

It had a circulation of 230,000.[15] For those interested in studying the Bible in depth, there was the 32-lesson *Ambassador College Bible Correspondence Course.* Over the course of 30 years, between 1954 and 1984, more than 2 million people enrolled in the course.[16] By the time Mr. Armstrong died, the course had been produced in seven languages and was attracting more than 200,000 applicants for enrollment each year.[17] In 1985, the church distributed more than 1 million lessons.[18]

Then there were the many books and booklets—more than 40 million of which had been distributed over the course of Mr. Armstrong's 50-year ministry.[19] The most requested book was *The United States and Britain in Prophecy*—mailed to 6 million people. The most popular booklet was *The Seven Laws of Success*, requested by 3 million.[20]

Between 1980 and 1984, the church distributed 361.6 million books, booklets, magazines, newspapers, lessons and letters. According to the *Pastor General's Report,* "This huge amount of literature would fill to capacity a train 6½ miles long with 624 boxcars ...."[21]

Add to those boxcars the record numbers from 1985, which was, in the words of the WCG's mail processing director, "the greatest time of harvest that the work has experienced in this age. Records were established by wide margins in nearly every category of mail and phone calls."[22] That year, the church answered 1.1 million phone calls, received 6.7 million pieces of mail and added 2.1 million new names to its database. The church responded to this flood of requests by distributing 85.9 million publications, which represented a 15.8 percent increase over 1984.[23]

And of the millions of requests back in 1985, one title came from the lips of new contacts, subscribers and church members more than any other: *Mystery of the Ages.* Written during the last year of his life, Mr. Armstrong considered it the "best work of [his] 93 years ...."[24] From September of 1985, when the book arrived from the printer, to December that same year, 740,000 people wrote or called for *Mystery of the Ages,* making it by far the fastest-moving publication the church had ever produced.[25]

All this is what Mr. Armstrong bequeathed to his successor.

THE BETRAYAL

Now fast forward 20 years. Membership ranks in the WCG have dwindled by 70 percent. (As of 1997, Mr. Tkach Jr. said the church had lost about 70,000 members.[26] It has undoubtedly lost many more since then.) The income has plummeted by about 95 percent. The *World Tomorrow* program vanished from the airwaves in 1994. Ambassador College, providing liberal arts training to some 15,000 students over five decades, is now defunct: The Pasadena, California, campus closed its doors in 1990; its sister campus in Big Sandy, Texas, followed suit in 1997. The *Good News* was discontinued in 1990, while the *Plain Truth* barely survives with a few thousand paying subscribers. This is a colossal disaster by any business standard.

Then there is *Mystery of the Ages:* Tkachism took over in 1986 and the book was gone by early 1988, even though more than 1.2 million copies had been distributed—a phenomenal success by any measure.

All the unique doctrines of the Worldwide Church of God have been changed. All of Mr. Armstrong's literature has been retired. All the operations he established have been either drastically downsized or phased out altogether. Most ministers and members have either fled or been excommunicated for resisting change.

And through it all, a tight-knit band of Tkach loyalists weathered the spiritual storm and the devastation left in its wake, all the while amassing a small fortune by selling off all the goods and property Mr. Armstrong once used for God's work.

Today, in the WCG, THERE IS NO WORK—just truckloads of money brought in from the fire sale. They have sold off nearly everything that had any monetary value—summer campsites, fall festival sites, furniture, fine art, business equipment, books—everything. They even auctioned off personal gifts that world leaders had given to Mr. Armstrong. In 2000, they sold the Big Sandy campus for $8.5 million.[27] In 2004, they offloaded the fire sale's biggest prize: their headquarters property in Pasadena, including the world-renowned Ambassador Auditorium. Church officials were ultra-secretive about the final sum they collected for their crown jewels, but it was probably in the neighborhood of $60 to $70 million.

Whatever the final price, it was enough to make Bernie Schnippert positively giddy. "We are in a very good position financially," the church's director of finance told the *Pasadena Star-News* in May of 2004. According to Schnippert, the church now had enough to meet the church's financial obligations and then some.[28]

"Administrative Nightmare"

In *Transformed by Truth*, Joseph Tkach Jr. is quite critical of Mr. Armstrong's governmental structure. "It is said that power corrupts, and absolute power corrupts absolutely," he wrote. "Mr. Armstrong may have never wielded absolute power in our church, but by the same token, there weren't many who would challenge him on an issue. No doubt that is one reason why he earned a reputation 'on the outside' as a theological despot."[29]

Later, he wrote that Mr. Armstrong "was most definitely and absolutely in charge of our church. … He was the founder, and he came on the scene as this transcendental figure whom most of our members saw as having all authority and power …."[30]

In another book, written by Tkach Jr.'s right-hand man, J. Michael Feazell said Mr. Armstrong "seemed oblivious to the administrative nightmare his one-man-show style of leadership created."[31]

I can't figure out how a worldwide work that helped millions of lives—through the airwaves, with free literature, international humanitarian projects, a famous concert series, youth programs, two colleges and a high school—could ever be characterized as nightmarish, yet that is the way WCG officials today represent that history. In listening to them, you get the impression they had NO CHOICE but to remain in this church, as if Mr. Armstrong handcuffed them to the chairs at church services.

"How could the church have lied to me all these years?" Feazell asked in his book. It's one thing to disagree with what Mr. Armstrong believed and taught—a lot of people did—but to say the church *lied?* "I felt taken advantage of," Feazell continued, "spiritually and emotionally RAPED." (Emphasis added throughout book.)

Raped? Because he chose to remain in a church that he could have walked away from at any time? He's comparing his upbringing in the WCG to a woman being *forcibly* raped by a sexual pervert? Feazell wrote,

> It seemed as though my life had been robbed from me. I could have gone to a state college and had a real career and maybe even been a real Christian. I was angry. I was confused. I was depressed. And I was disgusted with the seductive assault on the true gospel waged by Herbert Armstrong's "one and only true church."[32]

I'm disgusted too, that he would compare Mr. Armstrong's *religion* to the despicable deeds of a rapist.

ONE LONG "PROCESS"

When Tkach, Feazell and their associates grabbed hold of the reins from a tyrannical despot who forced his subjects to submit, one wonders why the system of government Mr. Armstrong set up in the church wasn't the first doctrine they changed.

Feazell insists that right after Mr. Armstrong died, one of Tkach Sr.'s "first goals was to dismantle the authoritarian approach to government in the church ...."[33] Yet, according to Feazell, one of Tkach Sr.'s first courses of action was to tone down authoritative language in a *speech club manual*—not exactly earth-shaking in its magnitude.

Later in his book, Feazell admitted that when Tkach Sr. died in 1995, he "delegated the same unchecked authority to his son, Joseph Tkach Jr., making him the third pastor general of the church."[34] Think about that—even though one of his "first goals" as pastor general was to supposedly "dismantle" the church's authoritarian government, Joseph Tkach Sr. died with the SAME "unchecked authority" he had inherited from Mr. Armstrong nearly 10 years earlier. And as Feazell noted, the father passed those same powers down to his son, who, at 43 years of age, became SUPREME HEAD of the Worldwide Church of God in 1995.

"The younger Tkach," however, "immediately adopted, voluntarily, a consensual style of leadership and began to act only with approval from the church board of directors," Feazell wrote.[35] But did he make any permanent REVISIONS to the powers of pastor general? According to Feazell, the younger Tkach "began the process" of revising the church bylaws in 1996. Yet, when asked in July of 2002—six years later, during a court deposition—if Tkach Jr. had the same absolute power he inherited in 1995, Feazell said that "may well be true."[36] That admission was six years after the younger Tkach "began the process" of revising the bylaws—a full *16 years* after his father set out to "dismantle the authoritarian approach to government in the church."

REAL TRUTH EMERGES

Why did it take these men *so long* to make this change? For one, Feazell wrote, the decision to finally *begin* the process in 1996 "was made easier by the fact that rigid doctrinal opposition in the administration no longer existed."[37]

WHAT A SHOCKING AND SHAMEFUL REVELATION.

Writing as Tkach Jr.'s right-hand man, Feazell admitted that one reason Tkachism was so slow to relax the church's rigid stance on absolute power was the STRONG OPPOSITION *within the church* against doctrinal reform! It was only after that opposition was REMOVED that the Tkaches could then finally consider the prospect of relinquishing their total control.

Tkach Jr. said essentially the same thing in his book. Writing in 1997, he acknowledged that the church was even then working to change the way its government operated. "We do not believe that one form of church government is more biblical than another," Mr. Tkach wrote, "and are taking steps to decentralize our ecclesiastical structure."[38]

Later in the book he wrote, "There is no question that [Mr. Armstrong's] administrative and organizational structures allowed unbiblical teaching to be believed and perpetuated." So he blames Mr. Armstrong's authority as the reason why "unbiblical" teachings were believed and perpetuated. Tkach then wrote, "In His mercy God has *changed our doctrines first,* and we are NOW working to change our governmental structure and polity."[39]

In other words, once the changes had been made and the opposition removed, it was time to consider restructuring the government.

But how can he condemn the hierarchical government Mr. Armstrong supposedly employed to perpetuate his beliefs and, in the very same paragraph, consider that SAME hierarchical form to be divinely *inspired* because it was used to dismantle everything Mr. Armstrong stood for? Why is Mr. Armstrong's approach likened to rape, whereas Tkach's is a sign of God's love and mercy?

BECAUSE THAT'S WHAT JOSEPH TKACH SAYS—THAT'S WHY. *He just knows.* Never mind Mr. Armstrong's legacy—that he left behind a unified, financially solvent church with a committed membership devoted to supporting a worldwide work. Never mind Tkachism's legacy of destruction—of excommunicating people by the thousands; dividing families; destroying marriages; closing colleges, youth programs and foundations; and wasting away hundreds of millions of dollars.

Never mind all that—*just believe what Tkach says.*

As members in the church taken hostage by Tkachism, *that* was our ONLY CHOICE, or else we were FORCED out.

I repeat: WE WERE FORCED OUT! It was *Tkachism,* certainly not Mr. Armstrong, that FORCED its will on the members of the Worldwide Church of God.

LEGACY OF ABUSE

According to a document produced in 2002, Feazell said that Mr. Armstrong "had complete authority doctrinally and administratively. Disloyalty among ministers was dealt with by firing and expulsion from the church fellowship."[40] The exact same thing can be said about the Tkaches, as Feazell later admitted in a court deposition: "Any minister of any church is required ... to teach what the church's doctrines are ...."[41] And if someone "teaches contrary to church doctrine [in the WCG], then they are subject to being disfellowshiped."[42] And many were. *How many* is an open question, but it isn't going far out on a limb to suggest that the Tkaches were responsible for forcing more people out than Mr. Armstrong ever was—*by far*. According to Feazell, since the Tkaches took over, more than half of the church's membership and ministry has either left or been shown the door.[43]

Leaving aside the numbers, keep in mind the big picture. Think about the *way* Tkachism preserved loyalty to its administration. Under Mr. Armstrong, at least members and ministers had the benefit of knowing what they were getting into. A prospective member, for instance, could have seen Mr. Armstrong on television, requested literature and then arranged for a visit with a WCG minister. If he chose to, that individual could then study for baptism and finally become a member of the church. All along, the member would have known exactly what he was signing up for.

The same would have been true for WCG ministers under Mr. Armstrong. Most were probably trained at the school Mr. Armstrong established to support the work of the church—Ambassador College. All of them had a thorough understanding of the church's doctrines. If a minister, over time, decided he didn't agree with Mr. Armstrong's teachings and started causing division, he would leave or be disfellowshiped. As Feazell acknowledged, *any* minister of *any* church should be required to teach his church's doctrines. But again, at least that minister knew what he was getting into from the beginning. Mr. Armstrong was the founder—what he taught is what the church believed. If the minister once agreed with Mr. Armstrong's teachings and subsequently changed, why stay in Mr. Armstrong's church? How is it forcing your will on that individual to tell him, *if you don't preach the doctrines of this church, you don't belong here?*

With Tkachism, however, the element of FORCE was clearly at play. At the point of Mr. Armstrong's death, there were 120,000 people in the Worldwide Church of God who, to some degree or another, agreed with Herbert W. Armstrong's teachings. But at the very top of that church's governmental pyramid, surrounding Tkach Sr. was a band of men who never agreed with those teachings but somehow remained in the church. And after the founder died, these men, with Tkach's blessing, determined to change the very *core beliefs* of a church that had existed for over 50 years.

And since these changes were made FROM THE TOP DOWN, by men with unchecked authority, ministers and members alike were left with only one option: They had to abandon the fundamental truths they had proven and believed and taught *for years* while inside the Worldwide Church of God and accept Tkach's new teachings—or they were FORCED out by excommunication.

In my mind, *that* is using authority forcefully and abusively.

POWERLESS

Feazell explained in his book, "Ironically, the same authoritarian governmental structure that created the heretical environment in the first place *was necessary to correct it.*" They were justified in using absolute power, Feazell says. "Tkach would not have been able to implement the massive doctrinal transformation that characterized the later years of his administration without the unfettered hierarchical authority delegated to him by Armstrong."[44]

Realize just how stunningly blunt this admission really is. He knows—he's ADMITTING—that without TOTAL POWER, their transformation would have never happened! The church membership simply would not have allowed it! But by God's "mercy," they were able to use absolute power to force it down our throats—or else show us the door.

Feazell admitted that "change of such magnitude"—like what happened in the WCG—"virtually demands a hierarchical, authoritative form of church government ...."[45] Furthermore, he wrote that "without such total authority, *the changes in doctrine and direction would never have happened.*"[46] He's not saying *might,* or *perhaps,* or *maybe.* Without absolute power, the Tkach transformation would NEVER have happened.

THAT *is abuse of power.*

Feazell wrote about seven dynamics that accompany an organization in the midst of massive change. Under his sixth point, he wrote, "WCG members were frustrated with their sense of *powerlessness.* Not only did they have NO VOICE in the decision to change their cherished doctrines, but in a church culture that valued being able to understand and explain one's beliefs, they feared that they could not adequately understand the new doctrines."[47] The entire church membership, he says, cherished their old teachings—

couldn't understand the new—and were POWERLESS to prevent the changes from happening.

THAT *is abuse of power.*

Feazell's seventh point is this: "If you take the pressure off, people will revert to their old behavior. People tend to hope the crisis will just go away. If we were to stop teaching the changes right now and invite members to go back to the old doctrines, I am convinced that a certain percentage would do so."[48]

And these men think *Mr. Armstrong* used his office to forcefully pressure people into believing a certain way?

IT'S ALWAYS SOMETHING

At a 2002 deposition, we asked Mr. Tkach Jr. about the much-anticipated changes he had vowed to make in church governance. "Were those changes effected by the end of 1997 or early 1998?" we asked, referring to what he indicated in his book.

To which he responded, "No."

And what had they done in the five years since Tkach released his book? "We've had discussions," Tkach said. "[W]e've produced a manual, and *we won't make those changes until we conclude the sale of our property in Pasadena.*"[49]

Quite a coup: Force new doctrines into the church environment and give the members "no voice" in determining the church's course. Do away with the church's work—the television program, most of the literature, the colleges, the high school, the cultural foundation and so on. Excommunicate "disloyal" ministers. Drive out "divisive" members by the tens of thousands. *Remove all resistance.* Then sell off all the church's assets—including multiple millions of dollars worth of real estate in Southern California and Texas.

THEN, and only then—MAYBE—consider changing the way church government is administered.

NEW FINANCIAL MODEL

In the same *Worldwide News* (the in-house church newspaper) in which the WCG reported the sale of Ambassador Auditorium and the

Pasadena property, the church's controller, Ronald Kelly, announced plans for a new financial model. "As a result of the successful sale of the east campus and the sale of a portion of the west campus," Kelly wrote, "we are now beginning plans to implement our long-desired decentralized financial model."[50]

Keep this in mind: They had abandoned the headquarters-oriented work way back in the mid-1990s. The church's mission, like many other Christian denominations, was to develop congregations of worship at the *local* level. Again, Tkachism had completely done away with the "worldwide work" concept that Mr. Armstrong employed. There was no work, except at the local level. Congregations worked to develop their own identities.

BUT THE MONEY—*by the tens of millions*—kept flowing into the Pasadena "headquarters" even as late as 2004. Think about that. By 1995, virtually everything in the church had been decentralized—all except for the authoritative government and the financial model!

In his article, Mr. Kelly mentioned that the process of decentralizing the financial model had begun in 2003. That year, Pasadena collected $18.6 million in revenue. From that, they returned $1.5 million back to congregations—*a meager 8 percent.*

But as of June 2004—with the Pasadena property pulling in an estimated $70 million for Tkachism—NOW church administrators were finally prepared to decentralize the financial model so that members' tithes and offerings could actually be put toward the work that the church was doing at the local level.

Now, with his absolute, unchecked authority still intact, Joseph Tkach could divvy up the fortune acquired by selling off property paid for by the tithes and offerings of members who had supported the work done by Mr. Armstrong.

Once the spoils are dispersed, maybe then he'll be ready to decentralize the church's *government* model.

Then again, maybe not.

TWO

LEGACIES

"[W]e are acutely aware of the heavy legacy of our past. ... We have much to repent of and apologize for. We were judgmental and self-righteous .... So to all ... who have been casualties of our past sins and mistakes of doctrine—I extend my sincerest heartfelt apologies."

— JOSEPH TKACH JR.
Plain Truth, *March-April 1996*

TKACHISM has portrayed Herbert W. Armstrong's legacy as that of an ignorant, wild-eyed religious fanatic who used his power to abuse people. The problem with that portrayal, besides being false, is that it represents a minority viewpoint, even among members and former members of the Worldwide Church of God. In *Transformed by Truth,* Tkach wrote, "While a *large number* of the letters we have received over the past few years can be characterized as angry and hostile, we always have gotten a *few* precious letters from members encouraging us to maintain our current course."[1] He doesn't give exact figures, but admits that a "large number" of letters they receive are from members who are upset about what Tkachism has done.

Tkach said that church attendance peaked at 150,000 in 1988, two years after Mr. Armstrong died.[2] By the time Tkach wrote his book in 1997, WCG attendance had dwindled to about 58,000—an attrition rate of over 60 percent. Yes, their "remarkable" transformation, as Feazell wrote four years later in his own book, resulted "in the exodus of more than half of the church's members and clergy ...."[3] Today, that mass exodus must surely be nearer to 75 percent. That's not to say that *all* those who left did so in order to uphold Mr. Armstrong's teachings. But neither did they hang around to lend their support to Tkachism.

In 1996, Mr. Tkach Jr. wrote a "Personal" in the *Plain Truth,* where he offered a pathetic apology on behalf of Mr. Armstrong, *who had been dead for 10 years.* "We have much to repent of and apologize for," he said, explaining that the church had been "judgmental and self-righteous." He then rattled off a number of "flawed" doctrines Mr. Armstrong taught. "These teachings and practices are a source of supreme regret. We are painfully mindful of the heartache and suffering that has resulted from them," he wrote, without elaborating on HOW, exactly, people *suffered* as a result of what Mr. Armstrong taught.[4]

"We've been wrong," he told subscribers, before concluding with this: "So to all members, former members, co-workers and others—all who have been casualties of our past sins and mistakes of doctrine—I extend my sincerest heartfelt apologies."[5]

"Casualties," like "rape," is inflammatory. But instead of dwelling on that, let's consider another interesting angle to this transformation. By the time Tkach wrote this apology, ALMOST ALL *Plain Truth* readers from Mr. Armstrong's era had long since CANCELED THEIR SUBSCRIPTIONS. Judging by the circulation nosedive after 1985, it seems the real "casualties" were among *Plain Truth* readers who were uninspired by Tkachism.

Under Mr. Armstrong, the *Plain Truth* was a popular international magazine with an ever-increasing circulation. Tkachism ruined all that, and then apologized for what Mr. Armstrong did?

THE MOST REMARKABLE STORY NEVER READ

The fact that so many have been turned off by Tkachism hasn't exactly discouraged WCG officials from working hard to spread their "Armstrong was a crazed fanatic" gospel. Tkach Jr.'s 1997 tell-all book, according to the inside flap of the cover jacket, tells a "remarkable story of how the Worldwide Church of God was transformed by truth." According to the church newspaper, the book discusses the "miraculous reformation" within the WCG after 1985.[6]

Tkach himself described their transformation this way in the *Christian Research Journal*: "*Many* are now advising us that PROFOUND COURSE CORRECTIONS OF THIS MAGNITUDE are WITHOUT HISTORICAL PRECEDENT, at least *since the days of the New Testament church.*"[7] He's talking about a transformation so unusual and massive that nothing in the history books can even compare to it.

Predictably, a number of evangelicals raved over Tkach's book. Dr. Ruth Tucker called it a "landmark book." Pastor Gordon Kirk said the book painted a "picture of one of the most dramatic works of God in our century." He described Tkach's behind-the-scenes account as "compelling," "convicting" and "awesome." Dr. James Kennedy said the changes in the WCG were "more intensive than those that brought about the Protestant Reformation."[8]

Granted, you wouldn't expect them to promote their book with lukewarm reviews, but still, "without historical precedent"—more revolutionary than *even the Protestant Reformation?*

That is quite a story to tell. And according to Mike Feazell, quite a lot of people would be interested in a story like that. "There is a great deal of curiosity about what God has done within the WCG. Former members, former *Plain Truth* readers, former listeners to our television program, as well as the greater Christian world are all interested in the how and why of what happened."[9]

I actually agree with that. I believe there *is* a huge audience out there curious about the *how* and *why* of their transformation, but not from Tkach's angle—*that Armstrong was uneducated, taught heresy, etc.* Mr. Armstrong's small circle of critics said those things for as long as his work existed. There's nothing original about that story.

But what about making an appeal to Mr. Armstrong's *legions* of followers—the tens of thousands of members who actually *liked* his teachings, the hundreds of thousands of co-workers and donors who, though not members, *liked* his message enough to support it with donations, the *millions* who followed his ministry on television or who read his literature? What about appealing to *that* mass audience, among which there must be many wondering, *how did the Tkach administration manage to hijack the Worldwide Church of God and, in effect, excommunicate Herbert W. Armstrong post mortem?*

Now THERE is a story worth telling.

But Tkach's story? If anything, it is unremarkable—unless, of course, you happen to be one of his evangelical friends, like Don Jacobson, president of Multnomah Publishers, responsible for distributing Tkach's book. "We view the publishing of *Transformed by Truth* as a stewardship responsibility," Jacobson told the *Worldwide News*. "Telling the story of the sweeping changes and movement of the Spirit of God within the Worldwide Church of God is one of the most exciting projects with which we have ever been involved."[10]

But not everyone was as excited about the book as this small publisher of mostly religious materials. According to the *Worldwide News*, by early 1998, the first printing of the book had sold out and a second printing was underway, but the article did not comment on how many copies were initially printed.[11] According to a Multnomah representative, they printed and distributed a total of 30,000 copies of the book before it went out of print in 1999.[12] In 2001, the WCG offered the discontinued book online for free.

That same year, Mike Feazell finished his version of their "remarkable" story in *The Liberation of the Worldwide Church of God*. Eddie Gibbs, of Fuller Theological Seminary, said he believed Feazell's book was "destined to become a standard work, which church historians and religious sociologists will continue to consult for years to come."[13]

Dr. James Kennedy, who also plugged Tkach's book, said of Feazell's, "This is the most astonishing change that I have ever seen or heard of in any religious group." Another friend of the transformed church, Ruth Tucker, said, "Never before in the history of Christianity has there been such a complete move to orthodox Christianity by an unorthodox fringe church."[14]

Tkach Jr., even after interest in his own version of the story had fizzled, had high hopes for Feazell's. "We expect that his book will have a strong impact on making many more people aware in a positive way of the changes that have occurred in the Worldwide Church of God," he told the *Worldwide News*.[15]

But again, besides church historians, sociologists and the WCG's evangelical friends, hardly anyone else cared enough to pay $20 to read about the WCG's "miraculous" journey.

During a 2002 deposition, Feazell seemed very uncomfortable answering questions about book sales and the royalties he received for writing it. He said the royalties fell between the 5-to-15 percent range. The book's publisher, Zondervan, gave him a cash advance of $8,000 for his manuscript, which would count against whatever he collected from royalties. And at the time of Feazell's deposition, the book having been available nearly a year, Feazell still hadn't made enough in royalties to cover the advance.[16]

According to a Zondervan representative, they printed 6,000 copies of the hardcover edition in 2001. That version is now out of print. In 2003, however, Zondervan produced a paperback version, with a print run of 4,200. According to their representative, they sold about 3,000 of these to bookstores. As of January 2006, Zondervan had 740 of the paperbacks still in stock.[17]

As much as the WCG and other evangelicals hyped *Transformed by Truth* and *The Liberation of the Worldwide Church of God,* the final sales numbers had to be disappointing. Apparently, their "remarkable" transformation into any old mainstream denomination—"without historical precedent" in modern religion—is a story that didn't much resonate with the general public.

MR. ARMSTRONG'S "REMARKABLE" BOOK

When the *Plain Truth* finished its serialized version of *Mystery of the Ages* in November 1986, Mr. Tkach Sr. introduced the last installment by saying it was a "remarkable book" that was "in a very real sense" Mr. Armstrong's "last will and testament."[18] He said that Mr. Armstrong did not underestimate the value of the work.

And indeed, whenever Mr. Armstrong talked about the book, he heaped praise upon it. Soon after Mr. Armstrong began work on *Mystery of the Ages* in 1985, he told the church membership that it would probably be the "most important book" he had ever written.[19] In the Author's Statement of the book, Mr. Armstrong proclaimed, "Time may prove this to be the most important book written in almost 1,900 years."[20]

According to Joseph Tkach Jr., Mr. Armstrong perfected these
kinds of hyperbolic "hooks" while working as a young advertising
salesman in the 1920s.[21] "Unfortunately," Tkach wrote, "he brought
that sales mentality into the founding of our church."[22] Regarding
the "time may prove" statement, Tkach said, "This was an introductory statement he had used previously in substantially similar
terms for a number of booklets and books."[23]

In other words, Mr. Armstrong supposedly said those things
about *everything* he wrote. *It was a sales technique,* we're supposed to
believe. "He was excited for the people who would read the book,"
Tkach's father explained in 1990. "And he simply got carried away
in his description of it," Tkach said, barely three years after he
called the book "remarkable."[24]

One could be forgiven for seeing a similarity between "time may
prove this to be the most important book written in almost 1,900
years" and the statement Tkach Jr. made about the WCG's transformation: "[C]ourse corrections of this magnitude are *without historical precedent,* at least *since the days of the New Testament church.*"[25]
The big difference, of course—*and substantially so*—is that *masses* of
people were actually interested in reading *Mr. Armstrong's* "remarkable" work.

The church initially printed 150,000 copies of the hardcover
version of *Mystery.* They distributed a complimentary copy to every
family in the church. A publishing house in New York—Dodd,
Mead, Inc.—distributed the work to bookstores in the United States
and Canada. The church sent 1,000 advance copies, along with
press kits, to reviewers all across America. One positive review for
Mystery of the Ages appeared in *Library Journal,* a publication that
libraries rely upon to determine which books to order. The journal
praised Mr. Armstrong for presenting the church's doctrines in a
"clear and straightforward style" and recommended libraries order
it for either their religious or public sections.[26]

In November 1985, the church offered *Mystery of the Ages* to
480,000 *Good News* subscribers. According to the *Worldwide News,*
within a 10-day period, nearly 100,000 subscribers requested the
book.[27] By the end of that year, about 50 percent of the subscribers
sent in requests, which shattered a 21-year-old record in the church,

set in 1964, when 41.4 percent of *Good News* subscribers requested *God Speaks Out on the New Morality.*[28]

That wasn't the only record to be broken that year. Before 1985, the one-year record of book distribution was 635,000 copies of *The United States and Britain in Prophecy.* In 1985, 740,000 people requested *Mystery of the Ages*—and the book wasn't even released until September of that year.[29] That is *740,000 requests in just four months' time.* As the *Pastor General's Report* noted, "This book is quickly becoming one of the most highly acclaimed and sought-after pieces of literature Mr. Armstrong has written."[30]

The records continued on into 1986. After Mr. Armstrong died on January 16, the church prepared a special tribute to be broadcast on *The World Tomorrow* television program. Airing the weekend of January 25-26, it was the first time the church ever offered *Mystery of the Ages* (softbound) on television. It resulted in the highest response ever for *The World Tomorrow,* when 107,000 viewers requested the book by early February.

A year later, in 1987, another program that offered the book to viewers generated 59,000 calls. Later that year, a summer re-run of that same program brought in 37,000 more requests. By that same time, mid-1987, there were 5,000 copies of the book in U.S. libraries.

All totaled, by early 1988, about 1,245,000 copies of *Mystery of the Ages* had been distributed worldwide.[31]

Quite unlike Tkach's and Feazell's books, Mr. Armstrong's "remarkable" book actually produced remarkable results. Of course, WCG officials today might argue that it's an unfair comparison. By the time their books rolled off the presses, the church's media machine and subscriber base had all but vanished. Mr. Armstrong, on the other hand, benefited from a sprawling, worldwide work that had attracted a huge following over the course of 50 years.

But THAT'S EXACTLY THE POINT. Mr. Armstrong's whole work—his writings, his sermons, his institutions, *his entire life*—had a hugely positive impact on millions of human beings who wanted to be *part* of that work. Of course there were the occasional critics who disliked Mr. Armstrong's theology. As the *Pasadena Star-News* wrote the day after Mr. Armstrong died,

[T]hose who choose—or who believe they are divinely chosen—
to spread the message of monotheism in the world are bound
to endure more than their share of mortal vicissitudes. Many of
these men and women, however, leave a legacy that makes all their
suffering worthwhile. Herbert W. Armstrong was such a man.[32]

There were obstacles and hardships along the way—critics
and skeptics—but his LEGACY made all the difficulties worthwhile.
That's how the newsmedia in Mr. Armstrong's own backyard represented his legacy.

Yet, 10 years later, Joseph Tkach Jr.—the man sitting in the same
office Mr. Armstrong established—felt it necessary to apologize for
Mr. Armstrong's "heavy legacy" of "heartache" and "suffering."[33]
Tkachism, we're to assume, has brought nothing but joy and peace
into our lives. Notice what Tkach wrote in the *Christian Research
Journal* in 1996:

> The leadership and faithful members of the Worldwide Church
> of God are deeply grateful for God's mercy in leading us into
> the light. Yet our progress has not been without costs. Income
> has plummeted, costing us millions of dollars and requiring us
> to lay off hundreds of long-time employees. Membership has
> declined. Several splinter churches have broken off from us to
> return to one or the other of our previous doctrinal and cultural
> positions. As a result, families have separated and friendships
> have been abandoned, sometimes with angry, hurt feelings and
> accusations.[34]

Only in the upside-down world of Tkachism can *Mr. Armstrong*
be blamed for all that. But Mr. Armstrong wasn't the one who caused
the income to plummet. He wasn't responsible for reducing the
headquarters staff from 1,000 employees down to 50. He wasn't the
one who drove out 75 percent of the membership. Mr. Armstrong
didn't abolish all of the church's teachings, prompting splinter
groups to break away, thus destroying families and friendships.

Mr. Armstrong caused none of that. *Tkachism* is responsible for
that.

"A Giant of a Man"

Judging by the large outpouring of response to news of Mr. Armstrong's death, evidently, dozens and dozens of prominent leaders from around the world had nothing but deep respect for Mr. Armstrong as a man and high praise for his work.

The king of Thailand, Bhumibol Adulyadej, said that Mr. Armstrong, "through his understanding, wisdom and humanitarianism, has sought to give encouragement and assistance to people all over the world, particularly to Thailand where he has devoted much of his time and resources thereby becoming a close and valuable friend of our country."[35]

Otto von Hapsburg, then member of the European Parliament, sent this message: "Deeply shocked by news of the death of unforgettable Mr. Armstrong. Am with you all in prayers and hopes for successful continuation of his life's work."[36]

Prince Raad of Jordan, along with his wife, called Mr. Armstrong a "great humanitarian and philanthropist, a loss the world can ... ill afford at times such as these"—to repeat, a loss THE WORLD can ill afford![37]

Teddy Kollek, mayor of Jerusalem at the time, wrote, "One could only be deeply impressed by his vast efforts to promote understanding and peace among peoples. His good deeds were felt in many corners of the world"[38]—except, apparently, within the Tkach household. According to Tkach Jr., Mr. Armstrong's church was "judgmental," "legalistic" and "self-righteous"—fostering attitudes of "superiority."[39]

Jerusalem's mayor disagreed. So did California's attorney general, who, at the time, said Mr. Armstrong's "long and productive life leaves a lasting benefit for many." Pasadena's mayor—the man living right there in the same city, with an up-close view of the Worldwide Church of God, called Mr. Armstrong a "giant of a man who provided leadership of goodwill and principle."[40] City officials in Pasadena absolutely loved Mr. Armstrong and his work. Myron Stolp of the Rotary International in Pasadena said just after Mr. Armstrong died, "I can scarcely name an activity in which Ambassador has not in some way been involved!"[41] Cy Graph, president of the Pasadena Chamber of Commerce at the time, said, "In his own quiet way Mr.

Armstrong has done more to promote positive relations between countries than has the [U.S.] State Department."[42]

Even the leader of the free world at that time weighed in on the positive impact Mr. Armstrong had on his church and all Americans. U.S. President Ronald Reagan sent this note to the WCG upon hearing that Mr. Armstrong had died: "To the congregation of the Worldwide Church of God: Nancy and I join all those mourning the loss of Herbert W. Armstrong. As founder and leader of the Worldwide Church of God, Mr. Armstrong contributed to sharing the word of the Lord with his community and with people throughout the nation. You can take pride in his legacy. Our prayers are with you. God bless you."[43]

Yet, just 10 years later, the pastor general of the Worldwide Church of God—the very church Herbert Armstrong raised up—apologized to *Plain Truth* readers for all the "heartache" and "suffering" Mr. Armstrong had caused.

Why should we believe him? Well, because HE SAYS SO—that's why! And what's more, he enjoys enthusiastic support from evangelicals like Ruth Tucker and Hank Hanegraaff. They all think Mr. Armstrong's legacy was "heavy" with heartache and suffering.

President Ronald Reagan, on the other hand, said we should take pride in Herbert Armstrong's legacy.

I'm going with President Reagan's endorsement.

LIFELONG LEGACY

In the autumn of 1926, Mr. Armstrong was challenged by his wife, Loma, into an almost night-and-day, intensive study of the Bible. He wrote, "My research was totally different from that of students in a seminary. They absorb what they are taught in the doctrines of their denomination. ... But I had been called specially by the living God. ... I was taught by Christ what I did not want to believe but what He showed me was true!"[44] Mr. Armstrong never claimed to be a Bible scholar—at least not in the sense that he had been trained in a seminary or by a theologian. But he looked at that as a tremendous advantage. Having avoided seminary training, his approach to Bible study was without personal bias or prejudice.

He didn't preach what *someone else* said he should preach about the Bible. He relied solely *on the Bible.*

As God opened Mr. Armstrong's mind to the truths of the Bible, He also opened doors so Mr. Armstrong could teach those truths to a large audience.

What many remember as one of the top religious programs on television in the 1980s, *The World Tomorrow,* actually began as a small radio program in Oregon back in January 1934. The *Plain Truth* began one month later, with Mr. Armstrong rolling a couple hundred copies off an archaic mimeograph machine. By the time of his death, that monthly magazine was sent free to more than 8 million subscribers worldwide.

In 1939, Mr. Armstrong started the *Good News*—a bulletin, established mainly for members and co-workers of the church. Like the *Plain Truth,* it eventually developed into a full-color magazine and peaked with a circulation of over 1 million about a year and a half after Mr. Armstrong died.

In the spring of 1946, only 12 years after his work started, Mr. Armstrong saw that if the work was ever to span the globe, he needed more help. To train that help, he needed to raise up a college. The vision for this educational institution was clear in his mind even before it opened. And it resulted in not one, but *three* Ambassador College schools. The headquarters campus in Pasadena opened its doors in 1947; sister campuses opened in Bricket Wood, England, in 1960, and Big Sandy, Texas, in 1964.

As the college developed and grew, so did the work of the church. In 1953, the radio program began airing in Europe on Radio Luxembourg. Two years later, in 1955, *The World Tomorrow* appeared on television for the first time, although it lasted for only a brief span of time.

The *Plain Truth* went full-color in 1965, 31 years after its inception. The church also began publishing the magazine in German, French, Spanish and Dutch during the 1960s. By 1967, *The World Tomorrow* was poised and ready for another venture into the world of television—only this time, it would enjoy rapid growth.

In the 1960s, Mr. Armstrong sought to put into stronger action what he termed God's "way of *give*"—the way of godly character, generosity, cultural enrichment, true education; of beautifying the environment and caring for fellowman. He began undertaking humanitarian projects, helping select pockets of the underprivileged around the world. In 1975 he formalized the organization of these activities by founding the Ambassador International Cultural Foundation, or AICF. The AICF set up mobile schools in Buddhist Thailand to teach illiterate farmers how to raise crops of healthful food rather than illegal drugs. It funded and staffed schools for the disabled, archaeological digs of biblically significant sites and anthropological excursions. Its activities stretched from Bombay to Brussels, the Philippines to the Netherlands, Tokyo to Cairo; they reached Okinawa, Nepal, London, Jordan and Jerusalem.

As these philanthropic endeavors multiplied, they produced an interesting, unforeseen side effect: Doors began to open for Mr. Armstrong to meet high-ranking officials in these foreign countries. Leading individuals welcomed him openly, even taking an interest in his opinions, hosting dinners in his honor. Soon opportunity opened for "testimonial dinners," hosted by such officials, where they would invite their influential friends to hear Mr. Armstrong speak for 35 to 45 minutes. Mr. Armstrong took these occasions to preach the gospel of God's coming kingdom, speaking in plain terminology they could understand. These dinners opened the way for personal appearance campaigns, where Mr. Armstrong would speak to hundreds of thousands of leading people in various countries. Bringing his hope-filled biblical message of how God will soon *solve* the insoluble problems of humankind, he became widely regarded as "an unofficial ambassador for world peace."

The AICF also launched a bimonthly magazine, *Human Potential,* which was later renamed *Quest.* It was produced for subscription by heads of state and top officials and professionals worldwide and included many articles written by and for them. In its first issues appeared a Japanese leader's view of Israel, an Egyptian official's perspective on the Middle East, a case for international law written by a World Court justice. Reports on archaeology, nature, the wonders of the human mind and body, historical expeditions, arts and cultures of the world all appeared alongside articles of a moral and spiritual nature.

Thus, even as Mr. Armstrong "rubbed shoulders with and come to know the totally illiterate and poverty-stricken poor," as he expressed it *Mystery of the Ages,*[45] particularly via some of the humanitarian projects he undertook and oversaw personally, he also gained considerable credibility, favor and even prestige among the world's elite. He spent much of the 1970s traveling the globe to spread the gospel message to kings, presidents and other heads of state—all while writing vigorously for the many church publications. Through his travels, Mr. Armstrong met with royalty including the late Japanese Emperor Hirohito, the late Ethiopian Emperor Haile Selassie, King Bhumibol Adulyadej of Thailand, and the late King Hussein of Jordan. He had an endearing relationship with Egyptian President Anwar Sadat before his assassination in 1981. He later gained an audience with Sadat's successor, Hosni Mubarak. Mr. Armstrong discussed the cause of world evils with former Japanese Prime Minister Eisaku Sato and met with six successive Japanese prime ministers as well. He was on very friendly terms with then-President Ferdinand Marcos of the Philippines and was awarded the Presidential Merit Medal in 1983. Other heads of state Mr. Armstrong visited include Israeli prime ministers Menachem Begin and Golda Meir, Thai Prime Minister Prem Tinsulanonda and British Prime Minister Margaret Thatcher.

Throughout all these meetings, Mr. Armstrong never deviated from his purpose of freely sharing and spreading God's way of life.

Performing Arts

In 1972, Mr. Armstrong broke ground for the construction of Ambassador Auditorium in Pasadena. He dedicated this beautiful building, constructed with some of the finest materials on Earth, to the great God. At its grand opening in April 1974, the Vienna Symphony Orchestra performed under the direction of Carlo Maria Giulini.

Over the next 20 years, multiple hundreds of performers, including famed opera stars like Luciano Pavarotti, Placido Domingo, Joan Sutherland and Beverly Sills, delighted audiences from all over Southern California and beyond inside Ambassador

Auditorium. In what some have referred to as the "Carnegie Hall of the West," renowned performers such as legendary pianists Arthur Rubinstein and Vladimir Horowitz, and celebrated cellists like Yo-Yo Ma and Mstislav Rostropovich left audiences spellbound. Jazz icons Frank Sinatra, Benny Goodman, Bing Crosby and Sammy Davis Jr. also showcased their talent in "Pasadena's crown jewel." Other famous performers who graced Ambassador's stage include Andrés Segovia, James Galway, Marcel Marceau and Bob Hope. Pianist Alexis Weissenberg said, "I cannot adequately explain Ambassador to other artists who haven't performed there. It goes beyond the beauty of the place, the fantastic acoustics. It's also the people one deals with there. It's unique in the music world."[46]

Yet another legacy that was neither heavy nor burdensome.

After 2,500 concerts and recitals, it was the *Tkaches* who shut down the famous performing arts series in 1995, saying they could not afford to subsidize the program and that it "had nothing to do with the mission of the church" anyway.[47] "News of Ambassador's closure," the *Los Angeles Times* reported, "rumbled through Pasadena's business and political circles like an EARTHQUAKE."[48] The community was terribly disappointed. In fact, one reason it took so long for the WCG to sell the Pasadena property is the resistance that city officials put up over proposals to turn the campus into a residential community.

"Our mission in the building is over; we aren't going to keep it," Bernie Schnippert, the church's director of finance and planning, told the *Los Angeles Times* in 2002. "If it is not bought by the city or bought by a benefactor, the church will tear it down."[49] Quite a legacy! They actually gave the city an ultimatum: *Either buy Ambassador Auditorium for the appraised value of $22 million, or else we'll demolish it!* In the end, city officials held firm and prevented the auditorium from being sold to a developer. This forced the WCG to divvy up the property and sell off the parcels piece by piece. Harvest Rock Church bought the auditorium in 2004 for a little more than a third of the appraised value.

After the sale, like a good politician, Schnippert changed his tune. "The Ambassador Auditorium has *always* been an important part of the Worldwide Church of God's ministry," Schnippert told the *Worldwide News*. "We are pleased that this religious and cultural jewel will continue to be used for the glory of God."[50] He said this just two years after threatening to demolish the structure.

It makes you wonder what Pasadena city officials think about the legacy of Tkachism.

POWER STRUGGLE

During the 1970s, internally the church withstood its share of controversy and dissension. Much of it happened in Mr. Armstrong's absence. During this controversial decade, he was away from head-quarters traveling about 300 days a year.

In 1974, 35 ministers revolted and took a few thousand members with them. Soon after, Mr. Armstrong's son, Garner Ted, attempted to wrest control of the church from his father. In Mr. Armstrong's absence, the younger Armstrong began changing many of the core doctrines of the church and pursuing accreditation for Ambassador College. This, Mr. Armstrong would write later, led to church teachings being watered down and permissive behavior on campus at Ambassador.

Shortly thereafter, Garner Ted was disfellowshiped from the church. Unfortunately for the work, the troubles did not stop there. During the autumn of 1978, six disfellowshiped WCG members began to plot a conspiracy against the church in the form of a class action lawsuit. Mr. Armstrong wrote in the June 24, 1985, *Worldwide News,* "This resulted in an ex parte order by a judge. Secretly without prior notice, deputies on order of the attorney general's office swooped down on the church on the morning of January 3, 1979."[51] This launched what became the single greatest attack against the Worldwide Church of God to that point.

A FIGHT FOR GOD'S CHURCH

Perhaps at no time is the true character of a leader unveiled more than at a time of crisis. The year 1979 was such a time in the WCG. Those familiar with the WCG during those days witnessed first-hand Mr. Armstrong's fighting spirit. The main accusation Garner

Ted brought against the church was his father's "lavish spending." The charges (which were later thoroughly disproven) prompted the state attorney general to appoint retired Judge Steven Weisman as the receiver of the church. On the morning of January 3, Judge Weisman entered the wcg headquarters in Pasadena and summarily "fired" Herbert Armstrong, or so he thought. At the time, Mr. Armstrong was residing in Tucson, Arizona, which somewhat shielded him from the state of California's assault.

Describing Mr. Armstrong's reaction to these events, Stanley Rader wrote in his book *Against the Gates of Hell,* "Problems have never upset Mr. Armstrong, and he reacted even to this serious threat with serenity, courage and confidence."[52]

Two and a half weeks later, church members demonstrated their unwavering support for Mr. Armstrong by gathering at the headquarters campus in Pasadena. The slow trickle of people soon turned into a flood that converged upon the Hall of Administration. Members brought food and bedding to lodge in the church's offices in order to prevent the receiver from taking control of wcg property. Mr. Armstrong did not organize the event. None of the church leaders anticipated it. It was a spontaneous reaction of faith and courage by those members who set out to defend Mr. Armstrong and the wcg.

After the gathering of thousands of members, church officials organized a church service in the Hall of Administration where the receiver was supposed to come in and work. By this time, news of the attempted overthrow had gone national. It was being covered by many major newspapers.

Mr. Armstrong responded in a live telephone hook-up to Pasadena from Tucson: "The people of God have always been willing to suffer whatever they have to do for the living God! And I tell you, this has drawn us together." He advised the members to "be subject to the powers that be," but that "we are to obey God rather than man." He said, "[I]f we have to begin to suffer the persecution of being thrown in prison, I will be the first to be ready to go. The living God is fighting this battle for us ...."[53] That evening, the headline for the late edition of the *Los Angeles Times* blared, "Ready for jail—Armstrong."

Herbert Armstrong fought diligently against the state's unconstitutional attack. In the process, the wcg received enthusiastic
support from dozens of churches that recognized the danger of
such an attack. This support came from different churches with
different teachings, but which all held to the same constitutional
right to freely practice their religion.

On October 14, 1980, the state dropped the case against the wcg
when the legislature passed a law barring the attorney general from
investigating religious organizations the way they had the wcg.

Commenting on how Mr. Armstrong faced this struggle,
Stanley Rader wrote, "Over the years of my close association with
this remarkable man, I have noted abundant evidence that he is the
embodiment of his own message of hope and trust that the living
God will provide man with the wisdom to prevail over obstacles."[54]

If anything, the California attack revitalized the aging apostle
and strengthened the church. The period between 1979 and 1986
was truly the church's finest hour—the era of its greatest-ever
growth.

"Incomparably Richer"

Perhaps none was as deeply impacted by Mr. Armstrong's legacy as
those who worked right alongside him. After Mr. Armstrong died,
many of these faithful supporters recorded their thoughts for the
Worldwide News tribute issue of February 10, 1986.

Larry Omasta worked closely with Mr. Armstrong on the television program. "Mr. Armstrong knew," Omasta wrote, "that the
camera lens represented a world that needed the message he had to
deliver. That, I think, is what made him such a compelling speaker.
He did not speak at his audience—he spoke to them."[55]

A wcg evangelist, Norman Smith, had worked with Mr.
Armstrong on the radio broadcast back in the 1950s: "Mr.
Armstrong was a towering influence in our lives. The personal
memories we each have of his powerful broadcasts will be an inspiration to continue and complete the work we are given to do."[56]

Dexter Faulkner, executive editor for the *Plain Truth,* said, "Mr.
Armstrong was a seasoned professional communicator, widely

recognized for his outstanding ability in writing and advertising. ... [H]e was interested in what God wanted in the church's publications. And he insisted that every headline, every article, every advertisement bring this world a little closer to God's Kingdom."[57]

Ellis La Ravia, vice president of the Ambassador Foundation, said, "His example of drive, enthusiasm and determination in God's service set the standard for all of us. He always gave God credit for everything. He left high standards. He will be missed."[58]

Roderick Meredith, a professor at Ambassador College at the time, referred to Mr. Armstrong as a "second father" for many of the college students. According to Dr. Meredith, Mr. Armstrong "was a human dynamo, working, driving and building a dedicated organization through which Christ could work to impart His message to this generation. ... As with any other truly great man, there will never be another like him."[59]

Leroy Neff, former treasurer for the WCG, said, "No one I have known has had such singleness of thought and purpose. Most of his thoughts and conversation related to God's work and God's Word. ... I found him to be the most generous person I have ever known."[60]

Frank Brown, regional director in Britain, Scandinavia, East and West Africa and the Middle East, said he felt Mr. Armstrong's greatest attribute, "apart from his desire to do God's work, was his clarity of vision. He had the rare ability to think far in the future and envision not only what God was leading him to do, but its ultimate outcome. Mr. Armstrong was a visionary. ... Those of us in the church today are all incomparably richer for having a part in Mr. Armstrong's vision and reality of the future. He was loved. He will be missed."[61]

No one in that tribute issue mentioned anything about Mr. Armstrong's "heavy legacy" of heartache and suffering or his self-righteous judgmentalism.

COURSE ALREADY CHARTED

Ironically, that same "heavy legacy" Tkach Jr. loves to pin on Mr. Armstrong was responsible for appointing his father to the office of pastor general. And at the time of his appointment, Tkach Sr. seemed proud of Mr. Armstrong's legacy. "What an impact Mr. Armstrong had on my life!" he wrote. "Because of his yieldedness, God was able to use him in a profound way to proclaim the most important message the world will ever hear."[62]

The day Mr. Armstrong died, Mr. Tkach told the headquarters staff, "The admonishment is now for those of us still living who now have a task that is set before them, a course that has already been charted by God's apostle. We need to maintain that course and not deviate from it one iota."[63] At Mr. Armstrong's funeral, Mr. Tkach prayed, "We readily admit and acknowledge that there is no man who can fill his shoes, but, Father, we aim to follow in his footsteps."[64]

Of course, that never happened. As we will see, Tkachism deviated off course *even before Mr. Armstrong died.* Today, the church is completely transformed. Its mission has changed, its doctrines are different, its traditions are gone—its very identity is transformed. And all these changes, Tkachism admits, have brought about "catastrophic results."[65]

How then is it possible to pin the blame for this destruction on Mr. Armstrong? It's the *legacy of Tkachism*—not Mr. Armstrong—that RUINED THE CHURCH. If we judge by fruits, we become acutely aware of *Tkachism's* heavy legacy. It's Tkachism's self-righteous judgmentalism that brought so much heartache and suffering into the lives of thousands of members, former members and co-workers who loved Mr. Armstrong and faithfully supported his work.

THREE

THE SELF-
APPOINTED
APOSTLE

*"For some years now, there have been some, like vultures,
waiting for me to die. They would like to come back and take over
the leadership of the church in my stead."*

— HERBERT W. ARMSTRONG
Worldwide News, *June 24, 1985*

GARNER Ted Armstrong was the man many believed would succeed his father as pastor general of the Worldwide Church of God. A gifted speaker, he was the church's presenter on the *World Tomorrow* program for many years. So when Herbert W. Armstrong, in 1978, had the gut-wrenching duty of disfellowshiping him for abusing authority and conspiring to water down doctrine and take over the church, he did so with a heavy heart.

Coming out of the 1970s, Mr. Armstrong's primary concern was on getting the church back on track. "God Almighty and Jesus Christ were virtually thrown out of the college," he wrote, "and were rapidly being thrown out of the church!"[1] Approaching 90 years of age at the time, Mr. Armstrong was also concerned, understandably, about who his successor might be. Spiritually speaking, he always believed that Jesus Christ, not any man or group of men, would choose his successor. But at the same time, he wasn't naive—he knew, human nature being what it is, that certain men *strongly* desired his office. His son had already conspired to take over, but failed.

So in 1981, with the aid of his legal advisers, Mr. Armstrong drew up provisions in the church's bylaws that would prevent an imposter (like his son) from gaining control of the church. In the event of his death, the church's Advisory Council of Elders—at that time, a board of nine senior ministers, all personally selected by Mr. Armstrong—would be vested with absolute and total authority to designate a successor. Should Mr. Armstrong die, no one could claim to be his rightful successor without the Advisory Council's backing.

Four years later, even with this fail-safe plan in place, Mr. Armstrong was still uneasy about the question of his successor. "In a few days I will be 93 years of age," he wrote to the church in mid-1985.

> For some years now, there have been some, like vultures, waiting for me to die. They would like to come back and take over the leadership of the church in my stead. I have been deeply concerned about this, but in no sense worried. This is the church of God, not of any man. Jesus Christ is the living Head of this church. I am not.[2]

Mr. Armstrong then reiterated the provisions drawn up in 1981: "If Christ should remove me, He will direct the Advisory Council of Elders to select *one of them* to continue leading you until the coming of Jesus Christ in power and in glory."[3] So for the last four years of his life, it was generally understood within church circles that the Advisory Council—which had expanded from 9 members to 14 by mid-1985—would be responsible for choosing a successor—*not Herbert Armstrong.*

Nine days before he died, however, Mr. Armstrong changed his mind.

CHOOSING A SUCCESSOR

On Tuesday night, January 7, 1986, a nurse wheeled Mr. Armstrong into the elevator of his two-story home in Pasadena, California. Waiting for him downstairs, on a couch in Mr. Armstrong's study, were the director of Church Administration, Joseph Tkach, and Mr. Armstrong's personal aide, Aaron Dean, both of whom were on the Advisory Council. Across campus, on the fourth floor of the Hall of Administration, there sat 11 other Council members, along with the church's legal adviser, Ralph Helge, listening in via telephone hook-up. (Another Council member, Dibar Apartian, arrived late at the Hall of Ad and did not hear the discussion.)

In the days leading up to this teleconference, Ralph Helge, with Mr. Armstrong's approval, had been working to amend the church's bylaws to allow Mr. Armstrong to name his successor *personally*. Helge had also prepared the paperwork whereby Mr. Armstrong would officially designate the new pastor general.

According to Helge, Mr. Armstrong decided toward the end of 1985 to select the successor himself rather than leave the task in the hands of the Council. Why the change? Helge said it was for the church's protection—to prevent anyone from casting doubt on the validity of the Council's choice.[4] Apparently, Mr. Armstrong wanted to remove all doubt as to who his successor would be. Indeed, in those final resolutions, he expressed concern about those *on the outside*—specifically his disfellowshiped son, Garner Ted Armstrong—attempting to create confusion and cast doubt upon the successor's credentials.

Mr. Dean, however, believes Mr. Armstrong had serious concerns about some on the *inside* as well—particularly Roderick Meredith. "He just might succeed in getting control," Mr. Armstrong told him, "and he should never, ever be over the church."[5] Dean's recollection mirrors closely with what Mr. Armstrong privately wrote to Meredith in 1980, after sending him to Hawaii on a mandatory, six-month sabbatical. "In brutal frankness," Mr. Armstrong wrote to Mr. Meredith, "you lack the charisma to lead God's work. You do not attract—as I said before, you REPEL people. You are a harsh taskmaster over those under you. That is your record!" Later, he wrote, "You have a will to lead, but not the qualifications."[6]

By the time Mr. Armstrong was about to die in 1986, Rod

Meredith had returned to the Council of Elders. And with Council members like Raymond McNair and Dibar Apartian firmly in Mr. Meredith's camp, Mr. Armstrong had reason to worry. "That's why he decided to name someone," Dean said in a telephone interview, "because he didn't want Rod taking over, or someone else."[7]

But as it turns out, naming someone himself didn't exactly remove all cause for concern either. Ralph Helge said Mr. Armstrong got feedback from several members of the Council regarding who should succeed. Dean said he "changed his mind several times about who would be in charge."[8]

PASSING THE BATON

According to Aaron Dean, when Mr. Armstrong decided upon Joseph Tkach as his successor, it came with certain strings attached. For one, Tkach would be elevated to the office of pastor general, *but not his staff.* "If you bring your staff up, they'll lead you astray," Mr. Armstrong told Mr. Tkach. The church's founder wanted Tkach to rely heavily on the Advisory Council, Dean said.[9]

The decision to appoint Mr. Tkach as successor was drawn up in official church documents on January 7, 1986. Mr. Armstrong called for an Advisory Council meeting that same day. Since many Council members had not seen him in weeks, he wanted them to actually hear his voice of approval for the amendment to the bylaws and the appointment of Tkach. "He didn't want an accusation that Ralph Helge and Joe Tkach just got together and wrote a letter and Mr. Armstrong never heard of it and all of a sudden he dies and bingo, here it is," Dean said.[10]

Aaron doesn't remember whether he or Ralph Helge read the final resolutions at that meeting. But it wasn't Mr. Armstrong; he was too weak. He did, however, have enough strength to greet the Council and assure them that the documents had his blessing. He asked the members to give Mr. Tkach their full support. "[I]t was a very moving event," Helge said in 1998. "[H]e was passing the baton to Mr. Tkach."[11]

Yet, ironically, in the very documents Mr. Armstrong approved for the sake of *establishing* Tkach's godly authority, what stands out most is the one office he did *not* transfer to his successor. Tkach would assume all the titles and offices Mr. Armstrong held *except the spiritual rank of apostle.*[12] So Mr. Armstrong never laid hands on him. He never ordained him as an apostle. What he did that January 7 was *appoint* Joseph Tkach to succeed him as pastor general. That's it.

INFORMING THE CHURCH

After Mr. Armstrong verbally stated his intentions before the Council, Mr. Dean suggested he also inform the church membership of his decision—again, in order to leave little room to question the line of succession. Problem is, Mr. Armstrong had become so weak, he couldn't write or dictate a letter. So Aaron Dean wrote one in his stead, dated January 10, 1986. Above Mr. Armstrong's signature, Mr. Dean wrote, "This is my first letter to you in 1986, and could very well be my last. Now in my 94th year I am in a very physically weakened state enduring severe pain and with virtually no strength whatsoever." Then later,

> After much counsel and prayer over the past months God has led me in announcing a decision last week to appoint Mr. Joseph W. Tkach, director of Church Administration, to the office of deputy pastor general, to assist me while I am in a weakened state, and should God choose to take my life, to place himself totally in Christ's hands to lead God's church under Christ, succeeding me as pastor general, in the difficult times ahead.[13]

Aaron read the letter aloud to Mr. Armstrong and assured him that he wouldn't send it out unless he felt like Mr. Armstrong completely understood its meaning. "I read the whole thing to him and at a couple spots he squeezed my hand and then he actually added a word at the end. So I knew he understood it," said Dean. The letter was mailed January 10.[14]

Four days later, on Tuesday, January 14, Ralph Helge told the media about the designation of Mr. Tkach. According to the

Associated Press, "Although the designation of Tkach was effective immediately, he would assume the various offices and titles of the church leader only if Armstrong dies."[15]

Two days later, on Thursday morning, January 16, 1986, Herbert W. Armstrong died at 5:59 a.m. He was 93 years old.

PREPARING THE CHURCH

News of Mr. Armstrong's death among church members was not shocking. He was old and had been seriously ill for the last 5½ months of his life. On August 3, 1985, he left Pasadena on a round-the-world trip. He intended to visit the church's youth camps in Minnesota and Scotland before meeting with world leaders in Japan and South Korea, but upon his arrival in Minnesota, his temperature rose by about two degrees and would not subside. So he canceled the rest of his trip and flew home.

After two weeks in bed, his temperature dropped somewhat—at least in the mornings; usually by mid-afternoon, it would again rise. This fluctuation enabled him to get in some office work during the last part of August and all of September.

On Monday morning, September 9, Mr. Armstrong appeared before the college's sophomore class to present his new book, *Mystery of the Ages*. The following week, September 16, Mr. Armstrong delivered what would be his final sermon before church members.

Sunday, September 29, was the last day Mr. Armstrong made it outside of his home. It was the day before the church began its week-long fall festival. Of course, even after he missed the entire festival, church members remained hopeful that God would revitalize him. Mr. Armstrong himself hoped for a positive turn.

But after two more months of the same deteriorating health, he candidly alerted church members about his declining physical state in a December 9 letter he dictated to Aaron Dean. "I had hoped for a turn to the better—so that I could return for daily work in my office—and a recovery from this illness, but unfortunately, that has not occurred."[16] He told the members he had been in bed clothes and robes since September 30—more than two months.

"Frequently I have very serious and painful angina attacks of the heart," he continued. "I have been able to make certain necessary decisions in brief telephone contact with those at the office and will continue this as and when my very limited physical strength permits."[17] He described his involvement in the day-to-day church operations as "very limited." He hadn't taped a television program since August.

According to Ralph Helge, by the point of the January 7 Advisory Council meeting, "you kind of knew in your heart … that he probably would die."[18] Aaron Dean figured his death was inevitable, which is why he composed the January 10 letter for Mr. Armstrong.

TKACH SHOCKED

The day Mr. Armstrong died, Mr. Tkach wrote to the church membership and co-workers, "I am deeply saddened to have to inform you that Herbert W. Armstrong's illness has *ended in the manner least expected by all of us.*"[19]

Of course, God could have intervened to extend his life for several more years. But that a 93-year-old man *would die*—after being confined to his bed for four months with constant fever, low blood volume and heart disease—isn't exactly shocking, particularly after the entire church was told that he may not live to "write" another letter.

Mr. Tkach, like everyone around Mr. Armstrong at the time, *must* have expected him to die. But maybe he wanted to be perceived as humble—as if becoming pastor general was the furthest thing from his mind. Whatever the reason, Tkach's first comment as pastor general was strange.

THE RANK OF APOSTLE

Mr. Armstrong may not have ordained Tkach as an apostle, but that didn't stop the successor from taking matters into his own hands. After becoming pastor general, Mr. Tkach appointed Larry Salyer to replace him as the director of Church Administration. Larry Salyer, in turn, submitted a piece for the *Pastor General's Report* in which he explained how Mr. Tkach was fulfilling the office of apostle. According to Aaron Dean, that happened about a month or so after Mr. Armstrong died. When it did, Dean told Tkach that it didn't seem right for a man Mr. Tkach just promoted to then turn around and tell everyone that his boss was an apostle. According to Dean, Mr. Tkach agreed and decided to shelve Salyer's write-up.[20] But as it turns out, it was set aside only temporarily.

Mr. Tkach announced his new spiritual rank at a regional directors conference in Pasadena, on November 21, 1986, *only 10 months* after he had been in office. Tkach's announcement cleared the way for Salyer's piece to be pulled off the shelf. Salyer wrote to the ministry the next month,

> During the last several years Christ saw to it that Mr. Tkach was pressed into daily contact with Mr. Armstrong and was directly involved in virtually every major decision. Mr. Armstrong delegated to Mr. Tkach ever-increasing responsibility for gathering facts and implementing his decisions. In the final weeks of his life Mr. Armstrong specifically instructed Mr. Tkach in the responsibilities of pastor general, sharing many personal experiences with him. And before his death he appointed Mr. Tkach as his successor and saw to it that the passing of the baton was legally documented and announced to the church.[21]

What he failed to mention is that within those same legal documents, Mr. Armstrong SPECIFICALLY mentioned that Mr. Tkach would succeed him in every office *except* apostle. Later, Salyer continued,

> It has become obvious to the leading ministers at headquarters that Mr. Tkach is doing, as Mr. Armstrong was before him, the work of an apostle. ... Christ has chosen him and sent him forth as an apostle to carry on His work, supported and reinforced by the whole church, as co-workers with Christ.

To leading ministers at headquarters, it had become OBVIOUS, after only *a few months,* that Joseph Tkach was an apostle. Mr.

Salyer then encouraged the WCG ministry to explain in sermons Mr. Tkach's newly established office.[22]

The next month, in the church's newspaper, there is a reference to Mr. Tkach as an "apostle" buried on the back page of the issue. In commenting on Gerald Waterhouse's tour of Australia, Robert Fahey said he "showed clearly how God carefully selected and trained Mr. Tkach for the responsibilities he now has as the apostle of God's end-time church, taking up the baton from Mr. Armstrong."[23] In the issues that followed, Mr. Tkach's new spiritual rank worked its way to the front page of the church paper—splashing across headlines: "Spirit is catalyst of unity, says apostle in Pasadena"; "Christ's apostle 'deeply inspired' by trip to Jordan, Egypt, Israel."[24]

With Mr. Armstrong, it wasn't until after *17 years* of service in God's work that one of his top ministers put forward the idea that Mr. Armstrong was serving as God's apostle. Herman Hoeh, one of the first four Ambassador College graduates, made the suggestion at a fall festival in 1951. Yet, as Mr. Armstrong later wrote, the whole idea came as a complete shock. He shook his head in "astonishment" upon hearing it and rejected it entirely.[25]

It was only after looking back on the *fruits* of his ministry—of proclaiming the gospel message of the Kingdom of God to the world—that Mr. Armstrong admitted to fulfilling the office of apostle. "Never in my life had I thought of occupying such an office," he wrote three years after that 1951 festival.

> But in the light of events, the fact of how God has set up His church today has become self-evident to all. It is God's doing. If one does find, unexpectedly, that God has set him in such an office, there is only one choice—he must accept it with full humility, realizing personal lack, and surrendering the self totally to God as an instrument in His hands, relying wholly upon God for guidance and every power and need.[26]

The word *apostle* means "one sent forth." Once Mr. Armstrong realized that God was indeed sending him forth into all nations with the true gospel message, then his thinking about the apostleship began to change. The "fruits," as he often would say later in life, proved which office he fulfilled.

Mr. Tkach didn't care so much about fruits. He just wanted the office. Like Simon Magus, who lusted for the power and authority of the first-century apostles,[27] Mr. Tkach had a burning desire to be one too—even *before* Mr. Armstrong died. "He asked for it and Mr. Armstrong refused," Dean says. "In fact, he asked several times."[28] Mr. Armstrong then took the extraordinary step of clearly stating in the final resolutions and directives he left the church that Joseph W. Tkach would succeed him in all his offices and titles, *except* the spiritual rank of apostle.[29]

As it happens, that's the one title Mr. Tkach wanted most. So right after Mr. Armstrong died, he *made himself* an apostle.

FOUR
CREDENTIALS

"In conducting his studies, however, Armstrong had no seminary training and lacked any disciplined study of church history, biblical interpretation and original languages of Scripture."

— MICHAEL FEAZELL
2002

BESIDES wanting to be an apostle, Joseph Tkach Sr. also liked the idea of having an impeccable resume. "They were trying to create a legend out of him from the word *go*," Aaron Dean remembers. Ellen Escat, Mr. Tkach's administrative assistant, even asked Aaron to "make Mr. Tkach look like Mr. Armstrong" when discussing him in sermons or conversations.[1]

If, in fact, Tkach was self-conscious about his qualifications for being pastor general, you can understand why. Mr. Armstrong, in addition to having established the church, was a prolific teacher and writer, a distinguished author, a famous television personality and an unofficial ambassador for world peace who was known among kings, prime ministers and presidents.

Mr. Tkach wasn't even well known *within the Worldwide Church of God*. He rarely wrote for church publications. WcG *ministers* knew him because of his position in Church Administration. But most of the church membership had never even heard him speak before he became pastor general in 1986.

TKACH'S LIFE IN THE CHURCH

Considering he succeeded someone as prominent as Herbert W. Armstrong, Joseph Tkach Sr. had very little written about his background, even within the church's vast literature base. With Mr. Armstrong, one could quickly pull together piles of information for a biography. With Mr. Tkach, that task is nearly impossible.

What little background information there is about Tkach was mostly written around the time he became pastor general. The most informative piece is a short article that appeared in the *Worldwide News,* "Passing the Baton," by Jeff Zhorne and Michael Snyder.

Mr. Tkach was baptized in 1957 and spent his early WCG years in the city of his birth—Chicago, Illinois. He became a deacon in 1961 and a local elder in 1963—the same year the church employed him to work full time in the ministry.

His three years as a local elder in Chicago were unusually productive, according to the *Worldwide News* synopsis: "The pastor general established churches in South Bend, Fort Wayne and Indianapolis, Ind.; Rockford and Peoria, Ill.; Davenport, Iowa; Grand Rapids, Mich.; Milwaukee, Wis.; Cincinnati, Ohio; and St. Louis, Mo."[2] That a *local elder*—and a *new* one at that—would ESTABLISH 10 congregations across seven different states, is something that just didn't happen in the WCG during the 1960s. My own father started attending services in St. Louis *in 1961*—two years *before* Mr. Tkach even became a minister. So there is no way he could have "established" that congregation. "The only time I remember seeing him in St. Louis was for softball tournaments," my father remembers.[3]

Someone might have alerted the WCG's editorial staff about this attempt to pad Mr. Tkach's resume after "Passing the Baton" ran in the *Worldwide News.* By the time the information appeared in the *Good News* four months later, it had been revised, saying Mr. Tkach "helped" establish those congregations—which might be closer to the truth, but still seems like a stretch.[4]

In 1966, according to the *Worldwide News,* the WCG moved Mr. Tkach and his family to Pasadena so he could go to Ambassador College (AC). The article says "he attended for three years before being assigned to serve with [Roderick] Meredith in the Los Angeles, Calif., church."[5] Tkach Jr.'s book says his father and mother "took classes for three years, intending upon graduation that my dad be sent out to pastor a church. Instead, he remained in Pasadena and eventually pastored a church there."[6]

The way Tkach Jr.'s book is worded gives the impression that his father graduated from Ambassador, which he didn't.

As it happens, my father also went to Pasadena in the late 1960s and took classes for three years. He enrolled in the summer of 1967, one year after Tkach started his AC career. Both of them would have attended a small liberal arts college of about 500 students for at least two years together. And like Tkach, my dad was married at the time. And since most students were single, the Tkaches and the Flurrys would have been part of a fairly exclusive married student community between 1967 and 1969.

My father was photographed as a freshman in the 1968 Ambassador College envoy. Because he had previous college credit transferred to AC, he was on the three-year graduate program. So the following year, in the 1969 envoy, he can be found within the junior class. And in the 1970 edition, he is included within Pasadena's graduating senior class.

Mr. Tkach, however, cannot be found in *any* of the college envoys between 1966 and 1970. "I don't remember ever seeing him in a class," my father says. He does recall seeing Tkach from time to time around the Pasadena campus, but not as a regular student.[7]

In fact, Mr. Tkach did not come to Pasadena in 1966 as an AC student. The church had experienced rapid growth during the 1960s. It wasn't like the 1940s and '50s, when *nearly all* the leaders of the church were young men, in their 20s, who graduated from Ambassador College. During the 1960s, with bigger field congregations, there were more potential leaders, many of them already married and with grown children, who had developed in the local area without Ambassador training. To provide these men with some headquarters training, the superintendent of the U.S. ministry at the time, Roderick Meredith, established a one-year program for their benefit. Approved by Mr. Armstrong, the program called for a handful of local elders to come to headquarters for a year, where they could audit Ambassador College classes and receive on-the-job training in Meredith's Los Angeles congregation, which had 1,100

members. The idea was for them to get a year of training at headquarters before rotating back out into the field to work as an associate pastor and eventually a pastor.

In the case of Mr. Tkach, according to Meredith, "He was never
a good speaker, but Mr. Blackwell [Tkach's district superintendent]
pressured and pressured me to bring him to Pasadena because he
was a hard worker." And he did work hard, Meredith remembers.[8]
But Mr. Tkach also had his limitations.

"When we brought him out, we found that he was not an intel-
ligent person and he did not know his Bible that well," Meredith
said. As to why Mr. Tkach stayed in California instead of going
back out to the field, it *wasn't* because there was a need in Pasadena.
According to Meredith, "We found Mr. Tkach couldn't really rotate
through and go to the field because we couldn't really trust him to
visit [the church members] on his own very much. So we assigned
him to visit the widows in just non-threatening type visits. So he
got the reputation of being the great loving minister to visit the
widows frankly because we couldn't let him do too much else."
According to the superintendent of the ministry at the time, the
reason Mr. Tkach stayed in Pasadena is because he "did not qualify
to be sent out as a pastor."[9]

As for the Ambassador training, Meredith says Tkach did sit in
on some of the Bible classes, but not for credit. He can't remember
if he audited any classes after that initial year, but during his "three
years" at Ambassador, according to his boss, he never attended full
time, he didn't take any classes for credit and "he definitely did not
graduate."[10]

So the impression the Tkaches gave, that Sr. went to Ambassador
College for three years *before* being assigned to pastor congregations,
is not true. Tkach was assigned to Mr. Meredith in 1966 upon his
arrival to Pasadena. And for the next several years, he worked with
widows so as to not be a liability elsewhere.

He was raised to the rank of preaching elder in 1974, after being
a local elder for 11 years. Throughout the 1970s, Tkach continued
as an assistant pastor in various congregations in Southern
California.

When California's attorney general's office tried to seize control of church operations in January 1979, Joseph Tkach was an assistant pastor for the Pasadena A.M. congregation. After church members spontaneously descended upon the headquarters property to show their support for a church under fire, Mr. Tkach and a deacon named Joseph Kotora hastily set up the Hall of Administration lobby for a makeshift church service. Dean Blackwell gave a sermon before the "sit in" congregation that day, and Mr. Tkach closed the service with prayer.

Tkach's involvement in the 1979 crisis did not escape Mr. Armstrong's attention, even though Mr. Armstrong was living in Arizona at the time. In July 1979, he appointed Mr. Tkach as director of Ministerial Services (later named Church Administration). Then, on September 27, 1979, in Mr. Armstrong's Tucson home, the church founder raised three individuals to the rank of evangelist—the highest ecclesiastical office in the church (besides Mr. Armstrong's). The new evangelists—Ellis LaRavia, Stanley Rader and Joseph Tkach—had all played a role in defending the church against the state's unconstitutional attack.

Besides heading up Church Administration, Mr. Tkach also became associate pastor of the Pasadena P.M. congregation—the headquarters congregation Mr. Armstrong pastored. In 1981, Mr. Armstrong selected Mr. Tkach to serve on the Advisory Council. These were Mr. Tkach's primary responsibilities for the final years of Mr. Armstrong's life.

SKETCHY EDUCATION

Besides adding to his exploits in the church, it appears that Tkach's handlers also wanted to create a legend out of his life *before* conversion—particularly his academic background. In light of Mr. Armstrong's views about modern education, one wonders why Mr. Tkach seemed so self-conscious about his formal education. Mr. Armstrong viewed his lack of training at an "assembly line" university or seminary as an advantage. Mr. Tkach, however, wanted scholarly credentials, even if he had to invent them.

After becoming pastor general in 1986, for some reason, he wanted the brethren to think that he was born in 1926. "Passing the Baton" gives precise dates for Tkach's baptism, ordinations and marriage. But no birth date is given—it just says he was 59 at the time he became pastor general.

The WCG's personal correspondence department produced a "Letters Series" in 1989 in which there is a fact sheet about Mr. Tkach's background for people who requested such information. That letter, prepared three years after Mr. Tkach took charge, says he was "born in 1926," but does not give the exact day or month of his birth.[11]

According to his birth and death certificates, however, Mr. Tkach was born on March 16, 1927, which means he would have been 58 when Mr. Armstrong died—not 59. By the time Mr. Tkach died in 1995, after critics had exposed these birth date inconsistencies, the WCG got the date right in a *Worldwide News* article by Jeff Zhorne.[12] Tkach Jr. also corrected the date in *Transformed by Truth*, justifying the mix-up this way: "As was common in those days, the doctor didn't get around to filling out a birth certificate until a *few months* after my dad's birth."[13] In fact, according to the birth certificate, the doctor filed the information just *eight days* after Tkach was born.

As far as why they wanted him to be a year older, it's hard to say. With the correct date, he would have finished high school early, soon after his 17th birthday. So maybe they wanted him to be an 18-year-old graduate. In any event, he did finish high school in 1944. He graduated 155th in a class size of 349, from Tilden High School in south Chicago.

The following year, in January 1945, he ran off and joined the Navy as a 17-year-old. So maybe they tried to make him 18 for that reason. But Tkach admitted to *Plain Truth* readers in 1986 that he ran away from home and was "under age" when he joined the Navy.[14]

It's just an odd "fact" to lie about. But why they stuck with the 1926 birthday for the first several years of Mr. Tkach's pastor generalship, when they could have gotten the correct date from his driver's license, is inexplicable.

Continuing with the timeline, according to Jeff Zhorne, Tkach served in the U.S. Navy during World War II, from January 17, 1945, to July 22, 1946.[15] Mr. Tkach, however, wrote in the *Worldwide News* that he returned from the war to Chicago on December 21, 1945, which would have limited his service in the Navy to 11 months.[16]

From 1946 to 1950 is when the biography gets real sketchy. In reading what the WCG produced, you are left with the distinct impression that Mr. Tkach went to college during those four years. In "Passing the Baton," for instance, it says that after Tkach received a naval certificate in "basic engineering" in 1945, he then returned home to attend the Illinois Institute of Technology in Chicago, where he studied industrial management. After that, he was hired by Hupp Aviation in 1950.[17]

Upon searching their archives, however, representatives at the Illinois Institute found no record of Joseph Tkach ever having attended there. His career at the Illinois Institute, apparently, was not unlike his "training" at Ambassador College.[18]

LACK OF SCHOLARSHIP

Writing in 2002, Michael Feazell criticized Mr. Armstrong because he "had no seminary training and lacked any disciplined study of church history, biblical interpretation and original languages of Scripture."[19] In his book, Feazell said that "Herbert Armstrong and scholarship did not mix well."[20] As if it mixed well with *Tkach*. Feazell wrote, "Many of Armstrong's doctrinal errors sprang directly from his ignorance of biblical scholarship and sound methods of biblical interpretation."[21] In *Transformed by Truth,* Tkach Jr. criticized Mr. Armstrong for his lack of training in "hermeneutics, epistemology, or apologetics."[22]

Of course, Mr. Armstrong would have responded to those criticisms thunderously, by pointing to the RANK IGNORANCE about God within scholarly circles. Critics may scoff at Mr. Armstrong's supposed lack of scholarship, but hundreds of thousands— including a great many world leaders Mr. Armstrong visited—would have considered Herbert Armstrong a Bible scholar and expert educator. Look at the fruits: Perhaps thousands of pamphlets, articles and letters, hundreds of booklets and seven books. Thousands of sermons. He produced and delivered 1,500 radio programs and nearly 200 television programs. He developed the curriculum for three colleges—giving what must have been thousands of class lectures himself. Objective observers, even if they disagree with his theology, would at least give him credit for all that he produced.

Compare that with Tkach Sr.'s exploits, even counting his fabricated academic record. Before taking over in 1986, he hardly ever wrote or spoke publicly. According to Aaron Dean, Mr. Armstrong actually took comfort in Tkach's average intellectual capacities, believing it would make him more prone to rely on the Advisory Council.[23] After becoming pastor general, Tkach's own son even admitted that his "dad was not known as a theologian."[24] Tkach's former boss, Roderick Meredith, evaluated Mr. Armstrong's successor more bluntly, saying he "did not speak well and I didn't realize how little he understood the doctrines."[25]

In light of Tkach's sketchy educational background, it's astonishing how often Tkach Jr. and Feazell have found occasion to ridicule *Mr. Armstrong's* lack of scholarship. But if Mr. Armstrong was uneducated, where would that leave Joseph Tkach?

THE REAL CHURCH HISTORIAN

In a 2002 deposition, we pointed Tkach Jr. to the statement about Mr. Armstrong's lack of seminary training and disciplined study of church history and then asked, "Could the same thing be said of your father?"[26] That question caught the younger Tkach completely off guard.

"No," he stammered, "not as precisely as that, no."[27] According to Tkach, his father spent more time studying church history than Mr. Armstrong. He later said that Mr. Armstrong "read mostly on philosophy,"[28] as if Joe Jr., who was born the same year Mr. Armstrong turned 59, knows everything the founder of the church *read*. When he spoke and wrote, Mr. Armstrong did, at times, refer to the written works that had made an impression on him. But how Tkach Jr. took these many comments to mean he read mostly philosophy, I'll never know.

In his *Autobiography,* Mr. Armstrong discussed his earliest plunge into the study of church history. His wife had challenged him to prove the biblical truth on the question of the Sabbath. In response to her challenge, he "spent a solid six months of virtual night-and-day, seven-day-a-week study and research" trying to prove that Sunday was God's day of worship. "I even studied Greek sufficiently to run down every possible questionable text in the original Greek."[29] He used Robertson's *Grammar of the Greek New Testament*. He also relied upon a number of other commentaries and Greek and Hebrew lexicons. He delved into several encyclopedias—Britannica, Americana, as well as the Jewish and Catholic encyclopedias.

"I read Gibbon's *Decline and Fall of the Roman Empire*, especially his chapter 15 dealing with the religious history of the first four hundred years after Christ," Mr. Armstrong wrote. "*I left no stone unturned.*"[30]

From that alone, you get the impression he read quite a lot more than just philosophy.

In *Mystery of the Ages*, Mr. Armstrong wrote, "Scholars and church historians recognize that events in the early Christian Church between A.D. 50 and 150 can only be seen in vague outline—as if obscured by a thick mist."[31] To support his conclusions, Mr. Armstrong relied upon the noted English scholar Samuel G. Green in his *Handbook of Church History*. He quoted from William Fitzgerald's *Lectures on Ecclesiastical History*, William McGlothlin's *The Course of Christian History* and Philip Schaff's *History of the Christian Church*.

In his booklets *The Plain Truth About Easter* and *The Plain Truth About Christmas*, Mr. Armstrong relied on Alexander Hislop's *The Two Babylons*.

Mr. Armstrong's study of church history is also reflected in the many writings he produced on the subject. In *Mystery of the Ages*, his longest chapter by far was titled "Mystery of the Church." He also wrote an eight-part *Plain Truth* series in 1979 on the "Proofs of God's True Church" and a 1984 booklet, *Where Is the True Church?* Included among his more than 1,500 radio broadcasts is an eight-part series on "The True Church."

Add to that the comprehensive works of Mr. Armstrong's *students*: Dr. Hoeh's booklet *A True History of the True Church* and article "Amazing 2,000-Year History of the Church of God," Dr.

C. Paul Meredith's book on the development of false Christianity, *Satan's Great Deception,* and Ron Kelly's thesis, "History of the Church of God."

Tkach Jr. boasted that his dad "read books" about church history, some of which weren't even published until after Mr. Armstrong died. Among the works Tkach Jr. cited were those of Methodist minister Justo Gonzalez.[32]

Mr. Armstrong studied Gibbon, Schaff, Fitzgerald, McGlothlin and Green and wrote extensively about the history of the church. Tkach Sr. studied Gonzalez and never wrote a thing about church history.

Of course, deep in his heart of hearts, Joe Jr. knows Mr. Armstrong's extensive research and training, as well as his productive life, towers above his own father's intellectual achievements. But the reason he raises the "uneducated" card in reference to Mr. Armstrong is because he *doesn't agree* with Mr. Armstrong's *explanation* of church history. Had he put it that way, at least it would have been honest. But to say that his dad studied church history and Mr. Armstrong didn't—that he read mostly philosophy?

Every present and former member of the Worldwide Church of God should *know* that is a lie.

DISCIPLINED STUDY

In the deposition quoted above, to support his father's credentials as being superior to those of Mr. Armstrong, Tkach Jr. claimed that besides his father's grasp of church history, Tkach Sr. went to Ambassador College. Our attorney then followed up with the question everyone on our side of the table almost blurted out: "Well, it would be sort of difficult to distinguish your father's educational background from Mr. Armstrong's wouldn't it, to say that he attended a college that Mr. Armstrong created and supervised?"[33]

Unbelievably, Tkach responded, "Not at all. Because in the college milieu, there was disciplined study. Mr. Armstrong never had that."

For the sake of argument, let's suppose Mr. Tkach actually attended Ambassador College for three years as a full-time student

and then graduated in 1969. Let's assume he was an active partici-
pant in the "disciplined study" of Ambassador life. How does *that*—
attending what Tkach Jr. now calls an "indoctrination camp"[34]
started by a heretic—qualify as disciplined study, while *establishing,
teaching at* and *supervising* that same college does not?

HERBERT ARMSTRONG AND J.H. ALLEN

In *Transformed by Truth,* Mr. Tkach Jr. wrote, "In fact, it is no
secret that Herbert Armstrong's *The United States and the British
Commonwealth in Prophecy* was copied from a book titled *Judah's
Scepter and Joseph's Birthright* by J.H. Allen."[35] He offers no support
for this plagiarism charge. It's just true because he says so—it's "no
secret"—*everyone* knows Mr. Armstrong "copied" it. But if you actually take the time to examine the two books, you will find that they
are entirely different. Yes, ENTIRELY.

Just because both books discuss the modern identity of the lost
10 tribes of ancient Israel does not mean Mr. Armstrong "copied"
Allen. If William Manchester and Martin Gilbert both write biog-
raphies about Winston Churchill, does that mean one plagiarized
the other?

And it's not like Mr. Armstrong tried to conceal the fact that
he read Allen's book when studying the subject of ancient Israel's
migration into Europe. He said, "It's true that I had read one or two
other writings and that book of J.H. Allen on the truth about the
lost 10 tribes."[36] But it would be a "bald-faced lie" for anyone to say
it was copied, Mr. Armstrong said.

"I examined this so-called Anglo-Israel theory," he continued.
"But I checked it very carefully with the Bible, and *I only believed
what I saw in the Bible.* I didn't believe and I threw out a lot of what
they had."[37] Isn't that the way any honest theologian would study a
biblical commentary or history? If it squares with the truth of the
Bible, then Mr. Armstrong was entitled to expound upon it just as
much as any other theologian.

J.H. Allen introduced his book by writing, "Although it is not
generally known, it is nevertheless true that God made two covenants with Abraham ...."[38] Compare that to the introductory state-

ment in *The United States and Britain in Prophecy:* "A staggering turn in world events is due to erupt in the next few years. It will involve violently the United States, Britain, Western Europe, the Middle East."[39] These opening remarks, like the titles for both books, highlight the *vast difference* between the two.

J.H. Allen organized his work into these three sections: 1) the birthright promise; 2) the scepter promise; and 3) the veil being lifted from the Abrahamic nations. The first two sections revolve around the promises God made to Abraham in Genesis 12 and how they played out in history. And to Allen's credit, he tried to be honest with the Bible as compared with secular history.

The third section is also mostly historical and secular. And when Allen does venture into explaining the prophetic significance, he veers way off course.[40]

Mr. Armstrong's book, on the other hand, is about a PROPHESIED CAPTIVITY to come upon our peoples unless we repent of our sins. That is the book's central focus from beginning to end.

In expounding on these end-time prophecies, Mr. Armstrong devoted some space in the book, between chapters 3 and 8, to establish Israel's present-day identity based upon Bible and secular history. These are crucial historical facts that must be explained for readers to understand the truth about end-time prophecy. J.H. Allen is to be credited for teaching the truth about some of these historical facts. But he certainly did not grasp the tremendous significance of this history as it relates to Bible prophecy.

And yet, that's what *the last six chapters of Mr. Armstrong's book* are devoted to—expounding upon the real significance of this history as it relates to end-time prophecy. In chapter 10, for instance, Mr. Armstrong wrote about how the birthright promises were withheld for 2,520 years. There is nothing like this in Allen's book. Another chapter asks the question, "Why did Israel lose its identity?" J.H. Allen not only failed to answer that question, he never asked it. Then Mr. Armstrong concluded his book by discussing what is prophesied to happen to the American and British peoples in the very near future—a conclusion that is not only different, but at complete odds with J.H. Allen's conclusions.

While it is true that Mr. Armstrong read *Judah's Scepter and*

Joseph's Birthright, along with other books about the "Anglo-Israel" theory, HE DID NOT COPY those works. Joe Jr. made that dishonest claim without any supportive evidence whatsoever, simply because he dislikes Mr. Armstrong and doesn't agree with the book that more than *6 million people* requested.

THE GHOST WRITERS

On page 66 of his book, Tkach Jr. wrote,

> When my dad did give a major sermon on doctrinal changes, he always read major portions of it, confirming in these people's minds that he was a mere dupe of the "gang of four." They circulated rumors that others were writing his articles for church publications and publishing them either without his knowledge or against his will. [41]

And that's true. I remember listening to a number of Mr. Tkach's taped sermons from the late 1980s and early 1990s—I even reviewed a few videotaped sermons. He would read and read, and oftentimes trip over words. I also remember the rumors vividly: *Who prepared this for him? And why doesn't he pull away from his notes?*

Later on in the book, after referring to these "rumors," Tkach Jr. wrote, "It didn't seem to occur to people that if my dad didn't like or agree with material Mike Feazell (who was his executive assistant and editorial advisor) or others *prepared for him,* he could have changed it or not used it at all." [42]

Yes—in the very same book Tkach Jr. accuses Mr. Armstrong of copying J.H. Allen, he admits that his own father had his sermons *prepared for him.* Then he justifies that by saying his father *didn't have to* use those pre-prepared sermons if he didn't want to.

And it wasn't just Tkach's *sermons* that others prepared. Tkach Jr. continued, "My dad hired Mike Feazell to assist him, especially in *writing* and *theology,* and he could have fired him at any time. My dad spent hours every day with Mike, working out details of *letters, articles* and *sermons.*" [43] In 2002, Feazell admitted that as

Mr. Tkach's assistant, he was primarily "responsible for editing and drafting his written material."[44]

Rod Meredith remembers how awkward and embarrassing it was to see Tkach Sr. ramble on using someone else's material:

> In the sermons in Pasadena, when he got away from his manu-script—which was written at times by Larry Salyer, at times by Robin Webber, and most of the time later by Mike Feazell, who wrote virtually all of his articles—why then, he would start shouting and they would bawl him out backstage, "Dad, why did you get away from the script?" And so it was kind of embarrassing.[45]

The men who assisted Mr. Tkach justify these actions by saying that he just wasn't a good communicator. Mike Feazell wrote, "Because Tkach Sr. did not possess the same facility of written and oral expression as Armstrong, *he had to rely heavily on others* for his *written communication* to pastors and church members."[46] His own son admitted that Tkach Sr. wasn't a *theologian*—and that others prepared his sermons and articles—that when he gave sermons, he was "anchored to his [actually someone else's] notes."[47] Mr. Tkach's personal assistant, the one who prepared his sermons and articles, readily admits that Tkach was *not* a good communicator—whether in writing or verbally. And the WCG's own website says Mr. Tkach didn't have the "magnetic personality that Mr. Armstrong did."[48]

It's all kind of pitiful, isn't it? Tkachism has worked so hard to make Mr. Armstrong out to be an unqualified, uneducated ignoramus. And yet, look at the one who led them through their transformation.

FIVE
TKACH'S FELLOWS

*"I know Gerald Flurry very well. … How could he carry on
for Mr. Armstrong? He wasn't even trained around him, much less at
his feet. Wasn't even trained close to him. Wasn't even trained
at his coattail. Wasn't trained within arm's reach."*

— GERALD WATERHOUSE
Sermon, *January 25, 1992*

THE day Mr. Armstrong died, Mike Feazell and Mike
Rasmussen, who both worked for Mr. Tkach, "went up to my
office and took all my files out of my drawers," Aaron Dean
remembers. He said, "I got called by Brenda Yale and Donna—the
secretary up there—and they were crying. And they said, 'What's
going on? They're treating us like criminals.'" [1]

Bob Herrington, one of Mr. Armstrong's four nurses, remembers well his first encounter with the new administration. As
Mr. Armstrong's primary nighttime caregiver, Herrington lived
in an apartment adjacent to Mr. Armstrong's home. He was at
Mr. Armstrong's bedside the morning he died. And, according to
Herrington, "I was evicted before the day was through. Somebody
came over to me and said, 'We have important people coming to
town—we're going to need that apartment.'" [2] Herrington wouldn't
reveal who told him to leave, but whoever it was also insisted that
Herrington *not* attend the funeral, so as not to attract the atten-

tion of the press. So, a few days after Mr. Armstrong died, Bob Herrington packed his things and moved to Texas.

According to Aaron Dean, these incidents highlight one of the first promises made to Mr. Armstrong that Tkach broke. Mr. Armstrong wanted *his* staff to assist Mr. Tkach, *not* Tkach's staff. But contrary to the assurances he had given to his predecessor, Mr. Tkach (or perhaps his staff) made it clear on January 16 that, despite Mr. Armstrong's warnings, *Tkach's staff was coming with him.*

TKACH'S PERSONAL ASSISTANT

Michael Feazell's family moved to Pasadena in 1957, when he was 6, so he could attend the WCG's Imperial Grade School. He was educated by the church's grade school, high school and college, finally graduating from Ambassador in 1973.

After graduation, Feazell worked for one year at Imperial Schools as an elementary teacher. In 1974, he moved to Yuma, Arizona, and taught fifth grade at a local elementary school for four years. During the summers, he worked for the WCG's youth camp in Minnesota, where he was in charge of the camp store. In the fall of 1978, the church again hired him full time, to work at Ambassador's Pasadena campus as a tennis instructor and equipment manager.

Then, coincident with Tkach Sr.'s appointment over Ministerial Services in 1979, Feazell catapulted up the WCG hierarchy. Tkach brought him on board first as a special projects coordinator and later as personal assistant. Feazell was not a minister at the time he joined Church Administration.

Feazell had been a friend of the Tkach family for a number of years. He met Tkach's son, Joe. Jr., at Imperial High School in 1967, where both of them were attending as tenth graders. They later attended Ambassador College together in Pasadena and graduated together in 1973. During the summer months of his college years, Feazell even lived with the Tkaches. In many ways, Joe Sr. was like a father to him.

For a period of seven years at Church Administration (late 1979 to early 1986), Mr. Feazell assisted Tkach Sr., maintaining consistent communication with the WCG ministry in organizing the

Ministerial Refreshing Program, ministerial transfers and ministerial assignments for the Feast of Tabernacles.

When Mr. Tkach became pastor general in 1986, Mr. Feazell continued serving as his personal assistant, but focused instead on preparing Tkach Sr.'s articles and sermons.

HEAD OF THE MINISTRY

Like Feazell, Joseph Tkach Jr. was born in 1951 and grew up in the Worldwide Church of God. His family moved to Pasadena in 1966 when Mr. Meredith accepted Tkach Sr. into the one-year program for local elders. After Joe Jr. graduated from Ambassador in 1973, he married Jill Hockwald. He worked as a ministerial trainee for the church between 1973 and 1976, serving in Indiana, Michigan, California and Arizona. He was ordained as a local elder in the summer of 1976. Months later, his employment with the church was terminated due to budget cuts. Though no longer paid by the church, he continued serving as assistant pastor for the Phoenix East congregation in Arizona. He was later removed from this position in July 1978, two months after he divorced his first wife at the age of 26.

Between 1978 and 1986, Joe Jr. lived in relative obscurity within the Phoenix East congregation as a local elder. He married for a second time in 1980. He was employed as a social worker until 1984, and then worked for Intel until 1986.

After his father succeeded Mr. Armstrong in January 1986, Joe Jr. began a sharp ascent up the WCG hierarchy. His father appointed him assistant director of Church Administration in August 1986, where he worked for Larry Salyer. (Salyer had replaced Tkach Sr. as head of Church Administration once Tkach became pastor general.)

Eight months after moving to Pasadena, in April 1987, Mr. Tkach Sr. raised his son to the rank of *pastor*. Later that year, in November, Joe Jr. was again promoted. Tkach Sr. decided to reorganize Church Administration into two branches—the U.S. ministry and the international ministry, with Joe Jr. in charge of the former and Larry Salyer the latter, effectively making Salyer the assistant to

Joe Jr. Thus, in a matter of 15 short months, Joseph Tkach Jr. went
from being a non-salaried, local church elder—the lowest-ranking
spiritual office in the WCG—to the pastor-ranked director over the
WCG's ministry. This meteoric ascent put him in charge of approximately 1,200 WCG ministers in *less than a year and a half.*

He was 36 years old.

HEAD OF MEDIA OPERATIONS

Bernard Schnippert, another college friend of Joe Jr.'s, graduated
from AC in 1971. After serving in the personal correspondence
department for a short time after graduation, Schnippert went into
the field ministry for a few years, serving in Edmonton and Calgary
in Alberta, Canada. By the mid-1970s, poor health forced him to
take a two-year paid leave of absence.

In 1977, he returned to work in Pasadena as an assistant to
Dr. Robert Kuhn, where he was responsible for coordinating the
Systematic Theology Project (STP). Garner Ted Armstrong later
presented the infamous STP at a ministerial conference in January
1978, shortly after his father had left town. The STP was a scholarly attempt to liberalize or alter many of the church's doctrines.
It was prepared by a handful of WCG scholars, coordinated by
Schnippert, and carefully concealed from Herbert Armstrong. Once
Mr. Armstrong caught wind of the conspiracy, he ordered all of the
church's ministers to return their copies. He disfellowshiped Garner
Ted and Dr. Kuhn later that year. These two, along with other
disgruntled former members, then proceeded to launch the unsuc-
cessful civil suit against Herbert Armstrong and the Worldwide
Church of God in January 1979.

Bernie Schnippert somehow escaped the STP fallout and
remained within the WCG. He spent the next eight years seques-
tered in a small congregation in Las Vegas, before getting a call from
headquarters in April 1987. He was offered a position in Pasadena
assisting Dexter Faulkner in Editorial Services. His primary title
was that of international booklet director. A few months after his
arrival at Pasadena, on August 1, Mr. Tkach raised Mr. Schnippert
to the rank of pastor.

The following month, Mr. Tkach made this remarkable announcement in the *Pastor General's Report:*

> As God grants greater and greater impact to the *World Tomorrow* television program, the *Plain Truth* magazine and our other publications, both in the United States and internationally, I have come to see the vital necessity of establishing thorough coordination among the four crucial and closely interrelated departments of Mail Processing, Editorial Services, Publishing Services and Television Production.[3]

To that end, Mr. Tkach selected Bernie Schnippert to fill the newly created position of director of Media Operations.

In other words, instead of assisting Dexter Faulkner in Editorial Services (which he had done for all of three months), Schnippert was now Faulkner's boss—*as well as Richard Rice's, Ray Wright's and Larry Omasta's*—three other department heads.

Thus, the man who coordinated the Systematic Theology Project in 1977 was now director of all the church's media operations nine years later—just a year and a half after the death of Herbert Armstrong.

HEAD OF THE COLLEGE

Donald Ward is another key personality who rose to prominence within the WCG during the tumultuous 1970s. Highly educated, Ward was admitted into Ambassador College, Big Sandy, in 1969—and already equipped with a master's degree from the University of Southern Mississippi. He started teaching at Big Sandy one year after his arrival as a student and later obtained a doctorate in education from East Texas State University in Commerce in 1973.

After being named the associate dean of faculty for Big Sandy that same year, Dr. Ward played a key role in Ambassador's pursuit of accreditation throughout the mid-1970s. Early in the process, he explained in the college's newspaper that to become an accredited liberal arts college, Big Sandy would have to offer at least four majors, which would necessitate the addition of many new courses, and also beef up its faculty credentials and library services.[4]

In 1976, Dr. Ward became Big Sandy's academic dean, but only for a year because of Mr. Armstrong's decision in 1977 to close Big Sandy. In March 1978, however, Garner Ted appointed Dr. Ward as vice president of Ambassador's Pasadena campus. One month later, in April, Ted elevated him to the office of president, in hopes that Dr. Ward's credentials would help the college become accredited. Their plan was to close up operations in Pasadena and consolidate in Big Sandy as an accredited institution.

The elder Armstrong wrote extensively about the state of the college during this tumultuous time period. He said the campus was a "shambles of immorality and secularism. Illicit sex was rampant."[5] Garner Ted had been keeping major decisions from his father—decisions "he was unauthorized to make."[6] Ted either shipped out or demoted old-timers and replaced them with yes-men. According to Mr. Armstrong, Ted surrounded himself with "men he thought would be loyal to him personally above being loyal to the church and to God."[7]

As with the STP, once Mr. Armstrong awakened to what was happening to the college, he intervened swiftly and decisively.

> On May 8, last month, I learned that my son had appointed a man I do not even know as president of Ambassador College. I then wrote him that this was the last straw—of his assuming authority never given to him to make major decisions.[8]

Incredibly, the hiring of Dr. Ward was the last straw that resulted in Garner Ted being fired!

Mr. Armstrong later wrote about these traumatic years for the church and college:

> The liberals at Pasadena wanted accreditation. They did not want to be accredited as a Bible college, but as a full competing college or university. As such the college would fall under the rules of the secular accrediting society, which would more or less determine policy and curricula. ...

Ambassador College had been destroyed as God's college. In 1978 ... I had to completely close Ambassador College at Pasadena, starting all over again, as in 1947, with one freshman class. The colleges in England and in Texas had already been closed.[9]

Despite all this, however, Dr. Ward managed to escape the accreditation fallout. He settled into a low-profile position as pastor of a congregation in East Texas.

When Big Sandy reopened in 1981, Dr. Ward returned to his previous position of academic dean, serving under Leon Walker, the deputy chancellor. Ward held that position until late 1987 when Tkach Sr. called him. At the time, Dr. Ward had been working under Rod Meredith, the deputy chancellor at Big Sandy. At the Pasadena campus, Raymond McNair was the deputy chancellor. When Mr. Tkach appointed Dr. Ward to the position of vice chancellor over *both* campuses in 1987, he became *Meredith's* and *McNair's* SUPERIOR.

The following year, in 1988, Ambassador College again began its active pursuit of accreditation—and just like in 1978, Dr. Ward was at the helm. Their plan—surprise, surprise—was to close operations in Pasadena and consolidate in Big Sandy as an accredited institution.

OUT WITH THE OLD

So, in *less than two years* after Mr. Armstrong's death, Don Ward was president of Ambassador College, Bernie Schnippert headed all the media operations, Joe Tkach Jr. was in charge of the ministry and Michael Feazell was the pastor general's executive assistant and ghost writer.

Another personality who would figure prominently in the new administration was Greg Albrecht, who was dean of students at AC Pasadena throughout the 1980s. In 1990, Bernie Schnippert moved Albrecht into Editorial Services, where he would later be given charge of the church's flagship magazine, the *Plain Truth*.

All five of these scholars were made evangelists *after* Mr. Armstrong died in 1986.

And what of the *other* evangelists—those raised to that position by Mr. Armstrong? They quickly faded into the background, just like in the 1970s. In July 1986, Mr. Tkach removed Leslie McCullough from his position as deputy chancellor at Big Sandy and shipped him off to head up the small regional office in South Africa.

To replace McCullough, Mr. Tkach moved Rod Meredith from headquarters to Big Sandy. Three years later, after Tkach decided to close the Pasadena campus and focus its accreditation pursuit on Big Sandy, he brought Meredith back to Pasadena and tucked him away in an insignificant position within the editorial department.

Weeks after Mr. Tkach catapulted Dr. Ward to vice chancellor over the colleges, ahead of Mr. Meredith and Mr. McNair, Tkach shipped McNair to the New Zealand regional office.

We won't take space to elaborate on a number of other examples, like Richard Ames, Herman Hoeh, Ellis La Ravia, Leroy Neff and Gerald Waterhouse—but suffice it to say that all of these men, who were prominent evangelists at the time of Mr. Armstrong's death, faded from view and settled into much less significant roles once Mr. Tkach stepped into office and brought up his staff.

There are a few exceptions, like old-timers Dean Blackwell (who has since died) and Ron Kelly (who was the church's financial controller until 2005, when he retired), but for the most part, when Tkach Sr. took over, he brought in a whole new administrative team.

It's interesting now as I look back on this history because one of the biggest criticisms the Tkach administration had against my father, after they fired him in December 1989, was that he was a relative nobody—a lowly field minister who never served under Mr. Armstrong. And while that may have been true, one wonders what Mr. Armstrong would have thought of the upper echelons of the wcg administration at the point of my dad's firing.

Donald Ward over the college?

Joe Jr. in charge of the ministry?

Michael Feazell writing articles for the pastor general?

Bernie Schnippert heading the church's four main departments?

By the end of 1989, Tkach Jr. and Feazell had been delegated enough authority to fire two field ministers on the spot—my father and his assistant John Amos—ministers who had been serving full time in the church for two decades. Had Mr. Armstrong been present at the firing, he may not have recognized my father and Mr. Amos.

But I'm not sure he would have recognized the two men firing them either.

SIX
FINGERPRINTS

*"The admonishment is now for those of us still living
who now have a task that is set before them, a course
that has already been charted by God's apostle. We need to
maintain that course and not deviate from it one iota."*

— JOSEPH W. TKACH
The day Mr. Armstrong died

IN his 1997 book, Joseph Tkach Jr. wrote, "Early on, there were some astute members who saw that the first two or three changes we made required that other changes would soon have to be made. They accurately predicted most of the corrections we announced in the following three or four years. Yet *at the time we saw none of this.*" According to Tkach, when their critics predicted further changes, "We steadfastly denied we *were even thinking* about such changes ...."[1] He said further that NONE of the WCG leaders even had any of this in mind—meaning the church's transformation—*as late as 1991.*[2] It was all just an innocent coming-of-age story, we're supposed to believe.

The problem with that theory is that what happened in the Worldwide Church of God *after* Mr. Armstrong died is what *almost* happened to the church in the 1970s, *before* he died. In fact, it was Mr. Armstrong's declining health back then which had Garner Ted and others chomping at the bit to transform the church. The imminent likelihood of Mr. Armstrong's death helped expose the true colors of Garner Ted and his fellows. Indeed, had not Mr. Armstrong recovered from heart failure in 1977, the church's transformation would have occurred a decade earlier than it did.

Tkach Jr. acts as if they had no clue, even as late as 1991, about what they were doing or where the church was headed.

Yet, what Donald Ward did to Ambassador College between 1989 and 1994 is EXACTLY what he *almost* did in 1978 under Garner Ted. *Exactly!*

And we're supposed to believe that Bernie Schnippert's work on the Systematic Theology Project in 1977—a scholarly attempt to liberalize the doctrines of the church—had no influence on his work 10 years later, when he returned to Pasadena to take charge of the editorial, publishing, television and mail processing departments?

The principal players in the Tkach transformation left their fingerprints ALL OVER THE CRIME SCENE during the 1970s! But unlike Garner Ted and a few others, THEY NEVER GOT CAUGHT. They fled the scene once Mr. Armstrong showed up physically revitalized and determined to prosecute the guilty. Joe Jr. got laid off, went through a divorce and hibernated in Arizona. Feazell—also laid off—went to Arizona to teach fifth graders. Schnippert settled into a small congregation in Las Vegas. Dr. Ward moved to East Texas.

Then, after Mr. Armstrong's failing health finally got the best of him, they returned from hiding and IMMEDIATELY went to work on accomplishing what they and others *almost* did in the 1970s.

That's not to say that *all* of Tkach's fellows were staunch supporters of Garner Ted's coup attempt. Some of the personalities changed. But in looking at the events from the mid-to-late 1980s, we find many of the same fingerprints that were left on the 1970s mess.

The most significant and obvious difference, of course, is that after January 16, 1986, Mr. Armstrong wasn't around to restrain the rebels.

IDENTITY OF BABYLON

The early to mid-1980s might well be considered the golden years for the Worldwide Church of God. At the same time, however, Mr. Armstrong's overall health was in decline. His eyesight got so bad that, without the assistance of Aaron Dean, he would not have been able to complete *Mystery of the Ages*. Yet even with Dean serving as his eyes and ears those last few years, Mr. Armstrong did not see everything that was going on behind his back.

On December 17, 1983, Mr. Armstrong gave a sermon in Pasadena titled "Mission of the Philadelphia Era." He read from a three-volume, extra-large-print version of the Bible—and even then, he needed a magnifying glass. During the sermon, he listed a number of truths God had restored to the Worldwide Church of God over the course of his ministry. Toward the end of his message, Mr. Armstrong discussed RELIGIOUS DECEPTION and the IDENTITY OF MODERN BABYLON and its daughter churches (Revelation 17:5). He said, "Well, brethren, all those things have been *restored* …."

The following year, on March 10, Mr. Armstrong reiterated many of these restored truths in a sermon he gave in Chicago. He also discussed the list at a ministerial conference over the summer. Then, in *Mystery of the Ages,* he wrote in 1985, "At least 18 basic and essential truths have been restored to the true church."[3]

But Mr. Armstrong never produced a written list himself. That task was left to the church's editorial department. Richard Rice, who managed the church's mail processing center, was the first one to compile a written list of the truths. It appeared in the *Pastor General's Report* a few months after Mr. Armstrong died. Although the list wasn't numbered, it included 18 points. The list church members are much more familiar with appeared five months later in the *Worldwide News,* with a short introduction by Mr. Tkach.[4] According to Tkach, Editorial Services had prepared the list— and for the first time, it was numbered—there were 18 points of restored truth.

But there is NOTHING in Rice's list or the one introduced by Tkach that says anything about the *modern identity of Babylon.* That's because editors had been hard at work, *even before Mr. Armstrong died,* REVISING and OMITTING much of the church's teaching about ancient Babylon and the development of the modern Babylonian religious system.

The biggest revision in church literature appeared as early as 1982 in *The Bible Story.* Basil Wolverton, a nationally known artist and WCG minister, began work on the project in 1958. Originally appearing in the *Plain Truth* in monthly installments, *The Bible Story*

was converted into a six-volume set of books during the 1960s.
Mr. Armstrong assigned the project to Mr. Wolverton because of
the tremendous need to properly teach children the truths of the
Bible. "Bible stories up to now," Mr. Armstrong explained, seemed
to have "no mission but that of providing exciting entertainment.
Biblical incidents are taken out of context, their real connection
with the very purpose of life ignored." Furthermore, he wrote, "In
my research into the history of education, the truth emerged of the
diabolical master conspiracy for deceiving the whole world."[5] Thus,
Mr. Wolverton set out to tell the story of the Bible factually and
chronologically, and in a way that would be interesting and understandable for children. Yet the series was not intended for children
alone: It provided a basic understanding of the thread of the Bible
for all interested readers, including many thousands of adults.

Chapter 5 of the 1960s version contains quite a lot of history
regarding the establishment of civilization after the Noachian Flood.
It discusses how Noah preached God's truth and prophesied about
a coming Messiah. "But something happened back then to cause
men to believe that the son of a god had come to Earth shortly after
the flood," Wolverton wrote.[6] It went on to explain how Nimrod
and his wife, Semiramis, established a Babylonian religious system
as a great counterfeit to God's true religion. "There, in ancient
Babylon," wrote Wolverton,

> were born the false beliefs that have wormed their way into
> almost every religion. Even today millions and millions of
> people who may want to live according to the right ways are not
> aware that their manner of worship follows very closely that of
> ancient idol worship and pagan rites begun at Babel.[7]

Virtually all of this critical history—Nimrod's plans to rule the
Earth; his wife's successful attempt to make a false god out of her
slain husband—was removed from the 1982 version of *The Bible
Story*. It was edited out four years after Mr. Wolverton died—and a
full four years *before* Mr. Armstrong died. There, in a 1982 publication, is evidence of Tkachism—conveniently enough, at about the
time Mr. Armstrong's eyesight went bad.

After Mr. Armstrong died, the editorial staff saw fit to remove any reference identifying modern Babylon as a truth restored to the church. They did this despite Mr. Armstrong's repeated references to this point the last two years of his life.

The wcg's new explanation about the history of Babylon and its prophetic significance immediately surfaced in other church literature once Mr. Armstrong died. In *The Plain Truth About Christmas*, for example, Mr. Armstrong had written,

> Nimrod, grandson of Ham, son of Noah, was the real founder of the Babylonish system that has gripped the world ever since— the system of organized competition—of man-ruled governments and empires, based upon the competitive and profit-making economic system. Nimrod built the tower of Babel, the original Babylon, ancient Nineveh, and many other cities. He organized this world's first kingdom.[8]

That entire paragraph got chopped out of the "updated" 1987 version, which is a major change when you consider what the church had long taught about the system Nimrod established.[9]

All well BEFORE, if Tkach Jr. is to be believed, "we were even *thinking* about such changes."

REVISIONIST HISTORY

In 1984, the wcg produced a booklet titled *The History of Europe and the Church,* written by Keith Stump. The booklet, written when Mr. Armstrong was nearly blind, is full of politically correct language that Mr. Armstrong never would have approved. For example, it attributed the cause of World War I to a "bloody event" in Sarajevo and the fact that great powers were "caught in the webs of their alliances."[10] Mr. Armstrong—and every other honest historian—would have blamed Germany for starting that war. But shortly before and after Mr. Armstrong died, wcg scholars attempted to revise that history.

Worse than that, they also revised the church's prophetic teachings about Germany. Less than four months after Mr. Armstrong died, Church Administration informed its ministers that several books would need to be "updated." Page 93 of Mr. Armstrong's *United States and Britain in Prophecy* said, "Israel had been removed from Palestine more than 130 years and had long since migrated, with the Assyrians, north (and west) of Assyria's original location."[11] In the 1986 version, editors rewrote it to say that Israel migrated north OF Assyria, as opposed to WITH. The significance of this change is made obvious by the other edits in Mr. Armstrong's work. On page 147, Mr. Armstrong wrote,

> Ezekiel was among the Jewish captives after their captivity, which occurred more than a hundred years after Israel's captivity. By that time the *Assyrians* had long since left their land on the southern shores of the Caspian Sea and migrated northwest, finally settling in the land today called *Germany*.[12]

In the 1986 version, all references to "Assyria" and "Germany" were removed from this passage. There is no mention of the Assyrians migrating to a land called *Germany* today. Then they completely removed this paragraph in the 1986 version:

> The Assyrians—before 604 B.C.—left their land north of Babylon and migrated northwest—through the lands that are now Georgia, the Ukraine, Poland, and into the land that is called Germany today. Today the descendants of those Assyrians are known to us as the German people.[13]

Again, these edits were made *within months* of Mr. Armstrong's death—perhaps set in motion even *before* he died. Reading the 1986 version of *The United States and Britain in Prophecy* for the first time, a new reader would have had NO IDEA that Germany today ascended from Assyria anciently—a teaching that essentially identifies Germany in Bible prophecy. For those even vaguely familiar with Mr. Armstrong's prophetic teachings, this represented a MONUMENTAL change in the church's teachings.

Of course, Tkach Jr. had *no idea* that a change this significant would have a profound impact on the church's prophetic teaching—or so he would have us believe.

MYSTERY OF THE AGES, SOFTBOUND

On September 9, 1985, Mr. Armstrong handed out the first hard-cover copies of *Mystery of the Ages* to the sophomore class at Ambassador College. Two months later, in November, the soft-bound version of the work arrived from the printer.[14]

At first glance, there appears to be no difference between the two versions. Though the softbound is 66 pages shorter than the hardcover, its smaller font size and line spacing accommodates more text on each page. Nevertheless, someone in the WCG—certainly not Mr. Armstrong—saw fit to alter certain statements having to do with race.

On pages 122 and 123 of the softbound version, they left out statements saying that Adam, Noah and Jesus were white. They even omitted a reference to ancient Israel being Caucasian. On page 143, they also removed a reference to ancient Israel being "racially" separate from other peoples.

On page 124, they omit a reference to Nimrod being "black," even though the Bible identifies his father Cush as a black man.[15]

In light of accusations the Tkaches would make years later, that Mr. Armstrong was racist, these edits—made *before Mr. Armstrong died*—are quite revealing. There, visibly present in November of 1985, are the fingerprints of Tkachism.

BIG SANDY CAMPUS

In the same December 1985 letter in which Mr. Armstrong informed the church about his rapidly declining health, he also made an important decision regarding Ambassador College:

> ... I feel God has led me in deciding that it is necessary that we close the operations at Big Sandy, Texas, after the end of this present school year. The certification of the college requiring the pursuing of accreditation, the financial needs of the first commission of the church, and the needs of the ministry made this decision necessary. The trained ministry at the campus in Big Sandy are sorely needed elsewhere because of the thousands of prospective member visit requests. I have ordered

implementation of this decision to the appropriate officials involved.[16]

The same announcement appeared later that week in the *Pastor General's Report*. Two weeks after that, Richard Ames, director of admissions at AC, told the ministry that all applications for Big Sandy had been re-directed to the Pasadena campus.[17] In the December 30, 1985, *Worldwide News,* Aaron Dean wrote a front-page article encouraging the church's youth to become educated whether they were able to attend Ambassador College or not. Mr. Dean referred to the closure of Big Sandy in the article and commented on how only a few of the church's young people would be able to attend AC.[18]

Two and a half weeks later, Mr. Armstrong died. Two months after his death, the newly appointed pastor general of the church, Joseph W. Tkach, paid a visit to the Big Sandy campus. During his trip, Mr. Tkach met with the college's deputy chancellor, Leslie McCullough, and its faculty members. According to the March 24, 1986, *Worldwide News,* "The pastor general updated the ministry and faculty on events taking place in God's work, including the status of the Big Sandy campus."[19] Of course, the "status" of the campus was pretty clear in the weeks prior to Mr. Armstrong's death: It would be closed.

Around the time of his Big Sandy trip, if not during, Mr. Tkach ordered a feasibility study "to determine the best use of the campus facility and to look long-range at the needs of the church and college in Texas."[20] He wrote to the ministry a few days after returning to Pasadena, saying, "The trip was most enjoyable and certainly informative for me as I am in the process of making decisions about the future of the campus."[21]

Five weeks after his Big Sandy visit, incredibly, Mr. Tkach announced plans to keep the Big Sandy campus open:

I have instructed Mr. Les McCullough and Dr. Don Ward to apply for state certification so that we may operate the college in Big Sandy, Texas, at least one more year. Last December, Mr. Herbert Armstrong wrote to the brethren that "the certification of the college requiring the pursuing of accreditation, the financial needs of the first commission of the church, and the needs of the ministry" made necessary the decision to close the operations of Ambassador College in Big Sandy, Texas. Since that time I have found that we can be certified for another two-year period without having to pursue accreditation.

This will allow the current freshman class to graduate in Big Sandy, and give us time to see what direction God will lead us regarding the future of the campus there. The state's decision on certification will not be final until July, but as of now we plan to operate next year. Of course, if certification is denied, we will go ahead with plans to allow qualified Big Sandy students to finish in Pasadena over the next two years.[22]

According to Dr. Ward, who heard the April 15 announcement via telephone hook-up in Big Sandy, Mr. Tkach's announcement was greeted by "thunderous applause that went on for a great while." Mr. Tkach asked the combined groups of faculty and students to pray that God's will be "revealed to me." He said that he was committed to "do whatever is best for God's work."[23]

Not four months earlier, one of the main reasons Mr. Armstrong gave for closing the campus was to DO WHAT WAS BEST FOR THE WORK—its "financial needs" and the fact that Big Sandy's ministry was needed elsewhere. What a MONUMENTAL SHIFT in priorities for Mr. Tkach—and just three months after Mr. Armstrong died!

Dr. Ward, of course, NEVER DREAMED that such a stunning reversal might eventually result in shifting the entire focus of the college onto Big Sandy and in the pursuit of accreditation.

Or did he?

DIFFERENT EMPHASIS FOR COMMISSION

The scripture Mr. Armstrong almost always used to describe the church's commission is Matthew 24:14: "And this gospel of the kingdom shall be preached in all the world for a *witness* unto all nations; and then shall the end come."

For example, in the February 1972 issue of *Tomorrow's World,*

Mr. Armstrong identified Matthew 24:14 as "the very prophecy defining our COMMISSION for this latter day."[24] In a co-worker letter dated September 17, 1982, Mr. Armstrong said, "Jesus' sign [that] we are near the end of this world (Matthew 24:14), which you have backed me in proclaiming to the world—the gospel of the kingdom of God—has been going to the world in great power!"[25] In a 1983 sermon, Mr. Armstrong clearly defined the commission for the church: "Today's mission of the church you will find in Matthew 24 and in verse 14."[26] Mr. Armstrong wrote in *The Plain Truth About Healing*: "The great commission and ministry for God's church today is in Jesus' prophecy concerning it in Matthew 24:14."[27]

In his first sermon as pastor general, *given just two days after Mr. Armstrong died,* Mr. Tkach said,

> In the Synoptic Gospels, OUR COMMISSION IS CLEARLY STATED— which just means a general view of our responsibilities. Turn to Matthew 28. Here we're told, in verse 19, to "Go ye therefore, and *teach all nations,* baptizing them in the name of the Father, and of the Son, and of the Holy Ghost." Our commission here is directly from Christ. We are an extension of the early New Testament Church, who never did complete the commission.[28]

This scriptural citation represented a disturbing shift in focus. Mr. Armstrong may have occasionally *associated* Matthew 28:19-20 with the church's commission, but it was not the primary passage he referred to. He repeatedly emphasized that the church had been commissioned to preach the gospel message to this world *as a witness.* With that as its focus, as Mr. Armstrong would then explain, *God would provide* members and co-workers who responded to the warning message.[29] Certainly, the church then had an obligation to teach and train those who responded to God's call, but this was secondary to the church's main mission— preaching the gospel of the kingdom of God as a witness. Mr. Armstrong explained:

> The two spiritual areas, which are the real purpose and mission of the church, are, one, proclaiming the good news of the

kingdom of God for a witness to the nations of the world ....
Now the *second mission* of the church is to feed the flock, as
Jesus said, on the spiritual food of the Word of God.[30]

To be fair to Mr. Tkach, in that same sermon, he did quote from
Matthew 24:14 right at the end of the message. He said, "We have a
commission to preach the gospel as a warning message to a dying
world."[31]

But he then wrote just a few days after that sermon: "My faith
and confidence are in Jesus Christ's sure and infallible promise,
built into the *very commission* He gave His church: '... Lo, I am with
you always, even to the end of the age' (Matthew 28:20)."[32]

Shifting the work's *emphasis* to the SECONDARY MISSION of feeding
the flock, as opposed to preaching the gospel to the world, HAD A
DEVASTATING, DOMINO-LIKE EFFECT ON NEARLY EVERY ASPECT OF THE
WORK. *It turned the church inward*—leading to a focus on Ambassador
College, local congregations and personal evangelism. Proclaiming
the gospel message as a witness took a back seat to the inward
needs of the church.

MYSTERY OF THE AGES SERIALIZATION

As I mentioned, editors had made subtle changes to the softbound
Mystery of the Ages even before Mr. Armstrong died. Much more
significant than that, however, are the deletions made in the serialization of the book in the *Plain Truth* magazine. Mr. Armstrong actually
started the project, beginning with the July 1985 issue. He wanted
the message of the book to reach the "largest audience possible,"[33]
and the *Plain Truth* circulation was around 8 million at the time.

Because of the length of the book, serializing *Mystery of the
Ages* took a year and a half (from July 1985 to December 1986). As
with any serialization, one might expect editors to condense some
portions of the text. But to do so in a way that completely alters the
author's clear intent cannot be considered an *abridged* version of the
original text—rather a *corrupt* version.

The most glaring deletion occurs at the end of chapter 6—
"Mystery of the Church"—in the July-August 1986 *Plain Truth*

installment. In the book, the section begins with the subhead, "Restoration of God's Truth to Church." In the first paragraph under the subhead, Mr. Armstrong begins by summarizing the history of the church of God—from the first century to the time of the end. In the book, he wrote, "From the year 1931, exactly 1,900 years (a century of time cycles) from the foundation of the church, this small remnant of the original true church of God began to take on new life *as the Philadelphia era.*" Those last four italicized words are left out of the serialization, which is significant, as anyone ever associated with the WCG would know.

From that point in the text, editors saw fit to delete a number of specific prophecies in the serialization, beginning with this one:

> It had come to the "time of the end." A new spiritual vitality was infused into it. The time had come for Jesus' prophecy of Matthew 24:14 to be fulfilled—"this gospel of the kingdom shall be [proclaimed] in all the world for a witness unto all nations; and then shall the end come." Such vital truth that had been lost was gradually revealed and proclaimed.[34]

In light of what we covered about the church's commission, the significance of this omission is obvious. The *Plain Truth* version then omits six paragraphs about the Philadelphia era and the leader who God prophesied to raise up during that era (Mr. Armstrong, as the church had always believed). Mr. Armstrong wrote,

> To this era—or to its human leader—God had set before it an open door .... This church and/or its leader had but little strength. Neither were of great and powerful stature in Satan's world but those of this era were faithful to the Word of God. Though much of the original gospel truth, imparted to the original apostles by Jesus in person, had been lost, it was restored through the Bible to this era of God's church who were faithful in keeping it.[35]

That is missing in the serialization version. And so is this next paragraph:

It is revealed in Malachi 3:1-5 and 4:5-6 that God would raise
up one in the power and spirit of Elijah, shortly prior to the
Second Coming of Christ. In Matthew 17:11 Jesus said, even
after John the Baptist had completed his mission, that this
prophesied Elijah "truly shall first come, and restore all things."
Although it is plainly revealed that John the Baptist had come
in the power and spirit of Elijah, he did not restore anything.
The human leader to be raised up somewhat shortly prior to
Christ's Second Coming was to prepare the way—prepare the
church—for Christ's coming, and restore the truth that had
been lost through the preceding eras of the church. Also a door
was to be opened for this leader and/or the Philadelphia era
of the church to fulfill Matthew 24:14: "And this gospel of the
kingdom shall be preached in all the world for a witness unto
all nations; and then shall the end come." [36]

After these deletions, the serialization then continues:

It was to be at a time when, for the first time in the history
of mankind, the weapons of mass destruction were produced
that could erase all humanity from the Earth (Matt. 24:21-22).
This also was to occur just before the Second Coming of Christ
(verses 29-30).
  These prophecies have now definitely been fulfilled. The true
gospel has been restored and has now gone in power into every
nation on the face of the Earth. [37]

For a person reading *the book*, "these prophecies have now definitely been fulfilled" refers to Matthew 24:14, Revelation 3:7-13,
Malachi 3:1-5, Malachi 4:5-6 and Matthew 17:11! In reading the
serialization, however, you don't even know what prophecies Mr.
Armstrong is referring to. To delete all the prophecies and then
say, "These prophecies have now definitely been fulfilled," MAKES NO
SENSE.
  Within a few months of assuming his new position as pastor
general, Mr. Tkach had already signed off on eliminating some of
the strongest statements Mr. Armstrong made in *Mystery of the Ages.*

And these just happened to be statements about Mr. Armstrong's office, his prophesied role in world events and his God-given commission.

"BROAD IS THE WAY"

Besides the serialization, several other examples from 1986 demonstrate Tkachism's intention to generalize teachings that had traditionally been clear-cut, specific explanations of Scripture.

In addition to *Mystery of the Ages,* Mr. Armstrong wrote a handful of booklets the last year of his life—one of which is titled *Are We In the Last Days?* After he died, editors renamed the booklet *The World Won't End This Way!* Here is how they explained this change: "The old title was an excellent way to present the topic to an earlier generation. But the new generation of television viewers simply did not respond to this prophetic title as they do to other brochures and booklets on prophecy."[38] The old version was supposedly requested less, and Tkachism knew the exact reason why. The *title* was outdated.

In another booklet, *Ending Your Financial Worries,* Mr. Armstrong made the tragic error of saying that America is the "wealthiest nation on Earth." WCG scholars gleefully noted that "smaller nations have a significantly larger per capita annual income than does the United States."[39] This may seem like a meaningless change, but again, those with a general understanding of Mr. Armstrong's theology immediately realize the impact these little adjustments had on major doctrinal positions. Mr. Armstrong often referred to America as the single greatest nation on Earth—thanks, in large part, to its phenomenal wealth. That's because the Bible actually *prophesied* of America's assent to greatness in this end time. Mr. Armstrong explained these prophecies in his book *The United States and Britain in Prophecy.* Knowing what eventually happened to that book, you can get an idea of where they were going with these 1986 edits.

In 1986, editors were also hard at work revising one of Mr. Armstrong's biggest books—*The Incredible Human Potential.* On page 5 of that book, commenting on Simon Magus and his deceptive work to pervert the true gospel during the first century, Mr. Armstrong wrote,

> There ensued "the lost century" in the history of the true church of God. There was a well-organized conspiracy to blot out all record of church history during that period. A hundred years later, history reveals a "Christianity" utterly unlike the church Christ founded. [40]

Drawing upon research from scholars and church historians—like Edward Gibbon, who referred to a "dark cloud" that hung over the first age of the church—Mr. Armstrong coined the expression "lost century" to describe the sparse historical record of the early church. For WCG scholars in 1986, "the lost century" was "hardly appropriate." After all, they reasoned, John's writings were recorded during this time—and Polycarp followed in John's footsteps. So how could that historical period be considered "lost"? So they rephrased it as "an obscure period in the history of the true church." While they felt like that was more accurate, the change unmistakably de-emphasized Satan's conspiracy to blot out a true record of church history.

In *What Do You Mean—"The Unpardonable Sin"?* Mr. Armstrong wrote,

> In John 7:31, it is recorded: "And many of the people believed on Him ...." But were they really Christians? *Notice, beginning with John 8:30: "As He spake these words, many believed on Him. Then Jesus said to those Jews which believed on Him, If ye continue in my Word, then are ye my disciples indeed ...." But they did not actually believe Him! They believed on Him—that He was a great teacher, as a man—they believed on the person—like millions today. But they did not believe Him—did not believe what He said—His message—His gospel.* To these same people, who "believed on Him," Jesus said, just a few verses farther on, "... but ye seek to kill me, because my word hath no place in you." [41]

By removing all the italicized words in 1986, editors agreed that it would read more "smoothly."[42] It also removed a reference to "millions today" being deceived in the same manner as those in Christ's day.

Years later, Tkachism would often ridicule Mr. Armstrong's teaching about the whole world being deceived (Revelation 12:9). Thus, viewing these selective 1986 edits in hindsight, their intent to undermine Mr. Armstrong's teaching is clear.

OTHER CHANGES IN 1986

Tkachism changed the church's teaching about the human spirit within months of Mr. Armstrong's death.[43] In explaining why they changed the wording in *The Incredible Human Potential* to reflect the new teaching, they said it read "smoother," whereas Mr. Armstrong's explanation had "puzzled a number of readers."[44] That Mr. Armstrong's teachings could now be altered for no other reason than because they "puzzled" readers must have had liberals in Pasadena eager for the next round of changes.

They also changed the meaning of the Hebrew word for *God* in 1986. Anyone who ever heard Mr. Armstrong discuss who and what God is undoubtedly remembers him explaining the meaning of *Elohim,* as he did in *Mystery of the Ages:*

> ... a noun or name, *plural in form,* but normally *singular in gram-matical usage.* It is the *same sort of word as family, church, group*— one family consisting of two or more members—one church composed of many members—one group of several persons.[45]

They first introduced their different understanding of the word *Elohim* when they reprinted two other writings of Mr. Armstrong's— *The Incredible Human Potential* and the booklet *Why Were You Born?* They altered the definition this way: "... a noun, plural in form, but with either singular or plural usage."[46] They left out the fact that the Hebrew word is like the English words *family, church, team* or *group.* And instead of it being "singular in *grammatical* usage," as Mr. Armstrong said in *Mystery of the Ages,* it had an "either *singular* or plural usage."

Years later, when the Worldwide Church of God adopted the trinity doctrine, it argued that *Elohim,* as it is used in Genesis 1:1, refers to a SINGLE DEITY.[47] The WCG *officially* accepted the trinity doctrine in 1993. But like with so many other doctrinal revisions, fingerprints appeared several years earlier. In this case, it was 1986, when they CHANGED THE DEFINITION of *Elohim.*

CHRIST'S AGENDA?

On the day Mr. Armstrong died, Joseph Tkach promised to maintain the founder's course and "not deviate from it one iota." Yet he clearly started breaking promises that very day.

In 1995, after supporting and defending the Tkach administration for nearly a decade, David Hulme had finally had enough of the doctrinal transformation. He wrote this in his resignation letter to the elder Tkach:

> The most disturbing aspect of our recent conversation on the eve of Passover, is that with some pride you stated that you had agreed with Richard Plache and Al Corozzo in the 1970s with regard to the place of the law in the Christian life. You said you agreed with them (and therefore disagreed with Herbert W. Armstrong) but felt that they were ahead of their time, and that nothing could be done. I remind you that Richard Plache was one of the prime movers in a 1975 attempt to overturn Sabbath observance in Britain. As a result he was put out of the church, along with Charles Hunting and David Ord, by Mr. Armstrong. If you agreed with these men as you claim, did you inform Mr. Armstrong of your radically different stance any time before his death?"[48]

In his response to Hulme, Tkach Sr. did not deny that these conversations took place. He just said that Hulme had misrepresented his comments. But notice what else Tkach wrote:

> I was trying to point out to you that challenges about the validity of certain doctrines, challenges that were raised by

leading ministers of the church in the 1970s, caused me to realize that there were indeed doctrinal questions that had never been adequately answered. [49]

Notice! From Tkach's own pen (or whoever wrote the letter for him) we discover that these were questions raised *in the 1970s*. They were raised by "leading ministers" at the time (many of whom were disfellowshiped by Mr. Armstrong, he failed to mention). And they were questions, at least in Tkach's mind, that had never been adequately answered. This "nagging realization," Tkach admitted, "troubled me." And so what did he do? "My response at the time," he explained, referring to the 1970s, "was to simply put the subject '*on the shelf*' and give it little thought until years later, when I found myself, as pastor general, responsible for the spiritual instruction of the church and challenged on many of the SAME POINTS."[50]

Can you believe that? He readily admitted to setting controversial subjects on the shelf "UNTIL YEARS LATER"—*when Mr. Armstrong was no longer in control!* But the idea that he or anyone ever had an agenda? "Preposterous," he says. "It was *Christ's* agenda." That's all it was—*an innocent coming-of-age story about Jesus Christ leading a wayward church out of darkness and into the glorious light.* They NEVER had *any* of this in mind. *None* of them did.

Isn't that amazing?

SEVEN
RIDDLED
WITH ERROR

"[T]hese things that [Mr. Armstrong] had written in that book [Mystery of the Ages] were never central—we never used the term 'central' to our teaching. They were just his interpretations of Scripture …."

— JOSEPH TKACH JR.
Deposition, *September 8, 1998*

URING my father's firing on December 7, 1989, the subject of *Mystery of the Ages* came up. My father strenuously defended its content, arguing that it should not have been discontinued. Joseph Tkach Jr. told him it would be impossible to distribute it, as the book was "riddled with error." That statement shocked my father. The church membership had been told the book was discontinued because it was expensive and its content could be found in other literature. But on that winter night inside Tkach Jr.'s office, the real reason emerged.

Nine years later, during a deposition, when asked if he had used the phrase "riddled with error" during the firing, Tkach said, "I believe those were my exact words."[1] According to Tkach, Gerald Flurry felt that *"Mystery of the Ages* should be promoted more than it was being promoted, and I told him that it had too many errors … to promote it the way he thought it should be …."[2]

We have already examined a number of changes that took place in 1986. Tkachism continued dismantling doctrines throughout 1987 and the first half of 1988—when they removed *Mystery of the Ages* from circulation. Based on what Tkach Jr. told my father in 1989, the changes were so numerous and far-reaching that *Mystery of the Ages* could not be used in any form. It was, as he said, "riddled" with error.

NAMES AND DATES

As noted in chapter 6, Tkach's fellows wasted little time altering the teachings in *The United States and Britain in Prophecy*. Besides removing all references to ancient Assyria being Germany today, editors also had trouble with the way Mr. Armstrong delineated between Israelites and Jews.

As Mr. Armstrong taught, "It is wrong to call the Jews of today 'Israel.' They are not the nation Israel—they are Judah! And wherever Israel is today, remember that Israel as a national name does not mean Jew!"[3] Editors removed these kinds of statements from the 1986 version, presumably to avoid offending Jews. Yet Mr. Armstrong was not trying to offend anyone. He was simply making this key distinction in support of the book's central point:

> Jews are Israelites, just as Californians are Americans. But most Israelites are not Jews, just as most Americans are not Californians. The Jews are the house of Judah only, a part of the Israelites. *But when these people are spoken of as nations, rather than as collective individuals, the term "Israel" never refers to the Jews.* "House of Israel" never means "Jews." The three tribes at Jerusalem under the Davidic king are called, merely, the house of Judah.[4]

The italicized sentence, the most critical point in the paragraph, is what editors removed from the 1986 version.

Earlier in the book, when Mr. Armstrong expounded on Genesis 48—where Jacob passed on the birthright blessings to Ephraim and Manasseh—he explained that, in verse 16, it was these two lads who were named Israel, not the descendants of Judah. Later, Mr.

Armstrong asked, "Who, then, according to your Bible, is the real Israel (racially and nationally) of today?"[5] Ephraim and Manasseh of course! But these sorts of statements needed to be removed because, according to wcg scholars, they had been a "source of criticism."[6] *A source of criticism?* This is the central point of the entire book![7]

They also had a problem with captivity dates for Judah (604 to 585 B.C., according to Mr. Armstrong) and Israel (721 to 718 B.C.). In the latter case, editors chose 721 alone as the date for Israel's captivity. As for Judah's, they decided to leave the attacks on Jerusalem by Nebuchadnezzar as "generally ... UNDATED" in the 1986 version of the book.[8]

The significance of these changes has much more to do with prophecy than it does with assigning dates to ancient events.[9]

Of course, Tkach Jr. says they had no idea where changes such as these were leading. But the truth is that these massive edits, starting in 1986, damningly reveal the mindset of the same people who completely rejected the book a short two years later.

ONE SMALL BOOKLET, ONE GIANT REVISION

About six months after they made the changes covered above, wcg editors SLASHED MORE THAN TWO THIRDS of the text from the 1986 version of *The United States and Britain in Prophecy*—reducing the 184-page book to a meager 53 pages.

Absent from the 1987 version are the Introduction, the first two chapters and the last fourth of the book. The last four chapters of the book, in fact, are summarized in five pages in the 1987 version. Editors essentially pulled out what prophetic teeth had been left in the 1986 version. And the tiny bit they left in was highly sanitized—making it much less personal for the modern descendants of Israel ("we" and "us" were changed to "they" and "them").

When the Tkaches announced that the book had been downsized, they explained that the larger edition had "become prohibitively costly to mail in vast areas of the English-speaking world."[10] So they made the small version *only* for areas with high postage costs. But—get ready for this—once they finished it, they discovered it was "Mr. Armstrong's style at its best"! It was "so effectively written and to the point" that Mr. Tkach decided to make the small version available for EVERYONE—*conveniently making the book version dispensable.* That's how they explained it to the membership in 1987—that the booklet version was BETTER and that it would save the work postage costs. NOTHING was mentioned about the doctrinal transformation the text had undergone since Mr. Armstrong died.

The following year, in mid-1988, even the 53-pager failed to survive the editor's knife. After a tumultuous two years in print after the death of Mr. Armstrong, editors finally laid to rest *The United States and Britain in Prophecy* permanently, even though members would not find out the real reason for its removal until years later.

Tkach Jr.'s biggest beef with the book is how Mr. Armstrong's teaching supposedly "worked to foster racial prejudice."[11] In *Transformed by Truth,* he wrote, "Within two years of Mr. Armstrong's death, several church leaders began discussing Anglo-Israelism[12] with my dad."[13]

He says *within two years.* In fact, by the time two years had passed, two thirds of the material had already been CHOPPED OUT—and the entire book was buried a few months later. Significant changes to the text, as we have seen, were made *immediately* after Mr. Armstrong died. It was as if the destruction of this truth had been planned all along and that the only obstacle preventing it from happening was Mr. Armstrong being alive.

Indeed, the blueprint for the book's demise had been drawn up a decade earlier. Writing about *The United States and Britain in Prophecy* during the liberal era of the 1970s, Mr. Armstrong told the church, "[M]y son, assuming an authority never delegated to him, had this most important booklet *cut down to almost nothing,* then PUT OUT OF CIRCULATION ENTIRELY!"[14]

Isn't that incredible? It happened the EXACT same way after Mr. Armstrong died. Yet the Tkaches claimed they had no idea where the massive 1986 edits were leading.

JESUS CHRIST'S SACRIFICE

Many commentators analyzing the WCG's transformation out of

"Armstrongism" point to March 1987 as the watershed event that began the process of re-evaluating everything. We have already seen how the changes were actually in full swing long before this. That said, however, the early-1987 change regarding Jesus Christ's sacrifice and divine healing was huge.

Mr. Tkach Sr. first introduced the subject in the March 18, 1987, *Pastor General's Report,* sent to the ministers of the church. He explained the change one week later to the entire membership.[15] Tkachism has led people to assume, incorrectly, that the "healing change" meant that it was no longer a sin for wcg members to go to doctors. But Mr. Armstrong NEVER said it was a sin to go to doctors.

In his booklet *The Plain Truth About Healing,* Mr. Armstrong actually said we *need* doctors for a variety of things. He wrote,

> The great advances in the medical field enable man to do for his human family many things he could not do 50 years ago, short of actual healing. God does for us (often by miracle) that which we are unable to do. God gave man talents, mind-power (physical) and *abilities that He intended us to use and develop* under His guidance, and always for His glory and toward our development in the holy, righteous character of God.[16]

Earlier in the text, he said "[I]t is true that today most doctors prescribe medicines that are NOT poisons but rather are designed to help nature do its own healing." He asked, "Do we ever need doctors?"

Answer: "Yes we do—but the true people of God do not need them to *compete* with God as our God-healer ...."[17] Mr. Armstrong's teaching on this subject was similar to any other church doctrine: PUT GOD FIRST. And even then, if someone lacked faith in God, he actually *encouraged them* all the more to put their trust in doctors!

> If a church member simply lacks the faith to be healed by the living Christ—if he has more faith in medical "expertise" than in God and God's promises—God's church will not judge or condemn him if he puts himself or his child under medical

treatment. If that is the best he has faith in, better let him have what help man can give, rather than no help at all![18]

With Tkachism, on the other hand, church members *did* often judge each other—and usually the ones judged most harshly were those who chose *not* to rely on doctors for "healing"! In some cases, ministers even refused to anoint members, despite God's clear command in James 5:14, because the members did not first go to a doctor.

Setting aside Tkachism's misinterpretation of what Mr. Armstrong actually taught on the subject of healing, there were in fact definite changes made in the church's doctrine in March of 1987. The most significant of these had to do with Jesus Christ's sacrifice.

Mr. Armstrong taught that the way we are freed from the penalty of sin (eternal death) is by Jesus Christ's shed blood. Christ died in our stead. Divine healing is based on the same principle. Prior to His crucifixion, Jesus was beaten and scourged. Numerous scriptures explain the reason for this terrible scourging: It was so we might be healed.[19]

Nothing underscores the differentiation between the scourging and the crucifixion like the Christian Passover. At this ceremony, as New Testament scriptures explain, Christians are first commanded to eat broken bread, which symbolizes Christ's beaten and broken body. Then we are to drink a tiny glass of wine, which represents Christ's shed blood.[20]

Along these same lines, Mr. Armstrong taught that since God's law is spiritual,[21] transgressing against that law constitutes *spiritual* sin—the penalty for which is eternal death. In like manner, man's physical body functions according to definite *physical* laws. Transgressing against these laws also exacts a penalty—in this case, sickness and disease. In other words, sickness and disease come as a result of *physical* sin.

Jesus Christ died so that the penalty for spiritual sin, eternal death, might be paid and that we might receive the gift of eternal life.[22] He was beaten before He died so that the penalty for physical sin—sickness and disease—might be paid in full so we can be healed. Jesus Himself explained in Luke 5:17-26 that healing is the forgiveness of physical sin.

With Tkachism, there is no such thing as physical sin. There may be a cause for physical sickness, but it is not physical sin. Therefore, Jesus was not beaten for our healing. His broken body has "far more significance," Tkach said.[23] The sacrifice of Jesus should not be separated according to the broken body and the shed blood, he said. Both blend together as one supreme sacrifice. Furthermore, while Mr. Armstrong believed it is always God's will to heal (although it is up to God to determine *when*), Mr. Tkach said healing was not a promise from God, but rather a *blessing*—and that it was not always God's will to grant that blessing.

You can find this kind of reasoning in the Systematic Theology Project, produced by wcg liberals during the 1970s. In attempting to water down God's emphatic promise in James 5:14-15, the stp said, "Although this one statement appears to be written without qualification, the condition 'if it be God's will' was no doubt tacitly understood."[24] Of course, you cannot find a statement like that—"if it be God's will"—anywhere in the Bible regarding God's promise of healing. But liberals in the 1970s believed that condition was tacitly understood. Mr. Tkach agreed and changed the church teaching in 1987, after Mr. Armstrong died.

The new teaching about Christ's sacrifice and physical sin had a profound impact on the church's literature inventory. In his book, Tkach Jr. said, "In 1989 we stopped circulating booklets that taught what we had come to believe was a flawed understanding of divine healing."[25] In truth, that process began immediately after the change was made in March 1987. It began with Mr. Armstrong's booklet *The Plain Truth About Healing*. Upon making the change, Tkach Sr. explained,

> The healing booklet will have to be temporarily withdrawn until edits and revisions reflecting this new understanding Jesus Christ has given to His church can be made. References in our literature to "physical sin" and Jesus' body being broken for the limited purpose of paying the penalty for "broken physical laws" will also have to be revised.[26]

Three weeks after Mr. Tkach wrote that, *The Principles of Healthful Living* booklet and the reprint article, "The Plain Truth About Fasting," were removed from stock. They also announced that Lessons 12, 23 and 25 of the correspondence course had been shelved in anticipation of being revised.

In 1988, *What Is Faith?, The Plain Truth About Easter* and *The Wonderful World Tomorrow* were all discarded because of "incorrect" explanations on healing and Christ's sacrifice. They were later revised and re-issued, *carrying Mr. Armstrong's byline,* yet containing new doctrinal teaching that Mr. Armstrong would have rejected.

In *Mystery of the Ages,* on pages 64-68, Mr. Armstrong discussed a dramatic personal example of healing that would either have to be re-worked or removed entirely, based on Tkach's new teaching. The section on page 211, under the subhead, "Jesus Beaten for Our Healing," discusses physical sin and healing as forgiveness of sin. On page 317 is a reference to healing and repenting of sin. Likewise, on page 319, Mr. Armstrong refers to the *laws* of health. All of these references would have to be removed for *Mystery of the Ages* to survive.

The ripple effect of this new teaching was huge.

"Messenger" Becomes "the Church"

Joseph Tkach Jr. would have us believe that when editors chopped all that material about "Elijah" out of the 1986 *Mystery of the Ages* serialization in the *Plain Truth,* there was nothing sinister behind the deletion. It was just an innocent effort to condense the text into the allotted space. They NEVER dreamed that their *teaching* on the subject would ever change. Yet, the following year, the church's Personal Correspondence Department (PCD) produced a form letter on the subject of the Elijah prophecy in Matthew 17. It read, "At the close of this present evil age, the message of 'Elijah' is again to be thundered to disobedient Israel as a witness and to prepare a people for Christ's Second Coming." [27] According to the letter, the WCG was delivering this message. Mr. Armstrong wasn't even mentioned. Yet most members would have been completely unaware of the new teaching, unless they happened to send a question to PCD about Matthew 17.

It wasn't until early 1988 that Tkachism finally got around to explaining the new teaching to a larger audience. Tkach Sr. wrote, "Jesus said that 'Elijah' was to 'restore all things,' or get things ready. John, in his day, prepared those who listened to him ...."[28] And what about the "other man"—the *latter-day* fulfillment of these prophecies? Tkach explained: "Just as Malachi prophesied of John the Baptist [Malachi 4:5-6] and just as the angel Gabriel expounded [in Luke 1:16-17], a people would be prepared for God. From the Ephesian era until now, THE CHURCH OF GOD FULFILLS THAT ROLE OF PREPARING A PEOPLE FOR GOD."[29] So John the Baptist was the first-century Elijah and "THE CHURCH" is the end-time Elijah! John prepared the way for Christ's first coming, and *the church* prepares the way for His Second Coming. What began through John the Baptist, Mr. Tkach wrote, has "continued through the ages by the successive eras of the church of God."[30]

Incredibly, this momentous change in doctrine was passed off on the membership *as if it were something we had always known and believed.* Mr. Tkach introduced the article by saying the church had often focused on the "general principle" of these end-time Elijah prophecies—"that of strengthening family relationships, instead of the vital primary meaning of those verses ...."[31] In truth, the church had actually focused on the primary, *very specific* meaning of those verses—*that they referred to Herbert Armstrong and the work God did through him in this end time.* But in February 1988, Mr. Tkach not only made the rejection of that teaching formal—he made it sound like Mr. Armstrong taught the same thing.

What an impact this change must have had on the status of *Mystery of the Ages*—at that point still in circulation, though no doubt hanging by a thread. Right at the beginning of Mr. Armstrong's final book, on page 9, is a section under the subhead, "The Elijah to Come." In it, he again emphasized the duality of these specific prophecies—the first fulfillment being John the Baptist. Yet, as he so often explained, these prophecies also refer "to a *human messenger* preparing the way before Christ's now imminent Second Coming, this time in supreme power and glory as Ruler over all nations!" That statement was now at odds with Tkach's new teaching about *the church* being this "messenger."

Mystery of the Ages included another reference on page 251 about the "18 basic and essential truths" that were restored to the church through one man.

In chapter 6, we also discussed the significance of what Mr. Armstrong covered from pages 289 to 292 in *Mystery,* where he said "these prophecies have now definitely been fulfilled," referring to Matthew 24:14, Revelation 3:7-13, Malachi 3:1-5, Malachi 4:5-6 and Matthew 17:11.[32] (You will remember that all these prophecies were omitted from the 1986 serialization of the book.)

And then there is one final section at the end of *Mystery,* subheaded "Elijah to Come in Our Day." Mr. Armstrong wrote,

> John the Baptist was a voice crying out in the physical wilder-ness of the Jordan River, preparing the way for the First Coming of Christ, as a physical human being, to his physical temple at Jerusalem and to the physical people of Judah, announcing the advance good news that the kingdom of God would in the future be established. But also preparing the way before his Second Coming was a messenger of whom Elijah was a type. A voice crying out in the worldwide spiritual wilderness of reli-gious confusion, preparing the way for the spiritual glorified King of kings and Lord of lords to come in the supreme power and glory of God to his spiritual temple, the church (Eph. 2:21), to actually establish the kingdom of God.[33]

In many ways, changing the prophesied messenger from Mr. Armstrong to the church undermines much, if not all, of the mate-rial in *Mystery of the Ages.*

Adding all these changes together, it's no wonder Joe Tkach Jr., at the end of 1989, told my father that getting any further use out of *Mystery of the Ages* would be impossible.

RIDDLED WITH ERROR

Early on in *Mystery,* Mr. Armstrong spoke about the "Babylon of religious confusion," and how the seven basic mysteries would reveal why the religious world is so confused.[34] In his first chapter, on who and what is God, he explains how the ancient Babylonian mysteries worked their way into Christian dogma.[35] In the fourth chapter, on civilization, Mr. Armstrong explained how our civilization started with Nimrod and how the pagan religions of this world began with his wife Semiramis.[36] Yet, as we have already seen, the identity of Babylon had been watered down by Tkachism even before Mr. Armstrong died.

There is also material in *Mystery* identifying modern-day Assyria—they "settled in central Europe, and the Germans, undoubtedly, are, in part, the descendants of the ancient Assyrians," Mr. Armstrong wrote.[37]

There are the many other "lesser" changes the wcg made, as we have discussed in the last two chapters. When Tkachism altered the *Elohim* definition in 1986, their new understanding contradicted the definition found in *Mystery of the Ages* on pages 50, 94 and 135. Their revised 1986 teaching on the human spirit, as it differs from the animal brain, is different from Mr. Armstrong's explanation on pages 104, 105, 109 and 237 of *Mystery of the Ages.* In February 1987, editors removed all references in its holy day booklet to the Israelites killing the Passover lamb on the evening of the 14th of Nisan. This too contradicted what Mr. Armstrong wrote in *Mystery* on the bottom of page 53.

Add to this the discontinuation of literature. In September 1987, the wcg removed *The Incredible Human Potential* from circulation—offering no explanation for the move, except that "much of the material" existed in other available literature.[38] *The United States and Britain in Prophecy,* as we covered at the beginning of this chapter, made it through a significant revision in 1986, but then dramatically shrunk in 1987 and finally disappeared in 1988. And *The Wonderful World Tomorrow*—another major book written by Mr. Armstrong—had a fourth of its content cut in 1987 because of the "considerable savings" it would bring the work.[39]

All these changes, *all* these massive cuts in literature, happened *before* mid-1988. One could hardly describe this as a slow awakening to a new understanding. These men were pushing their program just as hard and as fast as they possibly could without revealing their full intentions.

It's no wonder the status of *Mystery of the Ages* had reached a critical crossroads for WCG officials by that time. *Mystery of the Ages,* as of mid-1988, was the church's best-known, most-requested book. On the other hand, Tkachism believed it was "riddled with error."

What would the Tkaches do?

EIGHT

DISCARD

"We have more than 120,000 copies of Mystery *…. Should we,
as we are about to do with the Easter booklet, destroy all existing
stock of these books and order new printings of them?"*

— **DEXTER FAULKNER**
Memo to Joseph Tkach Sr., *April 18, 1988*

A CCORDING to Joseph Tkach Jr., the reason the church
put *Mystery of the Ages* "on hold" in the spring of 1988 was
because "[t]here were enough historical errors," "other kind
of errors" and "misinterpretations of scripture" that it needed to be
corrected before the book could be used again.[1]

Of course, even before the book was officially "on hold," it
had become unpopular within the circle of decision-makers
in Pasadena. June 7, 1987, was the last time the book was ever
offered on the church's television program. (It was a summer re-
run that brought in more than 37,000 calls requesting the book.
The original program, which aired on January 25, 1987, generated
59,000 calls—the fourth-highest response ever. As an aside, the
highest weekend response ever came as a result of the January 26,
1986, tribute to Mr. Armstrong—one in which *Mystery of the Ages*
was the literature offered.)

The July 21, 1987, *Pastor General's Report* updated the ministry
on the library book program. Members had been working on the
project since mid-1986 and had distributed nearly 5,000 copies of
Mystery of the Ages to U.S. libraries. In December of that year, the

church newspaper informed members that *Mystery* was now available in Norwegian and French.[2] The Spanish and Italian versions became available in February 1988.[3]

This, from what we could find, is the last mention of *Mystery of the Ages* in any of the church's official literature. For most of the church membership and field ministry, it completely disappeared from view for more than a year.

At headquarters, however, there was no hotter topic than *Mystery of the Ages* throughout 1988. It was discussed in numerous meetings, interoffice memos and internal reports.

120,000 BAD COPIES

On April 18, 1988, Dexter Faulkner, Editorial Services manager, sent an interoffice memo to Mr. Tkach Sr., drawing attention to incorrect teaching about Christ's sacrifice in *The Wonderful World Tomorrow* and *Mystery of the Ages*. He attached photocopied pages from the *Mystery* section, "Jesus Beaten for Our Healing." Mr. Faulkner wrote,

> We have more than 120,000 copies of *Mystery* that contain the statement [about Christ's sacrifice]. Replacement cost would be around one dollar per copy. Shipping costs would be substantial because of the weight of the book.
>
> Should we, as we are about to do with the Easter booklet, destroy all existing stock of these books and order new printings of them?[4]

We have no record of whether Mr. Tkach responded to Faulkner's query by memo or verbally, if at all. But we can still piece together a pretty accurate record of what happened. Three weeks after the memo, in Bernie Schnippert's "Literature Coordination Report"—sent to department heads, regional directors and those involved in producing and distributing literature—we find that *Mystery of the Ages* had been put "on hold" in all languages, so that its content might be revised.[5] The following week, employees were told that, because of its "on hold" status, *Mystery* "should not be distributed."[6]

Then, on June 2, Mr. Schnippert lowered the boom on those 120,000 copies remaining in stock:

> All softbound copies of *Mystery of the Ages* in English, German, Norwegian and Spanish should be discarded IMMEDIATELY because they contain passages that do not correctly reflect the church's teaching about Christ's sacrifice.
>
> All hardbound copies of *Mystery of the Ages* should also be discarded.[7]

Roger Lippross, *Plain Truth* production director at the time, later indicated that this action was indeed taken. He said it was common, even under Mr. Armstrong's leadership, to withdraw literature from circulation for one of two purposes: to either retire or revise the publication. "In either case," he said, "the remaining inventory copies, but not archive, personal and research copies, would be disposed of …."[8]

Mr. Tkach Jr.'s recollection of these events, however, is much less vivid. At his 1998 deposition, he said that, from what he remembers, distribution of the book continued "until we almost ran out."[9] Later, after reviewing some of the documents quoted above, he said, "I really wasn't always aware of when they discarded it or when they didn't."[10]

TEMPORARILY OUT OF PRINT

Though Mr. Tkach Sr. signed off on destroying the 120,000 "bad" copies, he initially gave the impression he wanted the book to be revised and printed again.[11] Thus, in June 1988, Mail Processing designated the book's status as TOUT—temporarily out of stock.[12] Those who requested the book were given written notice saying it was currently out of print and being revised for re-distribution sometime during the first half of 1989. In its place, they offered the booklet *Your Awesome Future*.

In July, the future plans for the book were explained further:

"Last week, we decided to move the production of the core version of this book [*Mystery*] up to the No. 7 spot on the core production schedule. This will allow us to get this book back in print in all languages by early summer of next year." [13] The "literature core" was an initiative Mr. Tkach kicked off in 1987 to make the church's most important literature, about 50 titles, available in eight different languages. Their goal was to produce seven titles per year. Now that it was in position number 7, *Mystery of the Ages* was on the fast track, so to speak, to being revised.

In the rush to stay on schedule with the revision, on July 8, Lowell Wagner, in Editorial Services, distributed a questionnaire attached to a photocopy of *Mystery of the Ages* to a number of people who worked with the church's literature and in the letter-answering department. [14] He encouraged recipients to thoroughly review the book and to answer a number of questions like: *Does this literature contain any misstatement of doctrine or fact? Does it leave any false impressions, create any misunderstandings, or generate questions it doesn't answer? Does it contain any statements likely to cause unnecessary offense? Does this literature contain any unnecessary or irrelevant material you feel should be deleted before reprinting? Is the literary style interesting and pleasing overall?*

How incredibly revealing this questionnaire should have been to those editors who read it. Herbert W. Armstrong FOUNDED their church! *Mystery of the Ages* was his life's greatest work. Yet 2½ years after he died, Tkachism circulated this audacious questionnaire asking ministers if they thought the material in *Mystery* was "interesting" or "pleasing."

Years later, when asked why the questionnaire was distributed to the ministry, Tkach Jr. replied, "Rather than just have a few people give input on the errors they find, it was helpful to have a larger group of people comment on the errors they found." [15]

It wasn't sent with the intention of salvaging *Mystery of the Ages* at all. It just provided a way for Tkachism to get more headquarters personnel involved in ridiculing Mr. Armstrong's teachings.

MORE CHANGES

Meanwhile, changes in fundamental doctrines discussed in *Mystery of the Ages* kept barreling out of headquarters. In the summer of 1988, Mr. Tkach Sr. set off this bombshell:

> [W]e must also be willing to face the fact that the overwhelming weight of scientific evidence indicates that there do exist bones, bones like those of humans, that date to a time *before* the creation of Adam. These bones apparently belonged to creatures that had an appearance like man's. ... We should realize that it is not outside the realm of possibility that God created animals shaped like man in the times before the great destruction that preceded the re-creation. Nor is it impossible that these same creatures had certain skills for building.[16]

At the time, Dr. Herman Hoeh had been giving lectures before WCG ministers about "pre-Adamic" times. Another minister, Richard Burky, also advocated this idea of man-like builders who lived before Adam, in his paper that later circulated under the title "Creative Development."

Mr. Armstrong called these kinds of arguments by another name: "FENCE-STRADDLING THEISTIC EVOLUTION."[17] *God is Creator, but He's operating on a trial-and-error basis—using evolution, you might say, to sort of refine His product.*

It goes without saying that these theories markedly contradict huge sections in *Mystery of the Ages*.[18]

Mr. Tkach followed up his theistic evolution theory with another whopper two weeks later. In chapter 6, we noted how shifting the focus of the commission to "feeding the flock" turned the church inward. Predictably, it wasn't long before Tkachism rejected the gospel commission entirely.

"Just what is the 'great commission' of the church of God?" Tkach Sr. asked in August 1988. He continued,

> Has God given His church a great commission to preach the gospel to the world, and another, secondary or lesser commis-

sion to feed the flock? Is there in reality a "first" commission and a less-important 'second' commission? [19]

Later, he wrote, "It may surprise some to realize that the phrase *great commission* is nowhere found in the Scriptures. Nor are the phrases *first commission* or *second commission* found in Scripture." [20]

But they are found, *and scripturally explained,* in chapter 6 of *Mystery of the Ages.* The first, and great, commission of the church is to preach the gospel of the kingdom of God; secondarily, it is to "feed the sheep"—to spiritually nourish the body of Christ. [21] Mr. Armstrong believed that while both aspects of the dual commission worked together hand in hand, first priority had to be given to preaching the gospel. He often told members that their individual spiritual development depended upon how much their hearts were in the work—the first commission—of the church.

Mr. Armstrong wrote *Mystery of the Ages* with the "gospel message to the world" in mind. As the WCG continued its turn inward, such works became expendable.

AMBASSADOR COLLEGE CROSSROADS

When Mr. Armstrong decided to close the Ambassador campus in Big Sandy, Texas, he said it was because he wasn't about to pursue accreditation. He also said more resources were needed for the first commission of preaching the gospel to the world. [22]

Since Mr. Tkach began his pastor generalship with an entirely different focus—one that did not put top priority on the first commission—you can see why he so quickly reversed Mr. Armstrong's decision to close Big Sandy. The first commission needs were not as important to him as they were to Mr. Armstrong.

It didn't take long for Mr. Tkach's radically different views on accreditation to be exposed either.

While Mr. Armstrong did not discuss accreditation specifically in *Mystery of the Ages,* he certainly addressed the subject of education in this world compared to Ambassador College. Right at the start of his book, on page 1, he wrote that "higher education in the

Western world has sought to erase the mystery by giving its virtually unanimous acceptance to the theory of evolution."[23] Because of this false premise, he explained in the "Preface," higher learning has not been able to solve the greatest of all mysteries: WHO AND WHAT IS GOD.

Disproving evolution was a critical point on which Mr. Armstrong's personal conversion hinged. It was one of two disturbing challenges he confronted early in life, during an intensive six-month study. That study culminated in the beginning of the worldwide work God would raise up through him. "And let me add here," he wrote in *Mystery of the Ages,*

> that my study of God's revelation of truth has never ceased. Later Christ used me in founding three liberal arts colleges—including one in England. Through constant study, teaching and collaboration with spirit-minded faculty members in theological courses, my mind has remained open. And knowledge of God's revealed truth has increased.[24]

This was the model on which Mr. Armstrong established Ambassador College. It was a character-building institution, with the Word of God as its foundation.[25]

These are some of the reasons Mr. Armstrong was dead-set against accreditation. He did not want the approval of men if it meant lowering God's standard at the college. He would much rather be *unaccredited* before men than to compromise with God's Word. Indeed, as we have seen, he was prepared to *close* Big Sandy entirely should Texas law require certified schools to become accredited!

Beginning in the fall of 1988, Mr. Tkach, Dr. Ward and company set out to strip away everything that made Ambassador College unique, despite their persistent claims to the contrary. This one decision led to a whirlwind of activity and change in the church—all revolving around Big Sandy. In 1988, they decided to pursue accreditation for Big Sandy. In 1989, they decided to consolidate both campuses in Big Sandy. In 1990, they closed the Pasadena campus. In 1994, after wholesale changes in the school—

altering the curriculum, increasing student enrollment, building dozens of new structures, introducing inter-collegiate sports—the college finally obtained accreditation.

But getting back to 1988, de-emphasizing the importance of preaching the gospel to the world as a warning while focusing energy and resources inward to expand the college activities did not bode well for the survival of Mr. Armstrong's most important book.

"CHRISTIAN DUTY" TO TURN YOURSELF IN

As you might well imagine, by this point there were a number of dissenting voices within the church's ranks—although not nearly as many as there should have been. Some ministers were beginning to question the church's direction—even refusing, in some instances, to preach the "new truth" coming out of Pasadena.

To these ministers, Mr. Tkach's message was clear: GET BEHIND ME OR GET OUT. In 1988, he wrote to the ministry:

[I]f you have any doctrinal area that you do not understand properly, you have an obligation to contact Church Administration and discuss the matter. It would be dishonest and divisive for a minister to refuse to address with his congregation a doctrinal point of significant import to the church because of his personal disagreement, and to fail to notify his superiors of that disagreement.[26]

This is one reason so many ministers buckled under the weight of these many changes—they knew if they didn't declare their support for them from behind the pulpit, it could well cost them their jobs. Tkach continued,

If a matter is unclear to you or deeper understanding is needed, it is your *Christian duty* ... to call Church Administration for guidance. It is spiritually inexcusable for you to permit your lack of understanding or disagreement to become a source of division among the membership in your local congregation.[27]

If they didn't agree with the church's direction, they had a Christian duty to turn themselves in. Tkachism, we would find out years later, had a great fondness for the term *Christian duty.*

NINE

INCIDENTAL
POINTS

"The fundamental truths of God's Word are contained in Mystery of
the Ages. *But we must realize that some of the peripheral or incidental
points it contains give occasion to critics to fault the whole book, as well
as inadvertently misleading readers on a few points."*

— JOSEPH TKACH SR.
Pastor General's Report, *February 14, 1989*

NOT surprisingly, Mr. Tkach decided against revising
Mystery of the Ages. Bernie Schnippert had the honor of
making the first official announcement on December 2,
1988—albeit only to church employees involved in producing and
distributing literature. He wrote, "Mr. Tkach decided last June to
stop distributing *Mystery of the Ages* [actually, he placed the book
on hold May 13, then discarded the inventory on June 2] because
of sections that no longer properly reflected the church's teaching
on *certain subjects.*"[1] In actuality, the only specific reason offered
in those earlier reports was that it needed to be revised "to better
reflect the church's teaching *about healing.*"[2] Now the reasons had
broadened to "certain subjects."

"For now," Schnippert wrote, "Mr. Tkach has decided not to
reprint the book."[3] And with that, the wcg had finally made it
official. The book's lifespan within the church had lasted from
September 1985 to May 1988—a run of only 32 months. Years later,

they would spend more than twice that amount of time fighting us in court to *keep* the book out of print!

Mr. Schnippert offered this explanation in his December 1988 report: "When Mr. Armstrong compiled *Mystery*, he drew material from other booklets, booklets that are still in print. In that way, *Mystery* will not actually go out of print since parts of it are already contained in other booklets."[4] This is one of the first instances where they used the "while we've made a change, it's not really a change" excuse. This tactic would be repeated again and again for three more years, in an effort to hide their massive doctrinal transformation from the church membership. Schnippert gave this example as support for the fact that *Mystery* would "not actually go out of print":

> The same sort of situation exists with *The Incredible Human Potential*. As early as 1982, Mr. Armstrong had sections of the book produced as booklets. *Your Awesome Future, What Science Can't Discover About the Human Mind, Human Nature—Did God Create It?*, and *World Peace—How Will It Come?* were all originally part of *The Incredible Human Potential*. Mr. Armstrong used these booklets frequently on the telecast. And although *The Incredible Human Potential* is no longer in print as a book, much of it is still being used in booklet form.[5]

Tkachism latched on to this excuse early on and milked everything it could out of it. *But the same message is available in other literature,* they often said.

Mr. Armstrong did extract some material from *The Incredible Human Potential* to produce smaller booklets for the television program. But to say that, because of these booklets, "much" of the book was still being published was terribly misleading. To then use the same excuse for retiring *Mystery* was even more ridiculous in light of the long list of changes that had been made.

After Schnippert's December 1988 announcement, Mail Processing updated its staff on procedures regarding the book. "Both versions of the *Mystery of the Ages* book [softbound and hardbound] have been out of stock for a few months"[6]—*discarded* or *destroyed,* actually. Those requesting the book would now be sent a postcard saying, "This publication is no longer available and there are now no plans to reprint it."[7]

PREPARING THE CHURCH

Almost seven months elapsed from when *Mystery* was put "on hold" to when they said there were "no plans to reprint." Then, after that, it took Church Administration another *60 days* to inform the field ministry about the decision and an additional 20 days to tell the membership.[8] By stark contrast, Joseph Tkach Jr. fired my dad on December 7, 1989, a year after they killed *Mystery,* and news of the disfellowshipment hit the *Pastor General's Report* just 12 DAYS LATER.[9]

But upon deciding not to reprint Mr. Armstrong's best and most popular work—even long after destroying all remaining inventory copies of the book—church leaders waited *nearly three months* before telling the membership. The reason they took so long is because they wanted to prepare the church for an announcement this earth-shaking.

At the outset of 1989, Mr. Tkach Sr. wrote to the ministry, "One area that I want to stress is that of putting undue emphasis upon Mr. Herbert Armstrong or upon me. In the church of God, human leaders are never to become objects of reverence or devotion bordering on worship."[10] Previously, we have noted Mr. Tkach's attempt to demote Mr. Armstrong post-mortem—even rejecting his prophesied role as the end-time "Elijah." At the same time, Mr. Tkach wasted little time in assuming the spiritual rank of apostle, just 10 months into his pastor-generalship. What's interesting about the above statement is that Mr. Tkach presents himself as co-equal with Mr. Armstrong. Don't put "undue emphasis upon Mr. Herbert Armstrong *or upon me,*" he said. From what I remember, *he* was the only one putting undue emphasis on himself. Mr. Tkach continued,

> It is not appropriate, for example, to assign various scriptures to Mr. Armstrong *or me personally* as though our leadership were

specifically prophesied in the Bible. Besides being erroneous and spiritually presumptuous, this kind of thinking only serves to falsely brand God's church as a cultish sect that worships its human leaders.[11]

I remember Dean Blackwell once delivering a sermon in which he went through Joshua 1, likening Mr. Tkach to Joshua, who succeeded Moses anciently. Outside of general references like that, I certainly don't remember any minister ever assigning *specific* scriptures to Mr. Tkach and his leadership. That Mr. Tkach would now consider this a problem was simply an attempt to de-emphasize Mr. Armstrong's importance while elevating his own, and in a manner that seemed both humble and wise.

On the other hand, Mr. Armstrong, Mr. Tkach and just about every minister in the wcg had, *for many years,* assigned various scriptures to Mr. Armstrong and *his* leadership. That Mr. Tkach would now equate this with *worshiping* a human being is absurd. Jesus is the one who said that Elijah (not the "church") "shall first come, and restore all things."[12] Was it erroneous and spiritually presumptuous for Jesus to say this? Or for the disciples to believe it? They knew that John the Baptist was the first-century fulfillment of this prophecy.[13] In fact, *Mr. Tkach* even said John the Baptist was the prophesied messenger to prepare the way before Christ's first coming. Was it erroneous and spiritually presumptuous for him to assign various scriptures to *John the Baptist*—a mere human? Was Mr. Tkach worshiping John the Baptist?

Mystery of the Ages has more to say about various scriptures assigned to Mr. Armstrong than any other book or booklet he ever wrote. Mr. Tkach now deemed these sections of the book erroneous and spiritually presumptuous. What members did *not* know at the time was that Mr. Tkach now believed the WHOLE BOOK had so many errors that a revised copy couldn't even be printed.

MYSTERY OF THE AGES REVISED

Two weeks after his comments about assigning scriptures to names, Mr. Tkach began the PGR by writing, "I am thrilled to announce that our new booklet *Who Was Jesus?*, written by Paul Kroll, is now printed and ready for mailing!"[14] The publicity the church gave this booklet is not unlike that which Mr. Armstrong heaped upon *Mystery of the Ages* when it was first released. All members and co-workers automatically received a copy. The church offered the booklet on television. Mr. Tkach also offered it to all *Plain Truth* subscribers in his semi-annual letter. He went on to write, "I believe this will be one of our most vital and important pieces of litera-ture as we continue to do the job of preaching and teaching the full gospel of Jesus Christ—the unparalleled good news about the salvation of mankind through Jesus, and His prophesied Second Coming to establish the kingdom of God."[15]

The problem with *Who Was Jesus?* wasn't so much the content (although it does contain some unbiblical teachings), it was the new *direction* or *focus* of the message. It was moving away from the message Jesus actually preached to focusing primarily on the messenger.

In *Mystery of the Ages,* Mr. Armstrong wrote about a "violent controversy" that erupted in the early years of the first-century church. The dispute centered on whether the church should proclaim the gospel OF Christ or merely *a gospel* ABOUT Christ. The gospel about Christ won out—leaving only a faithful few to proclaim the true gospel OF Jesus Christ.[16] Mr. Armstrong wrote about this false gospel, in some detail, on pages 278-279 of *Mystery of the Ages.*

Our purpose in this volume is not to help you prove which gospel is true. But suffice it to say, had Mr. Armstrong lived long enough to compare *Who Was Jesus?* with *Mystery of the Ages,* he would have made this conclusion in the strongest possible terms: *Who Was Jesus?* is ABOUT Christ, whereas *Mystery of the Ages* contains Christ's message—the gospel *Jesus Christ preached.*

It is not coincidental that Mr. Tkach delayed the *Mystery of the Ages* announcement until AFTER *Who Was Jesus?* was printed. He needed a replacement for *Mystery of the Ages.* He just couldn't, in good conscience, make all the editorial changes necessary to keep *Mystery of the Ages* afloat. And aside from that, the whole focus and intent of the church's work had changed. Nothing reflects this better than comparing *Who Was Jesus?* with *Mystery of the Ages.* So, on the eve of announcing that *Mystery of the Ages* was now dead and buried, Mr. Tkach said he was THRILLED to announce that "one of our most vital and important pieces of literature" was now ready for distribution. In that way, *Who Was Jesus?* served as the revised edition of *Mystery of the Ages.*

PASSING THE BUCK

As would become customary with major changes in the church, Mr. Tkach had someone else break the news about *Mystery* being discontinued. Though Mr. Tkach had personally opened the January 17 PGR with his "thrilling" announcement about *Who Was Jesus?,* in the next issue, he delegated the job of telling the field ministry about *Mystery of the Ages* to Larry Salyer, who wrote,

> *Mystery of the Ages* is among the most expensive pieces of literature we have recently published. We have offered this book to the public many times through the telecast, the *Plain Truth,* coworker letters and semi-annual letters. While it is not completely accurate to say that we have saturated our audience with these offers, we have made more offers for this book and have distributed it more than any other in the past four years.[17]

Actually, the book had been distributed less than three years.

Mr. Salyer then factored in another reason for its removal: "Because *Mystery of the Ages* covers so many doctrinal subjects and is so costly to publish, obviously we want it to be completely accurate theologically. This is important, also, because our literature faces an ever-increasing critical review from outsiders." To his credit, he at least slips in part of the real reason, indicating it wasn't "completely accurate." But later, Salyer wrote, "Please do not tell prospective members to request copies of *Mystery of the Ages,* because we do not have any in stock. We do not plan to print more until editorial and budget questions have been resolved."[18] Actually, they had destroyed all remaining stock and told employees there were no plans to reprint.

Breaking down Salyer's comments, he identified three reasons for *Mystery's* removal: 1) too expensive; 2) distribution had reached *near*-saturation point; and 3) not completely accurate theologically.

Let's look at these three reasons more closely.

TOO EXPENSIVE

In his 1998 deposition, Mr. Tkach Jr. backed up Larry Salyer's assessment, that the book was too expensive. "It's much easier to give away 10 booklets that cost a dime each to produce than it is to give a book that costs 10 bucks to produce. It's just that simple."[19] But it's not as simple as he made it sound because *Mystery of the Ages* never cost that much to produce. When Dexter Faulkner asked Tkach Sr. about what to do with the 120,000 unusable copies in 1988, he said the replacement cost for the book would be "around one dollar per copy."[20] With that in mind, using Joe Jr.'s hypothetical, sending *Mystery of the Ages* may have been *more* cost-effective than 10 booklets.

Nevertheless, when we asked if printing and distributing the book was a "financial drain" for the church, Mr. Tkach Jr. said, "Absolutely."[21] Why, then, had it not been a huge financial drain for the church before 1988? "Because the income was sufficient to—to go ahead and do that," said Tkach. Later, even after realizing that the income in 1988 was actually one of the "peak years" for the church, Tkach stood by the "too expensive" excuse: "… expense was absolutely an *equivalent reason* to the errors that we first were aware of in '88," he said.[22]

Of course, Tkach HAD to say this or else admit that Larry Salyer misled the ministry in 1989. Yet, a quick look at the figures removes the smoke screen. The cost for printing and distributing *Mystery* was not exorbitant—not when compared to a 10-booklet equivalent—and certainly not for a multi-million-dollar organization at the peak of its income.

NEAR-SATURATION POINT

Writing in the *Pastor General's Report* nine months before Mr. Armstrong died, Joseph Tkach Sr. referred to a sermon Mr.

Armstrong had recently given in which he had mentioned *Mystery of the Ages.* "I know this book," Mr. Tkach wrote, "will prove to be another major step forward for God's church and the spreading of the gospel *around the world.*"[23]

Mr. Armstrong's vision for this book's impact was also worldwide. "I candidly feel it may be the most important book since the Bible! ... We want to reach the largest audience possible with this book."[24]

It is true that the church used nearly every means possible to promote the book once it was completed in September 1985—television, the church's literature, direct mail, newspaper advertisements, bookstores, etc. Never had the church distributed so many copies of a single book so quickly.

But did it reach the "largest audience possible" in its short life span of about 2½ years? Is it fair to say that the church's audience had nearly been saturated with offers for the book? Did it prove to be the major step forward in preaching the gospel *around the world* like Mr. Tkach said it would be in April 1985?

The main reason Mr. Tkach developed his "literature core" plan in April 1987 was because there were *fewer than a dozen booklets* available in ALL eight languages in which the church printed—English, Dutch, French, German, Italian, Norwegian, Spanish and Portuguese. And while English obviously had the most literature available, Mr. Tkach could not see the work really making a "coordinated worldwide" push unless all the church's major literature was available in all eight languages. This is why he set the goal for 50 pieces of literature to be printed in all eight languages.[25]

By the time *Mystery of the Ages* had been put on hold in mid-1988, the book had been translated and printed in at least six of those eight languages. The first translated version of *Mystery,* from what we found in the church's newspaper, was the French version.[26] They distributed it to French-speaking brethren at the Feast of Tabernacles in 1987—two years after Mr. Armstrong first handed out the English translation of the book. The French version was later mailed to 1,900 people who had requested it. Their names had been put on a waiting list until a translated copy was available.

The Norwegian version of the book rolled off the presses

sometime after that 1987 Feast, in the fall. The initial printing was for 21,000. Advertising for the book began in the March 1988 Norwegian *Plain Truth*.[27]

The Italian and Spanish versions of the book were released on February 26, 1988. There is no mention in the *Worldwide News* of when the Dutch and German versions were printed. But judging by the length of time it took for the other four, mentioned above, to be completed, it was probably late 1987 or early 1988 before they were finished.

Which brings us to the point. Only *a few months* after these translated copies were finished and printed, Mr. Tkach put *Mystery of the Ages* "on hold" in ALL languages! They had *just completed* six of these translated versions, and then the whole project was swept aside because, according to Larry Salyer, they had reached *near* saturation point with their audience? That couldn't possibly have been true for the foreign-language areas.

Two months before Salyer's comments, when Bernie Schnippert told headquarters employees about the removal, he admitted,

> We are all aware that this decision will have its greatest impact in the non-English areas which may not have as much of *Mystery* in print in other booklets as do we in English. This fact was considered very carefully before the decision was reached. But we believe that in time the further production of core booklets will increase all international inventories to the point that the essential elements of our teachings, if not the exact words used in *Mystery,* will be available in all areas.[28]

The "exact words" of *Mystery* available in other literature?

At least he acknowledged the great impact this decision would have on the non-English areas. Schnippert continued, "This was a case where the need for a unified approach and considerations of accuracy had to take precedence over individual circumstances."[29]

Yet the whole purpose for the literature core was so the work could "realize a truly unified and coordinated worldwide media effort."[30] And how could *Mystery* NOT be considered a "core" publication? *Mystery of the Ages* is a magnificent summary of all Mr.

Armstrong's work and teachings. To have that book available in all eight languages, which it nearly was, would have been a major step forward for the work in spreading the gospel around the world. This was Mr. Tkach's goal for the core literature initiative. But the English version is the only one that even got off the ground—and even then, it was short-lived.

According to Roger Lippross, the WCG's literature production director at the time, the church distributed 1.245 million copies of the hardcover and softcover editions of *Mystery of the Ages*.[31] By comparison, the church distributed more than 3 million copies of *The Seven Laws of Success* and 6 million copies of *The United States and Britain in Prophecy*.[32] Mr. Armstrong wanted this to reach the "largest audience possible" and the book only went to less than half the number of people that received *The Seven Laws of Success*.

Yes, distribution of *Mystery* got off to a phenomenal start. Yes, it was the fastest-moving book the church had ever produced. But it certainly had not reached a near-saturation point. In fact, the INCREDIBLE response to the book for 32 months makes the decision to remove it that much more ridiculous!

Nearly a year after *Mystery of the Ages* had been released—after being distributed to all church members, offered on the television program and to *Plain Truth* readers—Richard Rice wrote in the *Pastor General's Report,*

> The comments we continue to receive about *Mystery of the Ages* show that it is STILL having a powerful impact on the lives of many. Readers consider this book the apex of Mr. Armstrong's writings. The brethren often say they have never seen God's plan unfold as clearly as in the pages of this book.
>
> Many people who were never interested in religion before have been moved to ask for ministerial visits after reading it. ... *Mystery of the Ages* continues to be an effective tool in spreading the gospel.[33]

Implying that the book had run its course, nearly saturating the church's audience, while it was still flying off the shelves, is patently dishonest. The reason the Worldwide Church of God retired its most popular piece of literature is because they believed it had so many doctrinal flaws that it simply could not be revised without turning it into a completely different book.

NOT COMPLETELY ACCURATE

Larry Salyer offered this as an example of why *Mystery of the Ages* wasn't "completely accurate theologically":

> In chapter 2 on page 70 (page 59 of the softbound edition), we find the following statement: "What was God's ultimate objective for the angels? Beyond question it is that which, now, because of angelic rebellion, has become the transcendent potential of humans." The impression may be perceived by some to be that God was initially going to reproduce Himself through angels and, since they failed, the opportunity was given to humans.[34]

Actually, Mr. Armstrong was quite clear in his book that *because of angelic rebellion,* God set out to reproduce Himself through man. He wrote,

> To fulfill his purpose for the entire vast universe, God saw that nothing less than himself (as the God family) could be absolutely relied upon to carry out that supreme purpose in the entire universe. ...
> God then purposed to reproduce himself, through humans, made in his image and likeness, but made first from material flesh and blood, subject to death if there is sin unrepented of— yet with the possibility of being born into the divine family begotten by God the Father. God saw how this could be done through Christ, who gave himself for that purpose.[35]

Mr. Armstrong *repeatedly* made the point, and backed it up with scriptural passages like Hebrews 1:1-8, that God never offered this potential to angels.

What Tkachism had a problem with in the above quote is the fact that God enacted His purpose through man *because of* angelic sin. They had no problem accepting that God initially created a pre-Adamic, animal-like man with architectural skills. But how dare Mr. Armstrong teach that man was created on Earth to succeed where the angels failed!

Mr. Salyer said, "Another area of concern is the sensitivity surrounding any discussion of the races."[36] Of course, much of what Mr. Armstrong had to say on the subject of race had already been edited out of the softbound version. So this seems picky.

Outside of the above quote and the sensitive statements made regarding race, the only other inaccuracy Salyer addressed was how Mr. Armstrong "quoted freely" from Alexander Hislop's *Two Babylons*.[37] In actuality, Mr. Armstrong referred to Hislop on two occasions and does not quote him once.

These all, taken at face value, would have to be considered minor points that could have been easily fixed (assuming, of course, that they are even errors in the first place). But remember, *Mystery of the Ages* was "on hold" for more than six months, awaiting the chance to be revised, before Mr. Tkach decided it would be retired permanently.

MR. TKACH FINALLY SPEAKS

Nine months after he directed Bernie Schnippert to put the book on hold, Mr. Tkach finally broached the subject of *Mystery's* status. He addressed the ministers first in the *Pastor General's Report* and the membership one week later in the *Worldwide News*. Mr. Tkach began his column by saying, "It is critically important that God's church never be in a position of continuing to put out what may be misleading or inaccurate material once we have become aware of it. God expects us to continually be growing in understanding and knowledge. Mr. Armstrong often reinforced that concept."[38] To that point, that's about as close as any of them got to the real reason for removing the book. It contained "misleading" and "inaccurate" material. But in removing these supposed errors, Mr. Tkach said he was only following Mr. Armstrong's example. This excuse would be used repeatedly in the years that followed—*Mr. Armstrong made changes and so do we—what's the big deal?*

Mr. Tkach then downplayed the significance of the errors in *Mystery*.

> The fundamental truths of God's Word are contained in *Mystery of the Ages*. But we must realize that some of the peripheral or incidental points it contains give occasion to critics to fault the whole book, as well as inadvertently misleading readers on a few points.[39]

But it was the Tkaches who were misleading people! Everyone close to them knew how they felt about *Mystery of the Ages*: It WAS "RIDDLED WITH ERROR." Yet, in telling the brethren why it was discontinued, he talked about "incidental" points that could give critics the wrong impression.

Mr. Tkach did not elaborate on any of the "peripheral or incidental points" that needed changing. Instead, he devoted much space to explaining how much of the church's literature had become "dated."

MYSTERY OF THE AGES—OUTDATED?

"We must ... face the fact," Mr. Tkach wrote, "that literature written in the early to late 1950s does not always have the same impact today as it surely had then." He continued,

> Mr. Armstrong was explaining the truth to different audiences with different kinds of understanding than we face today on the brink of the 1990s. It behooves us now, as God leads us, to present the truth of His Word in a format that will reach people in a world that has traveled 30 to 35 years down the road of secularism and spiritual ignorance, and that is looking beyond into the last decade of this century.[40]

Later, after explaining how they had been taking a "serious look" at the church's body of literature, Mr. Tkach wrote, "A manner of presentation that worked in 1959 may have less impact on a reader in 1989." Understandably, he continued, this process of updating would be difficult for some church members.

I'm sure you feel, as I do, a certain nostalgic reluctance to revise or retire some of the booklets that the church has used for years and that we have all learned and grown from. But healthy change is a part of growth, something that has long been a vital part of the production of the church's literature.[41]

Mr. Tkach concluded by making this unbelievable comparison: "No one would argue that we should still be producing such booklets from the past as *1975 in Prophecy* or *Hippies—Hypocrisy and 'Happiness.'*"[42]

He actually equated the removal of *Mystery of the Ages* with discontinuing *Hippies—Hypocrisy and "Happiness."* Mr. Armstrong finished *Mystery of the Ages* less than *three years* before Mr. Tkach removed the book. That he could even imply it was outdated in 1989 is truly ridiculous.

Mystery of the Ages is not a pamphlet attacking a social evil that took place in 1963. Neither is it a booklet outlining prophetic trends in the lead-up to 1975. *Mystery of the Ages* is a 363-page book explaining the church's ENTIRE BODY OF BELIEFS—*every major doctrine!* In fact, what's most notable about the book is how *timeless* the content really is.

Mr. Tkach wrote, "I heard one man say, 'But we're taking Mr. Armstrong out of everything.' How short-sighted and imperceptive!" Actually, that man, whoever he was, turned out to be quite the visionary. "Mr. Armstrong's teaching will always be a part of us," Mr. Tkach insisted, even though *Mystery of the Ages, The Incredible Human Potential* and *The United States and Britain in Prophecy* were already gone for good.[43]

THE REAL REASON

Putting together comments from Bernie Schnippert, Larry Salyer and Joseph Tkach, we now have these five reasons offered in 1989 for the removal of *Mystery of the Ages:* 1) content available in other literature; 2) too expensive; 3) distribution at near-saturation point; 4) content outdated; and 5) incorrect peripheral or incidental points.

Yet, the documented evidence points to one reason—and one reason only: Tkachism had MAJOR problems with the book's doctrinal teachings by early 1988. Notice what Church Administration told the field ministry just a few months after all these excuses were given:

> Apparently a number of ministers have recommended obsolete literature to prospective members. These recommendations include two books, *The Incredible Human Potential* and *Mystery of the Ages*, and the booklet *The Book of Revelation Unveiled at Last* [discontinued in December 1988]. It obviously creates an uncomfortable situation when these [prospective members] are told that the recommended literature is not in print.
>
> Please consult the updated lists of current literature that we publish twice a year before recommending a book or booklet.
>
> In addition, it is inappropriate to photocopy and distribute obsolete articles. If the literature is not on our current literature index, THEN IT SHOULD NOT BE USED.[44]

Now please again examine the five reasons they discontinued *Mystery*. You couldn't logically cite any of those as reasons why someone could not at least obtain a photocopied version—or possibly borrow the book. The reason obsolete literature was not to be used, *under any circumstances*, is because it was doctrinally wrong! It was, as Tkach Jr. stated dogmatically, *in private*, later that year, "riddled with error."

While working on this chapter, someone forwarded me an e-mail they had sent to the WCG on June 27, 2003, asking this question: "Why did the church really discontinue Herbert Armstrong's teaching?"

Paul Kroll replied three days later: "[T]he reason the Worldwide Church of God had to discontinue many of them is because they were in error from a biblical perspective, and some were legalistic in nature."[45]

Would to God they had been that honest in 1989.

TEN

THE AGENDA

"One of our greatest challenges has been trying to explain these doctrinal reforms to outsiders while maintaining our credibility internally, and some groups have greatly hindered our efforts by their reporting."

— JOSEPH TKACH JR.
Transformed by Truth

O N December 17, 1994, Joseph Tkach Sr. delivered a landmark sermon, bringing out into the open several far-reaching doctrinal changes that centered around a "new" (actually mainstream) understanding of the Old and New Covenants. According to his son, "[I]t once and for all convinced the skeptics within our own church that the changes were for real and that they were permanent."[1] Later, he wrote,

> [M]any of our members didn't believe that the changes they were seeing in the church were real. Just as evangelicals have a hard time believing that the Worldwide Church of God has moved into orthodoxy, many of our members had a hard time believing their church was moving away from its peculiar doctrinal distinctives.[2]

Why would *their own members* have been skeptical about the changes being "for real"? Why would they find it difficult to believe the church was moving away from its past teachings?

It's because after making the changes, *the Tkaches* then reassured the membership that NOTHING HAD REALLY CHANGED. And when rumors would circulate that more changes were coming, the Tkaches kept saying, "We will never change that"—right up to the point of actually making the change.

The change regarding the Old and New Covenants is one such example. Throughout 1994, Tkach Sr. VEHEMENTLY DENIED rumors that the church was on the verge of doing away with its teaching on Sabbath observance, the holy days and the law.

Mr. Tkach gave a sermon in Pasadena on April 30, 1994 (a tape of which was later played in all WCG congregations), in which he denounced "rumormongers":

> They have no compunctions at all about exaggerating. Like I read from this list of rumors that are going around: We're going to start keeping Christmas, and we're changing the Passover, and we're making changes to please the Protestants to get accreditation. … [W]e're going to do away with the Sabbath, we're going to do away with the holy days and we're going to do away with the law.[3]

At the Ambassador College commencement exercises on May 20, 1994, Mr. Tkach quoted Ted Koppel, who said, "What Moses brought down from Mount Sinai were not the ten suggestions. They are commandments." Mr. Tkach said,

> Notice he used the word *are* and not *were,* because they are still in existence today, in spite of what others accuse us of saying— "that we are doing away with the law and the commandments of God." Again I say, "garbage."[4]

In an article written around that same time, Mr. Tkach assured the church membership that.

> we are also committed to upholding and walking in all the ways of God, including the observance of the Sabbath, the fourth of the Ten Commandments, as well as the annual festivals, during which we celebrate God's plan of redemption and salvation of humanity through Jesus Christ.[5]

Later that year, on November 12, Mr. Tkach made several more strong statements in a Pasadena sermon: "Yes, we should keep the law"; "I'm not trying to minimize the importance of the law"; "I'm not trying to minimize the importance of the Sabbath."[6]

Three weeks later, speaking in Washington, D.C., Mr. Tkach asked, "Does this mean that we are no longer obligated to obey the law?" His answer: "God forbid!" He later said, "Christ is saying the New Testament gospel is not contrary or contradictory in any way, shape or form to the Old Testament law."[7]

Then, on December 17—*just two weeks later,* and after a string of denouncements against those spreading "lies" and "rumors"—Mr. Tkach *did away* with the church's teachings on clean and unclean meats, tithing, the Sabbath, holy day observance and the law. This, according to Tkach Jr.'s book, is when skeptics in the church *finally* knew that the changes were for real.

Is it any wonder why church members might have thought such changes would never take place?

MASS EXODUS

After Mr. Tkach's "Old Covenant/New Covenant" sermon, some 20,000 people left the Worldwide Church of God. Many of them settled into the newly established United Church of God—originally headed by David Hulme. In his resignation letter to Mr. Tkach, Hulme wrote,

> Several months ago you told me, "This church has been far too Old Testament, but I couldn't tell the members that. No, not for five years." I was surprised at the time, but not knowing what you meant exactly, I let it aside. Since then I have noticed that you have often responded with a categorical denial to the accusation that there is an agenda of doctrinal changes. Yet in discussion with one minister last December you described the change on tithing from gross to net (announced in the December 6, 1994, PGR) as simply a "stepping stone" to voluntary tithing. This certainly sounds like an agenda. As you know, many have feared that "agenda" involves a move into the Protestant mainstream.[8]

Mr. Hulme had been a headquarters insider for some time—for many years heading up the communications and public affairs department in Pasadena. In fact, during the late 1980s and early 1990s, Mr. Hulme was often the one who contacted outside organizations to inform them of the "positive" changes in the church. The church, at that time, desperately wanted to remove the "cult" label many outside groups had pinned on it. So Mr. Hulme would not have been considered an ultra-conservative by any means. Early on, he was very supportive of the church's changes—at least judging by his comments as the church's spokesman. Yet, by 1995, *even he* concluded that the Tkaches had an agenda from the beginning. Hulme continued,

> The fact that [Mr. Armstrong] chose you on the basis of continuity of doctrine and practice when in fact you believed very differently, in my mind casts serious doubt whether he would have appointed you if he had known your beliefs. That you differed so much from your predecessor explains why almost every doctrinal and administrative change caused me to inform you that something was very wrong. It is only in the light of your comments about Richard Plache and Al Carozzo, however, that I have put it all together. Apparently you and I were not agreed in the first place. I thought you were upholding Mr. Armstrong, but it now appears you were not. By your own admission you were simply biding your time.
>
> No wonder that my many protestations about radical change were never answered, and the changes proceeded as if no input had been given. And yet you continued to insist that nothing had really changed very much. Why? Prior to December 1994 did you feel it expedient to create the impression publicly that nothing had really changed in the church's view of the law? Was the time still not right?[9]

As we noted at the end of chapter 6, Tkach responded by admitting there was an agenda, but that it was *Christ's* agenda. As if Jesus Christ would repeatedly try to deceive WCG members with lies and hypocrisy.

PLEASE BE HONEST

Three months after my dad was fired, Dennis Leap, a WCG local elder serving in Buffalo, New York, resigned from his post and joined the Philadelphia Church of God. He sent a letter to the WCG brethren in his area to apprise them of why he was leaving. In his letter, Mr. Leap gave three reasons for his departure: 1) the WCG's discontinuation of *Mystery of the Ages*; 2) drastic changes in fundamental WCG doctrines; and 3) the WCG's compromise with the truth in order to win favor with the world.

Mr. Leap was the first WCG minister to leave the church after my dad and Mr. Amos were disfellowshiped. So it was big news for our little church. And I'm sure it bothered WCG officials in Pasadena. Joseph Tkach Jr. decided to answer Mr. Leap's letter himself on April 20, 1990. He wrote,

> Your first point concerned our discontinuing distribution of *Mystery of the Ages*. ... This book was discontinued because we have more economical ways of providing *exactly the same message* to subscribers and members. The doctrinal message of the book *is not being changed or stopped.*[10]

Would Jesus Christ say the "exact same message" of the book was being disseminated four months after firing two ministers and saying the book was "riddled with error"?

Tkach Jr. continued scolding Mr. Leap, "[D]on't pretend to others that you are continuing to follow Mr. Armstrong's way. Please be honest about it."[11] How ironic that statement turned out to be. It is now clear that this accusation is precisely what *Tkachism* was doing at the time Joe Jr. wrote his letter—dishonestly giving the impression they were continuing in Mr. Armstrong's steps. Tkach Jr. wrote, "[N]one of the 'seven mysteries' explained in [*Mystery of the Ages*] has been changed or deleted."[12] The book was riddled with error and had too many doctrinal flaws to be reprinted or even revised, yet Tkach Jr. said that NONE of the seven mysteries had been changed or deleted?

Jesus Christ would not have given that false impression.

ASSIGNING SCRIPTURES TO NAMES

The Tkaches were also dishonest and deceitful with the way they changed the teaching about assigning scriptures to names. Seven months *before* Mr. Armstrong died, Mr. Tkach Sr. identified Mr. Armstrong as the prophesied Elijah who came in this end time to restore all things.[13] He reconfirmed this teaching shortly *after* Mr. Armstrong died, when he listed the "18 Truths" in the church's newspaper, the *Worldwide News*. In that article, Mr. Armstrong is referred to as "someone who would come in the spirit and power of Elijah" and who restored "all things to the church."[14]

Then, as we noted in chapter 7, on February 9, 1988, Mr. Tkach explained the end-time Elijah prophecy much differently than anyone in the church *ever* had. He said "the church" now fulfills the role of the end-time Elijah[15] and palmed it off on the membership as if it were something we had always known and believed.

On January 3, 1989, Mr. Tkach took it a step further—saying it was "not appropriate" to assign scriptures to Mr. Armstrong as though his leadership was prophesied in the Bible. In his 1990 letter to Mr. Leap, Tkach Jr. explained what his father meant by saying it was inappropriate:

> The intent was not to question whether the end-time Elijah prophecies were being fulfilled. Indeed, church literature had mentioned over a period of many years that these prophecies were being *fulfilled by the "work."* Mr. Armstrong, as human leader of the church, obviously was primary in accomplishing the prophesied task. HE DID NOT, however, claim to be the exclusive fulfillment of the end-time Elijah office. ...
>
> Mr. Armstrong *illustrated* his calling and work by *comparing* it with the work of Elijah and Zerubbabel at times. Lessons can be illustrated by these comparisons. But, SOME HAVE GONE MUCH FURTHER THAN MR. ARMSTRONG HIMSELF DID in such labeling ....
>
> It may surprise you to learn that it has never been a doctrine of the church that men's names should be applied to scripture. No member of the church has ever been required to believe that Mr. Armstrong was "Elijah" or "Zerubbabel" to be in good standing. Mr. Armstrong would have bristled with indig-

nation had anyone tried to require that! He knew the difference between an illustration and a doctrine ....

While we have attempted to curtail speculation about individuals fulfilling specific prophetic roles, there has been NO FUNDAMENTAL DOCTRINAL CHANGE IN THIS AREA. It has *always been known* that both Joshua and Zerubbabel were typical primarily of Christ."[16]

First of all, while Mr. Armstrong certainly acknowledged the indispensable role of the church in *supporting* him, he did, nevertheless, teach that his specific office and role was prophesied in Scripture, as reflected by the following passage:

> Remember, God does things in dual stages. ... As John the Baptist prepared the way, in the physical wilderness of the Jordan River for the first coming of the human Jesus (both man and God), then coming to His material temple, and to His physical people Judah, announcing the Kingdom of God to be set up more than 1,900 years later, so God would use a human messenger in the spiritual wilderness of 20th-century religious confusion, to be a voice crying out the gospel of the Kingdom of God, about the spiritual Christ, coming in supreme power and glory to His spiritual temple, to actually establish that spiritual Kingdom of God. ...
>
> Has this happened, in your days, and has God brought you into this prophetic fulfillment as a part of it?
>
> Has *anyone else* done it?[17]

As Mr. Armstrong explained in *Mystery of the Ages,* it works like an organized team—with the coach and the players mutually depending on one another. But there is just one leader—one apostle. And for many years, the church taught that many prophecies referred to Mr. Armstrong's office and work *directly*—and then to the church secondarily, or indirectly. The Tkach administration confirmed this fact before and after Mr. Armstrong died.

Then on February 9, 1988, Mr. Tkach Sr. said the "Elijah" prophecy referred to the church IN GENERAL—*from the Ephesus era in the first century until now.* He didn't even mention Mr. Armstrong as part of the fulfillment! And then in his letter to Dennis Leap, Mr. Tkach Jr. falsely stated that the wcg had *always* taught this, saying there had been "no fundamental doctrinal change in this area."

NOT JUST AN ANALOGY

In a 1991 *Worldwide News* article by David Hunsberger, we find the same false impression perpetuated more than a year after Tkach Jr.'s letter to Dennis Leap. Hunsberger wrote, "[Gerald Flurry] says that Mr. Armstrong was the prophesied Elijah ...."[18] Yes, and so did Mr. Tkach—not to mention Mr. Armstrong, Gerald Waterhouse, and just about every other well-known wcg minister. Hunsberger went on to write:

> Malachi foretold that an Elijah would come to prepare the way for the Messiah. Jesus said (and Mr. Armstrong taught) that this was fulfilled by John the Baptist, who prepared the way for the Messiah's first coming (Matthew 11:14-15; 17:12-13; Mark 9:13).
>
> Mr. Armstrong taught that he, with the church, was also fulfilling a *type* of the work in preparation for the Second Coming of Christ.[19]

Here again you see the teaching watered down significantly from what Mr. Armstrong actually believed and taught. And like Tkach Jr., Hunsberger led the reader to believe that this was something the church had *always* taught—even under Mr. Armstrong. Later, Hunsberger wrote, "Mr. Armstrong drew an analogy between his own work and that of Zerubbabel, but he did not believe that Zechariah predicted an end-time Zerubbabel who would finish building the church ...."[20]

That is completely false. Mr. Armstrong did not just draw an analogy between his work and Zerubbabel's. He believed his work, *supported* by the church, was the fulfillment of a VERY SPECIFIC PROPHECY.

To make a change in doctrine is one thing. But to make it and then say there is no change is lying. And the reason people lie is to cover up something—to obscure the truth.

This is important to understand: *At that time* in the WCG, the Tkaches *did not want the members to know* they had made such a radical change in their interpretation of these foundational prophecies. So instead, they first watered them down and then tried to sell the membership on it by lying that Mr. Armstrong had always taught it that way. Once the membership accepted this, then the administration could go all the way with the change—and with little or no backlash from the membership.

"I AM ELIJAH"

The extent of Tkachism's deceit is plainly evident in view of the way Tkach Jr. now remembers what the church used to teach about these end-time prophecies. Now that his motive has changed from trying to sell the church members on the changes to trying to paint Mr. Armstrong with the most extreme brush strokes possible, his descriptions are TOTALLY different. In his 1997 book, Mr. Tkach Jr. says, "Herbert Armstrong used to read Malachi 4:5-6 and say that it applied to him"[21]—not "him and the church" or "the church"—just "him." Tkach then proceeded to quote pages 290-91 of *Mystery of the Ages,* where Mr. Armstrong refers to several end-time prophecies that he believed he fulfilled, with the support of the church (the same section of *Mystery* that editors chopped out of the serialized version of the book *in 1986*).

Mr. Tkach continued, "Herbert Armstrong taught that he was the real fulfillment of this passage and that John the Baptist was merely an [sic] foreshadowing."[22] But wait a minute! Didn't Mr. Hunsberger say Mr. Armstrong taught that *John the Baptist* was the REAL fulfillment and that his own work was merely a "type" or an "analogy"?

Mr. Tkach elaborated further on Mr. Armstrong's teaching: "After his first wife died and the idea started to play in Herbert Armstrong's mind—as his own ego accepted the notion and certain people began to play on his ego—he began to accept that he was *personally* the Elijah."[23] (Emphasis in original.) Mrs. Armstrong died in 1967! This is when these ideas supposedly started playing in his mind. How then does Mr. Tkach explain his comments from 1990—that Mr. Armstrong DID NOT "claim to be the exclusive fulfillment of the end-time Elijah office"?

Mr. Tkach told Mr. Leap in 1990 that "some have gone much further than Mr. Armstrong himself did in such labeling." In 1997, Mr. Tkach had now swung to that very extreme. Mr. Tkach continues with this amazingly vivid recollection:

> In the sixties we would say that WCG was doing an Elijah-like work. In the seventies we said that Herbert Armstrong himself was fulfilling the role of Elijah. ... In the last two years of his life, in several sermons, he was even more explicit when he said directly, "I am Elijah." When Ron Kelly, one of our long-time ministers, heard Mr. Armstrong say this, he confessed to me, "I was alarmed when I heard him say, 'I am Elijah.' I could handle, 'I'm in the role of Elijah.' But 'I am Elijah'—what did he mean by that?"[24]

Some five years or so after all these sermons in which Mr. Armstrong supposedly said, "I am Elijah," Joe Jr. told Mr. Leap that Mr. Armstrong taught this: 1) these prophecies were fulfilled *by the work*; 2) he was not the exclusive fulfillment of the Elijah office; and 3) his calling could be *compared to* or *illustrated by* the work of Zerubbabel or Elijah. Even as late as October 1994, in another personal letter, Mr. Tkach Jr. wrote, "Mr. Armstrong taught that he was fulfilling *the role* of Elijah."[25]

Now, of course, Mr. Armstrong is supposed to have said, in "*several* sermons" no less, that "I am Elijah." He apparently believed, in a very literal sense, that he "was *personally* the Elijah."

In actuality, there are no sermons where Mr. Armstrong said anything like that. What Mr. Tkach now says in his book, in an effort to make Mr. Armstrong look like a wild-eyed, cult-leading fanatic, goes much further than anything Mr. Armstrong ever believed or taught.

On the other hand, what Tkach Jr. said in 1990—all but removing Mr. Armstrong from those end-time prophecies—also misrepresents the truth of what the church once taught. What Mr.

Armstrong believed is clearly explained in his co-worker letter from March 19, 1981.

The question is, why opposite explanations—*both of them false*—in 1990 and 1997? Well, in 1990, Tkach Jr. was trying to keep members from leaving the wcg. So he gave the false impression that they were only emphasizing something that *Mr. Armstrong himself taught*—which he didn't. Since that is of little concern today and since they have aligned themselves with other evangelical groups that consider Mr. Armstrong a heretic, Tkach now makes Mr. Armstrong out to be a crackpot—one who supposedly said, "I am Elijah—*personally.*"

The Trinity Doctrine

On March 6, 1998, Pat Robertson interviewed Joseph Tkach Jr. and Greg Albrecht on his television program, *The 700 Club.* They talked about the wcg's doctrinal transformation. In describing the changes that took place early on, Mr. Tkach Jr. said, "*Starting in 1989,* we REALIZED THAT THE TRINITY WAS CORRECT and that it's the only logical and historically [sic] way to explain that God is one in three." [26]

For background, let us briefly examine what Mr. Armstrong taught on this subject. In *Mystery of the Ages,* he wrote, "The trinity doctrine limits God to a supposed three Persons. It destroys the very gospel of Jesus Christ!" [27] In *The Missing Dimension in Sex,* he said, "God is not merely one Person, nor even limited to a 'trinity,' but God is a Family." He then said, "The doctrine of the trinity is false. It was foisted upon the world at the Council of Nicaea." [28]

Based on what Tkach Jr. told Pat Robertson, they realized Mr. Armstrong was wrong and that the trinity was correct in 1989.

In 1990, Philip Stevens wrote an article for the *Good News* titled "Who Was Jesus' Father?" Somehow, this statement managed to sneak by wcg editors: "The concept of a trinity is nowhere found in the Bible. ... The trinity hides from man God's plan of salvation. The trinity doctrine maintains that the Godhead is a closed unit into which no one else can enter." [29]

Three months after that article appeared in the *Good News,*

Michael Snyder wrote a letter to Watchman Fellowship, a cult-watching organization based in Arlington, Texas. Mr. Snyder said,

> The question of God's disclosure to humanity is still open and the church awaits further scholarly discussion in the field of dogmatics concerning this topic. The article "Who Was Jesus' Father?" from the November-December 1990 *Good News* has been declared officially null and void with respect to church doctrine.[30]

He later told the group, during a phone interview, "At one time the church lacked adequate scholarship and resources to fully understand how God's disclosure to humanity had a relationship to the church activity on Earth. Now, we have reexamined it and we have come to see that it is an open question."[31]

Of course, these declarations were made to outside organizations that were pushing for doctrinal reform in the WCG. As far as the church membership goes, very few, if any, would have known that the *Good News* article had been declared "officially" null and void.

Mr. Snyder also referred Watchman Fellowship to a study paper on the trinity written by the church's Greek scholar, K. J. Stavrinides. It was printed in the January-February 1991 *Reviews You Can Use,* which was sent to WCG ministers only. Dr. Stavrinides wrote, "The Worldwide Church of God teaches the full divinity of the Father, and of the Son, and of the Holy Spirit—the biblical foundation for all trinitarian discussions."[32] That is about as trinitarian as you can get. Yet, in that same issue, Mr. Tkach Jr. assured the ministry that the church's position on the trinity had not changed, but rather its *explanation* for disproving it.

Around the same time, in the spring of 1991, David Hulme and Michael Snyder, his assistant, took part in discussions with the faculty at the Trinity Evangelical Divinity School. During his presentation, Mr. Hulme said he had been invited to explain the church's position on a "number of things" and to update them on the "changes" in the WCG. He said he wanted to take them through "some of the more important changes that have occurred in the last four to five years." When he got to the subject of the trinity,

Mr. Hulme relied on Dr. Stavrinides' paper mostly, quoting several paragraphs from it, concluding with,

> Even though the Worldwide Church of God considers *some* positions on the trinity to be heretical (for example, all forms of Arianism), it sees the Eastern, Western, Protestant, and Modernist views of the nature of God as genuine attempts to reach a deeper understanding of God's nature.[33]

As you might imagine, with these types of comments being made to those *outside* the church, all sorts of "rumors" and "gossip" began swirling on the *inside. Was the* wcg *about to accept the trinity?* some wondered. Fortunately for members, Mr. Tkach Sr. stepped forward to set the record straight. Toward the end of the summer of 1991, he wrote an article in the church's newspaper titled "How Do You React to Change?" The article reflected much of the wcg's latest discussions with *Truths That Transform*, Watchman Fellowship and the Trinity Evangelical Divinity School. Mr. Tkach clued the membership in on the church's new position on man's destiny to NOT become God. "No human being can be equal with God," Mr. Tkach explained.[34] "Our inheritance is to be children of God, definitely the supreme pinnacle and crowning glory of God's creation, *but not literally to be God himself.*" Later, he explained, "We are, and will be, members of the family of God. But even when we are changed, we will still be distinct from the eternal, uncreated, without beginning, supreme and sovereign God."[35]

Just so the reader knows, Mr. Armstrong never taught that man was destined to be on God's level, insofar as rank, position or experience. He taught that we would be on God's level in the same way a newborn son is on the same level as his human father—all members of *one family.* But Mr. Tkach said it was now inappropriate to use the father-son analogy to define our relationship with God.

In drawing these distinctions between man and God, the stage was now set for closing off the Godhead to three beings in one. As Mr. Armstrong correctly noted, the trinity limits God. It does away with the family of God.

At the end of his article, Mr. Tkach answered the critics (such as the PCG) who were saying the WCG was rejecting all the doctrines that made it distinct and different from Protestant churches. He then listed a number of distinctive doctrines that still made the WCG unique. Incredibly, included in the list, is this emphatic statement on the nature of God: "We DO NOT BELIEVE the doctrine of the trinity."[36] Never mind that in a personal letter to Watchman Fellowship, Michael Snyder declared a *Good News* article "null and void" because of its comments in opposition to the trinity doctrine. Nor that, according to Snyder, the subject of "God's disclosure" was now an "open question" in the church. Neither did Mr. Tkach mention that the church now taught the "full divinity of the Father, and of the Son, and of the Holy Spirit—the biblical foundation for all trinitarian discussions"—as Dr. Stavrinides had explained to the ministry months earlier. Nor did he draw attention to the fact that David Hulme had been involved in several discussions with trinitarians at the Trinity Evangelical Divinity School.

When you say, "We do not believe the doctrine of the trinity" without qualification, doesn't that imply that the church rejects all forms and practices of the trinity? As far as unsuspecting members were concerned, putting Tkach's "We do not believe the doctrine of the trinity" statement together with the November-December 1990 *Good News* article (declared "null and void" privately, but not in a church publication), the church was teaching the very same thing it had *always* taught about the nature of God.

One former WCG member wrote Mr. Tkach Jr. about what he perceived to be two different messages coming from the church— one to outside organizations in the evangelical world and a different one to its own members internally. Tkach Jr. had this response:

> You also enclosed an interview with Mr. Michael Snyder and Dr. Ruth Tucker. In order to understand the statements made in this interview, we must first comprehend the atmosphere in which the interview took place, the people involved, and the purpose.
>
> Mr. Snyder is the spokesman for the Worldwide Church of God in relation to queries asked from sources outside the church. As such, he cannot answer questions directed at him

by such sources with "in-house" terms, language, and phrase-ology. Dr. Ruth Tucker is a professor of the Trinity Evangelical Divinity School. Mr. Snyder had to address her questions in terms she would understand so that she could comprehend his answers.

Furthermore, it is an unfortunate fact that in the past some in the church chose to *phrase our beliefs* in ways that were not entirely correct. For example, the church has never believed in the concept of the trinity *as embraced by many other churches.* Quite frankly, those other churches cannot themselves agree on the exact nature of God. However, in our attempts to disprove their theories, we used some faulty reasoning of our own. This did not mean that we were wrong in rejecting the trinity doctrine, it merely meant that some of the proofs we tried to use to support our beliefs were invalid.[37]

Classic Tkachism: *While we have made some changes, there is no real change.* WCG members heard these excuses for ALMOST 10 YEARS! *We are not changing core doctrines—only re-phrasing our beliefs to be more accurate technically. The reason it sounds like major changes are being made when you hear interviews with outside organizations is only because of phraseology, not because there is any real change. We must use different terms with outside observers or else they wouldn't understand.*

Eventually, of course, the church's official statements to its membership gradually caught up with what they had been telling outsiders all along. Five months after he unequivocally said that the WCG did not believe in the trinity, Mr. Tkach wrote,

The newly printed Statement of Beliefs of the Worldwide Church of God will be mailed to you soon. ... Let me make a few comments about one portion of the Statement. In the state-ment about God, you will notice that the final sentence reads: "The church affirms the oneness of God and the full divinity of the Father, the Son, and the Holy Spirit." Someone may ask, "Does this mean we now accept the doctrine of the trinity?" No, it does not. The doctrine of the trinity in the Western Church attests the union of three Persons in one Godhead, so that the three are one God as to substance, but three Persons as to individualities. We do not accept that teaching; we believe that the word Person is inaccurate when referring to the Holy Spirit.[38]

In other words, *we have accepted the trinity, but don't misinterpret that to mean that we have accepted the trinity.*

In its August 1992 booklet *God Is …,* the church stated, "God is one being, one entity"—"the Holy Spirit is also God"—and "the Bible does reveal three entities within the one Godhead."[39] When referring to the booklet in the *Worldwide News,* Mr. Tkach wrote, "The doctrine of the trinity did not originate in paganism, as we have traditionally thought."[40] But did all these statements mean the church had now accepted the trinity? *Of course not,* they continued to tell the membership.

The following year, in August 1993, Mr. Tkach wrote, "Simply put, the Bible proclaims plainly and clearly that there is one and only one God. … When the Bible says that God is one, the word *one* does not refer to a 'God family,' but to one God." A little further in the article, Mr. Tkach wrote, "The Bible teaching is that there is one God who is the Father, the Son, and the Holy Spirit."[41]

And yet, two weeks after that was written, Mr. Tkach reassured members, "In our practice and experience *nothing changes.* … What we didn't previously understand was how to put our belief down on paper in such a way it didn't lead to biblical and theological problems."[42] Even as late as 1993, they were saying, "nothing changes." *They were only trying to get it completely accurate on paper.*

Were it not for Tkach Jr.'s interview with Pat Robertson years later—where he admitted they realized the trinity was correct in 1989—it might STILL be safe to assume (within the church, of course) that the Worldwide Church of God IN NO WAY teaches the doctrine of the trinity.

THE LIST GOES ON

Mr. Tkach Jr. foisted off a number of other lies on the church membership, as evidenced by another letter he wrote to a member on March 16, 1992. On page 5, he said,

> Those who minimize Christ and turn the focus on the gospel only to the millennial kingdom are not Christ's ministers. They have glorified themselves and created an empty religion of human works and fascination with speculative details of prophecy and with labeling and judging others.[43]

Was he putting down Mr. Armstrong, who taught that the true gospel was a message God the Father sent through Jesus Christ about the kingdom of God? Not at all! "The true church has *always believed* that Christ is the central figure of the gospel," Tkach Jr. wrote in the same letter. "You asked what the commission of the church is today. It is the same as Mr. Armstrong taught it was," he continued. Yet, later he told the member that Matthew 24:14 was not the church's commission—again giving the impression that Mr. Armstrong had always taught this himself. Finally, Mr. Tkach Jr. wrote, "Mr. Armstrong DID NOT DE-EMPHASIZE CHRIST!"[44]

That was in 1992. In his 1997 book, Tkach said Mr. Armstrong "programmed" WCG members "not to talk much about Jesus."[45] He said, "Rather than speak much about Jesus, we talked mainly about God. He was the Father, and He was in charge. ... Throughout most of our years as a church, we struggled with theological inconsistencies about Him. We never developed a consistent doctrine of Christ ... ."[46] Again, he told a member that Mr. Armstrong did not de-emphasize Christ in order to reassure him, at that time, that they hadn't really changed anything. And now? OF COURSE MR. ARMSTRONG DE-EMPHASIZED CHRIST!

Notice another comment Joe Jr. made in his 1992 letter:

> All people who have the Holy Spirit in them are part of the one true spiritual church because it is the Holy Spirit that puts one into the church (1 Corinthians 12:13). However, *Mr. Armstrong always believed* that there were true Christians who were not on the official membership roll of the Worldwide Church of God.

He spoke of the Church of God (Seventh Day) members as true Christians, for example.[47]

Yet, in his book, Tkach said the WCG under Mr. Armstrong was "*adamant* that God had only one true church in the world, and we were it."[48] We "spent decades living in a cave, hurling big rocks—boulders, if we could lift them—at anyone who passed by our fortress," he said.[49] We taught that the "unregenerate would ultimately be annihilated"[50]; that Sabbath-breakers "were condemned to the lake of fire."[51]

So in 1992, according to Tkach, Mr. Armstrong "always" believed there were true Christians in other churches. But in 1997, Tkach said Mr. Armstrong was "adamant" that his was the only true church.

One final example from Tkach Jr.'s March 16, 1992, letter to a WCG member:

> Do you know what "British Israelism" is? It is a racist doctrine that sees the British Empire as the kingdom of God on Earth and the whites as God's favorite people. Obviously this doctrine was more popular when England was more powerful! THE CHURCH HAS NEVER TAUGHT "BRITISH ISRAELISM." We have taught that descendants of Israel settled and populated much of Britain and the United States.[52]

This is a rare instance where Tkach Jr. actually got it right. Mr. Armstrong never used the terms "British-Israelism" or "Anglo-Israelism" to describe the church's teaching. Indeed, you won't find either of those terms in *The United States and Britain in Prophecy*—not once in 184 pages! Look for them in any other literature by Mr. Armstrong and you won't find them.

Yet, notice what Mr. Tkach Jr. wrote in his 1997 book: "British or Anglo-Israelism is a doctrine of little interest to most evangelicals. Some with a seminary or Bible college background might remember it as an esoteric doctrine associated with sects and cults, but for those of us in the WCG is was [sic] the central plank of our theology."[53] *Another remarkable contradiction.* In 1992, Mr. Tkach Jr. assured a church member that Mr. Armstrong NEVER taught "British

Israelism." In 1997, Tkach Jr. told the world that "British Israelism" was the WCG's "CENTRAL PLANK" doctrine. Now, all of a sudden, EVERYTHING Mr. Armstrong taught "sprang from this belief."[54] Why such a radical shift in Mr. Tkach's recollection? Because now that the WCG has completed its transformation, it is safe to call Mr. Armstrong a racist. So in place of "United States and Britain in Prophecy" they insert "British Israelism." That way Mr. Armstrong gets lumped in with all the others—many of whom actually are racist.

THEIR GREATEST CHALLENGE

By now you can see how convoluted and contradictory Tkach Jr.'s positions are. How could the explanation of Mr. Armstrong's teachings change so dramatically between 1992 and 1997 *when Mr. Armstrong died in 1986?* Mr. Armstrong left an incredibly thorough written account of what he believed and taught. But that has not stopped Joe Jr. from dramatically altering his explanation of those teachings—all depending on the *time period* and the *audience* he was addressing.

Notice what Mr. Tkach Jr. says in his book about the difficulty they ran into when trying to explain the many changes:

> Some cult watchers, ministries, churches, and pastors can be more of a hindrance when it comes to helping individuals or aberrant groups break away from their cultic theology and practice. One of our greatest challenges has been trying to explain these doctrinal reforms to outsiders *while maintaining our credibility internally,* and *some groups have greatly hindered our efforts by their reporting.*[55]

The reason he blames outside groups for hindering their efforts to make doctrinal changes within the church is that they reported what was actually happening! This became problematic for Tkachism because they were telling these outside groups about all the changes—even telling them that more were coming—while at the SAME TIME *telling their own members that nothing was changing! They* are the ones who hurt their own credibility—by *lying.*

In his book, Tkach Jr. explained how their church leaders, in the early 1990s, kept contacting evangelical groups in order to keep them apprised of the changes in the WCG: "As one thing led to another, we finally said, 'You know, Hank Hanegraaff is a person we should talk to. We think he'd listen.'"[56] Greg Albrecht wrote a letter to Hanegraaff on January 5, 1994, and included with it an updated edition of the church's *Statement of Beliefs*. He concluded his letter by requesting to meet with Mr. Hanegraaff. As Tkach Jr. wrote in his book,

> A few days later Hank's office called Greg to set up a meeting. From the first time we met, Hank recognized the enormity of our task [of changing the many fundamental teachings of the church] and understood that we were facing some tremendous battles. After thoroughly quizzing us about our faith and expressing satisfaction with our answers, he invited us to be guests on his radio program. *Our fellowship was not ready for that at the time.*[57]

Can you believe that? Joseph Tkach Jr., Greg Albrecht and Michael Feazell had no qualms about pouring their hearts out to Hank Hanegraaff, as long as it was in private. But they weren't about to go on the radio with their "we've joined mainstream Christianity" heart-to-heart. And why? Because *the membership wasn't yet ready.* The members, remember, were skeptical—they didn't even think the changes were for real! They heard Tkach Sr., all throughout 1994, deny that the church was about to do away with the law.

Then, on December 17, the membership finally heard the same news Tkach's fellows told Hank Hanegraaff a year earlier—that the WCG had now joined mainstream Christianity.

ELEVEN
DEATHBED REPENTANCE

"Not long before he died, Herbert Armstrong told my dad that some things in the church needed to be changed. He didn't make a list of the changes he had in mind, he simply said that 'things needed to be changed.'"

— JOSEPH TKACH JR.
Transformed by Truth

AFTER everything Mr. Armstrong said about *Mystery of the Ages* before he died—"most important book since the Bible"; "best work of my 93 years of life"; "the most valuable gift I could possibly give to you"—the fact that the Tkaches retired the work 2½ years after his death says a lot about what they really believed all along about Mr. Armstrong's teachings. But to retire the book *and then blame its removal on Mr. Armstrong,* after all those glowing, PUBLIC remarks, shows how far Tkachism was willing to go in order to deceive and lie—even if the lie was unbelievably absurd.

In 1990, Joseph Tkach Sr. said, "Mr. Armstrong himself told me that the book contained errors and that he needed to rewrite it." But, according to Tkach, Mr. Armstrong died before he could revise the book. "I felt that there was so much valuable truth in the book that we should continue using it anyway," Mr. Tkach said.[1] So according to the 1990 version of the story—get this—it was *Mr. Armstrong* who wanted the book shelved and *Mr. Tkach* who wanted to keep it in circulation! "After a while," Tkach continued, "I realized that the errors in the book could make the whole subject seem unreliable, and I had to do what I perhaps should have done to begin with."

As for Mr. Armstrong's profuse praise for the material in the book, Tkach said he "made some very strong claims regarding the book. He even called it the most important book since the Bible. This was an overstatement."[2] Yes, in the very *same article*, Mr. Tkach said Mr. Armstrong OVERSTATED the book's importance when it was released, yet *fully realized* there were errors in it and that it needed to be rewritten.

What Mr. Tkach failed to mention in that 1990 article is that *he too* got "carried away" in his praise for the book. On January 16, 1986, the day Mr. Armstrong died, Mr. Tkach called *Mystery of the Ages* Mr. Armstrong's "most powerful and effective book."[3] Ten months later, when he introduced the final installment of *Mystery* in the *Plain Truth* serialization, he wrote, "Mr. Armstrong *did not underestimate* the importance of this last work ...."[4] He said that 10 months AFTER Mr. Armstrong died. In 1990, Tkach made it clear that Mr. Armstrong DID overestimate the book's importance.

That Mr. Tkach would change his views about the book from 1986 to 1990 is one thing. But how could *Mr. Armstrong's* views change? HE WAS DEAD! Either he thought the book might be the most important since the Bible or else he considered it flawed and in need of a rewrite. It can't be both!

In his 1986 article, Mr. Tkach Sr. called *Mystery of the Ages* Mr. Armstrong's "last will and testament, to be passed on to those who would value it. ... He loved and respected his readers and, in a figurative sense, he remembered you in his will.[5]

All these comments were made *after* Mr. Armstrong supposedly told him the book CONTAINED ERRORS and NEEDED TO BE REWRITTEN. But in 1990, in response to criticism for removing *Mystery* from circulation, Mr. Tkach wrote,

> As I said, before he died, [Mr. Armstrong] told me that the book had errors and should be rewritten. The truth remains the truth, of course. The errors were the problem. But he did not get the chance to rewrite it. So what was I to do? *How could I before God*

continue to print the book, knowing it contains errors, and knowing Mr. Armstrong told me that he wanted to rewrite it?[6]

The thing is, *before God,* HE DID CONTINUE PRINTING THE BOOK! He distributed it around the world for TWO AND A HALF YEARS! What's more, even after this supposed conversation with Mr. Armstrong, Mr. Tkach referred to *Mystery of the Ages* as "powerful" and "remarkable," saying it was Mr. Armstrong's "last will and testament." He never once mentioned this conversation with Mr. Armstrong until four years after he died—*after* he had already discontinued the book—and *after* he had received criticism for doing so.

Don't blame me, Mr. Tkach responded to the critics. *I'm only carrying out Mr. Armstrong's final wishes.*

How absurd is that?

MR. ARMSTRONG BEHIND THE CHANGES?

Picking up on his father's sudden recollection four years after the fact, Tkach Jr. made even more sweeping statements in 1991. In a personal letter written late that year, he told a former WCG member, "On his deathbed, Mr. Armstrong himself commissioned my father to look into *the very changes we have made.* Therefore, we are following the wishes of Mr. Armstrong and, more importantly, God."[7] By that point in time, numerous changes had already been made and much of Mr. Armstrong's literature had either been revised or rejected. *And the Tkaches were actually trying to convince members that Mr. Armstrong had commissioned Tkach Sr. to make these changes.*

The following year, in November 1992, Mr. Tkach Sr. sent a video to all WCG churches in which he further elaborated on the supposed deathbed conversations he had with Mr. Armstrong. Here is what Mr. Tkach told the membership nearly *seven years* after Mr. Armstrong's death:

A number of these [changes], whether you want to believe it or not that's immaterial, I can't lose any sleep over that; I know what transpired with Mr. Armstrong.

When we were talking about a number of these issues, I said to Mr. Armstrong, "What you're bringing up here is really heavy, heavy information. It's a shame that we can't tape record this and preserve it for posterity."

And he said, "Well, okay." No, first he asked me why.

I said, "Well I know my limitations. I won't remember everything we're talking about." And I said, "Secondly, even more important, the people won't believe me!"

And so he acquiesced for a second and said, "Go ahead, get a tape recorder." So I went around into the kitchen and as I was dialing for the radio studio or TV, I don't remember, to ask someone to bring a tape recorder down, I heard his faint voice calling me back.

So I went back and said, "Yes sir."

He said, "On second thought, let's not do it."

I said, "Well, may I ask you why?"

He said, … "The people, God's people, His precious chosen people, are going to have to take it on faith, if they truly are converted."[8]

Mr. Tkach wanted this conversation recorded because he *didn't think the people would believe him.* So what Mr. Armstrong supposedly spelled out for him must have been MAJOR doctrinal changes. Later in the video, Tkach said,

Some of those things were so far over my head it's only within the last few years that they're beginning to come back. And that's what he told me. He said, "When it's time for you to remember a certain point, God's Spirit will bring it back as if we were just discussing it." And that's how things just come.[9]

Brilliant! It would all unfold just like it did with Jesus Christ's disciples, who couldn't understand certain things until after the Spirit of God filled the church on Pentecost in A.D. 31. The problem is, Mr. Tkach had received God's Spirit decades before these deathbed discussions. He had spent his entire adulthood in the Worldwide Church of God. He was well aware of the church's body of beliefs. That Mr. Armstrong's deathbed comments were so far over his head doesn't necessarily speak well of his overall grasp of doctrine.

What Tkachism told the WCG membership in 1992—nearly seven years into their administration—is this: On his deathbed, Mr. Armstrong commissioned the Tkaches to look into the "very changes" that had been made, which is pretty specific. What Mr. Armstrong brought up was such "heavy, heavy information" that Mr. Tkach wanted to tape record the conversation. Furthermore, the reason it took several years for Mr. Tkach to make the changes Mr. Armstrong supposedly wanted made is that the deathbed comments were "so far" over Tkach's head, they simply did not start coming back until years later.

RIDDLED WITH ERROR

In that same video, Mr. Tkach also made some UNBELIEVABLE comments about *Mystery of the Ages*. He said,

> The same thing with *Mystery of the Ages*. We do have that on tape—where he [Mr. Armstrong] admitted that it was "RIDDLED WITH ERRORS." We have it on tape where he began to extol the book and everything else when he was offering it to the student body as their textbook. And he told them that unfortunately the thing went to the printer before it could be properly edited and remove a lot of *our misunderstandings* in it. And it got printed.[10]

This was a sad case where the elder Tkach could not keep his lies straight. This happened quite a lot in those days, especially when Mr. Tkach would veer away from sermon notes someone else had prepared.

The video Mr. Tkach referred to was of Mr. Armstrong presenting the book to the sophomore class at Ambassador College on September 9, 1985, about four months before he died. In it, Mr. Armstrong was nearly overcome with emotion when he asked, "Will you forgive me if I get a little bit of a thrill that this is done; that this book is out now? Today is a pretty big day in my life when

I can hand copies of this book out to each of you." He spent quite a bit of time during that speech explaining how *Mystery of the Ages* came to be. He said he wanted the students' education to be as "complete as possible." Mr. Armstrong explained how some of the material in the book was from other books and booklets he had written while some material was brand new. He said, "The Bible is like a book that had been sort of cut up into about 2,000 or 3,000 pieces and you have to get them all put together in the right order or you can't understand them. This book puts them together." Later, he said *Mystery of the Ages* covers the "main thread" of the Bible. Reading it, he said, would "make the Bible plain and clear and understandable." He recommended that the students read the book a second and third time, saying that they wouldn't get the full meat of its message after just one reading.[11]

In a co-worker letter written just three days after Mr. Armstrong's address, he said, "Since last December I have been working diligently on the largest and most important book of my life. In real fact I feel I myself did not write it. Rather, I believe God used me in writing it. I candidly feel it may be the most important book since the Bible."[12] More than two months later, Mr. Armstrong called *Mystery of the Ages* the "best work" of his 93 years of life.[13]

Mr. Armstrong *never said,* or even remotely *implied,* that the book was "riddled with error." In 1992, Mr. Tkach made the embarrassing mistake of attributing this infamous statement to *Mr. Armstrong* when, in fact, it was said by *his own son.*

CAUGHT IN A TANGLED WEB

In the letter Tkach Jr. wrote to Dennis Leap on April 20, 1990, he said, "Mr. Armstrong commented shortly after [*Mystery of the Ages*] was published that the book was *outdated* and *needed to be rewritten* when he was up to the task."[14] Mr. Armstrong began distributing the book just *four months* before he died. It was his newest, just-published book—and yet, sometime during his last four months, the Tkaches say he supposedly discovered it was "outdated"? Actually, when Mr. Armstrong first handed out the book to the sophomore class at Ambassador, explaining that he had relied on various other writings of his to help produce parts of the book, he said,

> Much of it's been *rewritten*. It's all been reorganized and *updated*. It had to be different from any book ever written before. It had to contain parts of several different books that we had. But we had no book that I thought was fitting .... There were some things in other booklets. But there were *some things too that weren't written at all* and weren't in any book that I wanted in.[15]

In truth, Mr. Armstrong NEVER said the book needed to be rewritten. What he said was that more material could be *added* to the original text. Here is what he wrote in a letter to those who requested *Mystery of the Ages:*

> Since writing the book, I have written another booklet that well *could be the opening chapter of this book*. And indeed, MAY BE IN FUTURE EDITIONS. It is on the mystery of the Bible itself. This booklet is titled *The BIBLE—Superstition or Authority? ... and Can You Prove It?* Can you prove that the Bible is indeed the very Word of God, and the supreme authority in life, in right and wrong, by which every person ever born will be finally judged?
> I feel sure you will want to read this new booklet, especially in connection with *Mystery of the Ages*.[16]

The ONLY indication Mr. Armstrong ever gave about revising *Mystery* was the possibility of *adding* another chapter. Yet Tkach Jr. took that to mean "Mr. Armstrong realized that *Mystery of the Ages* had errors in it."[17]

In David Hunsberger's response to *Malachi's Message*, he also brought up the subject of *Mystery* and the sophomore address. He wrote, "Mr. Armstrong realized that *Mystery of the Ages* had errors in it. Even when he personally distributed it to the sophomore class, he told the students that a new edition would need to be written."[18] Again, there is a huge difference between *adding another chapter* and wanting to rewrite the book because of major flaws.

Notice another excerpt from a letter Tkach Jr. wrote in early 1992:

> Mr. Tkach spent literally hundreds of hours in personal talks with Mr. Armstrong during the last months of his life. Mr. Armstrong was well aware of a number of errors in his book and other doctrinal changes and corrections that needed to be made. He *personally* told Mr. Tkach to study into SEVERAL OF THESE MATTERS. [19]

Now put yourself in the position of a WCG member sitting in that church between 1986 and the early 1990s. First, Tkachism made all kinds of changes, but told the membership there were no changes. Then, in the early 1990s, they admitted there were changes, but insisted that Mr. Armstrong was behind them. In the case of *Mystery of the Ages,* they said Mr. Armstrong had wanted to "update" the book anyway. Then, later, they said Mr. Armstrong was well aware of all the "errors" in *Mystery.*

Judging by the evolving story coming from WCG officials, you can see why Mr. Tkach couldn't quite get the story straight during his November 1992 sermon. But the extensively written historical record speaks for itself. There is no way an honest observer, looking at all the facts, could say that Mr. Armstrong wanted to re-write *Mystery of the Ages* because of errors, let alone that it was "riddled" with them. Yet, that is exactly what church officials tried to convince the membership between 1990 and 1992.

COMING CLEAN

Skeptics in the WCG were finally convinced that the changes were for real in late 1994, but not because of a courageous sermon by Tkach Sr. No—they were convinced because that was the year *the Tkaches finally came clean.*

That same year, Tkachism also fessed up on the *Mystery of the Ages* rewrite. Joe Jr. wrote in September, "Certainly Mr. Armstrong would have withdrawn and rewritten his book *Mystery of the Ages had he been aware* of the errors it contained."[20] But I thought he *was* aware of the errors? Didn't they have it on tape where Mr. Armstrong admitted it was "riddled with errors"?

Tkach Jr. continued, "[Mr. Armstrong] did announce to students that he was going to rewrite the first chapter and make it chapter 2 [actually, he indicated that he would *move* chapter 1 to chapter 2, *not* rewrite chapter 1] while writing a completely new chapter 1. He never accomplished this goal, however, due to his illness."[21] It's not 100 percent accurate, but it is certainly much closer to the truth than what he said between 1990 and 1992.

By the time Joe Jr. wrote his book in 1997, their deceptive spin had come full circle. He wrote that Mr. Armstrong considered *Mystery of the Ages* his "crowning achievement";[22] "his opus magnum."[23] No mention of Mr. Armstrong being aware of all the errors—or even that he wanted it to be rewritten. Instead, Tkach Jr. spun the 1997 version of the story this way: "Herbert Armstrong considered the book *Mystery of the Ages* to be the great work of his life, the greatest book since the Bible."[24] As for the "deathbed" conversations Mr. Armstrong supposedly had with Mr. Tkach? Joe Jr. explains,

> Not long before he died, Herbert Armstrong told my dad that *some things* in the church needed to be changed. He didn't make a list of the changes he had in mind, he simply said that "things needed to be changed."
>
> What things might he have intended? WE CAN NEVER BE SURE—with one notable exception. Near the end of his life, Mr. Armstrong said that our stance on divine healing needed change.[25]

That's not what he said in 1991—how Mr. Armstrong supposedly commissioned his father to look into the "very changes we have made." In 1992, Tkach Sr. said he was anxious to get a tape recorder because of the lengthy list of changes Mr. Armstrong wanted made. Instead, Tkach had to work from memory. And many of the changes made several years after Mr. Armstrong died, so said Mr. Tkach, sprung from those deathbed conversations. According to Tkach Sr., they just popped into his head as Mr. Armstrong told him they would.

That was *then*. Now, however, we can *never be sure* what Mr. Armstrong meant when he said some things needed to be changed.

SOPHOMORE ADDRESS

Let's consider one last point with respect to Mr. Armstrong's address before the sophomores. In the early 1990s, the Tkaches referred to this address as proof that Mr. Armstrong knew about the "errors" in the book. Notice what Mr. Tkach Jr. wrote in a letter, March 16, 1992:

> Mr. Armstrong realized that *Mystery of the Ages* had errors in it. Even when he personally distributed it to the sophomore class, he told the students that a new edition would need to be written. His exact words were: "*I won't say it is inspired in the sense of the Bible. It's not perfect.* Then when we come to prophets like Isaiah, Jeremiah, and Ezekiel, and when we come to the New Testament books, God inspired them. They are the infallible words of God. I don't make any such claim for this book [*Mystery of the Ages*] whatsoever. I think in a way God inspired it, but not in the sense that it is the Word of God. *I fully expect that within a year there will be a second edition, that some improvements will be made in this book.*"
>
> Regretfully Mr. Armstrong did not live to produce a revised edition.[26]

Mr. Tkach Jr. referred to these "exact words" in several letters he wrote to church members around that time. David Hunsberger also referred to this quote in his 1991 *Worldwide News* article.[27] The problem with this quote is that it is a distortion of what Mr. Armstrong actually said.

Excerpts from his comments were played before the entire church at the Feast in 1985. The 20-minute video, which preceded Mr. Armstrong's sermon, introduced *Mystery of the Ages* to the church. In the video, the announcer referred to the book as Mr. Armstrong's "most important and significant work." And to reflect this high level of importance spiritually, the announcer described how Mr. Armstrong wanted *Mystery of the Ages* to be of the finest quality physically—with the title embossed in gold lettering and the cover in royal purple. Four lengthy segments from the sophomore address were interspersed throughout the video. Here is the one uninterrupted clip Mr. Tkach quoted from so often in the early 1990s:

> When the Bible speaks, that is God speaking, not a man. Now it's true Moses wrote the first five books. But it wasn't really Moses writing it. God was having him write it. And it was God writing it. But that was really inspired. And *then when we come to prophets like Isaiah, Jeremiah, Ezekiel, and then when we come to the New Testament books, God inspired them. They are the infallible words of God. This book is not. I don't make any such claim for this book whatsoever. But I think in a way God inspired it. But not in the sense that it is the Word of God.* It's as God inspired Herbert Armstrong. And I tried to yield myself to Him. And I hope I was able to yield myself, if not 100 percent, 97, and 98, and 99 percent. The Bible is like a book that had been sort of cut up into about 2,000 or 3,000 pieces and you have to get them all put together in the right order or you can't understand them. This book puts them together.[28]

Notice the italicized words in particular. Mr. Tkach Jr. does quote that correctly in his letter. But before it, he added, *"I won't say it is inspired in the sense of the Bible. It's not perfect"*; and after it he tacked on, *"I fully expect that within a year there will be a second edition, that some improvements will be made in this book."*[29] (Notice his letter again, quoted above, to see where he added these comments.) These words DO NOT APPEAR in the video that played during the Feast in 1985. Nor do they appear on the *World Tomorrow* television program that also broadcast excerpts of Mr. Armstrong's address.[30]

Now granted, the video the church produced for the Feast most likely did not include Mr. Armstrong's entire speech. So it's possible Mr. Armstrong could have made the statements Joe Jr. attributed to him. It's also possible that Mr. Tkach invented the comments.

The key point, though, is this: For several years in the early

1990s, the Tkaches continually pointed to this sophomore address as PROOF that *Mystery of the Ages* was not perfect; that it was not inspired in the same way the Bible was; that it contained "errors"; that Mr. Armstrong knew it needed to be rewritten; and regrettably, he just never got that chance since he died soon after it was published. That much we know, based on the letters Tkach Jr. wrote during the early 1990s.

But notice how Mr. Tkach Jr. remembers that same sophomore address today:

> When the book was published in 1985, Mr. Armstrong addressed a class at Ambassador College and handed out the book to sophomores and juniors, who were assigned to use it as a textbook. "This book is the greatest book since the Bible," he said, "and it was *inspired just like the Bible*."[31]

What a SHOCKING difference! As every member in the WCG should remember, when Mr. Armstrong spoke about the book's importance, he said things like, "I candidly feel it *may be* the most important book since the Bible"[32] or "Time *may* prove this to be the most important book written in almost 1,900 years."[33] He did not blast away with, "THIS BOOK IS THE GREATEST BOOK SINCE THE BIBLE" and he certainly didn't say it was "inspired just like the Bible"! The very address Joe Jr. is supposedly quoting disproves it! (Please read the quote from the video again and keep in mind that this was played BEFORE THE WHOLE CHURCH.) In his book, Mr. Tkach twists, distorts and even makes up material from that sophomore address to add color to his ever-changing story.

These examples illustrate how far Tkachism goes in order to mislead and deceive. How could Joseph Tkach Jr.'s memory of the sophomore address be so different between 1992 and 1997? Judging by Tkach's writings, it's as if Mr. Armstrong gave two different speeches.

TAKING THE CREDIT

The year after Joseph Tkach Jr. succeeded his father as pastor general of the Worldwide Church of God is when he issued his mea culpa in the church's magazine, the *Plain Truth,* saying the church had been "judgmental and self-righteous." They had "much to repent of and apologize for."[34]

He actually apologized on behalf of Mr. Armstrong for his "flawed" teachings—some 10 years after Mr. Armstrong died! But why didn't he mention that *Mr. Armstrong himself commissioned Joseph Tkach Sr. to make the very changes they made since 1986*? In fact, throughout the article of apology, Joe Jr. never even mentions Herbert Armstrong. Wouldn't he at least want the *Plain Truth* readership to know that Mr. Armstrong was behind "all these changes"?

Tkach Jr.'s book, *Transformed by Truth,* according to a July/August 1997 *Plain Truth* ad, details how "in 1995, only 10 years after Armstrong's death, the *leadership of the* WCG publicly renounced its unorthodox teachings and entered the evangelical mainstream."[35] In a 1997 *Worldwide News,* Tkach Jr. quoted from *Charisma* magazine, which said, "The Worldwide Church of God has made a dramatic shift away from *heresy* since the death of its founder, Herbert W. Armstrong in 1986."[36]

Now, of course, Joseph Tkach Jr. and the leadership of the WCG heartily congratulate themselves for the WCG's radical transformation. *If only they would have been so honest in accepting responsibility in the late 1980s and early 1990s.*

When Mr. Armstrong died, the Tkach administration had nothing but praise and adulation for him and for *Mystery of the Ages.* A few years later, after numerous changes in church policies and doctrines, the Tkaches denied there *were* any changes. They insisted that they were following right in the footsteps of Mr. Armstrong. Then, after the changes became obvious, they attributed them to what *Mr. Armstrong* supposedly said on his deathbed. Now, Joseph Tkach Jr. takes *full credit* for the transformation—even indirectly calling Mr. Armstrong a heretic!

It's almost comical, were it not so gut-wrenchingly tragic for tens of thousands of people whose lives have been ruined by Tkachism.

TWELVE
STEWARDSHIP

"You shall know them by their fruits."

— JESUS CHRIST

JOSEPH Tkach Jr. introduced the final chapter of his book, "The Enigma of Herbert W. Armstrong," with an "advisory" addressed to former and current members of the Worldwide Church of God. He said, "This chapter is not written to attack or belittle Herbert Armstrong in any way."[1] He then proceeded to attack Mr. Armstrong and to imply that all the allegations of critics were true.

The "enigma" chapter is where he quotes Mr. Armstrong as supposedly saying, "I am Elijah."[2] It's where he made the "absolute power corrupts absolutely" comment and then followed up by saying "there weren't many who would challenge" Mr. Armstrong.[3] He said, "As the Worldwide Church of God has been dramatically changed and as we have faced the emotional upheaval of finding out much of what we believed was wrong, we have also had to FACE allegations about Herbert W. Armstrong *and his son*."[4]

Allegations? Garner Ted was suspended from the church more than once during the 1970s for his sexual improprieties and later disfellowshiped for attempting to overthrow his father. But why would Tkach Jr. lump *Herbert Armstrong* in with his son throughout the "enigma" chapter? To assign GUILT BY ASSOCIATION—that's why. According to Tkach, because of these allegations about Mr. Armstrong *and his son,* "I felt the need to apologize and ask forgiveness about our past unbiblical teaching *and behavior.*"[5] It wasn't just Garner Ted's behavior he felt he needed to apologize for—*Herbert Armstrong's too.*

And all this is not meant to be an attack against Mr. Armstrong in *any* way? "God has not asked us to be the judge of Mr. Armstrong," Tkach said right before leveling the same judgmental charge against Mr. Armstrong that Garner Ted did in 1979.[6]

"We neither have nor promote an extravagant lifestyle," Tkach wrote. "We have divested ourselves, and continue to, of those things that are opulent and do not befit a church."[7]

And so the Tkaches sold off all the festival sites used by church brethren. They sold the campsites Mr. Armstrong built for teenagers. They shut down the college campuses Mr. Armstrong raised up for the work and for the young people. They sold the property and all the buildings used for preaching the gospel to the world. They sold the airplane Mr. Armstrong used to visit the brethren and world leaders. They auctioned off equipment, paintings, sculptures and personal gifts world leaders had given to Mr. Armstrong. They sold literature, libraries, instruments, pianos, chandeliers, candelabra and furniture.

And now Tkach Jr. points to their financial demise as proof of how sincere their intent was to transform the church. "At any time in the past several years we could have called a halt to the changes, turned back the clock, confessed that we were wrong, and tried to woo back disaffected members (along with their pocketbooks)."[8] They counted the cost, he says, and were willing to abolish Mr. Armstrong's ministry and work, even when they knew it would result in steep financial losses.

The facts, figures and time frame, however, paint a completely different picture.

A SHOCKING DIFFERENCE IN PRIORITIES

As we have already seen in this volume, Tkachism's intent to change major doctrines began just as soon as Mr. Armstrong died—even before. Together with the deceitful way they introduced changes, they also acted swiftly to slash several successful programs Mr. Armstrong had started.

For example, in September 1986, Tkach Sr. capped *Plain Truth* circulation at 7 million.[9] So within *eight months* of Mr. Armstrong's death, Mr. Tkach decided to slash the magazine's reach by more than 16 percent. Mr. Tkach explained, "We could very easily have a worldwide *Plain Truth* circulation of 15 million by this time next year. But would that be wise stewardship?"[10] He wrote,

> Now maybe there are some in God's church who think I should just let the *Plain Truth* magazine circulation increase as fast as we can possibly make it do so, and then trust God to send us the money to back that up. Maybe some think we should just go on more and more television stations, any time a new opportunity comes available.[11]

How RADICALLY different that line of thinking was from his predecessor's. Eight months before he died, Mr. Armstrong said "the way is now open to increase the *Plain Truth* circulation past eight million and upward to *twenty or more million* subscribers …."[12] Yet he was realistic and wise in his stewardship. He said the church "could not afford to take advantage of these doors" *unless the income increased*—which is *precisely* what happened after he died.

But Tkach made it clear from the very beginning that they weren't about to put additional income toward the church's first commission. Spending money on the WORK of the church—a work it had been doing for *decades*—in their view, was a huge waste.

DOWNSIZE

Three months after he put a ceiling on *Plain Truth* circulation, in December 1986, Mr. Tkach decided to reduce the *Good News* and *Youth* magazines to six issues per year, instead of 10. The church's newspaper, the *Worldwide News,* would continue to be published every two weeks, but at eight pages per issue, as opposed to 12.[13]

Mr. Tkach offered this odd explanation for the reduction in the church's periodic literature:

> I have been quite concerned for some time that many of God's people simply are not reading the *Good News* as they should and as a result are missing a wealth of the spiritual, Christian-living instruction about the application of God's law of love in their lives that they vitally need!"[14]

Four years later, Mr. Tkach discontinued the *Good News* altogether, making it even easier for members to keep up with their reading.

But back to 1986. Tkach cut *Good News* and *Youth* production by 40 percent, *Worldwide News* content by one third, and *Plain Truth* circulation by 16 percent—*all in his first year.* "God's Word is filled with principles about living within our means," he wrote, "of counting the cost and of careful consideration of a matter in prayer before making a decision."[15]

Yet even as Tkach was slashing programs, the residual impact of Mr. Armstrong's work was still making its mark on Pasadena. For example, nearly 2 million people telephoned the WCG in 1986, which was a 78 percent increase over 1985.[16] The church's income also grew, finishing 11.2 percent above 1985—at just over $182 million.[17]

In 1987, this same dual theme played out—cutting programs even as revenues increased. In May, Larry Salyer told ministers that "Mr. Tkach continues to review and evaluate the procedures and techniques we use in doing God's work. ... Under his leadership and with the improved communication and cooperation of the operation managers, the work is moving forward on many fronts."[18] Mr. Salyer went on to explain how they were working on a five-year plan that would facilitate "greater efficiency and productivity" in the work.

Yet that same month, *Plain Truth* circulation slipped to 6.9 million.[19] The following month, in June, they stopped printing the circulation figure in the table of contents. In its place, it said, "Over 20,000,000 *readers* in seven languages."[20] By the end of the year, even that line disappeared.

They also made a number of "design changes" in the *Plain Truth* over the last half of 1987. These changes, supposedly intended to give the magazine a "more modern, up-to-date appearance," also happened to "cut costs significantly."[21] In other words, they downgraded the quality.

At the end of 1987, Mr. Tkach wrote, "I have often said that we should strive to work smarter, not just harder. As faithful stewards, we should always be on the lookout for a better way—a wiser, more efficient or more productive way—to get any job done."[22] We heard a lot about *five-year plans, working smarter* and being *wise stewards* during the late 1980s—all of it implying that Mr. Armstrong mismanaged the church's revenue.

Mr. Tkach, we were told, was an expert when it came to management and working with employees. One WCG minister even remarked, "Mr. Tkach is a manager. Mr. Armstrong was not a manager. Mr. Armstrong was an entrepreneur—traveled all the time. He didn't like big meetings. Mr. Tkach thrives on them, meeting after meeting after meeting, day after day."[23]

Due to his management skills, Mr. Tkach supposedly saved tons of money during those years. In actual fact, the membership and revenue increased during those years, mainly due to the fruit from Mr. Armstrong's labor. By the end of 1987, church membership had climbed to 88,455[24] and the income increased another 5.5 percent to a record-high $192 million.[25]

The following year, at a regional directors' conference in Pasadena in June 1988, Mr. Tkach told the leading ministers in the church that he was "trimming the fat" in the work in order to increase efficiency and effectiveness.[26]

The thing is, in 1988 the church's revenue topped out at *$201 million*.[27] It was the first time ever to exceed $200 million and represented 4.8 percent growth over 1987. According to the church's treasurer, Leroy Neff, during 1988 they had "almost eliminated all long-term debt" and were on course to "pay as you go."[28]

Yet, by the end of 1988, Mr. Armstrong's three major books—*Mystery of the Ages, The Incredible Human Potential* and *The United States and Britain in Prophecy*—had all disappeared from circulation. The *Plain Truth* circulation had been pared down to about 6.5 million,[29] even though the church's worldwide membership had grown to 91,685[30] and its revenue was 23 percent higher than it was three years earlier, during Mr. Armstrong's last full year at the helm.

THE ENTOURAGE

Tkachism began 1989 by selling off the church's airplane, the Gulfstream III, for $12.5 million.[31] The year before, Tkach chartered a Boeing 727 for a trip to Australasia in order to see if it would be feasible to fly in a less-expensive aircraft. He wrote,

> As I have often explained, we are continually looking for ways to make the various operations of the work more streamlined and efficient. It appears that there may be a significant financial advantage to selling the G-III and buying a used, but well-maintained Boeing 727.[32]

Later in 1988, after unsuccessfully locating a 727 he liked, Mr. Tkach settled for the British-made BAC 1-11. It was only $3.4 million, a price tag he said would immediately "benefit" God's work. He wrote, "Also, the BAC 1-11 has room for all our necessary TV equipment and personnel, as well as any additional necessary personnel. The G-III, as many of you know, was extremely limited in seating and storage capacity."[33] But for an administration determined to "trim the fat," it seems like the smaller, more fuel-efficient G-III would have better suited their needs—especially since it was already paid for.

In looking at the size of Mr. Tkach's entourage, however, it's no wonder they needed to "save" money by purchasing a used, gas-guzzling commercial airliner with about four times the cabin space as the G-III. For the Australasian trip, when they chartered the 727, Mr. Tkach's traveling party included:

> Joseph Locke, his personal assistant; James Peoples, operation manager of the computer information systems, purchasing and travel departments, and his wife, Linda; Ellen Escat, the pastor general's administrative assistant; Michael Rasmussen, executive office aide, and his wife, Juli; Julie Stocker, an administrative assistant in Communications & Public Affairs; and Ross

Jutsum, director of the music department in Pasadena, his wife, Tammara, and daughters, Heidi and Lisa.

Also traveling on the 727 were Mr. Tkach's Gulfstream III crew: Captain Ken Hopke, co-captain Lawrence Dietrich, maintenance chief Dean Mohr and steward Jay Brothers.

The church's television crew included Mr. Halford and his wife, Patricia; cameraman Gary Werings and his wife, Gloria; and Steve Bergstrom, cameraman and remote operations engineer.[34]

Counting Mr. Tkach, *that's 21 people,* for a 21-day tour through Australia, New Zealand, Thailand and Sri Lanka—to *visit church areas.* After their first stop in Melbourne, the entourage picked up another four adults and two children to accompany them for the next leg of the trip.[35] *Might as well*—there was plenty of room on the airliner.

Compare that with Mr. Armstrong's six-day trip to Japan in March of 1985. He took Ellis La Ravia and Aaron Dean, their wives and his personal nurse, as well as the two pilots. Mr. Armstrong was 92 years old at the time—and blind. He had been pastor general of the church for more than 50 years. And on one of the last international trips of his ministry, he took *seven* people with him, counting the pilots.

It is also interesting to note that during the trip, Mr. Armstrong completed chapter 5 of *Mystery of the Ages,* as well as a letter to the church membership. He met with the president of an advertising agency working on behalf of the church in Asia. He met with the church's regional director over Australia and Asia. He had a private meeting with the Japanese foreign minister and later hosted a banquet for 200 government officials, diplomats and Japanese business people. The night after the banquet, Mr. Armstrong addressed the managers at Japan Life, whose chairman had visited Ambassador College earlier that year. Before ending the trip, Mr. Armstrong discussed, with a number of Japanese government officials, the prospect of supporting a project in China.[36]

Compare that with Mr. Tkach's first trip aboard the used BAC 1-11—a three-day trip to Washington, D.C., in early December 1988.

He attended two services on the Sabbath of December 3, giving the *announcements* at both the north and south churches in Washington. The two sermons were given by evangelists who accompanied Mr. Tkach on the trip. On Sunday, Mr. Tkach attended the Kennedy Center Honors ceremony and toured some of the sites in D.C. with his entourage. Traveling with Mr. Tkach over the weekend were the five-man flight crew, including a steward and a chef, Michael Rasmussen, David Albert and his wife, Richard Ames and his wife, Dibar Apartian and his wife, Leroy Neff and his wife and Wayne Shilkret.[37]

It seems like plenty of "fat" could have been trimmed from that weekend trip.

Eight days after returning from Washington, D.C., Mr. Tkach took the BAC 1-11 on a 13-day trip to the Philippines, Hong Kong and Malaysia. Besides visiting church congregations, Mr. Tkach and his entourage toured war memorials, museums, shopping districts and a floating village. Traveling with Mr. Tkach were the five-man flight crew, the three-man TV crew and Michael Rasmussen, Ellen Escat and Esther Apperson.

In July of 1989, for a 13-day trip through England, Belgium, Italy and Greece, Mr. Tkach took Michael Feazell, Joseph Locke, Michael Rasmussen, Julie Stocker, Mr. and Mrs. Apartian, Mr. and Mrs. Hulme, the three-man television crew and the five-man flight crew—17 in all.

To spend that much money for his traveling entourage—for hotel reservations, limousine rentals, food and incidentals—even as he repeatedly stressed trimming the fat and working more efficiently, didn't seem to phase Mr. Tkach. The way he saw it, he saved the work millions by trading the G-III for the BAC 1-11.

THE 1989 INCOME "DIP"

Three months before the European trip, Mr. Tkach excitedly told the brethren about the church's new five-year plan, which had been completed in April 1989. After highlighting key points from the plan in a *Worldwide News* article, Tkach wrote, "Our current income dip would be even more difficult for us if we hadn't already been putting into effect cost-saving measures planned last year."[38] Who knows *what* would have happened to the work without Tkachism's financial model.

He told members that if the dip continued, "severe cutbacks" would have to be made, perhaps in television. He said that if stations in their area stopped carrying *The World Tomorrow,* their pastor could arrange for video cassettes to be mailed to the congregation for a local viewing.

"We must avoid waste," he wrote. Then finally, "At this point normal reserves have disappeared to take up the slack, and we have now begun to dip into the reserves from the sale of the G-III aircraft." They sold the G-III in *January* and by April they were already dipping into proceeds from the sale!

That's how bad the "crisis" was in 1989.

In May, Mr. Tkach wrote, "With an annual budget of $160 million, a shortfall of even a few percent is significant." Then later, "I was disappointed to learn of some few who had simply become complacent and careless about tithing, not seeming to realize that one who is careless about tithing is robbing God."[39]

I'm not sure why he would have used the 1985 budget figure. Income the year before Mr. Tkach addressed the "shortfall" was actually $201 million. At any rate, he kept pounding away at the budget "crisis" throughout 1989.

Later in May, Tkach wrote, "I know we'd all rather see growth than cutbacks. But as I've said many times, God does expect us to live within our means, and we will certainly do that."[40] It was beginning to sound like a broken record.

Later that year, in September, Mr. Tkach admonished the brethren to brace themselves for additional cuts. "If God wanted us to step out in faith in order to grow as fast as possible, there would never be a need to count the cost, or to worry about being prepared to handle the growth," he wrote. "The church has done that occasionally in the past, but we have always ended up having to slash severely because the budget simply could not keep up. Like anyone, we should be able to learn from our past experience."[41]

It was yet another way to put down Mr. Armstrong and his supposedly poor managerial practices.

"I wish we could have a 10 or 12 million *Plain Truth* circulation right now!" Tkach exclaimed. "But I have to realize that we just can't afford it now. I am instead having to face the fact that we may need to trim the circulation slightly to afford what God has given us."[42]

By the end of the year, the total "dip" for 1989 actually amounted to another all-time high: $211,777,000.[43] True, that only represented a 5.2 percent increase over 1988. But as Mr. Tkach himself admitted, with a budget as large as the WCG's, "even a few percent is significant."

That same year, Larry Salyer told the church that *Mystery of the Ages* was "among the most expensive pieces of literature" the church had produced. Years later, Tkach Jr. said the book was a financial drain and implied that their income was not sufficient to sustain the project. Yet they announced the book's removal right as the church had reached its financial peak!

MORE MASSIVE CUTS

The 1989 budget "crisis" triggered many more cutbacks in programs Mr. Armstrong established. In January 1990, Mr. Tkach announced the decision to remove the toll-free number from the television program, which would save the work $3.2 million per year. Besides the cost savings, Mr. Tkach said the work would benefit from the decision in other ways too: "The small amount of extra effort that it takes to write instead of to call means that the seed (in this case, the *Plain Truth* subscription) will be falling on more fertile ground. This would mean a somewhat smaller *Plain Truth* circulation, but a higher-quality one."[44] Impeccable logic!

In March, the *Worldwide News* reported that the number of stations airing *The World Tomorrow* had fallen to 123.[45] Just one year earlier, according to the article, the program had aired on 232 stations. At the time Mr. Armstrong died, the number of stations totaled 382.[46]

In July, Mr. Tkach told the membership, "*Plain Truth* circulation, which we have had to trim from last year's level to stay within budget, stands at a strong 5 million!"[47] The year before, it was over 6 million.[48]

In September, Mr. Tkach announced that it was time for *The*

World Tomorrow and the *Plain Truth* to take on a more religious tone. He had come to see that with the old "more secular tone," the church may have been fishing in waters "where the fish have stopped biting."[49] And since the *Plain Truth* would now be more religious, he explained, they no longer needed the *Good News* magazine! "The new *Plain Truth*," he explained,

> will replace both the current *Plain Truth* and the *Good News* (which will no longer be needed with the new *Plain Truth* format). ... This revised approach will enable us to maximize effectiveness with less expense in the publishing, editorial and mailing areas of the work.

Since Mr. Armstrong believed his God-given commission was twofold, he established the *Good News* in 1939 in support of the church's secondary mission—to "feed the flock" spiritual meat.[50] While the *Plain Truth* was primarily used to preach the gospel of the kingdom to the world as a witness (the church's first mission), the *Good News* was intended more for church members and co-workers, although later in his ministry, Mr. Armstrong made it available to anyone who wanted to study God's word in greater depth.

But when the Tkaches changed the commission after Mr. Armstrong died, they lost interest in the whole concept of proclaiming a message to the world. So they made the *Plain Truth* more like the *Good News* and then nixed the *Good News* altogether, describing the move as a better, more efficient way to do the work.

By the end of 1990, Mr. Tkach reported, "We have reduced the circulation of the *Plain Truth* by changing its format to a more clearly religious, gospel-oriented approach."[51] The worldwide circulation had dwindled to 2.7 million.

Thus, 1990 began with a *Plain Truth* circulation around 6 million and the *Good News* at 1.1 million.[52] By the end of that year, the *Plain Truth* had been cut by more than half and the *Good News* eliminated altogether.

Yet, despite this staggering series of cuts, the church had a worldwide membership of 97,000 in 1990[53] and finished the year with virtually the same amount of revenue as it did the year before: $211,243,000. That amounted to 29 percent more than Mr. Armstrong's best year—and at a time when they were making a staggering series of cuts.

One wonders, where did all that money go?

AMBASSADOR COLLEGE

As noted previously, Mr. Tkach altered the course for Ambassador College within months of Mr. Armstrong's death, beginning with the decision in April 1986 to keep the Big Sandy campus open. In 1987, Mr. Tkach wrote, "Ambassador College is perhaps the most visible and high-profile representation to the general public of what God's church teaches and believes in."[54] Mr. Armstrong, while he placed a high value on the example Ambassador set for the church and the world, continually stressed that the college's primary purpose was to help *support* the WORK of the church.

When Mr. Tkach decided to pursue accreditation for the college in 1988, he wrote, "[W]e must recognize that Ambassador College now serves a greater and broader purpose for God's work than it did in its earlier days."[55] So they began pouring money into the college.

In Mr. Armstrong's day, the annual spending on the college had been about 10 percent of the overall budget. In 1989, that figure increased to 14 percent: Of the $210 million the church spent, $30 million went toward the college.[56]

In 1990, the church spent almost $222 million ($10.6 million more than it received)[57]—*17 percent* of which went toward the college. So in the same year they slashed just about every program due to the budget crisis, they upped their college budget from $30 million to $37 million[58]—a 23 percent increase. "During 1990," according to the *Worldwide News,* "the church funded approximately $15,663,000 of construction costs for needed dormitories, classrooms and offices to accommodate the consolidation [of both campuses in Big Sandy]."[59] That same year, the *Plain Truth* circulation *had* to be cut from 6 million to less than 3 million, they *had* to "trim" at least 122 television stations from the budget[60] and the *Good News* and the toll-free number *had* to be cut *entirely.*

Here is a simple comparison between budgets for 1987 and

1990. In 1987, Tkachism spent $180 million. The budget break-down looked like this:

Publishing—24 percent
Local congregations, field ministry—23 percent
Broadcasting and proclaiming the gospel—18 percent
Management and general—18 percent
Ambassador College—10 percent
Member assistance—4 percent
Ambassador Foundation—3 percent[61]

In 1990, after spending $222 million, the breakdown looked like this:

Local congregations, field ministry—26 percent
Publishing—19 percent
Ambassador College—17 percent
Management and general—17 percent
Broadcasting and proclaiming the gospel—14 percent
Member assistance—4 percent
Ambassador Foundation—3 percent[62]

Spending on Ambassador College in 1987 amounted to $18 million. Three years later, after huge cutbacks in preaching the gospel, the college budget had more than doubled.

Ambassador College had become Tkachism's baby.

COUNTING THE COST

In his book, Mr. Tkach Jr. piously compares himself and his fellows to the Apostle Paul, who "suffered the loss of all things" in order to "win Christ."[63] He wrote,

> Our membership losses have resulted in a corresponding drop in income. … With dramatically fewer members and greatly reduced income, expenses had to be cut as well. … We were forced to lay off most of our headquarters staff, cut circulation of [and later charge for] the *Plain Truth* magazine, sharply reduce subsidies to [and later close] Ambassador University, end our acclaimed performing arts series at Ambassador Auditorium, and sell off many of our assets [including the auditorium]. …

So you do the math. What do these figures tell you? If the changes in the Worldwide Church of God are some kind of con job—some cynical, conspiratorial plot hatched in secret back rooms—then we're not very adept at pulling it off.[64]

Let us then, as he suggests, do the math. First, consider the golden years of Herbert W. Armstrong's work in the Worldwide Church of God—after he set out to get the church back on track in the late 1970s and through to the mid-1980s, when the church experienced such abundant growth. During the last five years of Mr. Armstrong's ministry, between 1981 and 1985, this is the annual revenue he had to work with:

1981: $108 million
1982: $121 million
1983: $132 million
1984: $148 million
1985: $164 million[65]

It amounted to $673 million. Compare that with the *first* five years of Tkachism:

1986: $182 million
1987: $192 million
1988: $201 million
1989: $212 million
1990: $211 million[66]

Tkachism's five-year total AMOUNTED TO $998 MILLION. *Can you believe that?* They had about a *billion* dollars to work with their first five years!

Talk about *golden* years. This was when Tkach's entourage was living large! It's when they decided to close the Pasadena campus and pump all that money into Big Sandy. It's when they changed the commission and slashed spending on numerous programs established to preach the gospel to the world. It's when they reduced the *Plain Truth* circulation from 8.4 to 2.7 million and *The World Tomorrow* from 382 stations to about 100. It's when the *Good News* and Mr. Armstrong's books were retired permanently—*Mystery of the Ages* found to be "riddled with error."

And it's when they tricked members into thinking NOTHING had changed, except perhaps some *minor* things that Mr. Armstrong himself supposedly wanted to change.

Tkach Jr. wrote, "The Worldwide Church of God reached its peak attendance in 1988—two years after Mr. Armstrong's death—with 126,800 members and 150,000 in attendance. Those figures stayed relatively stable *until 1992,* when a slight dip was noted."[67] Isn't that amazing? It didn't even dip *until 1992.* They got the power they needed to do away with Mr. Armstrong's teachings in 1986 and the additional benefit of a membership and income *on the rise,* thanks to the popularity of Mr. Armstrong's teachings.

And you wonder why they didn't tell 150,000 church members *in 1988* that *Mystery of the Ages* was RIDDLED with error? *I can give you about one billion reasons why.*

Let's do more math. Consider the income for Tkachism's *second* five-year period, between 1991 and 1995:

1991: $197 million
1992: $191 million
1993: $176 million
1994: $165 million
1995: $103 million[68]

It wasn't until 1995 that the church's income *finally* fell below the revenue Mr. Armstrong generated in his last year. Of course, Mr. Armstrong's $164 million would have had more purchasing power in 1994—amounting to about $226 million. But still, Tkachism's revenue for 1994, the year Tkach Sr. gave "The Sermon," as his son called it, was *$165 million.*

Total revenue during their SECOND five years amounted to *$832 million.* Where in the world did all THAT money go? They shut down the Pasadena campus and the toll-free number in 1990. *The World Tomorrow* went off the air in 1994. The concert series ended in 1995. *Plain Truth* circulation had plummeted. About the only thing going for the church was the college in Big Sandy—and they decided to close that in 1997. Yet Tkachism had $832 million to work with during this second five-year period.

Tkachism is obviously *not* the story of a few courageous leaders who counted the cost and were willing to give up everything for the sake of God's truth. Between Mr. Armstrong's death and the year *Transformed by Truth* was released in 1997, Tkachism received *nearly $2 billion* of income. And that's just the revenue. The book value of all the property and equipment they inherited from Mr. Armstrong was $83 million, according to their 1987 audit.[69] And nearly all of that was paid for.

Adjusting figures for inflation, imagine if you inherited an estate today worth $150 million and you could count on it generating another 2½ to 3 *billion* dollars over the next 10 to 12 years. That's the position the Tkaches landed in when Mr. Armstrong died. Yet look at what they have to show for it.

You do the math. How could these men do *so little* with so MUCH? Couldn't they at least come out of it with a moderately successful college? Or a magazine that was at least popular within Christian communities?

Apparently not. In doing the math, we see that *everything* Tkachism did to "manage" the Worldwide Church of God has turned out to be a miserable failure. Living through it, we heard all about their five-year plans, their big ideas, the amount of money they "saved." But in the end, everything collapsed. And now they want us to view their repeated failures as validation for how courageous and sincere they were in pursuit of the truth, no matter the cost? These men didn't sacrifice anything—except the *lives* and *investments* tens of thousands of *others* made in support of Mr. Armstrong's work.

Had it happened in the corporate world, the CEOs and executives responsible for hijacking a corporation and then treacherously robbing its investors of their future would have been FIRED, if not *prosecuted* in a court of law.

But in the world of Tkachism, a giant, conspiratorial con job, hatched in the secrecy of back rooms and then carried out by cynical, self-righteous imposters, is hailed as a courageous success story of service and sacrifice for the good of mankind.

FUNDING THE PENSIONS

In recent years, Tkachism has harshly criticized Mr. Armstrong for never starting an employee retirement plan. "In the past," Tkach Jr.

wrote in 2003, "the Worldwide Church of God in the United States and elsewhere made no provision for the retirement of its employees. This was a decision made by others before the current administration and was inherited by us."[70] Of course, Mr. Armstrong always had a generous assistance program designed to help those in need. But it was funded by *tithe*-payers, and tithing is now bad, the Tkaches say. *So Mr. Armstrong just couldn't do anything right!*

"The results of these unfortunate policies in our past are now being remedied," Tkach continued. "We are making plans to enroll U.S. church employees in a retirement plan funded by proceeds from the sale of the Pasadena property."[71]

And they're to be commended for this new financial model? They stopped doing ANY KIND OF WORK in the early 1990s and wound up with perhaps $100 million worth of property and facilities just sitting there collecting dust. So they sold it all and placed the "bulk of the sale proceeds," according to Ron Kelly, in a formal pension plan for *current* employees.[72] They SOLD everything Mr. Armstrong and his faithful supporters built for doing *God's work* and then set aside the proceeds for those who stayed through the transformation and remained loyal to *Tkach*. There's nothing brilliant about that. It's more like a payoff.

Tkach Jr. called the church's lack of retirement funding an "unfortunate" policy that his administration inherited. To use that excuse in 1986, when his father took over, or even in 1995, when he replaced his father, is one thing. *But to blame Mr. Armstrong for the lack of pension planning in 2003?*

What, exactly, did the *Tkaches* ever do for their retirees between 1986 and 2003? Quite a few of the long-time ministers who stayed with the WCG began retiring during the mid-1990s, long before the property ever sold. Couldn't the Tkaches have taken steps in that direction years earlier, if it was such an egregious error made by Mr. Armstrong? As we have seen, the WCG was still collecting hundreds of millions of dollars each year in the early 1990s. They had more than $2 billion in revenue to work with between Mr. Armstrong's death and when they finally sold the property in 2004. Couldn't they have carved out some kind of pension plan from $2 billion?

Herman Hoeh, Norman Smith, Dean Blackwell and Richard

Rice—all long-time evangelists in the WCG—retired in *1996*. But it's supposedly *Mr. Armstrong's fault* that the Tkaches never got around to developing a retirement program until 2004—*18 years after Mr. Armstrong died?*

Dr. Hoeh was one of the first four to graduate from Ambassador College. Norman Smith was ordained as an evangelist in 1957—Dean Blackwell in 1964. All these evangelists, by the way, were in their 60s at the date of their retirements—Hoeh was 67, Smith was 66, Blackwell was 64 and Rice was 60.

Before the Tkach pension plan could move forward in 2004—contingent on the sale of the property, of course—the WCG had a "discretionary assistance program" in place for its former, retirement-age employees. According to Tkach Jr., 240 retired employees qualified for assistance as of March 2003, which cost the church $350,000 per month. On average, that amounts to $1,458 per month for each retiree, or $17,500 a year—not exactly a lucrative retirement package.

Perhaps that's why Dean Blackwell—an evangelist of 32 years—got a part-time job at a Dillards department store after he retired.

MR. ARMSTRONG'S RETIREMENT POLICY

Retirement was a rarity for WCG ministers before Mr. Armstrong died. I mean, unless you are physically incapable of working, how do you retire from serving *God?* Moses never retired. Neither did Peter, John or Paul. "The United States is the only nation on Earth that retires people at age 60 or 65," Mr. Armstrong wrote in 1979. "In the United States most have come to suppose that people naturally begin to lose their mental faculties even as early as 55."[73] Mr. Armstrong didn't subscribe to that line of thinking. He proved by his own work that the most productive years of life can be long after the "normal" retirement age. In fact, the work of the Worldwide Church of God really didn't go *worldwide* until *after* Mr. Armstrong turned 60.

And had Mr. Armstrong not been brought back to life in 1977, Garner Ted's liberals would have destroyed the church long before the Tkaches ever did. It was in August 1977, when Mr. Armstrong was 85, that his heart and breathing both stopped. He had no pulse—no blood pressure. A nurse frantically administered mouth-to-mouth resuscitation and massaged Mr. Armstrong's heart. After about a minute-and-a-half, he was breathing again on his own.

Seven months after his resuscitation, Mr. Armstrong said this to a group of WCG ministers in Pasadena: "Shortly after they'd told me what had happened [heart failure], I felt that if my work in God's hands were finished and God didn't have any further use for me in His work, that I would rather have remained dead."[74]

Like the Apostle Paul, he had a "desire to depart"[75] if God was finished working through him. But God wasn't, as Mr. Armstrong would later explain:

> It is now clearly evident that God brought me back for a vital purpose, by CPR, from death by heart failure. Had I remained dead the church of the living God would have been virtually destroyed by the liberal element that had crept in, especially in headquarters administration during my absence from Pasadena.[76]

And so, at 85 years of age, and in poor health, he took charge and single-handedly put the Worldwide Church of God back on track! Retirement was never an option—even if liberal ministers might have *wanted him* to retire. If God kept him alive, it was to WORK. "I never expect to 'retire,' though I passed the so-called 'retirement age' long ago," he wrote in 1971.[77] "I expect to stay in harness as long as I live."[78]

And because he did that, even after congestive heart failure, he not only removed the liberal element—HE LED THE WORLDWIDE CHURCH OF GOD INTO ITS GOLDEN AGE! Herbert W. Armstrong's greatest contribution to the Worldwide Church of God was made *after* God brought him back to life in 1977.

At the time Mr. Armstrong's heart had failed him, liberals had come close to destroying the church. The *Plain Truth* circulation had fallen to just over 1 million, the *World Tomorrow* program—with Garner Ted at the helm—could be seen on only 50 stations, and Ambassador College had turned into a secular institution.

While recovering in 1978, Mr. Armstrong stepped up efforts to write more for the church's publications. He completed work on his best book to that point, *The Incredible Human Potential*. To get the college back on track, he had closed Big Sandy and decided to start over in Pasadena with one freshman class, making sure that it began as *God's* college. On the TV program, he took over broadcasting responsibilities for the first time at age 85! In his early years, Mr. Armstrong pioneered the radio broadcast. But when it transitioned to TV in 1967, Garner Ted became the presenter. That changed abruptly when Mr. Armstrong fired his son in 1978 for trying to take over the work.

So his first year after heart failure was not easy to say the least. And the pressure only intensified in 1979 after Ted and other dissidents convinced California's attorney general to launch an assault against Mr. Armstrong and the church. Ted couldn't overpower his father from the inside, so he attempted to do so from the outside. But his attack again fell flat on its face in 1980.

And then the church really took off. The same year the state of California attacked, Mr. Armstrong reestablished the *Good News* magazine, which had turned into a cheap tabloid. He restarted it in 1979 with a circulation of 120,000.

As the church entered a new decade, Mr. Armstrong concentrated his energies on *family*. "The very foundation of any stable civilization is a solid family structure," he wrote in 1979.[79] He knew the church's stability depended in large part upon the strength of its individual families. His two-fold plan—Youth Opportunities United (YOU) for teenagers and Youth Educational Service (YES) for pre-teens—was designed to bring families closer together and to support parents in educating their children in the ways of God. In 1981, at the age of 88, Mr. Armstrong started a new magazine for young people—*Youth 81*. Later that year, he reopened the college campus in Big Sandy. He regularly visited the church's youth camps during the 1980s. In fact, it was while Mr. Armstrong was visiting the youth camp in Orr, Minnesota, in 1985 that he became too ill to continue with his travels, which prompted his early return to Pasadena and eventual death. His last field visit in 1985 was to a *youth camp*. Then, back in Pasadena, one of his last public appearances was before the *students* at Ambassador College, when he handed out *Mystery of the Ages.*

These many youth activities established and emphasized at the end of Mr. Armstrong's life had a tremendous impact on me personally. Besides drawing me closer to my parents, they strengthened my relationships with other like-minded peers who wanted to succeed in life and avoid the common pitfalls of youth in this evil age. I traveled all over the Northwest with my youth group for sports tournaments, dances, talent shows and other activities. After my father was transferred in 1985, I had the same experiences in Oklahoma, Texas and Kansas. I attended WCG youth camps in Minnesota and Texas and was accepted as an Ambassador student in Pasadena and Big Sandy. This was all during the 1980s.

It was the work Mr. Armstrong did at the *very end* of his life, as an elderly man, that impacted my life the most.

And like the youth programs, every other church activity enjoyed prosperous growth after God raised Mr. Armstrong back to life in 1977. By the time he finally died in 1986—at 93 years of age—the church's annual income had about tripled. And after taking over responsibilities as full-time presenter on *The World Tomorrow* at age 85, the program became one of the highest-rated religious programs on television. The *Plain Truth, Good News* and *Youth* circulations all skyrocketed.

In 1985, while nearly blind, Mr. Armstrong began yet another monumental project. "With the writing of the new book *Mystery of the Ages,*" he wrote, "God has helped me this year to do the best work of my 93 years of life!"[80] He did his BEST work during his 90s! In fact, before he died, Mr. Armstrong said he had understood more in the last 10 years of his life than he had all the previous decades put together.[81]

That's a tremendous level of achievement for a man who would have rather died at the age of 85. "It would be so nice if I could retire," Mr. Armstrong told a group of ministers in 1981, "because it's a pretty heavy load I have to carry. But I'm not thinking of myself, I'm thinking of what I've been called to do. And it must be done." [82]

With Mr. Armstrong, God's work always came first. "I don't dare slacken my efforts," he wrote in 1968. "Most men retire when 16 years younger than I [he was 76 at the time]. This work must go on!"[83]

As early as 1957, he wrote, "When a man decides he already has achieved success, and retires—quits—he never lives long."[84] Had Mr. Armstrong ever given up and retired, he would have died long before his 93rd birthday—just like three of those ministers who retired in their 60s have since died.

Mr. Armstrong kept right on serving God even as an elderly, blind man. And in doing so, he got the Worldwide Church of God back on track, defeated the state of California in a nationally known lawsuit, became one of the most popular religious personalities on television, nearly quadrupled the church's growth in every major category, raised up and promoted numerous youth programs, traveled the world to meet with presidents and prime ministers and wrote a 363-page book.

"FOR MANY PEOPLE"

Herbert W. Armstrong prepared his last will and testament on January 12, 1986—four days before he died. Knowing he was near death, his first directive was that Herman Hoeh officiate the funeral "without pomp and undue ceremony."[85]

In his second directive, he bequeathed all his property of "every kind and nature" to the Worldwide Church of God.[86] *Think about that.* He had been pastor general of that church for more than 50 years. And though it started pitifully small, at the time of his death, the church's annual income was $164 million. As founder and pastor general of the Worldwide Church of God, Herbert W. Armstrong could have amassed a personal fortune by the time he died. As it was, the house he died in belonged to *the church*. The plane he traveled in belonged to *the church*. The cars he commuted in belonged to *the church*. And what he actually did own at the time of his death— even though he had three living children—he left to *the church*.

Had he been in it for the extravagant opulence that Tkach Jr. accused him of, can you imagine what kind of retirement package he could have set up for himself after 30 or 40 years as pastor general? Yet, he served God and tirelessly worked right up until the day he died. And at his death, every material possession he owned went right back to the church.

In his will, he explained that he chose not to leave his descendants anything—not because of any ill will toward them—but because he believed they had "adequate means of their own" and because leaving what he had to the church would ensure that it "be put to more permanent and beneficial use *for many people.*"[87]

That about sums up Herbert W. Armstrong's legacy.

Even on his deathbed, his final wish was for everything he owned to go toward the work so that "many people" might benefit.

Mr. Armstrong put *God's* family and *God's* work first. And as difficult as that might be to grasp, looking at it humanly, isn't that what we should expect from a man of God? Jesus Christ, after all, said, "He that loveth father or mother more than me is not worthy of me."[88] That's what Jesus taught—and *lived*. On one occasion, referred to in the Gospel of Mark, Jesus was preaching to a packed gathering inside a home. A messenger interrupted Him to say that His mother and siblings were outside and wanted to speak with Him. Jesus then turned and looked over the crowded room in response and asked, "Who is my mother, or my brethren? And he looked round about on them which sat about him, and said, Behold my mother and my brethren!"[89]

Wouldn't you expect Jesus Christ to put God's family and God's work first? "I MUST work the works of him that sent me, while it is day: the night cometh, when no man can work," Christ said.[90] It wasn't an option for Him—He HAD to work. He never considered retirement. He kept right on working until the day mankind murdered Him for putting God first.

PUTTING GOD AND HIS WORK FIRST IS THE BASIC THEME OF THE BIBLE.

There is a reason Christ called this the first and great commandment: "Thou shalt LOVE THE LORD thy God with *all thy heart,* and with *all thy soul,* and with *all thy mind.*"[91]

God's love is unselfish, outgoing concern for *others.* It is GIVING—first to God, then to all of mankind secondarily.

Herbert W. Armstrong put this principle—THIS LAW—into action. He *gave* and *gave* and *gave* and *gave*. Then he died—

exhausted from the heavy load God had laid on his shoulders. But God brought him back to life—and though he would have rather died or at least retired, he kept right on giving for ANOTHER 8½ YEARS! His lifelong work of service and sacrifice for the good of *others* proved, as our Savior promised it would, that it truly is more blessed to give than to receive.[92]

God blessed everything Herbert W. Armstrong did.

Yet it didn't take long for Tkachism to ruin it all.

HISTORY REPEATED ITSELF

"I want you, brethren, to think about and understand what happened to God's church in the 1970s lest history repeat itself! I want you to see the 'fruits' of rebelling against God's way and God's government."[93] Mr. Armstrong issued that warning to the WCG less than seven months before he died.

He told us EXACTLY what would happen if we didn't learn the lesson of the 1970s. He wrote,

> The "fruits" of the rebel leaders and "liberals" of the 1970s should now be clear to all. After some 35 years of steady growth in all facets of the work of God's church, the rate of growth began to slow, then ceased entirely in some areas, and, finally, even decreases began to be experienced in the number of radio and television stations, *Plain Truth* circulation, number of prospective members, number of co-workers, amount of income for the work, etc.—all under the "leadership" of the liberal element. These are well-documented facts that cannot be denied.[94]

Facts are stubborn, but so is Tkachism. Even though the lessons had been thoroughly documented, they REFUSED to heed them and decided to go their own way after Mr. Armstrong died.

And history ended up repeating itself.

PART TWO
OUR CHRISTIAN DUTY

THIRTEEN
BREAKING
GROUND

*"God's headquarters has moved numerous times since
the days of Moses and the Israelites in the wilderness. ... Therefore,
if any departmental moves occur, they won't represent
the first time headquarters operations have moved ...."*

— JOSEPH TKACH SR.
Pastor General's Report, *December 19, 1989*

M Y father staunchly supported the changeover from Mr.
Armstrong to Mr. Tkach in 1986. He arranged for all the
church members in his Oklahoma City congregation to
sign a card encouraging the new pastor general to carry on with the
work. He also invited Mr. Tkach, if he could fit it into his schedule,
to visit the Oklahoma brethren.

After making church visits to Phoenix, Big Sandy, Chicago and
Anchorage in early 1986, Mr. Tkach accepted my father's invitation
and stopped in Oklahoma City on June 7, 1986. According to the
Worldwide News, quoting my dad, Mr. Tkach's sermon was "the type
of sermon that is good for the ministry and can pave the way ... for
the type of sermons we need to be preaching to God's people. It left
all with the feeling we need to become more on fire for God's work,
inspiring us to be more enthusiastic and involved."[1] Coordinating
the special weekend, my dad arranged for the churches to present
Mr. Tkach with an oversized greeting card that played "Hail to the
Chief," a fanfare often used for greeting U.S. presidents. The church

areas also presented Mr. Tkach with a gold-plated, brass center-piece as a gift of appreciation for his visit.

Certainly, my father was not against Mr. Tkach's appointment as pastor general. Even after my dad first began to notice disturbing changes coming out of Pasadena, he tried to push these concerns out of his mind. He firmly believed Jesus Christ was Head of the church. And if leaders at headquarters needed to be corrected for any of their new teachings, Jesus Christ would take care of it.

In the third year of Mr. Tkach's leadership, sometime in 1988, my dad's thinking began to change.

THE LAODICEAN ERA

Before Herbert W. Armstrong died in January 1986, the WCG membership had been warned many times about the final prophe-sied era of God's church before the Second Coming of Jesus Christ—called *Laodicea* in Revelation 3. This era is characterized by spiri-tual lukewarmness—God says the people are "neither cold nor hot."[2] They trust in material things "and have need of nothing."[3]

Dr. Herman Hoeh wrote in his 1959 booklet *A True History of the True Church:* "This frightful condition lies now ahead of us. Just as the remnants of the Sardis era of the Church exist side by side with the Philadelphia era, so we will continue our work to the very 'end time' when another group will appear ...."[4] As that statement reveals, we believed another group would appear *separate from* the WCG—though undoubtedly composed mostly of former WCG members.

But Mr. Armstrong had not ruled out the fact that the WCG *itself* might turn Laodicean, as the following statement indicates: "But, the bad news, as it appears today, my dear brethren, is that we, undoubtedly of the Philadelphia era ... are in serious danger of becoming also the Laodicean era. I am personally much concerned about that."[5]

It wasn't until 1988 that my father began to see this as a distinct possibility. In studying Revelation 2 and 3, he realized that most of the time, church eras DO go astray. And once he accepted that historical fact, his discernment sharpened. He then noticed many more teachings coming out of Pasadena that simply did not square with the Bible. By the end of 1988, he was fully aware of the evil lurking within the Worldwide Church of God headquarters.

At the outset of 1989, my father began searching the Scriptures for God's perspective on all the changes. Why were they happening? Where was it leading? What should we do?

TRANSFER TO BIG SANDY

The first time I ever remember my dad expressing dissatisfaction with headquarters occurred sometime in January 1989. As a freshman at Ambassador College, Pasadena, I had given some thought to possibly transferring to the Big Sandy campus for my sophomore year. I knew how my dad felt about the idea. Although he would have supported my decision either way, he had always wanted me to stay at the headquarters campus. Since that is where most of the top ministers in the church were assigned, he felt I could learn more in Pasadena.

During one particular phone conversation about Big Sandy, however, I was surprised to hear him encourage me to apply for the transfer. "Dr. Meredith is over Big Sandy," he told me. "I think he's more conservative than some of the ministers in Pasadena." He was careful not to say much more than that.

I didn't give much thought to his comment at the time. I was just excited that he was happy for me to apply for the transfer.

GETTING THE PGR

When Larry Salyer explained in the PGR why they discontinued *Mystery of the Ages*, it upset my dad terribly. But to read Mr. Tkach's own words two weeks later, in the February 14 report—how the book had "peripheral or incidental"[6] errors and that it was outdated—was just too much. He had to vent.

He received that issue of the PGR on a Friday and then called me that night, February 17, 1989. At first, he was careful not to seem too upset. After a bit of prying, though, I got him to reveal how he really felt. He said, "Some of the things ministers are saying today would have gotten them fired if Mr. Armstrong were around." I listened in disbelief. Could it really be that bad? He went on to explain that they had discontinued *Mystery of the Ages* because of "minor errors" and "money." This was the first time I had ever heard that. Here I was at headquarters and no one—none of the ministers, faculty, student leaders—had ever told me that *Mystery of the Ages* was discontinued. My father later said, "We may very well be in the Laodicean era." He also encouraged me to read the Old Testament book of Malachi—saying that some of the prophecy in that little book may be happening right now.

All of this was a lot for an unbaptized 19-year-old to digest. I tried to piece together my father's comments with other things I was aware of. Four weeks earlier, during announcements at services, Mr. Tkach told the brethren how upset he had been recently, when he discovered that one of his assistants had been going "behind his back," complaining about "changes" in the church. Mr. Feazell followed those announcements with a sermon titled "Eternal Truths." In it, he discussed a number of changes in the church, but reassured the brethren that some things would never change— these so-called *eternal* truths. A week later, on January 28, Dr. Herman Hoeh gave a sermon on "change." A number of us students had wondered if something big was about to happen.

For me, something big did happen on that night of February 17. The man I trusted more than any other human being on Earth had just told me the church I had grown up in was now headed in a dangerous direction. It scared me.

BEGINNING OF MALACHI'S MESSAGE

A few weeks after our phone conversation, my father began working on a manuscript to explain, from a biblical perspective, why the WCG was making so many changes. He now believed the church had indeed moved into the Laodicean era and that a number of Bible prophecies explained *how* and *why* it was happening.

We continued our occasional phone conversations, talking about school, family and areas of Scripture he had been studying— usually the minor prophets. But he never mentioned his paper.

When I told him I was accepted to Big Sandy on April 4, he was glad to hear that I would be coming home toward the end of summer—and that I would only be a few hours from home during my sophomore year. More than that, he was glad that I would be getting out of Pasadena—the seat of the anti-Armstrong liberalism, so far as he was concerned.

He and my mom arrived in Pasadena on May 16 for my sister's graduation. Once again, he made no mention of the manuscript. No one, except him, knew about it—not even my mom.

Meanwhile, rumors had been flying around campus that the church was going to put the Pasadena property up for sale. On Memorial Day, May 29, a few friends of mine went to a Dodgers game with Fred Stevens, the WCG accounting manager who assisted Leroy Neff, the church treasurer. I happened to ask Mr. Stevens about the rumors to sell the headquarters property. He said, "If anything like that ever happened, Mr. Tkach is not so dumb as to keep it a secret." He brushed aside these rumors as a "bunch of lies."

MY DAD'S INITIAL FEEDBACK

On Friday, July 14, I flew to Oklahoma to spend the rest of the summer at home. My dad picked me up at the airport and we drove directly to Robbers' Cave in southeastern Oklahoma, where my dad's congregation was sponsoring a youth campout for the Oklahoma area churches. It was a three-hour drive I will never forget.

For four months, my dad had been working on his paper, telling no one about it. He occasionally worked on it at home in his office, but that was inconvenient and nerve-wracking with my mom around. His favorite work place was a vacant building in Enid, Oklahoma, where he pastored a small second congregation of about 100 people. The church area rented a room in a vacant building for services and Bible studies and the owner liked the congregation so much, he just gave my dad a key and said he could use it whenever he wanted. Thoreau had Walden Pond—my dad had a remote second office in a small Oklahoma town. He may have looked funny hauling a typewriter in and out of that vacant meeting hall, but it worked well for him. He wrote the bulk of his manuscript at that secluded location, about an hour and a half from home.

When he picked me up on July 14, he had a rough draft of *Malachi's Message* tucked away in his briefcase, in the trunk of the car. During the drive, he told me about a number of other things going on in the church—again, things I was totally unaware of. He said several ministers in the field were disgruntled with the changes coming out of Pasadena. And adding to his comment months earlier, about the church being in the Laodicean era, he said he believed the church was headed toward a "definite split." He later said he wanted me to read something he had written that explained all of this. He had kept this conversation bottled up inside his mind for four months. I could tell that he was relieved, just having gotten it off his chest. The thought of reading his paper made me nervous.

What if, after all, my dad was wrong? What if God *was* behind all of the changes in the church? Whether I read the manuscript or not, I knew, based upon what he had already told me, that I needed to study more on my own. I needed to prove for myself who was right and who was wrong. I didn't want to just take my dad's word for it.

I put off reading it until Sunday morning, two days later. We had planned to head back home that afternoon. As I read, I could tell my dad was anxiously awaiting any kind of feedback. He was very fidgety—constantly in and out of the cabin, trying to "keep busy" while I took the time to read.

I got through about half of it before we had to gather our things to leave. "So, what do you think?" he asked when I stopped reading. "Well, that definitely will get you fired," I responded. Its content certainly rang true—it was *inspiring* in fact—but I couldn't yet commit to accepting the material without first digging into Mr. Armstrong's foundational teachings. How could I say the church had fallen away from the truth when I hadn't yet fully proven the truth in the first place? I was 19—interested in baptism—and had so much to learn.

He agreed that the content would undoubtedly get him fired.

But believing it was from God, he fully intended to deliver the message to church leaders in Pasadena—perhaps in January of 1991—the end of the work's third 19-year time cycle. That was still a year and a half off, I thought. In the meantime, I had some studying to do as a sophomore in Big Sandy.

We talked about his paper most of the way home. Even with my limited understanding, I felt pretty sure about one thing: that we were now in the Laodicean era. But was it my dad's place to warn headquarters and the church about this? This is the question I wrestled with most over the next several months. Why not some other minister? Shouldn't a high-ranking minister from headquarters do this? Why couldn't my dad just tend to his flock in Oklahoma and let someone else lead the fight?

"This Church Is Laodicean"

Mr. Tkach was in Big Sandy for my orientation on August 14. He gave an odd introductory message—considering it was the kick-off to another exciting school year. He seemed paranoid and defensive. He was upset that some people were criticizing him. He then proceeded to criticize Mr. Armstrong, saying that in the past we had focused too much on prophecy.

Later that week, I met a sophomore whose dad also happened to be a minister in the WCG. From what I could gather, it seemed like his dad was upset about the changes too. I remember feeling good about that—like I wasn't totally alone in this.

The next week, on August 22, I got a part-time job in the college library. For the most part, I was responsible for organizing and storing sermon, Bible study and forum cassette tapes. Many of the older tapes, by Mr. Armstrong and other leading ministers, weren't even available to students. But as tape librarian, I had access to the archives. This wonderful collection proved invaluable as the semester wore on. As changes worked their way into the church, I often made side-by-side comparisons between what they were preaching and what the church taught when Mr. Armstrong was alive.

On Sunday night, October 1, I called my dad to chat about college and church subjects. During our conversation, he told me that his assistant, John Amos, had heard headquarters intended to remove Dr. Meredith from his position as head of the school in Big Sandy. My dad went on to say that he wondered if I should continue on at AC after my sophomore year. That comment shook me more than the Meredith rumor.

Four days later, Mr. Tkach, via telephone hook-up, announced that Dr. Meredith was being "transferred" to Pasadena to "write articles." He was replaced by Dick Thompson. Gary Antion would move in from Pasadena to replace Mr. Thompson as dean of students.

The whole announcement was upsetting. But I couldn't help feeling excited as well. The rumor Mr. Amos heard was, in fact, true! To me, it indicated that there were some rumblings of dissatisfaction among the field ministers around the world—it wasn't just my dad! If there indeed was a split in the church, hopefully the majority would stand up for the truth, or at least maybe it would be a 50-50 split.

That night, I happened to be eating with a student named Rick. After everyone at our table had left, half joking, he told me the church had drifted into a "lukewarm attitude." Once he saw that I didn't disagree, he quickly turned serious. "This church is Laodicean," he said. "I don't care what anyone says. The same thing is happening now that happened in the 1970s, only this time, I'm old enough to see it"—this from someone I had just met! I immediately thought to myself, "Now here is someone I need to spend more time with." When his friend Chris joined us in mid-conversation, I politely changed the subject. Rick interjected, "Oh, don't worry, he thinks the same way I do."

This was too good to be true! Sure, the overwhelming majority of students thought Dr. Meredith's transfer was nothing more than "business as usual." But for me to stumble upon two students who were terribly upset by the news and felt that the church was Laodicean seemed like a miracle from God. I really needed those two guys. The three of us started listening to old tapes together. We dug up old literature in the library to get a good grasp of what Mr. Armstrong taught on all the church's foundational teachings. For the rest of the semester, the three of us were practically inseparable.

OUR LAST FEAST

My family came to Big Sandy for the Feast of Tabernacles in mid-October. My sister read my dad's manuscript during that Feast, giving us lots to talk about. She told me that while she couldn't refute anything in the paper, her only concern was, *why did it have to be Dad?* She and I were struggling to get past the same obstacle.

Before the Feast started, I gave my dad a copy of a video Rick had gotten hold of a couple weeks earlier. It was Mr. Armstrong's taped sermon from the 1985 Feast. This was the one preceded by the 20-minute segment about the uniqueness and importance of *Mystery of the Ages*, with footage of Mr. Armstrong addressing the sophomores. My dad added a couple of points from that video to his Feast sermon, given the fourth day of the festival, October 17, 1989. It was the last Feast message my dad would give in the Worldwide Church of God.

Later that Feast, when Mr. Tkach announced that the church would be donating $100,000 to victims of the earthquake in San Francisco, I distinctly remember my dad saying, "They can afford to make a huge donation for the earthquake, but they can't afford to print *Mystery of the Ages*." He was disgusted.

GETTING TURNED IN

Soon after I read the paper over the summer, my dad began discussing the disturbing direction of the church with his assistant pastor, John Amos. Mr. Amos was also upset with the church's direction and didn't know how God intended to fix the problem, until after reading the manuscript. He was so gung-ho for what my dad was studying and writing that it inspired my dad all the more to press on with the project, confident that God would back him in the end.

There were also several members in my dad's church area who were upset about the changes. But he was much more guarded around them—telling them nothing about his manuscript and only that "God would work things out." Three individuals, however, persisted in asking my dad to explain what was going on with the church: Don Avilez and Stuart Powell (both local church elders), and a deacon named Dan Elliott. My dad finally agreed to meet with them, along with Mr. Amos, on Sunday, November 5. (Mr. Powell and Mr. Elliott also brought their wives). During the meeting, which lasted for several hours, he told them why he believed these changes were happening. He later issued copies of the manuscript, suggesting they study it first before meeting with him again a few weeks later.

On the way home with Mr. Amos, my dad expressed concern, wondering if he had done the right thing. Much of the feedback at the meeting was encouraging—even enthusiastic. But it was clear that the five of them were shaken by my dad's explanation.

Their follow-up meeting had been set for early December. This time, when my dad and Mr. Amos arrived at the old building in Enid (the same one where much of *Malachi's Message* had been written), the two wives weren't there—only the three men. (Conversely, Mrs. Amos, who was now in full agreement with her husband's support of my father, decided to attend.) Don Avilez had taken the lead among the three men, saying that my dad was way out of line to criticize Mr. Tkach Sr. and headquarters. Though not completely shocked, my father and Mr. Amos were both deeply disappointed. My father asked the three men to return their manuscripts, which they did, and assured them that he would eventually deliver a completed copy to Mr. Tkach. Until then, he asked that they keep these discussions confidential.

Later that week, Don Avilez called Arnold Clauson in Cape Girardeau, Missouri. (Mr. Clauson had been the pastor in Oklahoma City before my dad replaced him in 1985.) Mr. Clauson then called Joseph Tkach Jr. in Church Administration on December 6.

The cat was out of the bag.

Moving Headquarters

Ironically, I actually saw Joe Jr.'s dad in Big Sandy the same day Joe Jr. saw *my* dad in Pasadena. (The big difference, though, was that I didn't fire *his* father.)

On December 7, 1989, Mr. Tkach Sr. was on campus for a groundbreaking ceremony. The day was cold, cloudy and damp—

which, as I look back on it now, seems fitting—considering what finally came of their big ideas for Big Sandy.

The church and the college had been going through so many changes—reopening Big Sandy, pursuing accreditation, closing Pasadena, etc. More and more of the church's focus had centered on the Big Sandy campus. Mr. Tkach wrote in the December 19, 1989, PGR:

> Under careful study is also the possibility of moving one or more major departments of the work to Big Sandy, where costs of construction are significantly less than in Pasadena, and cost of housing would be considerably more affordable for our employees.[7]

They actually gave strong consideration to moving headquarters from Pasadena to Big Sandy. He continued, "If God leads me to see that some parts of the work should be relocated in Texas, sale of any resulting unused facilities here would also help in the costs of building there." As it turns out, there actually was something to those rumors we had been hearing in Pasadena earlier in the year. Mr. Tkach even acknowledged the rumor mill in his column: "Now I realize that such moves may sound drastic at first to some (though I understand *rumors have been circulating for months*)." According to the report, Mr. Tkach had commissioned a "careful and detailed feasibility study" on the possibility of such a move back in the spring of 1988.[8] No wonder rumors had been circulating.

Later, Mr. Tkach said, "Big Sandy has served as a second headquarters for decades," which wasn't true. It might have been a second Ambassador College *campus*—but certainly NOT a second headquarters. It became obvious where Mr. Tkach was headed. "I believe God is now leading me to see that a consolidation of as many of our resources, personnel and operations as possible at our less expensive facility may make good sense in preparation for the bumpy economic times ahead," he said. The church was, after all, in the midst of a financial crisis in 1989.

He went on to explain that Mr. Armstrong himself moved headquarters from Oregon to California back in the 1940s. "God's headquarters has moved numerous times since the days of Moses and the Israelites in the wilderness." Thus, "if any departmental moves occur, they won't represent the first time headquarters operations have moved."[9]

Indeed, plans for this move were already well underway by the time Mr. Tkach informed the church of the "possible option" in December of 1989. The WCG had been busy buying parcels of land around its 1,600-acre campus in preparation for the massive move. Numerous buildings were being designed by architects. In 1990, the church hurriedly built nine new structures in Big Sandy, including five student residences and a 350-seat lecture hall.

But the centerpiece of this building program was the Hall of Administration—a three-story office building situated at the end of the main entrance on campus. This building, once the move was complete, would become the church's new headquarters.

What I find most remarkable about this history is that the very day Mr. Tkach broke ground on a new headquarters in Big Sandy, the church's headquarters actually did move—but not to Big Sandy. On December 7, 1989, the *real* ground-breaking ceremony took place in Pasadena, California—inside Joseph Tkach Jr.'s office. On that day, Tkach Jr. fired my father and John Amos.

That's the day headquarters moved from Pasadena, California, to Edmond, Oklahoma.

FOURTEEN
FIRST SIP OF A
BITTER CUP

*"I believe the church disfellowshiped me unjustly.
Mr. Tkach didn't even talk to me, even when this was the weightiest
of all decisions affecting my fate in this church."*

— GERALD FLURRY
Letter to Ralph Helge, *December 21, 1989*

THOUGH I didn't know it at the time of the groundbreaking ceremony on that rainy afternoon, my father and Mr. Amos were en route to Pasadena. Tkach Jr. had called the house that morning, December 7, demanding that my father and Mr. Amos be on a plane to California that very day if they had any hope of retaining their jobs.

After arriving in Los Angeles late in the afternoon on December 7, they checked in at Holiday Inn Pasadena. That night, for over four hours, they went round and round with Joseph Tkach Jr. and Michael Feazell. During that meeting, my father came to see that the situation inside the Worldwide Church of God was actually far worse than he had realized.

My father complained about *Mystery of the Ages* being discontinued and the TV program getting weaker. "So let me see if I understand what you are saying," Tkach said, dissecting my dad's comments. "You're saying that you can run the church better than my father can." They kept turning it into a personality thing because debating the real issues only exposed their true intentions. But my father stayed on point, persistently asking why *Mystery of the Ages* had been removed, which led to Joe Jr.'s astonishing "riddled with error" outburst.

Suffice it to say, there was no compromise on either side that night. Shortly before midnight, Joseph Tkach Jr.—a man who had been employed by the church for three years—fired and excommunicated my father and John Amos. At his deposition, Tkach Jr. acknowledged that it was entirely his decision to fire these two long-time ministers on the spot. His father, the pastor general of the church, was not aware of the firings until after they had already happened.[1]

Upon leaving Tkach Jr.'s office that night, my father prophetically warned Tkach, "This is the first sip of a very bitter cup you are going to have to drink." Quite a parting shot from a man who had just been fired! My father also assured Mr. Tkach that he would be one of the first ones to receive the manuscript, as soon as it was completed and printed.

LIKE NO OTHER HUMAN

On the disfellowship notice filed the next day, Tkach Jr. wrote that he fired my father for "heretical doctrinal differences."[2] (The same reason he gave for disfellowshiping my mother.) At his deposition in 1998, in trying to explain what this meant, he said my father "was meeting with church members and asking them to give donations to him …."[3] This wasn't true at all.

Later, he attributed this preposterous assertion to my father: "He claimed that he was being used by God in a unique way, different from any other human ever to have lived …."[4] As bizarre as that statement is, Tkach repeated it two more times at his deposition. Later, when asked if Mr. Flurry was disfellowshiped for engaging in heresy, Tkach answered, "Well, when someone tells you that they are being used by God in a way that no other human who has ever lived is being used, I would consider that to be a bit on the heresy side." And later, "Claims that you are uniquely used by God in a role historically different from any other human in all of history, I considered pretty heretical."[5]

This was Joe Jr., the psychologist, at his best. Of course, my father never said anything like that during their meeting. But this was Mr. Tkach's *interpretation* of what my dad said. After all, Gerald Flurry criticized the pastor general of the Worldwide Church of God. He wrote a paper in which he set out to explain *why*, from a biblical perspective, the changes were happening. He believed God inspired his paper. *Therefore, he must think he's the most important man to have ever lived on this Earth!* How ridiculous.

The irony is that Mr. Tkach Jr. has taken great pride in trumpeting the WCG's transformation out of "Armstrongism" as something that is "unprecedented" in the history of religion. There has never been an instance in the history of religion where an unorthodox religious sect has transformed itself from a "cult" to a mainstream Christian denomination. Where would the Worldwide Church of God—in fact, *Christianity*—be today without the heroic and historically unique courage of Tkachism?

OKLAHOMA CITY CONGREGATION

The same day my father and Mr. Amos traveled to Pasadena for their meeting with Joe Jr., Arnold Clauson, the previous pastor in Oklahoma City, was en route from Cape Girardeau, Missouri, to Oklahoma City to announce the firing before my father's congregations. (He actually left for Oklahoma City before my dad even arrived to Joe Jr.'s office.)

On Friday evening, December 8, Mr. Clauson arranged to meet with all the elders and their wives as well as one deacon from my dad's territory.

On Saturday, Mr. Clauson read the announcement about the excommunication before the Oklahoma City and Enid congregations. According to Clauson, the brethren were "totally shocked" by the news. "[M]ost had no idea anything of this nature was going on," he wrote to Mr. Tkach Jr.[6] This squares with what Dean Blackwell, sent from Pasadena to Oklahoma City the following week, also admitted—that my dad's congregations were left in stable condition.

Mr. Clauson did note these two areas of concern that some

members had picked up in conversing with my dad and Mr. Amos: "1) Questioning Mr. Armstrong's literature being dropped from circulation and/or being updated, and 2) the weakness of the *World Tomorrow* telecast." Later, he wrote that my dad and Mr. Amos

> apparently asked several members, especially those who came to counsel about this and that, to go back and re-read *Mystery of the Ages, The Incredible Human Potential, The Book of Revelation Unveiled at Last,* and the *Autobiography,* and then get back to them with comments.[7]

Imagine that—recommending members read Mr. Armstrong's most important and effective book. How telling Clauson's report is. In many ways, the church had already been transformed.

RALPH HELGE'S FIRST SIP

On the day of the firing, Ralph Helge wrote my father and demanded that he return any church member mailing lists he may have acquired over the years as a field minister.

> Should you fail to abide by the demands contained in this letter within five (5) days, we will have no alternative but to consider filing suit against you and all other persons involved in the removal and misuse of these confidential materials and to seek an injunction against your continued possession and use of these materials, as well as all other appropriate relief, including an award of punitive damages.[8]

This type of language from Helge is something we became quite familiar with years later in our *Mystery of the Ages* lawsuit.

On December 11, 1989, Mr. Tkach Jr. followed up Helge's threat by sending my dad a proposed "assistance agreement and release." He wrote,

> As you understand, Mr. Flurry, late last week you were dismissed from your employment as a minister of the church,

disfellowshiped as a member, and your ministerial credentials revoked, because of what the church considers as your adherence to heretical convictions, spreading of the same among members of the church and your refusal to repent thereof. ...

As you know, your employment was for no set term and terminable "at will" at any time, by either you or the employer with or without cause. According to the practice of the employer, your termination does not entitle you to any type of severance pay or other post-employment benefits.

As a matter of Christian love, however, the employer is desirous of helping you now that your employment with the employer has ended.[9]

But before he could receive the "Christian love" offering of $6,160, my father had to sign off on five conditions. For instance, the WCG wanted written release from any and all possible liability, like wrongful termination. They also expected him to return church stationery and business cards, ministerial manuals, his ordination certificate, all church equipment and furniture, and any written or computer-generated records that pertained to church membership.

On December 21, 1989, my dad informed Mr. Helge that he had decided to reject the $6,160 "assistance." He, nevertheless, agreed to return everything except his computer and his ordination certificate. The computer, he wrote, "will help me in getting future employment." Regarding the certificate, he said the church had no right to take it. "I believe the church disfellowshiped me unjustly," he wrote. "Mr. Tkach [Sr.] didn't even talk to me, even when this was the weightiest of all decisions affecting my fate in this church."[10]

Mr. Helge responded one week later and said he would discuss the matter with Mr. Tkach Jr. On January 23, 1990, Tkach Jr. sent my dad another release form, only this time, "as a matter of Christian love," they offered my dad a computer in return for his signature![11] It was virtually the same form, with much of the same language, only instead of offering the $6,160 in love, they offered an IBM-compatible computer. My dad decided to keep the computer and the ordination certificate and not sign the release. The WCG did not pursue the matter any further.

It is interesting, looking back, that Mr. Tkach Sr. never once communicated with my dad during this whole ordeal. For the most part, Tkach Jr. and Helge handled the situation. And seven years later, when the WCG filed suit against us over printing *Mystery of the Ages,* Tkach Sr. would again be missing from the equation, having died of cancer in 1995. The two principle players, without question, in the case brought against us in 1997, were Joseph Tkach Jr. and Ralph Helge.

Neither of them would have admitted back in 1989 that the situation they were dealing with was only the first sip of a bitter cup they would have to drink.

SMALL BEGINNING

My sister quit her job at Church Administration in Pasadena the day my dad was fired. She flew home the next day, using my father's plane ticket. My father, in turn, drove home in my sister's yellow pickup (which had now become the family car). He needed that three-day drive, halfway across country, to sort things out in his mind. So much had happened so fast. There were times when he just parked the car alongside the road so he could get out and walk for a while. On the one hand, he had never been more discouraged. The Tkaches were ruining the church he had devoted his life to. But he also believed that God had revealed the answer to why these things had happened. It was found within a manuscript that only a handful of people had even seen.

I was at the house the day my dad arrived—Sunday, December 10. (I came home for the weekend from college in Big Sandy after hearing that he was fired.) In waiting for him to arrive, I remember fretting over what I would say and how I could encourage him. When he walked in the door that afternoon, we were prepared to uplift him, as best we could, knowing he had just endured the most difficult trial of his life. Yet it was the other way around: It was actually *my dad* who lifted our spirits. My mom and I, at that point, were technically still associated with the WCG. (My sister severed her ties the day he was fired.) And yet, here was this fired, former minister of the wcg encouraging us!

My father, though tired and emotionally drained, had had three days to mourn the sad state of the Worldwide Church of God. He was now firm in his resolve to do something about the problem—to get his manuscript ready for printing—to warn as many who would listen that the church had drifted into the Laodicean era. This realization gave him a great sense of purpose and hope, motivated by relaxed faith—a firm belief that he was doing the right thing.

I left for Big Sandy that night as excited as I've ever been. I was beginning to see that God would not stand idly by and watch His church fade into nothingness. God always warns in love. And if that warning had to be delivered through my dad, better him than no one.

THE FIRST PRINTING

Two other families who had no prior knowledge of the manuscript immediately offered their support for my father and Mr. Amos. Together, these four families—just 12 people—met for the Philadelphia Church of God's first service on December 16.

On Wednesday, December 20, with the help of two other church members, Tim and Melody Thompson, the pcg became an incorporated entity. Back in Big Sandy, I clearly remember my surprised reaction to the news that the church was incorporated. *They only have 12 people,* I thought to myself. *How could they already consider themselves to be an official church?* At the time, I was planning to leave school at the end of the semester. But I hadn't yet fully committed to the pcg.

When I got home on Thursday, December 28, I could see that this little group of people had been working at a breakneck pace—especially my dad and Tim Thompson. Mr. Thompson entered my dad's typewritten manuscript into a word processor. He, my father and Mr. Amos then worked to proofread, edit and lay out a final version.

I started working my old high school job at Kinko's. Sometime during the second week of January 1990, I took a finished printout of *Malachi's Message* with me to work. Mr. Amos and my dad had accumulated over 900 addresses of wcg ministers and members—the bulk of which were from the areas around Oklahoma City and Columbus, Ohio (Mr. Amos's previous pastoral assignment).

We made 1,000 copies of that first version of *Malachi's Message*—spiral bound, with a brown cardstock cover. Though few would have considered it a book, it was at least a good-quality manuscript. Meanwhile, my dad prepared a personal letter to be included with the books sent to those in his former congregations: "Dear Oklahoma City and Enid Brethren," he wrote.

> So much has been distorted about what I said and did, that I felt this letter was necessary. I feel it isn't asking too much of you to allow me to set the record straight. I hope you will read what I actually said and did.
>
> Mr. Arnold Clauson was sent here by Mr. Joe Tkach Jr. Arnold had a meeting with the deacons and elders on Friday night, the 8th of December. He related some statements that Mr. Tkach Jr. said about me. (Mr. Clauson did not contact me while he was in Oklahoma City.)
>
> Here is some of what I was supposed to have said in the December 7 meeting in Pasadena with Mr. Tkach Jr.: 1) Gerald Flurry is supposed to have said he could "run the work better than Mr. Tkach does." Actually, I have never made such a statement in my life. Has any one of you ever heard me say anything like that? 2) Supposedly, I told Mr. Tkach Jr. to "shut up and listen to me." The truth is I have never told even a deacon or local elder to "shut up"—much less one of my superiors. I did not say anything even close to those statements in that meeting. 3) Also, he said that when I send in magazine articles, I demand that they be printed because people must read what I have to say. The truth is I haven't submitted an article in about six or seven years. And I have never demanded that any articles be printed. Why should this even be mentioned now, after such a long time? What is the motive?
>
> Any of you can verify what was said about me by asking your deacons and elders. But you have probably already heard

about these comments I was supposed to have said. The sad part is, these distorted statements filter down into the congregation. I ask you, brethren, in my almost five years of service here in Oklahoma, have statements like that ever been made by me? Did I ever conduct myself in that fashion?

Mr. John Amos knows those statements about me are not true. So does Jesus Christ ....

Would you please read the enclosed, finished message of Malachi. Then you can evaluate me by what I say—not what people think I said. Obviously, I don't want a stained reputation if it can be avoided.

The Oklahoma City and Enid churches went through terrible turmoil in the 1970s—more than most churches. I desperately wanted to avoid causing you any more problems. But trouble now could mean far less difficulty in the future. I hope that serving almost five years in this area has revealed my love for all of you.

The decision to take a stand on the issues presented in the message of Malachi was not taken lightly. Mr. John Amos and I have given up almost any physical security we had. It's hard on our whole families. As you know, my wife has had serious heart problems for years. Why would we decide to take such a stand?

Hopefully, no one will think I'm doing this for money. The church offered me $6,000 "assistance" or severance pay if I met several conditions, and also took my only car (I don't have a "second car"). I do not qualify to receive social security or unemployment compensation. Headquarters called the $6,000 a "love offering." That view was not shared by me, so the money was rejected.

None of this is mentioned for sympathy. I say it only to help you see my true motive. Jesus Christ has promised to provide our needs—so we don't worry about money (and believe me, we have very little).

You may think I have a government problem. If you will read the Malachi message—you will see that loyalty to government is my motive for doing this! Then you will also understand the real reason why I was fired.

Please search the scriptures as the Bereans did (Acts 17:11) and prove all things (I Thes. 5:21). Then pray for God to guide your every step. I believe Mr. Amos and I would die—if we had to—for what is written in the Message of Malachi. We desperately want you to make up your own mind—and not let others do it for you. That is a very biblical approach. ...

[P]lease don't believe me or any man—believe the Bible.

Love always,
Gerald Flurry[12]

With me now added to the original group, 13 of us gathered at the Thompson home Wednesday night, January 10. We packaged 921 copies of *Malachi's Message,* several hundred of which included the above letter. No one could possibly gauge what kind of response there would be to that first mailing. But we all knew that this was the beginning of something special. Finally, members of the Worldwide Church of God could understand what was happening to their church.

We delivered the bundles to the post office the next day, Thursday. Many of those books from the first mailing landed in mailboxes on or just before January 16, 1990—four years to the day that Herbert W. Armstrong died.

FIFTEEN
PEANUT SHELL

"I can't believe that anyone would think that ... Christ built this world-wide work through Mr. Armstrong and then blew it all. He didn't choose the right one! He should have gotten someone that's long-standing and that's going to last in a stable manner forever like a 'snow flurry.'"

— GERALD WATERHOUSE
Sermon, *January 25, 1992*

CHURCH Administration announced my dad's firing on page 6 of the December 19, 1989, *Pastor General's Report:* "It is our unpleasant duty at this time to notify you that Gerald Flurry and John Amos, former pastor and associate of the Oklahoma City and Enid, Oklahoma, congregations, and Laura Flurry, a former Church Administration employee, have been disfellowshiped."[1]

At the time, outside of Oklahoma, this announcement was not big news in the church. Even on the day it was announced, most congregations also received news of the possible headquarters move to Big Sandy, which largely overshadowed the fact that two unknown ministers from the Midwest had been disfellowshiped.

After our initial mailing of *Malachi's Message* on January 11, the WCG made this comment to the ministry:

> Many of you have called to advise us of the receipt of a manuscript written by Gerald Flurry. It appears that he mailed it to most church pastors, to many members where he and John

Amos previously served and to some people in neighboring areas. We thank you for your diligence in keeping us informed and in protecting the flock from heresy.

As always, we encourage your prayers to ask for God's protection over His people as well as to grant repentance to those who have deceived themselves into thinking their righteousness is greater than what God gives to the church.[2]

This was the extent of the wcg's response (or lack thereof) to the pcg in those early days. Nothing specific is said about the *content* of *Malachi's Message*—only that it was "heresy" and its proponents are self-righteous. In fact, the church would not address any specific content in the book for another year and a half. During that time, they largely ignored *Malachi's Message* and the pcg.

At the local level, however, the church did work quickly to troubleshoot isolated areas affected by pcg mailings. After Arnold Clauson announced the firings in Oklahoma City the weekend of December 9, Pasadena sent Dean Blackwell in for a week to help smooth the transition to its next pastor, Don Lawson, transferring in from Salt Lake City. Mr. Blackwell gave a sermon December 16 in which he tried to address some of the points raised in *Malachi's Message*, but he hadn't even read the book. He told the congregation that my dad had gotten a wealthy man to help him raise up the church, which was not true.

In the months that followed, Mr. Blackwell became the wcg's unofficial troubleshooter for areas affected by *Malachi's Message*—often ridiculing and belittling my father and the pcg because of how small it was and the fact that it was started by two unknown ministers.

But with every handful of people that responded positively to *Malachi's Message*, we received more new names and addresses. And as the message spread, the wcg gradually broadened its attack against the pcg—first in an indirect way, and then later, head on.

FIRST SIP OF BEING EXPOSED

When Mr. Tkach Sr. announced in September 1990 that the *Plain Truth* and *World Tomorrow* would adopt a more "religious" tone, he made it sound like times were changing and that their audience had changed, but in fact, the only thing that changed was the church's message. They no longer felt obligated to deliver the warning message of the gospel to the largest audience possible. Their focus had turned inward.

When Mr. Tkach elaborated on this change in the November 14, 1990, *Pastor General's Report,* he left little doubt about them now proclaiming a different message:

> First, the telecast is definitely not to copy the overly emotional character of certain other religious programs. On the other hand, it is also not to become confrontational, degrading others' sincerely held beliefs, condemning, nor filled with hyperbole about specific prophetic fulfillments.[3]

Mr. Tkach prefaced this major change by pointing out obvious flaws in two opposite extremes. Then he stressed that they were only seeking to find a proper balance between the two. It was another attempt to obscure the fact that they were making a dramatic change.

"Prophecy programs will present a balanced, overall perspective of the purpose and value of prophecy, instead of attempting to interpret specific prophecies," he continued. "Prophecy programs will not lose sight of the gospel message by trading the true gospel for a '10-nation/save-your-skin' gospel"[4]—an unmistakable smear against Mr. Armstrong's teachings.

Of course, the television program and the *Plain Truth* had already been watered down significantly, as my father had told Mr. Tkach Jr. a year earlier. Arnold Clauson, you will remember, even noted in his report to Tkach Jr. that my father felt that the TV program was too weak. And now, a year later, Mr. Tkach Sr. finally came forward and at least explained why the program had changed.

The Philadelphia Church of God, as small as it might have been in 1990, had already begun to expose the wcg's deceitful transformation. The more our message spread, the more it forced wcg leaders to put forward some sort of response.

"SELF-RIGHTEOUS" MINISTERS

Not long after explaining the new format for the TV program and the *Plain Truth,* Mr. Tkach Sr. complained about the attitudes of certain members and ministers who had been put out of the church. Some of the more vocal ones, he wrote in the PGR, believe "[e]very word of *Mystery of the Ages,* along with every word of every article and booklet Mr. Armstrong wrote, except those they are personally aware that he specifically changed himself."[5] He went on to say that these dissidents bolster their argument by saying the WCG had "gone from Philadelphian to Laodicean." He then mentioned how upsetting it was to find out how some of these former ministers were treating their brethren:

> The minister places himself on a pedestal, usually along with his closest elders and deacons. Some people are afraid to counsel with him because he is harsh and intimidating rather than considerate and approachable. Members who become close to the pastor in this little clique pull out all stops in their efforts to get and stay "in good" with the pastor. Many become men-pleasers in their attitudes toward the leaders who are in the "in" group. A certain smug attitude develops among those who are in this "righteous" group toward those who are trying to be faithful to the church. Confidentiality becomes a problem, because things discussed with the ministers may be shared in this clique.
>
> Let me stop right here to say that these things are abominable in the sight of God! They are the result of an arrogant, smug, deeply self-righteous and superior attitude that is the opposite of all that Jesus Christ taught and stands for! And all this sin-filled abuse of ministerial authority is cleverly disguised in a pious smoke-screen of somehow being "loyal" to Mr. Armstrong and teaching the real truth![6]

Strong words those! And since only a handful of ministers had left (or been fired by) the church at that time, that rebuke was aimed primarily at the "self-righteous" ministers in the Philadelphia Church of God.

"Churches That Splinter"

On May 4, 1991, Dean Blackwell gave a sermon in Columbus, Ohio, during which he went through a list of 23 "splinter" groups that had left the Worldwide Church of God over the years. His main point was to show how all these groups had come to nothing. Of course, the PCG was his main target in that sermon.

> Do you think a little group of 135 people is going to grow big enough to preach the gospel of the kingdom around the world for a witness when they say "Christ is coming back soon— Christ's coming is imminent"?[7]

Actually, the PCG had between 200 and 300 members at the time of Blackwell's sermon. Still, he wasn't impressed. Blackwell said,

> To me, one of the greatest blessings I've had in my job has been to go out into troubled areas when something like this happens and see if I can shut the door in the wolf's face. I hate to see God's people blinded and duped and deceived and hoodwinked and led off into a little fly-by-night peanut shell floating on a big ocean going nowhere doing nothing.[8]

He criticized the PCG—which began with 12 people and had only been around for 16 months—for not being on television or radio. "You're going to know the church by the work it's doing," he later said.[9] Yes, and we have said much the same for over a decade, as the PCG's work has continued growing, whereas the WCG stopped doing a work long ago.

Mr. Blackwell also made some astonishing statements regarding Ambassador College.

> People said Mr. Armstrong said we should never have accreditation. That's not so. I've been in on every ministerial meeting ever held since 1955, and I've got that big, fat, thick notebook where I took notes vigorously and I can stick your nose in that book and show you right in the notes.[10]

And yet, Mr. Armstrong wrote this to the ENTIRE CHURCH:

We could now qualify for accreditation both at Pasadena and
Big Sandy—but we shall not, because the government of the
colleges would have to be according to that which is in force
in this world's educational institutions—God's government
would have to go. We already have the highest accreditation of
all—that of Almighty God![11]

Later, Mr. Blackwell said,

They said we moved the college to Big Sandy and Mr. Armstrong
said to close it. That is ridiculous. Mr. Armstrong didn't do any
such thing. I don't know how these people 3,000 miles away
supposedly know what Mr. Armstrong said and I've been out
there [in Pasadena] 13 years. I ought to know what he said.
I've been in on all the meetings, the board of directors, and he
didn't say any such thing.[12]

Of course, we knew what Mr. Armstrong said because he wrote
it in a letter he sent to all church members and co-workers.

MALACHI'S MESSAGE FINALLY REFERRED TO

Not long after Mr. Blackwell's sermon in Columbus, the WCG finally
mentioned my dad by name in one of its publications—the *Worldwide
News*. The PCG had only begun just 18 months earlier—and with
just 12 people. During that first year and a half, we had only mailed
4,000 copies of *Malachi's Message* to WCG members. But the message
in the book had apparently sent enough shock waves through WCG
congregations that Pasadena felt compelled to address the subject
directly.

In June 1991, Mr. Tkach criticized former ministers who had
resisted changes as being only interested in gaining a following
for themselves. "One dissident says I am destroying everything Mr.
Armstrong did," he wrote. "In fact, I am doing exactly the same
thing Mr. Armstrong did—putting the word of God first."[13]

Mr. Tkach again chose not to mention my dad by name. He left that to David Hunsberger, who wrote an article on page 4 of the issue, titled, "What the Church teaches about Malachi and his message." Mr. Hunsberger wrote,

> In this article we will examine the claims of one critic of the church to show how his teachings contradict God's word and how the attitude displayed in his writing is an affront to the Holy Spirit and contrary to Christian principles.
>
> The subject for this study is a book titled *Malachi's Message to God's Church Today* © 1990 by Gerald R. Flurry.[14]

Mr. Hunsberger continued, "Mr. Flurry contends that since the death of Herbert W. Armstrong the church has changed 'away from the Philadelphia standard' and has become the Laodicean era."[15] Thereafter, he offers a response to some of the points raised in *Malachi's Message*. To his credit, at least Mr. Hunsberger attempted to address some of the content in *Malachi's Message*. Most ministers, like Dean Blackwell, simply ignored the content and focused instead on ridiculing Gerald Flurry.

"SNOW FLURRY"

For many years, Gerald Waterhouse was known in the WCG as the "traveling evangelist." He traveled the world visiting hundreds of congregations, helping keep the brethren focused on headquarters. He played a lead role in stirring up zealous support for Mr. Armstrong in the years following the 1970s crisis.

He tried to drum up similar enthusiasm for Mr. Tkach's leadership, but he lost much of his credibility when he found himself defending the very things he had condemned a decade earlier.

He had much to say about my dad in a sermon he gave in Tallahassee, Florida, on January 25, 1992:

> I can't believe that anyone would think that Christ, who said "I will build my church," and "I will never leave nor forsake it," and people come now and think that Christ built this world-

wide work through Mr. Armstrong and then blew it all. He didn't choose the right one! He should have gotten someone that's long-standing and that's going to last in a stable manner forever like a "snow flurry." You ever notice how long they last? They come down and, "Well, where was it? There was a flurry, I saw it right here."

Brethren, I want to make a strong point here. You need to grasp what people are hoodwinked by Satan the devil on. I know Gerald Flurry very well. I thought I did. I didn't know some of the things he was doing behind the scenes. But he was never around Mr. Armstrong's feet to be trained there. I was with Wayne Cole. We sent him up to [Washington] when I was with Wayne Cole in 1975. When the decision was made to send him, he was serving not in Pasadena, he was serving in [Norwalk]. We sent him up to Washington to handle those four churches: Yakima, Quincy, Tonasket and Pasco. That's where he was for about 10 or 11 years. Then he went over to Oklahoma City.

How could he carry on for Mr. Armstrong? He wasn't even trained around him, much less at his feet. Wasn't even trained close to him. Wasn't even trained at his coattail. Wasn't trained within arm's reach. He was miles away for about 13 or 14 years. Whom did God appoint to carry on for Moses? One trained at his feet: Joshua. That's the smart way to do it.[16]

First of all, Christ did say He would build His church,[17] but He did not say He would never leave the church! He said, "I will never leave YOU, nor forsake YOU."[18] Church history proves just the opposite of what Mr. Waterhouse said. God doesn't leave His people, but His people can leave Him! Read Revelation 2 and 3. Then read Revelation 2:5 and Ezekiel 8:6 where it shows God will forsake a church that forsakes Him.

According to Mr. Waterhouse, Gerald Flurry couldn't carry on for Mr. Armstrong because he wasn't at Mr. Armstrong's feet like Garner Ted Armstrong, David Antion, Albert Portune, Wayne Cole and Stanley Rader. Or what about David Jon Hill or Charles Hunting? Those men were all trained at Mr. Armstrong's feet. But does being so trained guarantee someone will remain faithful to the teacher? Judas Iscariot was trained at Jesus Christ's feet. Lucifer was trained at God's feet.

Mr. Tkach was indeed trained at Mr. Armstrong's feet. At a special service the day Mr. Armstrong died, Mr. Tkach said, "[W]e are a product of [Mr. Armstrong's] dedication and service. ... We can appreciate having the opportunity of being able to support and hold up the arms of the late Mr. Armstrong." At that time Mr. Tkach promised to stay on the path Mr. Armstrong had established. He said,

> And the admonishment is now for those of us still living who now have a task that is set before them, a course that has already been charted by God's apostle. We need to maintain that course and not deviate from it one iota.

Then, during the final prayer at Mr. Armstrong's funeral, Mr. Tkach said, "We readily admit and acknowledge that there is no man who can fill his shoes, but, Father, we aim to follow in his footsteps." [19]

Following on the "coattail" of Mr. Armstrong did not prevent Mr. Tkach from changing every major doctrine Mr. Armstrong established, even after Mr. Tkach said that the course had "already been charted," and that we were not to "deviate from it one iota."

MELTING AWAY

You get an idea of how the wcg reacted to *Malachi's Message* and Gerald Flurry those first few years. They ridiculed the Philadelphia Church of God, calling it a "peanut shell" or "snow flurry," because they thought—or at least they hoped—it would just go away.

But it didn't. Our work kept growing.

Ironically, it's the Worldwide Church of God that has been slowly melting away. Its income has plummeted. Its leaders have sold off all the property. There is no work being done. Even many of its leading men have died, including Tkach Sr. on September 23, 1995. Earlier that year, while operating on Tkach Sr.'s gall bladder, doctors discovered widespread cancer.

Yet, Mr. Tkach's physical demise is nothing compared to the spiritual disease he brought into the Worldwide Church of God. And those under him, instead of fighting against the cancer, actually helped it spread. As Mike Feazell said in his book, the church Mr. Armstrong devoted his life to building "had slowly ceased to exist."[20]

SIXTEEN
"LARGEST AUDIENCE POSSIBLE"

"... Mr. Armstrong persevered during the last year of his life to complete this, his last book. One of his last public appearances was to present it to the students of Ambassador College. But he also wanted to make it available to a much wider audience."

— JOSEPH TKACH SR.
Plain Truth, *November-December 1986*

L ESS than a year before he died, Mr. Armstrong summed up his prophetic message in a letter on February 25, 1985. "For more than 40 years now the *Plain Truth* has been proclaiming an outstanding series of Bible prophecies of something due soon to occur in Europe that will change the whole world and shake up the lives of every one of us." He continued,

> Daniel's prophecy in chapter 2 pictures 10 nations in Europe in our time right now, as the 10 toes on the two feet of the great symbolic image. Five of those toes picture five nations in Western Europe and five in Eastern Europe. Then is pictured a great stone, representing Christ at His soon Second Coming, smiting those toes, and coming to rule in the Kingdom of God over all those and all other nations on Earth. This is further

explained in the 17th chapter of Revelation, depicting those 10 nations of Europe uniting under the Roman Catholic Church. In the last decade certain leaders in Europe have been working feverishly to bring about such a reuniting of Europe.[1]

The prophesied rise of a European beast power—a teaching that embarrassed the Tkaches—was the beating heart of Mr. Armstrong's prophetic teachings. He continued in that same letter, "For some reason God has been holding back the fulfillment of this prophecy—but it is certain to occur!" God had been *holding back* the final development of this Euroforce, according to Mr. Armstrong. He then wrote, "Meanwhile God's work is growing now as never before. ... I am now hard at work on a new book. It probably will be the largest and most important book I have ever written. The title is *Mystery of the Ages*."[2]

While events were held back in Europe, they had accelerated in the church. Mr. Armstrong was hard at work on the most important book of his life.

REQUIRED READING

In *Mystery of the Ages,* Mr. Armstrong set out to explain the biblical truth about seven great mysteries man has not been able to solve: the mystery of God, the truth about angels and evil spirits, the mystery of man, of civilization, Israel, the true church and, finally, the mystery of the kingdom of God.

"These are the seven great mysteries that concern the very lives of every human being on Earth," Mr. Armstrong wrote in the preface of the book. "The plain truth of all these mysteries is revealed in the Bible, but none of the churches or theologians seem to have comprehended them."

"Why?" he asked. Because "the Bible is the basic mystery of all."[3]

In April 1985, Joseph Tkach Sr. told the ministers he believed *Mystery of the Ages* would "prove to be another major step forward for God's church and the spreading of the gospel around the world."[4]

That same PGR also reported that Mr. Armstrong's February 25 letter brought in the "highest response in several months." According to Richard Rice, many recipients wrote Mr. Armstrong to tell him they were eagerly looking forward to reading *Mystery of the Ages.*[5]

Mr. Armstrong finished writing *Mystery* on May 14, 1985. A few weeks later, on June 7, Mr. Tkach told ministers that they needed to constantly review the doctrines that had been restored to the church through Mr. Armstrong. He then referred to *Mystery of the Ages* and said "this is a book that *should be reread* as soon as we finish it the first time, in order to really soak up what God is teaching us."[6]

When Mr. Armstrong handed out new copies of *Mystery of the Ages* to the sophomore class at Ambassador College in September, he told them,

> I want to say that you need to read every word, and you need to go over it more than once. You aren't going to get the full meat of this book in one reading. This is a book that, after you've read it, you can read it a second time and then later a third time.[7]

In the book itself, Mr. Armstrong wrote, "As you read and reread this book, compare constantly with your own Bible."[8]

So this was not something Mr. Armstrong wanted the brethren to take casually. He admonished the membership to thoroughly go through the book over and again. After it was printed, it automatically became the most important piece of literature in the church. It was used as a textbook at Ambassador College. And it was required reading for all people interested in becoming a member of the church.

Six months after Mr. Armstrong died, Church Administration gave these instructions to the ministry about baptismal counseling:

> Although the reading of *Mystery of the Ages* and certain booklets and correspondence course lessons regarding the subjects related to baptism *should be required,* the complete reading of all of Mr. Armstrong's lengthier books is, in most cases, an unnecessary requirement for baptism candidates.[9]

Some ministers, apparently, were requiring prospective

members to read all of Mr. Armstrong's books prior to baptism. While that wasn't necessary, one clear exception was Mr. Armstrong's final book. EVERYONE HAD TO READ *Mystery of the Ages!*

Without missing a beat, the Philadelphia Church of God continued with this policy at its inception in 1989, even though the book had been out of print for over a year and a half. "Mr. Armstrong instructed the ministers to insist that every baptismal candidate read *Mystery of the Ages*," my father wrote in late 1989.[10]

At a 1994 ministerial conference, PCG minister Dennis Leap called *Mystery of the Ages* the "primer text prior to baptism." He then reminded our ministers about Mr. Armstrong's instructions that it be "required reading."[11]

My father reiterated this same policy two years later, telling PCG ministers, "Mr. Armstrong required that anyone who wanted to be baptized must read *Mystery of the Ages*."[12]

At the end of his life, without question, Mr. Armstrong considered *Mystery of the Ages* the most important and significant work available within the Worldwide Church of God. Even Mr. Tkach said so for at least a year after Mr. Armstrong died. And since the establishment of the PCG in 1989, my father has upheld *Mystery of the Ages* as essential reading for prospective members.

But Mr. Armstrong never intended this book to be for members only. In it, there is a message for all of mankind. This is why he devoted so much of the church's resources and money toward the printing and distribution of *Mystery of the Ages*.

"LARGEST AUDIENCE POSSIBLE"

"You could say that Mr. Armstrong was the art director as well as the author," said Greg Smith, the book's designer. "He met with several people from Editorial periodically to review the design, the paper stock, the typestyle and finally, the cover."[13] Mr. Armstrong considered these details extremely important because of his expansive plans for the book. For the cover jacket, he wanted something that looked regal, so he chose a deep shade of purple that had to be specially mixed at the printer. The title was printed with raised lettering, embossed in gold. The church printed 150,000 copies of the hardback version and hired a New York publishing house—Dodd, Mead—to coordinate the book's distribution.

The hardback copies were distributed to WCG members as well as regular donors and co-workers who supported the church. The church also produced a paperback version and advertised it in the *Plain Truth,* which had a circulation of about 8 million. It offered free copies by letter to 480,000 *Good News* subscribers as well as to viewers of the *World Tomorrow* television program. A condensed version (and corrupt, we later discovered) of the book ran serially in the *Plain Truth's* seven different language editions.

To reach an audience outside the church's sphere of influence, Mr. Armstrong offered the hardback version in book stores for $12.95. "This presents the book to an audience that possibly would not read or treat seriously literature received free of charge," wrote Michael Snyder in the *Worldwide News.*[14] The church then spent $400,000 to advertise the book—the largest advertising campaign ever for any church literature. It placed full-page ads in 27 major newspapers, including the *Wall Street Journal, USA Today* and the *Saturday Evening Post.* It also advertised in *Newsweek* and several other magazines and journals. The ad explained "why *Mystery of the Ages* could be one of the most important books of our day" and informed readers that the book was available in bookstores.[15]

In the church's 1985 Behind the Work video, the narrator noted, "Every effort is being made to make *Mystery of the Ages* available to the widest possible audience."[16]

This is what Mr. Armstrong wanted for a book this important. He wrote to church members and co-workers in September 1985, "We want to reach THE LARGEST AUDIENCE POSSIBLE with this book. I know you will feel the same way when you read it."[17] For a short while at least, it seemed like Mr. Tkach felt that way as well.

"MUCH WIDER AUDIENCE"

For at least 12 months after Mr. Armstrong's death, Tkach Sr. heaped praise on the book. On January 16, 1986—the day Mr. Armstrong died—Mr. Tkach told members and co-workers, "Even in the last year of his life, with declining strength, he completed with God's help, HIS MOST POWERFUL AND EFFECTIVE BOOK, *Mystery of the Ages*."[18] Later that year, Mr. Tkach wrote in the *Plain Truth*,

> Although in declining health, and for all practical purposes blind, Mr. Armstrong persevered during the last year of his life to complete this, his last book. One of his last public appearances was to present it to the students of Ambassador College.
>
> But he also wanted to make it available to a MUCH WIDER AUDIENCE. He decided *Mystery of the Ages* should be published by installments in the *Plain Truth*—a parting gift to the millions he had served through radio, television and the printed word during his long life."[19]

Mr. Tkach acknowledged that Mr. Armstrong wanted the book distributed far beyond church boundaries—that he viewed the book as a parting gift for "millions." So Mr. Armstrong approved the serialization project *and also* the bookstore distribution, the advertising campaign, the press release and the direct mail and *World Tomorrow* offers. Tkach continued,

> Shortly before he died, he said he had understood more in the last 10 years of his long life than in all the previous decades.
>
> *Mystery of the Ages* is the product of that understanding. Mr. Armstrong DID NOT UNDERESTIMATE THE IMPORTANCE OF THIS LAST WORK, for it contained vital keys to understanding the plan of God as revealed in the Bible. *Mystery of the Ages* in a very real sense was a last will and testament, to be *passed on to those who would value it*. As we come to the last installment of this remarkable book, we gratefully acknowledge our indebtedness to Herbert W. Armstrong, and his dogged search for the truth. He freely shared his understanding with us, and we have been privileged to make it available to you. He loved and respected his readers and, in a figurative sense, he remembered you in his will.[20]

A year and a half later, Mr. Tkach retired the book from circulation *permanently* and trashed 120,000 copies left in storage. But not for the Philadelphia Church of God, today Mr. Armstrong's last will and testament would be all but obsolete.

OUR BIG DAY

When Mr. Armstrong handed out new copies of his book to the sophomore class on September 9, 1985, he nearly shed a tear as he asked, "Will you forgive me if I get a little bit of a thrill that this book is done—that this book is out now? Today is a pretty big day in my life, when I can hand copies of this book out to each of you."[21]

Our "big day" came 11 years later, on December 20, 1996, when we received our first copy of *Mystery of the Ages*—reprinted for the first time by the Philadelphia Church of God. For about a year, my father had seriously considered the move. He had discussed the subject with a few of us ministers at PCG headquarters in Edmond.

He advised me to contact a Washington, D.C., copyright attorney who had been referred to us by the husband of our television time-buying agent. I contacted him by phone in November 1996 and explained our situation as thoroughly and succinctly as possible. I told him that we would most likely move forward on the project, but wanted to get some legal advice before proceeding further. While he didn't offer his opinion on the legalities of printing a discontinued work we didn't technically own, he did tell us that if we chose to move forward, we should prepare for the possibility of litigation.

I asked him how we should handle the copyright notice at the front of the book, which read "© Worldwide Church of God." For obvious reasons, we didn't want to print it that way. The attorney said that the copyright notice itself was of no special significance. The only issue, he told us, would be that of false attribution. In other words, by putting the WCG on the copyright notice, they could argue in court that they were falsely attributed to the reprinting project. We were happy with that since we didn't want their name attached to the project anyway. But neither did we want to give the impression that we owned the copyright (although we certainly believed we were the rightful owners of the material *spiritually*), which is why we didn't want to include the PCG's name on the notice. So we opted for "© Herbert W. Armstrong."

A few weeks after that phone call, my father and I met with Mark Carroll, the prepress production manager for the church's publications at that time. He worked for a printer in Arkansas, and my dad wanted to know if he would be interested in accepting the project. Mr. Carroll, a PCG member, was thrilled by the prospect of resurrecting Mr. Armstrong's body of literature. He gladly accepted and, by the end of that meeting, we ordered 20,000 copies of the book. We told Mr. Carroll to be discreet about the project, as we wanted to catch the WCG by surprise and make as big of a splash as possible at the start.

We didn't have the money to produce a hardback version, but we modeled our softbound after Mr. Armstrong's hardback in size and in number of pages. And, of course, we used the text from the hardback version as well, since the Tkaches had corrupted the softbound and serial versions.

The day we received our first copy from Mr. Carroll, we happened to be finalizing edits for the January 1997 *Trumpet*. We didn't count on the *Mystery* print run finishing as soon as it did, so we didn't have anything prepared for that January issue officially announcing this tremendous step forward for our work. We decided at the last minute, however, to at least produce a back cover ad offering our readers, for the *first time ever,* a free copy of *Mystery of the Ages.* It was headlined "Solve the Mystery!"[22]

Mr. Carroll told us the *Trumpet* would not arrive in mailboxes until mid-January. So we had a couple more weeks until we absolutely had to say something. Our own church members, let alone the Worldwide Church of God, had no idea all this was going on.

"BATTLE CRY"

At church services on January 4, 1997, my father held up a large book and excitedly told our brethren, "This is the *Mystery of the Ages*—OUR version of it." As he proceeded to tell the members about the ad to appear on the back page of the next *Trumpet,* gasps of amazement rippled through the meeting hall. He said, "Today we have decided to print that book and give it away free, and just simply take the consequences—if there are any. And that will be, of course, *entirely* up to God." Later, he told members he was more concerned about the consequences for *not* printing the book than he was for printing it. This is a theme that would surface time and again over the next six years: TAKING THE BATTLE TO THE WCG WITH OFFENSIVE STRIKES. "We will do what has to be done," my father said, "and then the ball is in [the WCG's] court, as they say."[23]

The other theme that would play out during that same period was FAITH. My father said in the sermon, "I feel that Jesus Christ is not going to tolerate that book not being printed any longer. I believe that. And I'm willing to base a lot on that." Later, he exclaimed enthusiastically, "That book belongs to us! God says so. And God will back and support us. He's promised to do that."[24] From the beginning, my father charged ahead with the full assurance that God was on our side. Added to that, we firmly believed that by suppressing the work of Mr. Armstrong, the WCG's actions violated the Constitution. But however this might unfold in a court of law, it was secondary to the premise underlying our action from the beginning—*that God wanted Mr. Armstrong's teaching disseminated.*

The *Trumpet* at that time had a modest circulation of nearly 60,000. Once subscribers started receiving their issue in mid-January, the requests for *Mystery* started pouring in. In the first week after the ad hit, we received 2,000 requests for the book.

Soon after the *Mystery* ad first appeared on the back cover of the *Trumpet,* we prepared something much more substantial for our seven-year anniversary issue in February. We put a picture of the book on the cover, over the headline, "Where We Are Going!" My father titled his Personal "The Largest Audience Possible." In it, he described a "new phase" for our work, where the focus of our message would now be aimed primarily at the world, as opposed to members and former members of the Worldwide Church of God. He wrote,

> *Mystery of the Ages* was like the magnificent SUMMARY OF ALL Mr. Armstrong's work—THE ACCUMULATED KNOWLEDGE OF HIS ENTIRE MINISTRY. This book, more than any other piece of literature, was what Mr. Armstrong and God's work were about. ... Mr. Armstrong wanted it to reach "the largest audience possible." ...

I BELIEVE "THE LARGEST AUDIENCE POSSIBLE" SHOULD BECOME OUR BATTLE CRY TODAY! ... This is our most critical hour. We must pick up the dropped baton and finish the gun lap! We must stretch and strain to win the greatest race we will ever run![25] [Emphasis in original.]

This became our battle cry in 1997: THE LARGEST AUDIENCE POSSIBLE. It was what Mr. Armstrong wanted all along. To *think* about what MIGHT HAVE BEEN, had the Tkaches just followed in Mr. Armstrong's footsteps, as the elder Tkach SAID he would do at Mr. Armstrong's funeral. It agonizes us to think about what the WCG *could have done*—with Mr. Armstrong's well-established, decades-long track record and all the personnel, resources, tools and income the church had at its disposal when Mr. Armstrong died. As it was, Tkachism quickly turned all the advantages of that multi-million-dollar media empire AGAINST its founder's message—even to the point of destroying *Mystery of the Ages* within 32 months.

Delivering that message to the largest audience possible was now left to a faithful few who sought refuge from Tkachism inside the Philadelphia Church of God. Our work in 1997—even after seven years of steady, upward growth—was a microcosmic version of the work Mr. Armstrong gifted to Mr. Tkach in 1986. Reaching the whole world using only a fraction of the resources and power the church once had in Mr. Armstrong's day would not be easy. And making matters more difficult, every step of our progress would be met with angry, hostile resistance by those bent on destroying Mr. Armstrong's legacy and betraying his ideals.

WE WERE AT WAR! But we knew what we were fighting for. And we had a battle cry.

"Are you ready? Am I ready?" my father asked in his *Trumpet* Personal. "We have an unparalleled opportunity. In terms of numbers of people, we can be the fewest people to do the greatest work ever on this Earth!"[26]

SEVENTEEN
BATTLE LINES DRAWN

"We feel it is our Christian duty to keep this book out of print ... because we believe Mr. Armstrong's doctrinal errors are better left out of circulation."

— JOSEPH TKACH JR.
Transformed by Truth

O N February 10, 1997, as my wife and I flew across the Atlantic to Europe for our honeymoon, WCG attorneys, including in-house lawyer Ralph Helge, crossed the street in downtown Los Angeles to file papers against the PCG in a federal court. Three weeks earlier, on January 21, Mr. Helge penned this letter to my father demanding that the PCG stop distribution of *Mystery of the Ages:*

Dear Mr. Flurry:

It has just come to the church's attention, through the January 1997 edition of your *Trumpet* magazine, that you are offering the book, entitled *Mystery of the Ages*, for distribution.

As you are well aware, the Worldwide Church of God holds the copyright of said book. We are assuming that you are distributing an infringing copy of the same. Therefore, we hereby respectfully demand that you immediately cease and desist from copying, distributing or advertising said book.

We would appreciate your advising us by what authority you are, without the permission of the church, copying and publishing said book?

Please advise us promptly as to your intentions in this matter. If we do not hear from you promptly we shall assume that you are violating the church's copyright in said regard and that it is your intention to continue to do so. In such case, we will take appropriate action without further notice.[1]

My father was already prepared for the consequences of his actions. If that meant going to court to fight for "said book," then so be it. He decided not to respond to Helge's letter. The battle lines were clearly drawn.

In its February 10 complaint, the wcg suggested that since the pcg might receive public donations for its free distribution of the book, these donations would *deprive* the wcg of the "benefits" of *Mystery of the Ages*. We were robbing them of income! They also claimed that because of our action, the relationship between them and their members had been injured. According to the brief, the wcg had already suffered "irreparable damage."[2]

Our offices didn't find out about the court filing until the next day, on February 11, when we received a letter from wcg attorney Benjamin Scheibe of the law offices of Browne & Woods in Beverly Hills. He informed us that on February 12, they would file an Ex Parte Application, asking the judge for a temporary restraining order that would immediately stop us from distribution.[3] (An *ex parte* order is a legal instrument made by or in the interest of only one party to an action, in the absence of the other party.)

To that point, our experience with law firms was minimal—limited to wills and trusts mostly. Now we found ourselves brawling with a church more than 10 times our size and represented by the same law firm that stood down the state of California when it attacked the wcg in 1979! Dennis Leap, who *became* the pcg legal department the day we found out about the lawsuit, called Terry Moyer in South Carolina. Married to our television agent, Mr. Moyer was one of the few lawyers we knew personally. (Terry is the one who recommended the D.C. attorney I called to ask about the copyright notice.) Though we had never solicited his legal services, we had met with him on several occasions. Terry agreed to represent us for a few days until he could track down a reputable law firm in Southern California.

Moyer responded to Scheibe's letter the next day: "Please be advised that the Philadelphia Church of God strongly objects to any ex parte proceedings and intends to fully and vigorously contest any and all claims asserted against it ...."[4] Two days later, on February 14, we found out that the ex parte hearing had been set for the following week, on February 18.

LITIGATION BEGINS

On Monday, February 17, on the advice of Terry Moyer, we hired the services of the Los Angeles law firm Munger, Tolles & Olson. Mark Helm, who had been appointed lead attorney for the case, had *one day* to prepare for the hearing. Terry quickly brought him up to speed on the most relevant details of this unusual case, via phone and fax. That night, Mark spoke with Dennis Leap over the phone for about an hour.

The next day, Mark Helm stood before Judge Spencer Letts in a Los Angeles courtroom without anyone from the PCG at his side. He was on his own, having had one day to prepare for this case. The judge had read the WCG's brief and wondered why there was nothing filed by the PCG. Mr. Helm explained to the court that he had only come on board with the PCG "recently" and didn't yet know all the facts. We simply did not have enough time to file a response. He was, however, able to offer this succinct explanation to Judge Letts:

> This is not a case where the Worldwide Church of God is exploiting the copyright in order to disseminate and earn profits from *Mystery of the Ages;* this is a case where they are trying to suppress and not disseminate Mr. Armstrong's books; that's our understanding.[5]

To which Judge Letts responded, *"That's mine as well."*[6] Our attorney was stunned by this response. *With only the WCG's brief to go on,* Judge Letts clearly and quickly established that in his view, the WCG had no right to suppress Mr. Armstrong's works! Later in the hearing, the judge turned to the WCG's attorney and said,

> You're not going to be dealing with a closed mind, but what I know about this case, but for what Mr. Helm [just] said, is what you've told me, and it raises, in my judgment, very serious questions and *very serious irreparable harm on the other side as well.* [7]

The way he saw it, they were guilty of what they accused us of doing! They caused us "irreparable harm" by attempting to suppress Mr. Armstrong's works.

In response to the judge's suggestion that the WCG would lose based on the merits of the case, WCG attorney Benjamin Scheibe exclaimed, "I'm somewhat at a loss with the Court's suggestion, [that] there's not a probability of success on the merits here." That became the WCG's typical response early on in the litigation—they reacted incredulously to anyone who viewed this case as anything other than a simple, garden-variety copyright infringement. *They owned the copyright, therefore we couldn't print the book.* It was as simple as that—*to them.*

But not us, nor to Judge Letts, nor, as would soon become clear, to many others in the legal world. This was an unusual lawsuit. It was a case where a religious entity was *using* its copyright to SUPPRESS a work it no longer agreed with. Here is how Judge Letts assessed the dispute in that first hearing:

> The copyright seems to me to have two primary purposes, neither of which are at issue here. One is to keep there from being confusion about who is the person publishing the work; the second is to keep strangers from profiting from the work. Neither of those is at issue with somebody who wants to suppress the work entirely. ... It wasn't a question of whether there would be two publishers, or three, but rather whether there will be one or none. [8]

Scheibe's persistence would not change the judge's mind. "I

don't think you are going to prevail on the merits," the judge told him. "I understand your position," he later said, "but I don't agree with it." Mr. Armstrong, Judge Letts said,

> didn't dream that by giving this copyright to the corporation, which was his corporation that reflected his religion, that those who would come after him would use their corporate power to suppress his religion or to keep any prior practitioners of his religion ... from making that book available on a continuous, freshly printed basis, I don't believe the founder dreamed that.[9]

Scheibe argued that the WCG hadn't suppressed or abandoned the work because they still had *archival* copies. Plus, there were some copies in libraries! Scheibe said, "[A]bandonment requires overt acts such as destroying the last copies of a work"—which, of course, is precisely what the WCG did with the 120,000 surplus copies it had in early 1988.

We bounced off the walls that day at our headquarters complex after receiving word that Judge Letts denied their request for a temporary restraining order. That first hearing emboldened my father—God had backed his leap of faith. He knew we might be in for a lengthy and bitter dispute. But after such an overwhelming victory that early in the case, he was all the more convinced that God would support our actions—as long as they pleased Him and we walked by faith.

Judge Letts set the preliminary injunction hearing for March 10.

MEETING THE ATTORNEYS

Two days after the ex parte hearing, Dennis Leap, my father and I flew to Los Angeles to meet our lawyers for the first time. Before entering their firm the afternoon of February 20, the three of us met to discuss how we might best explain our strategy to the attorneys. We also considered the immediate steps our church might take now that Judge Letts denied the WCG's request for a temporary restraining order. For one, my father wondered if we should immediately start offering *Mystery of the Ages* on our television program. My dad also directed me to begin work on an ad campaign in Southern California newspapers. "Now that we have absorbed their initial blow," he said, "we have to strike back." He believed newspaper ads in their own backyard would help to expose their hypocrisy and lies.

After lunch, we met with Mark Helm and Ruth Fisher at the Los Angeles offices of Munger, Tolles & Olson. Kelly Klaus, in the San Francisco office, listened in over the phone. That afternoon, and the following day, the three of us explained the history of our work and its intimate association with the teachings of Mr. Armstrong. We told them about how the Tkaches had gotten control of the WCG and repudiated Mr. Armstrong's teachings and disfellowshiped many of those who adhered to the founder's body of beliefs.

The attorneys, in turn, familiarized us with a litigation road map. While the judge's denial of the restraining order was indeed a victory, the war had only just begun. The stakes would be much higher at the March 10 hearing. Preliminary injunction hearings can go a long way toward deciding the outcome of a case, we learned.

After our meetings concluded on February 21, Mr. Helm contacted Scheibe to request discovery, a pre-trial procedure by which one side gains information held by the other. Within their complaint, the WCG claimed to own the copyright to *Mystery of the Ages* because at the time it was written, Mr. Armstrong was "an officer and employee of the WCG."[10] We intended to challenge that assertion by arguing that Mr. Armstrong was the one who *raised up* and ESTABLISHED the church. Saying he was a WCG "employee" implied that some higher authority in the WCG "hired" him.

CHURCH GOVERNANCE

The "employee" issue was a critical point early on in the case because of how often we repeated Mr. Armstrong's final instructions regarding *Mystery of the Ages*—to distribute it to the "largest audience possible." In response to this, the WCG tried to show that what Mr. Armstrong said was irrelevant, *legally* speaking, because he was under the *church's* control.

At his 1998 deposition, Ralph Helge admitted that while there was no written employment agreement between Mr. Armstrong and the church, it was "common knowledge" that he was an employee. When asked if there was any person in the wcg who controlled Mr. Armstrong's work, Mr. Helge said the church's board of directors had a "certain degree of control." Later, Helge said the board even had the authority to *fire* Mr. Armstrong.[11]

Our attorney, Kelly Klaus, then reviewed a number of important statements made by Mr. Armstrong at a ministerial conference in 1981 (a transcript of which is printed in the March 6, 1981, *Worldwide News*). In his lecture, Mr. Armstrong explained that the church of God is a *spiritual* organism, but UNINCORPORATED. There were, however, a number of "support entities" in the church, mostly physical, that *were* incorporated, including the Worldwide Church of God, a California corporation. The members of the Worldwide Church of God, Inc., Mr. Armstrong explained, "are the officers that sign the corporation papers."[12]

At his deposition, we asked Mr. Helge about which entity exercised control over the other—the spiritual or the incorporated? Mr. Armstrong said the latter was "incorporated *under myself.*"[13] What he meant by that, Mr. Helge testified, was that the incorporated entity was subordinate to the "spiritual entity"—*but not to Mr. Armstrong.*[14]

Fair enough. The wcg had always believed that the living, *invisible,* Jesus Christ headed the church. But we also believed that Christ works *through* physical men. And His human representative, prior to January 16, 1986, was Herbert W. Armstrong. If *anyone* understood that, it would have been Ralph Helge, since he was the one who helped Mr. Armstrong draw up the church's bylaws and articles of association. Mr. Helge testified that the unincorporated association—the *spiritual* organism, keep in mind—basically didn't have any temporal responsibilities. Regarding the corporate entity, he indicated that Mr. Armstrong did *not* have "absolute right to tell the board of directors to do this or that."[15]

We then referred him to the church's articles of association, which state that the "Church Authority" has control over the "ecclesiastical" and "temporal" affairs of the church. And what did it mean by "Church Authority"? Article 2.1 says it means the "power

and authority *vested in Herbert W. Armstrong* and his duly autho-
rized delegates," which included the Advisory Council of Elders.
Later, in article 5.2, it says, "The authority and power of Herbert
W. Armstrong to unilaterally exercise all the powers of the Church
over the ecclesiastical and temporal affairs of the church shall be
absolute and unqualified."[16]

That we were trying to convince Mr. Armstrong's own legal
adviser that the WCG's government structure was hierarchical
seemed absurd. *Everyone* in the WCG knew that! After reading the
church's articles of association during his deposition, Mr. Helge
said, "I don't think it's proper to look at it and interpret it that he
ran things like a despot."[17] Of course, that's the *exact opposite* of
what we were trying to say. Mr. Armstrong governed the church
like a loving father—always seeking a multitude of counsel. But he
did have final say—and since some of his last instructions to the
church had to do with distributing *Mystery of the Ages* widely, his
authority in the church was of special significance.

Ironically, Joseph Tkach Jr., Mr. Helge's own boss at the time of
his deposition, is the one who interpreted the church's governance
doctrine to mean that Mr. Armstrong was a despot. In his book,
Tkach Jr. said Mr. Armstrong "was most definitely and absolutely in
charge of our church"—so much so, he had earned the reputation
from critics outside the church as being a "theological despot." [18]
It is even more ironic that the "absolute authority" Tkach Jr. freely
condemns in his book is the very means by which Tkach Sr. landed
in the office of pastor general in 1986, not to mention Tkach Jr. in
1995. (The all-powerful "board" had no say in either appointment.)
It's also the means by which the Tkaches excommunicated *thousands* of WCG members who simply desired to adhere to the same
teachings they had always been taught by Mr. Armstrong.

Early on in the court case, Ralph Helge portrayed Mr.
Armstrong as just another church employee—hired or fired by THE
BOARD. It then followed, that the church—or THE BOARD—had final
say on this legal matter regarding *Mystery of the Ages*.

Outside of court, however, Tkach Jr. portrayed Mr. Armstrong
as a corrupt, theological despot who wielded absolute power within
the WCG.

Witnessing this duplicity up close in the early stages of the court case brought back painful memories of how the Tkaches forced their changes on the church back in the late 1980s. It didn't take long before we realized we were going to have to live through much of that late 1980s history all over again.

FORUM SHOPPING

In their discovery request, the WCG asked us for an accurate count of how many books had been distributed as well as the amount of donations the PCG received as a result of distribution. We wanted to complete this initial exchange of discovery by the end of the day on Monday, February 24, 1997, so we could meet our February 27 deadline for filing our opposition to their complaint.

The following week, on Tuesday, we had not yet received any documents from the other side. Mark again contacted them to remind them that our opposition was due in only a couple days. Scheibe said the WCG was having problems gathering the documents because much of it was tucked away in storage.

On Wednesday, the day before our opposition was due, we still hadn't received documents from the WCG. Mr. Scheibe said they needed more time to locate the documents and asked if we would be amenable to delaying the briefing and hearing by one week, assuming it was fine with the judge. We agreed and later the judge pushed the hearing back to March 17, which also gave us another week to prepare our opposition brief. Scheibe said he would have discovery responses to us by the end of the week.

Two days later, toward the end of the day on Friday, Scheibe left Mark a voice mail that knocked our socks off. He said the WCG had filed a motion to dismiss the lawsuit. Just *18 days* into the litigation, they had already given up! And we hadn't even received *any* items of discovery—nor had we filed one single opposition brief in court.

The next day, at our weekly church service, PCG members applauded the news.

The following Monday, March 3, Mark Helm called the WCG's attorney to make sure he understood Friday's voice mail correctly.

Scheibe confirmed that the California action had indeed been dismissed.

Later that day, at our headquarters offices in Edmond, Oklahoma, we were served papers by courier. The WCG filed a new complaint in *Oklahoma*. It was a stunning blow—although we weren't necessarily shocked that the WCG would resort to manipulating the system.

In its new complaint, the WCG said it dismissed the action in California because it learned that the Philadelphia Church intended to contest the case on the basis that it should not have been filed there—a blatant fabrication. In actuality, at the February 18 hearing, Mark Helm only reserved *the right* to dispute personal jurisdiction. He had only been hired the day before, remember, and he hadn't yet assembled all the facts of the case.

The WCG turned our reservation of rights into an attempt on our part to challenge jurisdiction.

But after the hearing, once Mark pressed Scheibe for discovery *on the merits,* it was abundantly clear that we intended to move forward and fight the action in California. Scheibe himself is the one who suggested we delay the brief filing by one week so that both sides might have more time to collect discovery. As it turned out, that one-week delay prevented us from ever filing our opposition on the merits of the case. That delay, brought on by Scheibe, gave the WCG another week to think about stuff they could make up.

The real reason they dismissed the action in California on February 28 and filed one in Oklahoma the next business day is because they were shopping for a judge who would support their position.

THE AD CAMPAIGN

Shifting venues enabled the WCG to beef up its argument since Judge Letts had made it clear that their case was weak. In the California filing, they said nothing about the WCG's repudiation of Mr. Armstrong's teachings. Their main thrust was that they owned the copyright and *that,* in itself, should prevent us from printing and distributing the book.

In the Oklahoma action, however, they were much more forth-right about their turn away from Mr. Armstrong's teachings. They admitted the church had "intentionally not reprinted the book" due to a modification in doctrine, but felt obligated to "protect" its copyright. They said that while the PCG is free to believe the book's teachings, we could not go so far as to publish it. To do that, we would have to come up with our "own original expression of the ideas."[19] Furthermore, the Oklahoma complaint said,

> Because of this change in belief, Worldwide Church suffers irreparable injury by Philadelphia Church's unlawful reproduction and distribution of *Mystery of the Ages* because it does so with the purpose of perpetuating beliefs no longer followed by Worldwide Church.[20]

Ah yes! The real truth emerges. They told Judge Letts they suffered "irreparable damage" because we had "profited" from distributing the work (the donation "profit" was actually *theirs,* in other words) and because they had been "forced to incur attorneys' fees."[21] Now their suffering stemmed from the fact that we were perpetuating beliefs and teachings *they no longer agreed with!* It was the closest they ever got in court to saying they wanted to suppress Mr. Armstrong's teachings.

Taking that as our cue, we quickly went to work producing newspaper ads while our attorneys began working with an Oklahoma lawyer to answer the WCG's latest complaint. On March 5, in a meeting with Dennis Leap and me, my father said he wanted us to look upon this second attack from the WCG as a "tremendous opportunity." We have to regain the advantage by taking the offensive, he said. He explained that he felt the WCG's biggest weakness was being exposed before the general public. It was before that audience that the WCG had bragged about the "unprecedented" transformation their church had undergone since Mr. Armstrong's death. Our job, my dad said, was to show how this was actually one of the biggest *betrayals* in the history of religion. He felt like newspaper ads would be the easiest and quickest way to get the true story out there. He advised us to come up with a provocative sounding headline—something like, "Why are they desperately trying to keep *you* from reading *Mystery of the Ages?*"

My dad put pen to paper and worked up a rough draft of the copy while I started working on the ad design. Mr. Leap and I helped with some of the research for the ad. After we polished it off, we consulted our attorneys about the wording. It had to be just right.

Then, on Tuesday, March 18, our first newspaper ad appeared on page 14 of the front section of the *Los Angeles Times* under the headline, "Worldwide Church of God says: You can't read this book!"[22] Next to the headline was a picture of *Mystery of the Ages.* In the days that followed, the ad also appeared in several smaller papers in Southern California, as well as the *Washington Post* and *Denver Post.*

Using less than 1,000 words, we summarized the history of Tkach's rejection of Mr. Armstrong's teachings and how more than half of the WCG membership had been driven out of that church— many of them excommunicated. We also discussed the most significant details of the lawsuit. "Although Mr. Armstrong's successors have seized his church and betrayed his ideals," the ad read, "they should not be allowed to silence his voice." It continued,

> If the Worldwide Church of God no longer has any use for *Mystery of the Ages,* it should not be allowed to keep the book from those who do.
>
> The Philadelphia Church and the Worldwide Church are in a battle over religious beliefs. Rather than try to persuade potential believers to adopt one of two competing approaches, the Worldwide Church wants to conceal one of them altogether. This can only be because it recognizes the power and clarity of Mr. Armstrong's vision, and lacks confidence in the appeal of its own muddled and compromised approach.[23]

We wanted to expose their religious censorship in public, within their own community, and plug Mr. Armstrong's wonderful book at the same time. As my dad told Mr. Leap and me in February, "An ad campaign will help us achieve our goal." *And did it ever.* Several thousand people responded to our campaign by requesting *Mystery of the Ages.* In the weeks that followed, we produced two follow-up ads. Together, all three ads appeared in over a dozen newspapers.

But much more important than that, at least with respect to the litigation, is how the wcg *reacted* to the campaign. Our ads got right under their skin and put them on the defensive, as my father predicted they would. Mr. Helge contacted the newspapers we used in the Los Angeles basin, demanding retractions and even threatening litigation.

THEIR CHRISTIAN DUTY

At about the time our first ad appeared in the *Los Angeles Times,* Joe Tkach Jr. was putting the finishing touches on his new book, *Transformed by Truth,* to be released later that summer. Our March 18 ad prompted him to add this footnote on page 203 of his book:

> In February 1997 we filed suit against the Philadelphia Church of God—one of our splinter groups headquartered in Edmund [sic], Oklahoma—to block the republication of *Mystery of the Ages.* The Worldwide Church of God still holds the copyright to this book, and we contend that no one else has the right to publish it. We feel it is our CHRISTIAN DUTY TO KEEP THIS BOOK OUT OF PRINT, not because we recognize "the power and clarity of Mr. Armstrong's vision" or because our church "lacks confidence in the appeal of its own muddled and compromised approach," *as an advertisement for the Philadelphia church claims,* but because we believe Mr. Armstrong's doctrinal errors are better left out of circulation.[24]

That one footnote was perhaps the wcg's biggest blunder during the six-year lawsuit. In the Oklahoma complaint, remember, they said we caused them irreparable injury for perpetuating beliefs they no longer followed. Now we had a much stronger statement, *and direct from their own pastor general,* saying they had a "CHRISTIAN

DUTY" to suppress Mr. Armstrong's written works! Our *Los Angeles Times* ad was just too nettlesome for Tkach Jr. to ignore.

The "Christian duty" statement put the WCG in a nearly indefensible position from the outset. How would they convince any judge or jury that they weren't really using their copyright to suppress Mr. Armstrong's writings when, in fact, their own leader said it was his "Christian duty" to keep the works out of print?

And it was all brought to the surface by one single newspaper ad. That is what provoked Tkach Jr. to spontaneously (and publicly) reveal his true motive for filing the lawsuit from the beginning. It wasn't *to protect what they considered to be a valuable asset,* as we would hear later. Nor was it because *they had big plans for* Mystery of the Ages *down the road—perhaps distributing the work again in some kind of annotated form.* And it wasn't because *they were intent on making all of Mr. Armstrong's works available through e-publishing for historical purposes and to accommodate the spiritual needs of our* PCG *membership.*

Those were all LIES that would resuscitate their case from time to time in the years that followed. But what *killed* their case from the beginning is when Tkach Jr., in a brief, angry reaction to a newspaper ad, sat in front of his computer and actually typed *the truth.* As ABSOLUTE RULER in the WCG, he admitted he had a "Christian duty" to destroy Mr. Armstrong's written works.

EIGHTEEN
ROUND ONE: PCG

*"While the Church is not presently reprinting these books, the board
affirmed that the Church has a continuing interest in his books and did
not, and does not, intend to abandon the copyrights."*

— WORLDWIDE CHURCH OF GOD BOARD MINUTES
April 2, 1997

I N Oklahoma, we immediately tried to alert the new judge, Vicki
Miles-LaGrange, to the WCG's antics in California—that Judge
Letts denied their application for a temporary restraining order
and indicated the WCG would lose on the merits. We explained how
the WCG lulled us into preparing our defense against the California
action, all the while planning to transfer the action to Oklahoma.
We asked Judge Miles-LaGrange to immediately transfer the case
back to California to "thwart WCG's blatant attempt at forum shopping."[1] On March 11, she denied our ex parte request, saying
she wanted to hear both sides out before making a decision. So
we pressed forward, now tackling the case from two angles—the
merits and the application to *transfer* the action back to California.
(Actually, we also introduced a third angle in Oklahoma. More on
this later.)

Now that we wanted to move the case back to California, the
WCG accused us of the very thing we were so upset about—"forum

shopping"! In opposition to our motion for transfer, the WCG's Oklahoma attorney insisted that

> this action was filed in this forum solely because Philadelphia Church preserved a personal jurisdiction challenge to the previous lawsuit filed in California. *Immediately* upon learning of such a challenge, Worldwide Church properly dismissed that action ... and filed this action in this judicial district where the Philadelphia Church is located.[2]

Later in the brief, their attorney made a point to say that we never even filed a response to their California action—failing to mention that two days before our response was due, even as we were pressing the WCG for discovery on the merits of the case, Benjamin Scheibe asked if we would delay our opposition by one week, as they were having "trouble" locating the requested documents. Then, on February 28 the WCG pulled the rug out from under us by dropping the California action.

THE OTHER ANGLE

While the dispute over the venue raged on, we continued working on the merits of the case—particularly our defense. As stated in our opposition brief, filed on March 24, we believed our action to distribute *Mystery* was protected by the free exercise clause of the First Amendment as well as the Religious Freedom Restoration Act—a law Congress enacted to help prevent other laws from stifling one's religious freedoms. And should the judge narrow the scope of the ruling to the copyright law alone, even within those bounds, we felt like our reproduction of the book was valid under the copyright's "fair use" doctrine. We also argued that, by its action, the WCG had abandoned its copyright to *Mystery of the Ages*.

More significant than this, however, is the *offensive* posture we took in our counterclaim. In the "prayer for relief," we asked the court to not only dismiss the WCG's claim, but to reward us with the rights to print and distribute 18 *other works* by Mr. Armstrong.[3] As with the advertising campaign, we again wanted to get ourselves on offensive footing. This was central to my father's strategy throughout the case—if the plaintiff would come on strong, we would meet the aggression head-on and take it a step further. As small as we were (compared to them) and even though a "defendant," he wanted us to continually wrap our minds around the fact that *we* were on the attack and that *we* would somehow come out victorious in the end. Thus, seven weeks after first getting our feet wet in this case—in any kind of litigation, for that matter—we unleashed a counterattack. They chose to come after us in an attempt to keep *Mystery* buried. We determined to defend against that action—*and to go after more literature* at the same time. Here are the works we targeted in our counterclaim:

> *The Ambassador College Bible Correspondence Course* (58 lessons)
> *The Incredible Human Potential*
> *The United States and Britain in Prophecy*
> *The Wonderful World Tomorrow—What It Will Be Like*
> *The Missing Dimension in Sex*
> *The Autobiography of Herbert W. Armstrong* (volumes 1 and 2)
> *The Plain Truth About Healing*
> *What Science Can't Discover About the Human Mind*
> *Pagan Holidays or God's Holy Days—Which?*
> *Does God Exist?*
> *Which Day Is the Christian Sabbath?*
> *The Seven Laws of Success*
> *Who or What Is the Prophetic Beast?*
> *Just What Do You Mean ... Born Again?*
> *Why Marriage! Soon Obsolete?*
> *The Proof of the Bible*
> *What Is Faith?*

We didn't realize it at the time, but my father's decision to go after these 18 works affected the lawsuit's final outcome *more than any other single event.*

END OF OKLAHOMA ACTION

During April and May, activity in the lawsuit slowed considerably, in part due to Judge LaGrange's busy trial schedule. On April 21, however, the wcg did file a motion asking the court to dismiss our counterclaim. They said there was no "case or controversy" regarding the additional 18 works we were now seeking. Their complaint had to do with *Mystery* only, they contended.[4] And of course, that was true. We just wanted to up the ante.

Six weeks later, incredibly, the wcg withdrew its opposition to our motion to transfer and *actually asked the court to go ahead and return the case to California*. It was another stunning turn of events—and this time not easy to explain. Maybe the wcg was frustrated over the slow pace of events in Oklahoma. Perhaps they realized how much easier it was to litigate from their home turf in California. Maybe they were resigned to the fact that they would lose at the district level—whether in Oklahoma or California—and were just eager to get the loss on the fast track so they could appeal it. Whatever the reason, we braced ourselves for fighting them in whatever venue it settled in.

Two weeks later, having yet to hear from Judge LaGrange regarding the motions to transfer or to dismiss the counterclaim, the wcg filed its reply to our counterclaim. According to the brief, the wcg denied that it "stopped printing" *Mystery,* but rather "chose not to re-publish or continue distributing the *Mystery of the Ages* for the present." It had only been *temporarily* put aside, they told the court. As proof of their new-found desire to use Mr. Armstrong's writings, they were able to put forward minutes from a board of directors meeting, where the subject was discussed. "[T]he Church continues to work with the text of the books in an ongoing manner for possible future use."[5]

You can see why the "Christian duty" statement, which landed in bookstores later that summer, was so critical to our case. They NOT ONLY STOPPED PRINTING *Mystery,* they wanted to *stop others* from printing it too—Tkach Jr. said so, *explicitly,* in his own book! But to serve their purposes in court, they made it sound like they had future plans for *Mystery of the Ages.*

On June 30, 1997, Judge LaGrange granted our motion to transfer the action back to California. Thus, we were back where we started.

STATUS CONFERENCE WITH JUDGE LETTS

Now that the case was back in California, we quickly filed a motion to make sure it returned into Judge Letts's courtroom, lest the wcg get away with its judge-shopping shenanigans. On August 18, Judge Letts was indeed appointed to preside over our case. Two weeks later, lawyers for both sides arranged for a conference call with Judge Letts to hammer out some divisive issues. Upset by the legal wrangling, the judge requested for both clients, with their attorneys, to appear in his court chambers for a status conference.

September 25, 1997, was the first of many times we would meet face to face with our opposition. I distinctly remember my initial exchange with Ralph Helge. "I enjoy your articles in the *Trumpet,* Stephen," he said, after meeting me for the first time. At the time, back in Edmond, we were wrapping up production on our November issue—in which I accused the wcg of deceitfully lying about Mr. Armstrong's teachings over the years. "Why did the Worldwide Church of God discontinue *Mystery of the Ages*?" I asked in an article titled "Lying Words." "The answer to that question varies, depending upon who you are, when you ask it, and whom you happen to ask."[6]

Inside the judge's chambers, after we complained about the wcg's removal of Mr. Armstrong's most important book, Mr. Helge exclaimed, *with a straight face,* "We've never had any intention or decision to *not* publish it!" We were flabbergasted, especially since Tkach Jr.'s book with the "Christian duty" statement had just been released.

Helge then let loose another corker, suggesting that we actually *submit an offer* to license the book from the wcg. Here again, in the light of Tkach Jr.'s "Christian duty" statement, any such offer would have been entirely futile. In fact, a month before Helge's bizarre suggestion in the judge's chambers, wcg officer Greg Albrecht sent this message to an individual seeking to reprint some of the church's articles and booklets: "[W]e cannot grant your request to publish our old articles and booklets. We hold the copyright, and do not allow others to publish our former teachings and doctrines *for a variety of reasons.*"[7]

Later in the lawsuit, in 1999, the wcg even acknowledged in its own court filing that any such offer would have been rejected:

PCG did not request permission; Flurry explained that others had requested such permission but WCG had refused to allow reprinting of the book. *Flurry understood that the WCG refused these requests in order to protect its copyright* in Mystery of the Ages, thereby establishing that PCG knew full well that WCG had no intention of abandoning its copyright.[8]

Here, the WCG actually pointed to the obvious futility of any such offer as *proof* that it had NOT abandoned its copyright. At the same time, they even tried to turn Tkach's "Christian duty" statement in their favor, saying it actually established "an intent to *enforce* the copyright."[9] *Think about that.* That Tkach Jr. said it was the church's "Christian duty to keep [*Mystery of the Ages*] out of print" only proved, they told the court, that the WCG still owned and, in fact, was using the copyright.

Of course, they were "using" the copyright, but only to prevent Mr. Armstrong's ideas from circulating.

TWO MAIN POINTS

When the WCG filed its original complaint in early 1997, it had to make two essential points, for the most part: 1) that the WCG owned the copyright to *Mystery of the Ages;* and 2) that the PCG had no lawful right to print and distribute the work.

The first point wasn't as straightforward as one might think. Since the original author of *Mystery of the Ages* was dead, the WCG had to show how copyright ownership had transferred into its possession. Early on, rather than rely on Mr. Armstrong's last will and testament, they tried to prove ownership by saying that everything Mr. Armstrong, as an "employee" of the church, wrote belonged to the church. They opted for this strategy because it would then make Mr. Armstrong's final wishes for the book seem inconsequential.

Obviously, Mr. Armstrong would have wanted the copyright to protect and preserve his material—not destroy it. But since he was only one "employee" working at a huge organization, "hired" to produce a book, what he wanted didn't much matter, as far as "the church" was concerned.

On the second point, the WCG had to prove the copyright law somehow precluded us from distributing *Mystery of the Ages.* That wasn't as straightforward as they made it out to be either, because we never claimed to be the actual owner of the copyright. And since we were not claiming ownership for ourselves, the WCG had to prove that what we did violated the Copyright Act—in particular, that it was *not* a "fair use" of the work.

FAIR USE

Irrespective of who owned the copyright to *Mystery of the Ages,* or whether the WCG abandoned it or not, if the court found our action to be protected by "fair use," it was a done deal—we could print the book. So the fair use doctrine was of prime concern for both parties in this first round of litigation.

Section 107 of the Copyright Act says that "the fair use of a copyrighted work, including such use by reproduction in copies ..., for purposes such as criticism, comment, news reporting, *teaching* (including multiple copies for classroom use), scholarship, or research, is *not* an infringement of copyright." Section 107 then notes four factors for a court to consider in determining whether or not the copied material is protected by fair use:

> 1) The purpose and character of the use, including whether such use is of a commercial nature or is for nonprofit educational purposes;
> 2) The nature of the copyrighted work;
> 3) The amount and substantiality of the portion used in relation to the copyrighted work as a whole; and
> 4) The effect of the use upon the potential market for or value of the copyrighted work.[10]

We felt like all four of these determinative factors leaned in our favor. On the first point, without question, the PCG had distributed *Mystery* for non-profit religious and educational purposes. We offered the book absolutely free upon request. Regarding the nature of the work, since *Mystery of the Ages* is a factual account of Mr. Armstrong's teachings, as opposed to a work of fiction, that generally broadens the scope of fair use. The third factor considers whether the amount copied is reasonable in relation to its intended purpose. And since we use the entire text for teaching and educational purposes, we felt it reasonable to copy all of it. Finally, on the effect our printing had on the potential market and value of the book, there was none. The WCG didn't value it—nor were they looking to market it. Indeed, they wanted to destroy it and keep it out of circulation forever. That was their story, judging by the huge amount of written statements and oral communication that circulated inside and outside the church.

For litigation, however, they invented another story.

THE "ANNOTATED" VERSION

Joseph Tkach Jr. wrote *Transformed by Truth* during the first six months of 1997—the same time period litigation got off the ground over Mr. Armstrong's writings. After completing a final draft for his book, he submitted it to the church's board and they all gave it a liability reading. According to Tkach, after a few minor changes to the text, the board approved its publication. When asked at his deposition if the board agreed with the text of the book, Tkach said "they all felt it was accurate."[11]

We then asked him if he felt it was his "Christian duty" to keep *Mystery of the Ages* out of print. To which he responded, "*Not necessarily.*"[12] A ridiculously lengthy exchange then followed as we tried to get Mr. Tkach to admit he meant what he said in his own book! During the exchange, Tkach did say it was important for his church not to distribute "lies." But he also said the WCG had an obligation to protect the church's "assets," including the copyrights in question.[13]

Besides that, he informed us that the WCG *actually had plans* to use *Mystery of the Ages* again! Apparently, there had been many discussions about producing an annotated text that would correct all the "errors" in the original *Mystery of the Ages*. Mr. Tkach could not remember when those discussions began, whether it was before the lawsuit started or after. Greg Albrecht admitted in his testimony that it was "probably *after.*"[14] Tkach also admitted the annotated version would not be a "high priority" since the church was in the midst of massive cutbacks and downsizing.[15]

THE ADVISORY COUNCIL OF ELDERS

Three months after Tkach and Albrecht enlightened us about the annotation "project," the WCG formalized the pronouncement in *made-for-litigation* minutes from an Advisory Council of Elders (ACE) meeting. Prior to the lawsuit's beginning, keep in mind, there was not one shred of evidence indicating any intention of ever using *Mystery of the Ages* again. All the evidence—a mountainous pile of it—pointed to the fact that Mr. Tkach's "Christian duty" statement accurately reflected the church's position. So without any pre-1997 evidence to support their "big plans" for the literature argument, they had to make this up as the litigation unfolded.

This is what prompted these hilarious minutes from their December 4, 1998, Advisory Council meeting:

> It was and is a common practice for the WCG or the college to retire works from publication, or to rewrite them, either to express the concepts contained therein differently, express facts more accurately, or because of a change in doctrine. WCG and the college would dispose of excess inventory copies of such works, but archive, research and personal copies would be retained. This procedure was in accordance with the long-standing custom, practice and procedure of WCG and the college.[16]

Notice how they equate the occasional modifications Mr. Armstrong made to the church's teachings to Tkachism's wholesale destruction of our entire belief system. It's like saying a homeowner's routine maintenance around the house is equivalent to one who later inherits the house, demolishes it, and then obliterates and hauls off the very foundation on which it stood. "We are changing at the very core of our church," Mr. Tkach said in 1997.[17] So it would not be correct to say, *as it says in those minutes,* that the church merely "*modified* its doctrines" after Mr. Armstrong died. When Joe Tkach Jr. begins his book by saying the WCG has "renounced" Mr. Armstrong's "unbiblical teachings" and "embraced Christian orthodoxy," those are not the words of a *modifier,* so to speak. Mr. Tkach said the wcg changes were so "radical" and "unprecedented" that evangelicals at first had a hard time *believing it was even true.*[18] In *Christianity Today,* Ruth Tucker said she was "taken aback" by the wcg's transformation—a journey that turned a "heretical sect into an evangelical denomination."[19] According to the Advisory Council minutes,

> Mr. Armstrong explained many times how his doctrinal under-standing changed in many respects over the years as he came to understand new biblical truths. In fact, he chided other churches over the years for being committed to creeds that prevented them from accepting new truth and changing.[20]

As if Mr. Armstrong would have fully supported their "modifi-cations." This is the same despicable reasoning we heard in the late 1980s when the church started dismantling Mr. Armstrong's teach-ings. *Why, we're just doing the same thing Mr. Armstrong would be doing today if he were alive.* Back then it was at least more plausible, albeit deceitful. But to rehash that lame excuse *in 1998* after so much had been written about this unprecedented transformation? In his book, speaking on behalf of the wcg, Tkach said, "Today we reject what is well known as 'Armstrongism,' that is, adherence to the teachings of Herbert W. Armstrong in lieu of biblical evidence to the contrary."[21] That doesn't exactly leave you with the impression they are just following Mr. Armstrong's example of modifying a few teachings here and there.

The minutes go on to list a few of the doctrines Mr. Armstrong changed (as if that somehow justified their repudiation of "Armstrongism"). And because he sometimes retired or rewrote church literature to more accurately reflect a new understanding in doctrine, it naturally followed that Tkachism was doing the exact same thing.

> In fact, it has been the intent of wcg to consider revising, editing, or republishing moa, and other works to which it holds

copyright, in some annotated or revised form, and to distribute the same either free of charge, or, if selling them, at a reasonable price as an income producing item.

Retiring *Mystery of the Ages* was only temporary, you understand, "until appropriate revisions could be effectuated."[22]

JUDGE LETTS'S RULING

The preliminary injunction hearing was set for the afternoon of February 8, 1999. That morning, before we appeared in court, my father told Dennis Leap and me, "Although I don't know exactly what will happen today, I feel strongly that something positive will result."

It was my second appearance in court across the aisle from the WCG's representatives—and it was every bit as memorable as the first encounter. The five of us arrived first—our two attorneys carrying three-ring-binders. The rest of us had notepads and pens. Moments later, after we settled in, WCG reps, together with their Hollywood lawyers, came bounding through the doors—wheeling in giant file boxes, carrying huge books and binders. (And funnier than that, they never once touched the boxes of documents during the hearing.) They looked like they were ready for all-out war. But in Judge Letts's courtroom, they were barely able to fire off one round. Not but five minutes into the hearing, both sides knew where the judge stood.

"First, I don't think this was work for hire," the judge said. "I think that it's rather clear that ... Mr. Armstrong was not an employee and that this was not work for hire."[23]

He went on to say that he thought the question of who owned the copyright was a "little more complex" than either side had explained in their briefs. He asked that if the copyright transfers to someone, who then repudiates the teachings of the book, would that change the nature of the copyright? Could the successor then actually use the copyright to abolish the book, as opposed to protecting the ideas of the author? In the judge's view, the answer was NO. In such a scenario, the judge wondered if the copyright could even exist anymore! But even if it did, he said the copyright laws would not allow the wcg to suppress a written work.

In his judgment, our use of *Mystery of the Ages* was "fair use" under the Copyright Act simply because the book was not otherwise available. Regarding the "annotated version," the judge said, "I cannot imagine that if somehow there were a copyright on the Bible itself that somebody could buy that copyright and simply then say, *I'll only permit my annotated version of that to be in use.*" In fact, as he later brought out, should they pursue the annotated project further, a case could be made that our distribution of the original work would actually *increase* the market for their annotated version.[24]

As to the prospect of the wcg licensing the works to us, the judge also expressed this view: "If you are in a circumstance where you're simply saying they can't be used, I don't think there's any question about that."[25] In other words, it would be futile to seek licensing from caretakers who want to destroy the work. The judge never bought into their litigation-driven plan to "use" the works again.

Thus, true to his prediction at the outset of the case, Judge Letts denied the wcg's motion for preliminary injunction on February 8, 1999—just two days shy of the two-year anniversary of the lawsuit's inception. In his written order on April 20, he said Mr. Armstrong had unilateral power within the wcg, that the church did not control Mr. Armstrong's work, and that Mr. Tkach Sr. disavowed *Mystery of the Ages* as a religious work, destroyed existing copies of the book and refused requests for permission to reprint it. Judge Letts also found that "the wcg has no plans to print or use moa as originally published" and that "although the wcg has indicated that it might publish an 'annotated' moa in the future, the wcg has not contracted with or otherwise arranged to have anyone write the 'annotated' moa."[26]

In his legal conclusions, the judge determined that *Mystery of the Ages* was not a "work made for hire" and that the pcg's distribution of the work was protected under the "fair use" doctrine of the copyright law.

As we listened to everything Judge Letts said in our favor during that February hearing, we were actually anxious for him to conclude so we could rush outside the courtroom and celebrate. Even then, after the proceeding, we managed to subdue our jubilation in the hallway, so as to not offend the WCG representatives. But once those elevator doors shut and we were all alone—"WOOOOOHOOOOOOOOO!!!" As our two attorneys high-fived each other, we couldn't help feeling like we had witnessed something truly historic for our work.

At church services that weekend, on February 13, my father heaped praise on the judge for grasping the spirit and intent of the copyright law. Certainly, Mr. Armstrong NEVER would have dreamed of using that law to prevent *Mystery of the Ages* from being distributed. The copyright law, after all, is supposed to protect an author's writings, not destroy them. At the end of his sermon, my father said,

> So we have to prophesy again and get this most important book that there is in this world, after the Bible, out to the largest audience possible, brethren. That's what God inspired Mr. Armstrong to write. That's what He wants us to do and what a glorious calling it is, to be able to do this work, and show the world how to have real peace and joy and happiness.[27]

The following month, my father told *Trumpet* readers that we had "just won the most important court battle in this modern age." He wrote, "Mr. Armstrong believed *Mystery of the Ages* was the most important book on this Earth after the Bible. ... Time will prove Mr. Armstrong to be right. ... Soon the whole world will understand how important this great book is. Then the Bible will no longer be a mystery to man."[28]

It was a momentous time for our church. We weren't out of the woods yet—the WCG's lead attorney, Allan Browne, had made it clear during the hearing before Judge Letts that the WCG was anxious to appeal the ruling to the Ninth Circuit as quickly as possible. But still, after a two-year, hard-fought struggle, we did pause long enough to savor our first-round victory.

NINETEEN

ROUND TWO: WCG

"Suppose the book contained the recipe for building a nuclear weapon, and it's out in publication—the author says, 'My G--, I don't want this floating around the world. I'm going to call back all the copies and destroy them.'"

— JUDGE SCHWARZER
Ninth Circuit oral arguments, *December 6, 1999*

"CAN all of you keep a secret?" my father asked while cracking a smile. "I've decided to print *The Incredible Human Potential* and *The Missing Dimension in Sex*," he announced to 150 teenagers at a youth camp in 1999.

It was yet another bold step forward. The counterclaim had not yet been settled in court. Added to that, the *Mystery* ruling was under appeal. Yet my father took the district court's judgment as yet another signal that God was behind us. Furthermore, it removed all doubt, at least in our minds, about the legality of our actions within the scope of copyright law. So we printed two more books in the fall of 1999. In 2000, we printed four additional works: *The United States and Britain in Prophecy*, *The Wonderful World Tomorrow—What It Will Be Like*, *Pagan Holidays or God's Holy Days—Which?*, and *Which Day Is the Christian Sabbath?*

Our decision to print more of Mr. Armstrong's writings could not have come at a worse time for the WCG. Here they were preparing to appeal *Mystery,* and now they had to confront another monster.

WCG APPEAL

The WCG's opening brief for appeal relied on many of the same arguments they used at the district level. If anything, they put a stronger emphasis on what Judge Letts had exposed as duplicitous. For instance, Ralph Helge had testified that the WCG board had a "certain degree of control" over Mr. Armstrong,[1] a notion Judge Letts never bought into. Yet the language in their appeal brief took it a step further: "WCG had the right to control Mr. Armstrong's work." They did admit that Mr. Armstrong exercised considerable direction over the church, but they likened this to the authority of CEOs "who manage their corporations with a very free hand, *as long as they enjoy the confidence of the board of directors.*"[2] Here again, the impression they left on the court was that the board could have fired Mr. Armstrong at a moment's notice, which contradicted their own bylaws.

By this point in the litigation, the annotation sham was also presented more convincingly. "Those who respond to the PCG's ads for MOA very likely are the same people who would be interested in WCG's *planned* annotated version or in any future *republication of the original version,*" they told the Ninth Circuit Court of Appeals.[3] Never mind the "Christian duty" to keep it out of print—now they indicated they might even republish the original version!

Their appeal also accused us of printing the book so we could rev up income. *The PCG might offer it free up front,* they told the court, *but the book only serves as an advertisement to "sell" our real product— getting tithe-paying members.* They said we deliberately misled the public by our alteration of the copyright notice in *Mystery.* This, they said, would give the impression Mr. Armstrong was affiliated with the PCG[4] (as if they would want him to be affiliated with the WCG).

We filed our answer to their brief on September 1. On the point about Mr. Armstrong's authority in the church, we said, "His control over the WCG's earthly organizations was absolute." We even quoted from the WCG's own bylaws, which showed that Mr. Armstrong was in charge of the "ecclesiastical and temporal affairs of the church." He was the only one *required* to be a member of the church's board. He never had an employment contract with the church. We explained that he "simply did not want" one.[5]

On the annotation idea, of course we noted that this was invented for litigation. "The first time the WCG ever considered or discussed the idea of an annotated MOA was after the PCG raised a fair use defense, which suggests strongly that the idea was minted for the purpose of overcoming a fair use defense." We pointed out how Tkach Jr. said the project would not get started "any time soon." And we also picked apart Greg Albrecht's testimony, since he was the one given charge of the "project": "Albrecht's efforts to 'contact potential authors,' trumpeted by the WCG, actually consisted of little more than making a few calls (none of which were returned) to a writer for a journal that is critical of Armstrong's teachings and chatting about an annotation with someone else during a coffee break."[6] Not exactly *concrete* plans.

As for all the money we were supposedly pulling in from *Mystery,* we told the court the WCG's argument was based on "anecdote and speculation"—certainly not hard evidence.[7] They ignored the fact that we had spent over $200,000 printing and distributing the book to that point—that we sent it free of charge and did not solicit donations from recipients. We also pointed out that one of the initial reasons the WCG gave for discontinuing the work was that it was *too expensive.*

ORAL ARGUMENTS

The Ninth Circuit called for both sides to appear in court for oral arguments on Monday, December 6, 1999. The purpose of oral arguments is not necessarily to cover the material contained in the briefs, but rather to give the panel of judges (in this case, three) one last chance to ask questions of both sides before making their judgment. The judges' concerns about the case are what dictate the flow of the debate. Both the plaintiff and defendant are given 20 minutes each to answer questions. So attorneys have to go in prepared to answer *anything*—and to do it in the clearest, most concise way.

My father, Dennis Leap and I arrived at Burbank Airport

Sunday night, December 5. We stayed at the Pasadena Holiday Inn. As it happens, it was the same hotel my dad and John Amos had stayed in 10 years earlier, the night they were fired. (We checked out of the hotel on December 7, the same day they had checked in a decade earlier.)

The next morning, after a 7 a.m. breakfast meeting, we left for the Ninth Circuit Court of Appeals. It was within walking distance from Ambassador College—just two blocks from the WCG's head-quarters. We were definitely on their home turf, so to speak. In fact, the Ambassador Foundation even participated in the official opening of the Ninth Circuit Court of Appeals back in February of 1986, just three weeks after Mr. Armstrong died.

But we couldn't help feeling like *we* were the ones with home field advantage. How ironic it was that Mr. Armstrong's successors left their executive suites that morning to walk across the street to the Ninth Circuit to fight in court for the right to keep Mr. Armstrong's works out of print! And what a privilege it was—an absolute honor—for us to be fighting against them; and on the same side *Mr. Armstrong would have been on.*

"A VIEW TOWARD REWRITING IT"

The judges started the proceedings promptly at 9 a.m. Judge Wallace Tashima headed the panel of three. He was accompanied by Judge Melvin Brunetti, to his right, and Judge William Schwarzer on his left. There were four cases on the docket that particular day. Ours was last, so we had to sit through three other boring arguments. After the first three cases, Judge Tashima called for a 10-minute recess at 10:40. We re-entered the courtroom shortly before 11:00.

Our time had come. Allan Browne started the proceedings for the Worldwide. Judge Schwarzer wanted him to address the subject of "fair use." He wanted Allan to explain why he thought PCG's use of the book violated the fair use law. Allan said that because we did not seek permission to print the book, we did not act fairly and in good faith.

But they say you've abandoned the book and rejected its doctrines, Schwarzer interjected. Allan said that wasn't quite accurate, which is when Judge Brunetti spoke up for the first time: "I thought [the WCG] rejected the doctrine of the book, and then ridded their inventory of the book except for archival purposes."

"They do not reject the entirety of the book," Allan responded.

"I thought that they disposed of their inventory," Brunetti shot back.

"That's true," Browne responded. "But this was done with a view toward rewriting it and annotating this book and putting it back out on the market."[8]

We couldn't believe it. Here was a book Joe Jr. said was "riddled with error" exactly 10 years earlier. "Mr. Tkach has decided *not* to reprint the book," Bernie Schnippert told WCG employees in December of 1988.[9] "It is critically important that God's church *never* be in a position of *continuing to put out what may be misleading or inaccurate material*," Tkach Sr. told the brethren in February 1989.[10] The church destroyed remaining copies in order to "prevent a transgression of conscience by proclaiming what the church considered to be ecclesiastical error," wrote the Advisory Council of Elders.[11] And "no one else has a right to publish it," Tkach Jr. said in 1997.[12]

But on a December morning in 1999, inside a comfortable courtroom with barely a couple dozen people present, we listened to Allan Browne tell the court that *Mystery of the Ages* was discontinued and destroyed with a "view" toward rewriting it and annotating it so that it could go back out on the market.

As we sat there, an infuriating fact of litigation began to sink in: Liars can pretty much say *whatever they want* before judges. It certainly doesn't have to be true. It just has to be supported by "evidence" *on record*. In this case, Browne's evidence was testimony from Greg Albrecht that they had contacted a few people, *after the litigation started*, about the possibility of producing an annotation. *That's it.* That's all they needed in order to introduce evidence that this oral argument—and indeed, *this whole appeal*—would hinge upon.

God's system of judgment, of course, is based on fruits.[13] And more than 10 years of fruits (or lack thereof) revealed the annotated project to be a blatant lie. But in man's system, ironically, judgment can be easily skewed by "evidence." When judged before men, you can get by with bad fruits and still convince human beings to accept a lie.

Judge Tashima asked Allan how they were coming along on the annotated project. "The record reflects that the church had contacted several potential authors; they had talked about the possibility of doing that; they actually went to the point of getting a cost estimate," he answered.[14] It was all so patently ridiculous that we might have laughed out loud were it not so terribly upsetting.

The other key argument Allan Browne made that morning had to do with the tremendous monetary benefit we obtained from distributing *Mystery of the Ages*. And here again, a cursory review of the *facts* in this case shows that one of the initial reasons the WCG gave for discarding the book was the exorbitant cost involved in printing and mailing it. For the PCG, however, the whole project was a cash cow, Allan said. He based his assertion on the fact that we had received letters from people who were so overjoyed we were printing the book that they actually included a donation. Imagine that—church-goers giving money to their church!

Judge Brunetti questioned Allan about the connection between sending out the book and someone donating, saying it shouldn't be considered a direct exchange since the book was offered freely. But Allan said we sent a card along with the book saying, "If you want to make a donation you can"[15]—which wasn't true.

Allan ended a couple minutes early in order to save some time for a rebuttal at the end.

"GETTYSBURG ADDRESS"

When Mark Helm rose to speak, my heart pounded in my chest. *This was it,* I thought. Everything was riding on his presentation.

He began by addressing the fourth factor of the fair use law: The effect of our use upon the potential market for or value of the copyrighted work. Judge Schwarzer peppered him with a string of arguments at the outset. After Mark mentioned the WCG's decision to remove the book from print, the judge asked, "But don't they have an interest in keeping it from being published?" He said, "There are things in that book that reflect adversely on the Worldwide Church. That seems to be clearly established."

Mark responded this way: "[T]here is no secret of the fact that they used to hold these views. In fact, they take great pride in the extent to which they've deviated from them. So I don't think that you can say ... *Oh this is some embarrassing thing that nobody knows about*."[16]

Later, Schwarzer pointed to a previous case where the court had ruled that using a copyright to hoard one's work was acceptable within the law.

But that, Mark explained, was ruled "on the assumption that people would make those decisions to try to maximize the value of the work."[17] In our case, of course, the WCG had been working for more than a decade to try to diminish the value of *Mystery of the Ages* and, in fact, deprive *everyone* from ever gaining access to the book.

Schwarzer then raised the question about church members and how the WCG and the PCG were competing for members in the "same market."

"The members who are interested in the Philadelphia Church are completely separate from the members in the Worldwide," Mark responded.

"They are using the same principles—they're using *Mystery of the Ages*," Schwarzer said.

"The point is, your honor, Worldwide Church is *not* using *Mystery of the Ages*," said Mark.

Schwarzer fired back, "Not now—but they did to get a lot of members in the past."

Mark responded,

That's right, and they've lost more than half of their members after they did the about-face in doctrine, which the record shows is unprecedented in the history of religion. We're not talking here about, they tinkered with this doctrine or they tinkered with that doctrine. No religious historian has been able to point to any church in the history of religion that has had a turn-about of this nature. Everything that made that church distinctive and fundamental has now been renounced. And it went from something way out of the mainstream of Christianity, now into just a regular old, mainstream Christian church. That's never happened before, your honor. And so, therefore, the members are not the same.[18]

As my father would later remark, "It was like listening to Lincoln's Gettysburg address. I wanted to take notes, but couldn't, for fear of missing one word."

Judge Brunetti interjected to point out that this would be a much different case if the WCG still used *Mystery of the Ages*. But since they weren't, the question Brunetti asked is, can the copyright holder keep the work out of publication and stop the fair use of it?

RECIPE FOR TERRORISM

Mark explained that the copyright laws are in place so that authors can "retain the economic benefits from the fruits of their labors." He said, "This is not a case where they are trying to get a return for their labors—it's a case where they're trying, based on their religious duty, to stop somebody else from using a work that is important to them."

Schwarzer then jumped back into the fray, sounding more and more like an accomplice of Joe Jr.'s:

Suppose the book contained the recipe for building a nuclear weapon, and it's out in publication—the author says, *My G--, I don't want this floating around the world. I'm going to call back all the copies and destroy them.* ... Now, does he have a right to prevent the fair use of that book because he thinks it's his Christian duty to keep it out of publication?[19]

This analogy angered my father. For Schwarzer to compare *Mystery of the Ages* to a plan for a nuclear weapon was a revealing swipe at Mr. Armstrong's teachings. And yet this is the same man who, moments earlier, said the WCG and the PCG were competing for members in the *same market*.

We were fighting for a religious text—written by an ambassador for world peace who traveled the world to meet with dozens of presidents, prime ministers and members of royal families—that was repudiated by Tkachism. It's a text that, notwithstanding the unprecedented transformation the WCG underwent, remains central to our religious practice. To compare that with a manual about how terrorists can produce nuclear weapons was terribly insulting.

DIVINE INSPIRATION

Judge Brunetti seemed satisfied with Mark's explanation about the WCG's renunciation of Mr. Armstrong's teachings and that it tended to support our argument. He then asked for Mark to express his view on the economic benefit we were supposedly deriving from the distribution. That's when Mark actually read what is printed on the slip mailed out with all copies of *Mystery of the Ages*—the one Allan said asked for donations in return. It says, "All of our materials are sent free of charge as a public service and it is our firm policy to never request donations or offerings at any time." Mark added, "Now, how you can construe that as a solicitation of funds I don't know."

Schwarzer then spoke up to say that he accepted the fact that our primary reason for sending out *Mystery* was to spread our religious message. But he added that we *did* derive some economic benefit from the work—simply because we did not have the time and resources to write our own. That's when Mark brought up the subject of divine inspiration. The PCG, he said,

> believes that Mr. Armstrong was inspired by God when he wrote the book. There is no rewriting of the book that can happen. They believe that this is God's word as was handed to Mr. Armstrong. So it's not a question of, *Oh, we're going to now make up some views that we think are like it.* Those are the views. And you can describe it either accurately or inaccurately, but those are the beliefs that they have and they can't be rewritten.

We couldn't have said it better ourselves.

BROWNE'S REBUTTAL

In Allan's rebuttal, he chose to answer the question about the effect the book had on their potential market. The markets for both churches are the same, Allan said.

> They have many of our former members preaching there. We do believe that with our annotated version of the book, we will hopefully be able to get some of these members back. We also believe that they have used this book ... to develop relationships with these other people—relationships that may transcend our ability to get these members back. That's what it's all about: Develop the relationship, and then once you develop the relationship, you start getting a stream of income, because they become a member.

If we can just get the annotated version into the hands of those who've left the wcg—then they'll come back.

Please.

Judge Brunetti saw right through it: "You seem to be arguing that the doctrine is very flexible and fungible, that all you have to do is mutate it a little bit and you get them back—is that right?"

Of course he didn't mean *that.* "But we have evidence," Allan said, "hard evidence, that says this is a market, these are people that we hope to get back into the fold."

With that, Judge Tashima asked perhaps his best question of the day: So what if you do get them back? What would you do then? "Would you sell them a copy of the book?" Ah yes! The million-dollar question. Let's assume you get them back. What then? Notice Allan Browne's "hard evidence" response: "We would hope to have them become members again—and in the past, we did sell this book. When it first came out, we sold it in book stores. Mr. Armstrong did, for $14.95 a copy. *So that certainly is a possibility.*"

A possibility? He concluded oral arguments by suggesting that the wcg *wanted their former members back,* and that if they returned, they could *possibly purchase the original version* of *Mystery of the Ages.* As if this unprecedented doctrinal transformation had all been a simple misunderstanding.

At 11:45 that morning, the court stood in recess. Although we would not find out about their ruling for several more months, the three of them most likely voted on the case that afternoon, before turning it over to clerks to write up the opinions. It all seemed to happen so fast—as if they were hastily casting their votes on a case that meant everything to us.

TELEVISION TAPING

Our television producer, Andrew Locher, was on hand during the trip so that we could double-up on productivity. We decided to tape a *Key of David* program across the freeway from Ambassador Auditorium that afternoon. My father spoke about Paul's letter to the Colossian brethren. Chapter 1 of that book even speaks about a mystery that has been "hid from ages."[20] Tying this in with *Mystery of the Ages,* my father thought it would be effective to deliver a message with Ambassador Auditorium in the background, since he intended to discuss a few details about the court case.

We set up our gear on the embankment beside the road, between the freeway entrance and a city street. According to Mr. Leap (the rest of us had our backs to the street), while we were taping Greg Albrecht pulled up in his car, stopped and rolled down his window. He sat there awhile to watch and then shook his head and drove off. We chuckled over that while packing up the gear after taping. Then, as we loaded it into our van, a Pasadena policeman pulled up and asked, "Is that camera gear in the bags?" I said, "Yes, we just finished taping a program across the street on that freeway embankment." He told us to hang on while he parked; that he needed to ask us a few questions.

When he got out of his car, he said someone at the wcg had phoned in a complaint saying we had "climbed their fences and were taping on their property." We explained that there wasn't even a fence by where we were and showed him the location we taped from. We *filmed* their property, but we certainly weren't *on* it. After hearing our side, the officer remarked, "Well, sometimes people twist stories when they make a complaint so that the police will respond faster."

And sometimes they'll even twist stories to get a favorable ruling in court.

A Chance to Eavesdrop

My father wanted to stay in the hotel room to rest that night, so Andrew, Dennis and I went out for dinner at a restaurant on Colorado Boulevard in downtown Pasadena. We left the restaurant at about 7:00 and were walking a few blocks to our van, which we parked on the street. Halfway there, while waiting for a green light at a crosswalk, we suddenly realized we were standing right next to Judge Schwarzer! There he was—the man behind the robe. He looked a lot smaller and skinnier, dressed in his casual attire. To think, when we saw him, he may have already cast his vote! We wouldn't hear about the outcome of our case for another 10 months. But on that night, at that street corner, we were standing next to someone *who knew*.

We walked behind him for about a block, before he veered off into a restaurant with his party. We entertained the thought of getting a table close to his in order to eavesdrop. Perhaps we would hear how he came down on the case. In the end, however, clearer heads prevailed. We moved on.

In court, before distinguished-looking judges in long, black robes, one sometimes loses sight of the fact that these are mere mortals. They might be well-educated in the universities of this world. But they don't know more than God. In the courtroom that day, it was hard for me not to worry—with Schwarzer talking about nuclear weapons and Tashima seemingly skeptical toward our position. But seeing Judge Schwarzer on the street that night comforted me. It reminded me that our fate would not be determined by distinguished looking men in black robes. It rested in the hands of the *living* God. We had relied on Him ALONE to this point—and we would continue to do so.

The Race Card

On September 18, 2000, the Ninth Circuit filed its opinion, voting 2-to-1 in favor of the WCG. Judge Letts's ruling was reversed. The Honorable William W. Schwarzer wrote the opinion for the majority. Schwarzer noted that the WCG discontinued *Mystery* for a variety of reasons, including that it conveyed outdated views that were *racist* in nature. Its Advisory Council of Elders indicated that the church stopped distributing MOA because of "cultural standards of social sensitivity" and to avoid racial conflict. The Council noted, "Insensitivity in this area is contrary to the doctrinal program of the WCG to promote racial healing and reconciliation among the races."[21]

That was on *page 1*. In their brief, the WCG had said *Mystery* had *social errors*. "For instance, increasing sensitivity to racial harmony meant that certain passages authored by Mr. Armstrong—who matured in a very different United States of the 1910s and 1920s—did not reflect WCG's aspirations for the late 1980s."[22] That's the way WCG attorneys explained it. Of course, we don't agree with that assessment at all. But *Schwarzer* advanced the WCG's critique to flatout say *Mystery of the Ages* is racist! It's not just outdated or insensitive—it's RACIST—it causes RACIAL CONFLICT! *Ralph Helge* wouldn't even take that position. Tkach Jr. would. But still, this was coming from a federal judge who was ruling on a matter regarding *copyright* law and whether or not printing an abandoned book is fair use.

At oral arguments the year before, Schwarzer clearly identified the "key issue" of the case: the application of Section 107 of the Copyright Act. Then why so much in his September 18 opinion on the inflammatory subject of race? He did address the matter of copyright law later in his ruling. But when he introduces his opinion, on page 1, with the "fact" that *Mystery of the Ages* is racist, one wonders if his personal views about the book or Mr. Armstrong skewed his judgment on a purely legal matter.

Maybe there really was something sinister implied by his "recipe for building a nuclear weapon" analogy the year before.

MARKETING DEVICE

As for the legal arguments Schwarzer made, he believed the "work for hire" issue was irrelevant since Mr. Armstrong bequeathed *Mystery of the Ages* and the rest of his estate to the WCG in his will. Whether he controlled the church, or vice versa, did not matter to Schwarzer. Mr. Armstrong's personal desires for *Mystery* to be

distributed widely did not matter either. What mattered was that
WCG owned the copyright.

The judge later elaborated on the four factors for determining
"fair use." The first factor, we believe, weighed heavily in our favor
since our use of the book was not for profit, but for educational
purposes. But the way Schwarzer saw it, we were profiting from the
book because in printing it, we had a "core text" that would attract
new members, who would then become tithe-payers.[23]

The second factor considers the work's nature—whether it is a
factual account or a creative work. And since the fair use doctrine
"recognizes a greater need to disseminate factual works," we felt
like this tilted in our favor also. Problem is, Schwarzer reasoned,
while PCG members might consider *Mystery of the Ages* factual,
those outside the church would consider it a work of *fiction*.[24]
Unbelievable.

The third factor, *the amount copied,* also weighed against our
use, Schwarzer said, since we copied the entire book. "PCG uses
the MOA as a central element of its members' religious observance;
a reasonable person would expect PCG to pay WCG for the right
to copy and distribute MOA created by WCG with its resources."[25]
While he doesn't see how fair use would allow wholesale copying
of *Mystery,* it is interesting that he accepted the fact that the book
is central to our religious beliefs. If that's the case, how is it fair to
say, in the very same opinion, that the PCG uses *Mystery of the Ages*
as a "marketing device"? Is the *Book of Mormon* a marketing device?
What about the *Catechism of the Catholic Church?* Do Mormons and
Catholics use those documents to make money? Or do they represent bodies of *belief*—religious *teachings* that readers may either
faithfully believe and follow, or cast aside as scripturally flawed? If
an individual donates to the Mormon Church because he believes
the *Book of Mormon* is the truth of God, is he practicing his religious freedom, or merely making a business transaction based on
clever marketing by a supposedly "nonprofit" Christian church?
Using Schwarzer's logic, how could a church *even be considered
nonprofit?*

It's not like the subject of tithing is unique to the Philadelphia
Church of God. Nearly every church in existence collects tithes

and/or freewill offerings from adherents who consider it part and parcel of their religious faith. The patriarch Abraham paid tithes to Melchisedec—and without ever having read *Mystery of the Ages*. Jesus told the Pharisees of his day to tithe.[26] Was He a salesman just marketing a product? The Hebrew words for "tithe" appear 41 times in the Old Testament—the Greek equivalent surfaces in the New Testament 10 times.

If *Mystery of the Ages* really is central to the Philadelphia Church of God's teachings and beliefs, as Schwarzer acknowledged in his opinion, then to say it is *also* a marketing device is tantamount to religious bigotry.

COMPETING MARKETS

On the fourth fair use factor, Schwarzer said there was "undisputed evidence" showing "that individuals who received copies of MOA from PCG are present or *could be* potential adherents of WCG."[27] Here again, he took Allan Browne's nonsense a step further. Allan said the WCG wanted to lure former members back into the fold and possibly even offer them *Mystery of the Ages* again. Schwarzer added that our distribution of the "racist" book might actually prevent people from joining the WCG!

"Because the Church plans at some time to publish an annotated version of MOA, it is entitled to protection of its copyright."[28] Schwarzer either bought into the annotated idea, or else he knowingly accepted the sham on account of what he believed to be the greater good—to prevent us from a "fair use" distribution of a "racist" book.

With that, the court granted the WCG's permanent injunction against our distribution of *Mystery of the Ages* and ordered the PCG to pay the WCG's costs for appeal. In addition, the case would be sent back to the district level for a damages trial to determine how much we owed the WCG for our "unauthorized" republication of the book.

DISSENTING OPINION

On the surface, about the only thing good to come from the Ninth

Circuit ruling was Judge Brunetti's dissent. Like Judge Letts in the district court, he put the lawsuit in proper perspective. Right at the outset of his opinion, he said, "The copyright dispute in this case *arises from a change in religious doctrine* of the Worldwide Church of God." Later, he wrote,

> When WCG changed its church doctrine and renounced much of Armstrong's teachings, the founders and believers of PCG were forced from WCG as they could no longer practice their religious beliefs as set forth in MOA. It was WCG's doctrinal shift and renunciations that created the PCG and its need to publish MOA. [29]

Indeed, were it not for WCG's unprecedented transformation, there would have never been a PCG!

On the four factors of "fair use," Brunetti saw it much differently than Schwarzer. The first factor, in Brunetti's view, weighed heavily in our favor. We are a non-profit organization, he said. And even if you take into account the donations that came in specifically for *Mystery* distribution, those monies did not come close to covering the overall costs for printing and distributing the book, Brunetti explained. He also drew attention to the WCG's own admission that *Mystery of the Ages* was a costly production, and one of the reasons it was discontinued in the first place.

The second and third factors were mostly irrelevant in this case, Brunetti wrote. But the fourth factor, as has also been established by the Supreme Court, is the "most important statutory factor." On this point, Brunetti once again placed the dispute in its proper context.

> WCG's decision to cease publication of MOA, destroy inventory copies, and disavow MOA's religious message in the context of its doctrinal shift as a church demonstrates that MOA is no longer of value to WCG for such purposes, regardless of PCG's actions. [30]

When judging by fruits, you see, this whole case ought to be rather simple to weigh in on. Brunetti continued, "Because WCG has admitted that it has no plans to publish or distribute MOA as originally written, there can be no market interference."

Regarding the annotation, like Judge Letts, Brunetti wrote,

> PCG's use creates a larger potential market for an annotation rather than interfering with it. Moreover, the failure of WCG to make any reasonable progress on the annotation over the course of a decade as well as WCG's belief that it has a Christian duty to keep Armstrong's doctrinal errors out of circulation tends to undermine the credibility of WCG's intention to publish any such annotation.

Brunetti's conclusion summed up the WCG position beautifully: "In this lawsuit, WCG appears less interested in protecting its rights to exploit MOA than in suppressing Armstrong's ideas which now run counter to church doctrine."[31]

To us, Brunetti's dissent was a shining bright spot in the lawsuit's passage through the Ninth Circuit. His remarks, like those of Judge Letts, emboldened our approach to this case. My father described Brunetti's opinion as a "powerful dissenting opinion" that had "great clarity." He said, "Perhaps this was inspired by God and something dramatic is awaiting us."[32]

The way we looked at it, of the four judges to hear the case, two of them saw right through the WCG's smokescreen and interpreted the fair use doctrine exactly the way we did. It's just that the other two made a two-thirds majority at the Ninth Circuit. But in a lot of ways, the views of Schwarzer and Tashima motivated my father more than that of the other two judges. "This is too outrageous for words," my father told our membership five days after the Ninth Circuit ruling. "It ought to outrage God's people! I think it's nothing less than scandalous for you to take and reverse the decision of a District Court with such reasoning as that." He was referring to the annotation sham in particular. Indeed, Schwarzer's words aroused a fighting spirit in my father not unlike the deceitful betrayal Tkachism did during the late 1980s. "I'll tell you this," my father continued,

if we're not willing to fight against such a blatant and a flagrant violation of our rights, I think something has to be wrong with us spiritually. This has made me mad! And I want to fight more than ever. ... I want to take them on. ... I want to represent the great God. I want to defend God. And it makes no difference who's out there fighting against God, that's what we're here for! That is what we are—defenders of the faith.[33]

HELGE INFORMS THE WCG MEMBERSHIP

Prior to the court of appeals ruling, most of the WCG membership was left in the dark regarding the lawsuit. Indeed, many of their own members had absolutely no idea their church was even in court. After their victory, however, Ralph Helge was quick to gloat before the membership.

> PCG does have certain limited rights to request the court to modify the opinion and for some other procedural matters, and we assume they will petition for such relief. However, for all practical purposes, [the Ninth Circuit's ruling] would seem to be final in all material respects.[34]

Two months later, Helge then backtracked in order to explain the church's rationale behind instigating litigation in the first place.

> I would like to *clarify* for the members of the WCG, and all others who may be interested, why the WCG filed this lawsuit in the first place. Having represented the WCG for about 42 years, I can say that it has only been in extreme circumstances that the WCG has ever taken the affirmative step of filing a lawsuit.[35]

He was responding to flack they were getting from their own members! Apparently, some couldn't understand why they would take us to court over something like *Mystery of the Ages*—a book espousing doctrine they disavowed and even ridiculed, as well as destroyed. Helge explained that the church had an obligation to protect its "assets." After all, if the PCG just helped itself to Mr.

Armstrong's literature, what's to stop us from seizing control of other property?

He then told members about the annotation project, which must have come as a complete shock to most of them. "Just before the PCG's inappropriate commandeering of WCG's copyrighted assets, the WCG's board of directors was considering what use they should make of these assets."[36] In actuality, the undisputed facts of the case reveal that it was just *after* we "commandeered the assets" that the WCG suddenly became interested in them. But I digress. According to Helge, the board

> even discussed whether it would be appropriate for the church itself to reprint and publish certain of such literary works, reprinting *Mystery of the Ages* in annotated form explaining to the public where the church is in disagreement with conclusions in the book.

And what did those discussions ultimately lead to?

> Unfortunately [these discussions] came to an abrupt halt when the PCG undertook, to use the federal court's language from its own opinion, an act of piracy. The WCG then *could not proceed* with its own considered action regarding the literary works *because to do so would give the false impression that the WCG was intimidated into doing so by the PCG's act of aggression.*[37]

Yet another chapter added to their fictitious story. They were *just about* to use *Mystery of the Ages* until we came along and preempted their plan, forcing them to set it aside in order to stand up to an aggressive bully.

OUR FINEST HOUR

A few days after the ruling, my father exhorted us to fight as if our very lives depended on it—and to do so with a positively optimistic outlook. "God is with us," he said.

On October 10, 2000, we submitted a petition to all 27 judges at the Ninth Circuit for a rehearing *en banc*.[38] But The Ninth Circuit rejected our petition on November 9. On the surface, it appeared the odds were stacked heavily against us—especially since the chance of ever being heard at the Supreme Court is 1.6 percent. (Of the 5,000 or so requests for appeal every year at the Supreme Court, only about 80 of them are accepted.) But we were excited by the prospect of just submitting our case before the highest court in the land. *What an honor,* we thought.

Beyond that, there was the counterclaim. As much as the WCG would have liked it to piggyback on top of the *Mystery* ruling, it was an altogether separate case. And the longer litigation wore on, the easier it would be for us to expose the annotation lie by pressing them on the "plans" for the project.

We also saw a brightly-lit silver lining in the damages trial, because it would be tried before a jury. All along, my father felt that if we could tell our story *before a jury,* and *expose* the WCG for what it deceitfully did to Mr. Armstrong's legacy, we would gain a distinct advantage. It's one thing for a high-ranking WCG official to distort the truth and change his story in a deposition that most people never see. But to be exposed as a liar before a 12-person jury and a packed courtroom is much different. And rest assured, even if only a damages trial, we were determined that those men would be brought before the jury to answer for what they had done.

And besides what might happen in court, who knew what might happen outside of court. As my father told PCG members, something "dramatic" was going to happen in this case. "This news could be the greatest blessing this church has ever had," he said. "A miraculous decision from God can change this little work as a winning decision … never would have." Hearkening back to the 1970s, when the state of California seized control of the WCG's assets and falsely accused Mr. Armstrong of all kinds of outrageous activity, my father said, "I've always thought that what happened when the state of California attacked the church under Mr. Armstrong, that that was the church's finest hour. … It unified God's people as nothing ever did."[39]

"It's not over yet," my father insisted. "We're going to win this thing in the end. *We absolutely know that.*"[40]

TWENTY

COUNTERCLAIM TO THE RESCUE

*"… Worldwide claims it is entitled to all the tithes and
other contributions given to the splinter group's church by people
inspired by copies of the book that the group printed."*

— WALL STREET JOURNAL
February 21, 2001

THE day after the Ninth Circuit filed its opinion, we stopped distribution of *Mystery of the Ages* and the other five works of Mr. Armstrong we had printed. My father then spent a few days weighing our legal options and beseeching God. On September 28, as we had grown accustomed to during the lawsuit, he came out of seclusion prepared for an offensive strike. He reminded Dennis Leap and me about what we had seen. God *inspired* Judge Letts to grasp the central points of our case, my father said. God *inspired* Mark Helm's oral argument at the Ninth Circuit. God inspired Judge Brunetti's dissenting opinion at the Ninth. "Remember *what we have seen* in this case and be encouraged by it," he said. He reminded us that Mr. Armstrong spent practically his entire life operating on the edge of disaster. "Everything," he said, "hinges upon *faith*."

With that in mind, he decided to resume distribution of Mr. Armstrong's works until issuance of the official court order to cease and desist (the appellate court's ruling did not serve as such an order). He was well aware that the WCG would probably point to this action as "proof" of our "willful intent" to break the law. But since the order requiring us to stop had not yet been issued, my father felt like it would be a lack of faith not to disseminate God's truth. Of course, once the injunction was filed, we fully intended to comply with the order at once. But until then, it was a race against the clock to see how much literature we could distribute before we were ordered to lock it up.

Our November 2000 *Trumpet* splashed this headline across the cover: "A Modern Day Book Ban." Inside the issue, we talked about *our* Christian duty and why we risked quite a lot in order to make *Mystery* available. We wrote,

> The Worldwide Church of God has no interest in ever printing *Mystery of the Ages* in any form. Even if they did attempt such a project, perhaps just to spite us, it would be the most scathing condemnation of Herbert W. Armstrong and his teachings that you have ever read—much the same as *Transformed by Truth*.
>
> That is why we feel it is our *duty* to make this book available to the general public—and at no charge. [1]

In the January 2001 issue, we ran a two-page spread advertising the 1980 version of *The United States and Britain in Prophecy*. We urged readers, "[I]f you don't have a copy of the larger version, please write for your copy *while you can*." [2] We knew the injunction would be filed any day, so we were trying to unload as many books as possible. That advertisement brought in more than 3,000 requests for the book.

The following month, we did the same thing for *The Missing Dimension in Sex,* admonishing readers, "It could be your last chance to ever get this book!" [3] Unfortunately, that issue landed in mailboxes too late. On the evening of January 29, 2001, the court-ordered injunction was finally filed. Technically, it barred dissemination of *Mystery of the Ages* only. But we chose to cease distribution of all Mr. Armstrong's works.

Thus, we were not able to satisfy thousands of requests for *The Missing Dimension in Sex*. So we directed all those who asked for the book to instead contact the WCG. We even gave them the WCG's address and phone number. Since the WCG now had big plans for Mr.

Armstrong's literature, we urged people to call the wcg to check on the progress of their plans for distributing Mr. Armstrong's works.

THE WALL STREET JOURNAL

To this point in the case, we had to purchase ad space to tell our story to a mass audience. So when *Wall Street Journal* reporter Jess Bravin contacted us in November of 2000, we were *ecstatic*. Widely read across business, financial and legal districts worldwide, the *Journal's* circulation was about 2 million. A full-page ad in a publication of its stature runs at about $175,000. So we knew that if we could get a fair story out of the deal, it could be hugely beneficial to our cause—*and free.*

Bravin was drawn to our case because of its uniqueness. "It was absolutely fascinating," he said, "two churches suing each other over inspired writings."[4] As to the legal questions in the case, he was fascinated by the "unusual collision between copyright laws, freedom of speech and freedom of religion"—all of which, he said, are protected by the Constitution.[5]

Our lawyers supplied him with the relevant legal briefs and opinions and we gave him a pile of Mr. Armstrong's literature as well as *Transformed by Truth.* After that, we didn't hear back from him for several weeks. For a while, he got sidetracked with the hotly contested U.S. presidential election of 2000. We were, nevertheless, anxious to hear back from him—and hopeful that his editors wouldn't nix the story.

Soon after the election crisis ended, he contacted Dennis to say he was moving forward on our story. He arranged to meet with us at our headquarters facility in Oklahoma. Arriving in Edmond on Friday, January 26, 2001, we guided him on a tour through our offices and facilities. That afternoon, he sat down to interview my father for more than two hours. During the interview, my father explained how he came into the Worldwide Church of God as a young man. He recounted the events surrounding his firing in 1989. In discussing the emergence of the Philadelphia Church of God after the split, he told Jess, "All we've ever wanted to do is continue with what Mr. Armstrong did." My father admitted that we are not what you would call a mainstream denomination. But like Mr. Armstrong, we do profess to be followers of Jesus Christ's message as revealed in the Bible, he said.

The next day, we invited him to attend our church services, where I happened to be giving the sermon. Having visited a WCG service the previous week, Mr. Bravin noted afterward how different the two services were. The WCG service had more singing and testimonials, whereas ours was more informative. I told him that the format for our service is exactly the way it used to be in the WCG.

That evening, we took him out for dinner and then invited him to a concert sponsored by our Philadelphia Foundation. Of course, we had no idea how we would be portrayed in his piece, but it was still exciting just to have him in town—and knowing that the court case brought it all about.

FRONT PAGE!

Jess called Mr. Leap late Tuesday evening, February 20, to tell us the story would appear the following day. I left for work at 5:30 the next morning and hurriedly stopped at a convenience store to get the paper. The clerk must have thought I was a bit odd, watching me rush into the store, grab a *Wall Street Journal,* and proclaim, "I can't believe it!" There, on the far-left column of the FRONT PAGE, *above the fold,* was a drawing of Herbert W. Armstrong prominently displayed at the beginning of the article. For me, even without reading the article, *that was enough* to make my heart race with excitement! I bought three copies and headed off to work, where I finally sat down to read the piece.

Bravin told the story of a church that disavowed the tenets of its founder after his death, even to the point of destroying his written works and preventing all others from printing them. "Through it all," he wrote, "a splinter group in Oklahoma continued to take Mr. Armstrong at his word. Wanting to provide new converts with all of Mr. Armstrong's insights, the group began to print *Mystery of the Ages* and give it away."

What resulted, he explained, was "an unusual legal challenge." He continued,

Worldwide Church hasn't lost sales of its founder's book because it never charged for it while publishing it, and certainly has no wish to sell it now; nor has its adversary ever sold the book. But *Worldwide claims it is entitled to all the tithes and other contributions given to the splinter group's church by people inspired by copies of the book that the group printed.*[6]

Just six paragraphs into the piece, he told readers about the WCG's determination to take tithes and offerings away from the PCG, which was exactly right. We didn't charge for the book, so what money was there to go after for "damages," besides the tithes and offerings of our membership?

From that point, he delved into a brief history of Mr. Armstrong's ministry, Tkachism, and the PCG's emergence onto the scene. Not all of this history was expressed very favorably toward Mr. Armstrong, but it clearly brought out the fact that we were following in Mr. Armstrong's steps. And he also made note of Tkach's "Christian duty" statement—something we never tire of seeing in print.

While some of the history could have been portrayed better, my father felt like we came out on top with respect to the legal coverage. Along those lines, my father noted, "I don't believe it could have been better balanced."

Our lawyers were elated by the article.

Mr. Tkach Jr. wasn't quite as happy with Bravin's work. According to Tkach, Bravin interviewed him and Greg Albrecht for "nine hours" and yet only quoted him twice. "Only one of the quotes was actually correct," he said in an interview.[7] Tkach also felt like Bravin's statement about the WCG going after our tithes and offerings was *misleading.* "The truth of the matter," Tkach said, "is that the Ninth Circuit Appellate Court ruled in our favor, and eventually Gerald Flurry's group will have to pay what is known as damages for the wrong they committed." He continued,

Normally, we might be entitled to the profits from the sale of the book. But since the book was given away and not often sold (except for a brief time in book stores) the court may accept as the measure of those damages the amount of money Flurry received that is traceable to the book, in other words, donations from people who got the book and sent in money. Obviously, this becomes a calculation of a dollar amount, not the actual checks of the donors somehow signed over to us.[8]

Regarding Bravin's comments about the wcg taking our tithes and offerings, psychologist Tkach said Bravin was speaking metaphorically, not literally. He later suggested that we sell off some of our property to pay off the damages.[9] Of course, there's little difference between proceeds from a property sale and tithes and offerings direct from members, because we would have never acquired the property in the first place without membership donations.

HARVARD LAW REVIEW

If the *Wall Street Journal* helped us get some good publicity on the outside, the *Harvard Law Review* gave us additional hope that things might turn around in court. The April 2001 issue of the well-known law journal criticized the Ninth Circuit for applying the copyright law *narrowly*. "By giving insufficient weight to the religious nature of the text," the article stated, "the court interpreted fair use in a manner that contravenes the goals of a doctrine designed to encourage, not hinder, the free expression of ideas."[10] Of course, this is what our lawyers had been arguing all along. Technically, yes, wcg held the copyright to *Mystery of the Ages*. But they were using it unlawfully— to suppress the free expression of Mr. Armstrong's ideas. "The most serious error in the court's analysis," the *Review* continued,

> was its failure to credit sufficiently moa's centrality to pcg, which led it to misapply the first fair use factor. Moa is required reading for those who seek baptism in the church, and church policy mandates reading the book before [attending] services because it "provides the key to understanding the Bible." The dissent recognized this centrality. The majority, however, treated pcg's copying and distribution of moa as a straightforward infringement case. It failed to recognize that to prohibit

PCG's use of the book would be to suppress both the unique expression of the ideas in the book and the ability of PCG's members to live according to their religious faith.

If the majority erred in not recognizing this centrality, it made matters worse by giving credibility to WCG's plans for producing an annotated version of *Mystery*.

> The court's assumption that WCG was not seeking to keep MOA from the public (or from PCG) rested on a tenuous belief in the sincerity of WCG's annotation plans; it then privileged those speculative plans over PCG's immediate, religious need for the book.

Like Brunetti, the *Review* noted that the WCG had no plans whatsoever to reproduce *Mystery of the Ages*—certainly not in the form Mr. Armstrong printed it.

> WCG withdrew MOA from circulation because its leaders believed they had a "Christian duty" to avoid propagating the book's doctrinal errors; the church's reasons for not wanting PCG to copy MOA were clearly not limited to market concerns.[11]

Precisely. They had no interest in exploiting the *Mystery of the Ages* "market." But now that they had convinced the Ninth Circuit to reverse, they were keenly interested in the donations of PCG members who were inspired by reading the book. As the case wore on, we felt that judges and juries would come to see the insincerity behind the WCG's litigation-inspired activities. They weren't interested in using the copyright law to protect the free expression of ideas. Their ambition was to suppress Mr. Armstrong's religious views and help themselves to some of our money in the process.

The *Harvard Law Review* concluded, "The court's failure to see the case for what it was—a church's attempt to suppress heresy by using copyright law—led it to overlook the purposes of the fair use doctrine and facilitate the monopolization of a religious idea."[12]

Hanging by the Counterclaim

In our appeal to the Supreme Court, we continued insisting that, their litigation ploy notwithstanding, the WCG had no intention of ever publishing *Mystery of the Ages:* "While anyone should be free to debate the validity of the creator's ideas, no one should have the power to suppress those ideas simply because he or she disagrees with them."[13]

On April 2, the United States Supreme Court let the Ninth Circuit's reversal stand, deciding not to hear our appeal. The court did not give a reason as to why the appeal would not be heard. But as hard as it is to get your case heard in Washington, it's all the more difficult when there is still litigation pending at a lower level. In our case, the damages trial had yet to begin.

Additionally, the counterclaim we filed against the WCG for 18 other works had yet to be resolved. So we remained hopeful that the high court would reconsider the case once everything else had been finally decided.

The damages trial was set to begin in February of 2001. And by this point in the case, Judge Letts had obtained a semi-retired "senior status," which allowed him to withdraw from his involvement in our case. Thus, to allow time for a new judge to be brought up to speed, everything was pushed back.

In a May 7 hearing, with Judge Christina Snyder now presiding over the case, our motion to add Congress's Religious Freedom Restoration Act (RFRA) to our counterclaim was approved. Congress passed the law to help protect religious practices from being burdened by other laws. In this case, the Copyright Act, as interpreted by the Ninth Circuit, prevented our free exercise of religion. Early on in the lawsuit, the constitutionality of RFRA had been called into question in other cases. And since Judge Letts did not consider it necessary for our case anyway, he disallowed its use for *Mystery of the Ages.* But since that time, the Supreme Court had upheld the law in certain federal cases. Unfortunately, because RFRA had been removed from our case, it was not used as a defense at the Ninth Circuit level. So this is why we wanted to re-insert it into our case. And while the new judge would not allow us to raise the RFRA defense in the damages trial for *Mystery of the Ages,* she did allow us to raise it as part of our defense in the counterclaim.

Meanwhile, the wcg pressed forward for summary judgment on the counterclaim. They argued, quite simply, that everything the Ninth Circuit ruled on the *Mystery* case should be broadly applied to the other 18 works we were seeking in the countersuit. Going into the lawsuit, one could easily assume that our best chance, *by far,* was to gain fair use to print *Mystery of the Ages,* especially in light of the high praise Mr. Armstrong and Tkach Sr. both had for the book and their mutual desire for its wide distribution in 1985 and 1986. But now four years into litigation, the legal landscape had changed.

You will recall that the first time we heard about the "annotated" *Mystery of the Ages* was during Tkach Jr.'s deposition on September 8, 1998. He admitted it wouldn't be a high priority, but that Greg Albrecht would be looking into it. Albrecht testified to making a few phone calls. That was enough for two judges at the Ninth Circuit to tip the scales on the fourth fair use factor in favor of the wcg or, "at worst, neutral." The fourth factor ("potential market"), you recall, is what the Supreme Court considers the "most important" of the four. And since the Ninth Circuit considered this the wcg's weakest argument, the annotation sham tilted the balances in their favor— even if *barely.*

All this now presented a problem for the wcg with respect to our counterclaim because there was no evidence of any plans for annotating those other 18 works. In fact, in the very same deposition where Albrecht fumbled through all the contacts he supposedly made regarding the annotated *Mystery of the Ages,* we asked him if the wcg had planned to publish any of the other works we had listed on our counterclaim. Besides possibly re-working the Bible correspondence course, Mr. Albrecht responded, "I know of no such plans at this time."[14] Thus, if the Ninth Circuit forced us to accept the annotated sham as a possibility, *fine.* We didn't believe it, but we had to live with it. But with respect to the *other* works, the man given charge of the *Mystery* annotation himself admitted there were "NO SUCH PLANS." These facts would push the fourth fair use factor in our favor, we argued. Did they now have annotation plans for *The Incredible Human Potential*? What about *The Missing Dimension in Sex? The United States and Britain in Prophecy?*

E-PUBLISHING

Besides showing the court that the wcg had no plans to produce any of the 18 works, we also reasserted the fact that it would have been futile for the pcg to obtain permission from the wcg to print the works. We continued to point to the "Christian duty" statement, as well as Albrecht's 1997 e-mail which said the wcg does "not allow others to publish our former teachings and doctrines."[15] To counter our futility argument, by the end of the summer in 2001, the wcg indicated in court filings that it would have, *all along,* objectively considered any offer to license the works of Mr. Armstrong. They went on to suggest that we should—*even then*—make them an offer. Furthermore, they produced board minutes saying that Tkach Jr.'s "Christian duty" statement reflected his own "personal" views, not an official church position.[16]

On October 19, 2001, the wcg's secretary of the board of directors, Matthew Morgan, wrote my father a letter. In it, Morgan explained that once the pcg began distributing *Mystery of the Ages* in 1997, wcg suspended all considerations regarding "how it could best utilize its copyright assets" (the book was an "asset"). But since the lawsuit had now been "resolved in favor" of wcg (with the Ninth Circuit's decision), wcg's board had now decided what to do.[17] *Drum roll, please.* Believe it or not, the wcg now had "plans" for Mr. Armstrong's other material! And it just so happened to be the exact same literature we were seeking in our counterclaim. *Mystery of the Ages* would not be available—just the ones that had *not* been resolved in court! They decided to make the 18 works available via the never-before-utilized world of "e-publishing."

So, to win *Mystery,* they told the courts about grandiose plans to "annotate" the book. Then, to explain why these plans never materialized, they said they *had* to be put "on hold" until litigation had been resolved. After the Ninth Circuit ruling, they turned their attention to the counterclaim, telling the courts about their concrete plans, *not* for *Mystery,* but *for the 18 works!*

Here is what Morgan proposed in his letter to my father: The PCG *would pay all of the WCG's costs* for publishing; we would *withdraw our counterclaim;* the WCG would still be able to claim damages over the *Mystery of the Ages* infringement; they would collect royalties for every document downloaded; and they reserved the right to stop publishing the books at a moment's notice[18] (perhaps after we withdrew our counterclaim!).

And they wonder why we wouldn't make them an offer.

On October 31, 2001, the WCG then informed us that all their communications concerning the "offer" would be presented to the court in response to our argument that it would be futile to request a license. Of course, that's the whole reason they floated the e-publishing scheme to begin with. It was yet another litigation ploy designed to undermine our futility defense. In his letter, Allan insisted that the PCG make a "direct, immediate and unequivocal response to the WCG's solicitation."[19]

The stage was set for our November collision to determine whether or not Judge Snyder would grant the WCG summary judgment on the counterclaim or if she would deny it and allow the case to go to trial. Matthew Morgan's letter was the WCG's last-ditch effort to persuade the judge to rule in their favor.

But she didn't.

In her November 14 order, the judge referred to our point that there was no evidence of plans to republish the 18 works in any form. She then referred to Morgan's letter and a subsequent WCG board resolution to "publish" the works in question. But because there were still several disputed facts along these lines, she ruled, "[T]he Court cannot find as a matter of law that summary judgment is appropriate on PCG's fair use claim."[20]

The case was going to trial! What this meant was that, as the WCG pressed forward in its damages trial over our copyright "infringement" of *Mystery of the Ages,* we pressed forward with our counterclaim seeking the right to distribute these other 18 works by Mr. Armstrong.

Thus, when all hope appeared to be lost—after the Ninth Circuit reversal, after the Supreme Court's decision to refuse our case—the countersuit came galloping in to the rescue. When my father made the decision to file the counterclaim, a mere seven weeks into the case, you will recall that it was because he wanted us to stay on the offensive. And were it not for that critical decision, our chances for victory, after the Supreme Court rejection in April 2001, would have been all but dead.

As it was, we now had life.

TWENTY-ONE
THE INFAMOUS PREFACE

"We're not going to make a deal with the devil."

— GERALD FLURRY
Sermon, *April 6, 2002*

B
Y early spring 2002, we decided it was time to call WCG's bluff. After conducting our own investigation at headquarters to determine from others in the publishing industry what a fair offer would be, we put WCG to the test of their willingness to consider an offer from PCG "in good faith."

My dad drafted a letter to Matthew Morgan on March 14. In it, we requested to print and distribute *Mystery of the Ages* and the 18 works we were seeking in our counterclaim. He mentioned to Morgan that Tkach Jr. had vowed in 1997 to keep these works out of print because of his "Christian duty." And yet, my father continued, the WCG had curiously made recent representations before the court indicating a willingness to license the works. He reminded Morgan of Mr. Armstrong's lifelong policy of giving away literature at no cost to the recipient. Nevertheless, "based on WCG's recent representations to the court, we are making an offer in good faith to license these works."[1]

We offered to pay the WCG a royalty of 10 cents for every booklet we distributed, 25 cents per book and 50 cents for each correspondence course sent out. My dad concluded the letter by saying,

WCG recently made an "offer" to have PCG underwrite the expense of so-called "e-publishing" most of these works. Aside from not being a license to PCG at all, this "offer" suffered from numerous problems, among them that WCG apparently could withdraw the works from circulation immediately upon the conclusion of the court case between our two churches. WCG's previously announced "plan" to produce an "annotated" version of *Mystery of the Ages*—which by all appearances was created solely to gain a litigation advantage and (to our knowledge) has never been pursued—informs our concern in this regard. This concern is reinforced by, among other things, the facts that, outside the court case, neither Mr. Tkach nor anyone else has renounced WCG's avowed "Christian duty" to keep Mr. Armstrong's works out of print; and that WCG does not (to our knowledge) "e-publish" any other work in which it claims to hold a copyright. I look forward to receiving your response to PCG's offer to license these works.[2]

In all the posturing WCG had made before the court—acting as if they were more than happy to license—they had actually *never even made an offer to license the works.* And NOW WE HAD.

Here is how Matthew Morgan responded on April 8:

As an initial matter, Mr. Flurry, with all due respect, I feel it is necessary to mention that your letter, after 12 years of silence, is belated and fraught with self-serving comments. Its obvious purpose is to gain some type of legal advantage. Nevertheless, we will afford the courtesy of a response regarding your inquiry about a license. So there is no misunderstanding, and although we do not address each one of your self-serving comments, they should be considered as denied.[3]

The bottom line, however, is this: They are the ones who brought the subject of licensing before the court, even though they never made an offer. They are the ones who tried to gain the upper hand in litigation. And no matter how "belated" our offer might have been, it was, nevertheless, a reasonable offer. And they rejected it flatly.

Morgan went on to explain how "valuable" Mr. Armstrong's writings were to the wcg, which is why they were now moving forward on the e-publishing front. "Therefore," Morgan wrote, "no need exists to engage in complicated negotiations over the terms of a license. Your church will now be able to purchase as many legal copies of the 19 works as it desires and finds necessary to fulfill all its *alleged* spiritual needs."[4] (The wcg had since added *Mystery of the Ages* to the list of works they intended to e-publish, after we assailed their initial offer to publish everything *except* the one book the Ninth Circuit had allowed them to suppress.)

After all their harping, *Make us an offer! Make us an offer!*, they now said flatly—no need for "complicated negotiations."

THE DEAL THAT ALMOST HAPPENED

Not long after my father sent the letter offering to license the works, he gave a sermon in Edmond in which he said it was impossible to make peace with a terrorist, using the example of Yasser Arafat. He said, "[I]f you give Yasser Arafat what he wants, he is *still* going to be trying to destroy Jerusalem and drive the Jews into the sea. That's his goal."[5] In tying this in with the court case, he went on to say, "Now we're not going to make a deal with the devil—we'll have to fight through courts and go through a lot of problems like that, but we're *not going to make a deal* with the devil ...."

By not making a deal, he meant that he wasn't about to make one concession after another in hopes that we would somehow fall back into the wcg's good graces. He didn't want the pcg to be put in a compromising position where the wcg could then turn around and pistol-whip us into submission.

That said, however, it did not mean his conscience prevented him from ever paying the wcg *money*. He had, after all, offered to license Mr. Armstrong's works just three weeks before the sermon quoted above. And a month before that, Dennis Leap told our *Trumpet* readers, "Unless the case is settled out of court, a damages trial must take place."[6] So we hadn't ruled out settling, it just had to be according to ironclad terms that would prevent wcg from jerking the rug out from under us later on, *after* litigation.

Soon after our court case began, we seriously considered buying the WCG's former college campus in Big Sandy, Texas. In May 1998, a little over a year after our lawsuit began, we anonymously offered them $5 million for the property, which they rejected. A year and a half later, with the property still on the market, we upped our offer to $6.5 million. A few days later, the realtor got back to our attorney and said that the WCG still considered the offer much too low and they didn't like the fact that we were concealing our identity. But they were listening.

In February 2000, the WCG opted to use an auction firm to sell off the property and all the materials inside the structures. In sensing that they might be getting desperate to unload the campus, we worked furiously the next few weeks, trying to arrange financing that would allow us to make a $7 million offer. We hadn't planned on attending the auction, but we felt that if we could give them an offer high enough to prevent them from having to auction off everything over the course of five days, that maybe we could sneak in and make a last-minute transaction.

As it turns out, that's exactly what happened—except Hobby Lobby is the group that swooped in with an $8.5 million bid on the eve of the auction. *We missed it by $1.5 million.*

Of course, a lot has happened since our initial disappointment after Big Sandy fell through. Using the benefit of hindsight, we now see that God didn't want us to have that campus.

But that's not the point. The *point* is that *we were prepared to pay the Worldwide Church of God 7 million dollars for the Big Sandy campus.* So it's not like we were averse to giving them money in exchange for property. It just had to be a clear-cut deal, with no strings attached.

The same was true with Mr. Armstrong's literature. Paying them for Mr. Armstrong's works did not violate our conscience. But the circumstances for any such deal had to be just right.

THE "HOOK"

Matthew Morgan concluded his April 8 rejection letter by saying, "[T]he WCG is extremely pleased that it's [sic] decision to publish, not only serves as the best means for the church to capitalize on its literary copyrighted assets, but also has the additional benefit of fulfilling your church's alleged spiritual needs as well."[7] They were now *extremely* pleased to be able to serve our ALLEGED spiritual needs! Several weeks later, we found out *why* they were willing to make the literature available online (besides to gain a litigation advantage): Every e-published work would include a treacherous preface written by Joe Jr.'s childhood buddy, Michael Feazell. This was exactly the kind of "deal" we wanted no part of.

Feazell began the preface by saying Mr. Armstrong was a "gifted communicator" who, after years of personal study, began teaching religious doctrines that were "at odds with traditional Christianity."[8] But because of his "enthusiastic preaching," he attracted millions of followers, Feazell concluded—as if *what* he taught was of little or no consequence. He was just enthusiastic.

After Mr. Armstrong's death, the church "carefully reviewed" his doctrines and replaced them with "theologically sound ones." Here again, we're not talking about *review, reform, modify* or even *replace. More like an unprecedented repudiation of foundational beliefs, the likes of which had never been seen in the history of religion!*

Mr. Armstrong developed his unique body of beliefs because of a "personal bias against traditional orthodoxy," Feazell wrote. That bias was imbedded into the "church's culture" and it gave Mr. Armstrong a "unique advertising hook that captured many people's interest."[9] According to *Webster,* "bias" is "a highly personal and unreasoned distortion of judgment." Feazell was saying that Mr. Armstrong's *unreasoned distortion of judgment* was the "hook" that caught people like fish. He just *hooked* people and reeled them in by his own craftiness and distortion of judgment. Of course, Feazell is entitled to his own opinion, but how vain and arrogant to utterly disregard the opinions of 80,000 others who were either forced out of the wcg or left in disgust.

Most of them don't believe they were duped by an advertising hook. If anything, they were duped and deceived by Tkachism.

Feazell continued, "In conducting his studies, however, Armstrong had no seminary training and lacked any disciplined study of church history, biblical interpretation and original languages of Scripture."[10] Of course, neither did Joseph Tkach Sr., as we noted in chapter 4.

Feazell went on to say that Mr. Armstrong viewed the adherents of other churches as "children of the devil." Talk about a personal bias! This is the preface to be included at the beginning of all the literature we were seeking, and its whole point was to make us look like a hate-filled cult. Yes, the Bible says Satan is "the god of this world"[11] and that the whole world is deceived.[12] To say otherwise is to reject the Bible as God's inspired word. But the Bible also speaks of *all* deceived people and churches eventually being given a chance for salvation.[13] We believe that too. Jesus Christ died for this world—not for one church only.[14]

We look upon all peoples of this world as potential sons of God, whether they are presently Catholic, Protestant, Muslim, Buddhist or atheist. Where else is there a Christian denomination with teachings that offer hope for all peoples everywhere—even those who die without ever having known Jesus?

Feazell continued in his preface,

Armstrong also had many unusual ideas about prophecy, and for some these may have been the most attractive doctrines of all. He taught that the United States and Britain are the modern descendants of the lost 10 tribes of Israel, and that most biblical prophecies therefore apply to the Anglo-Saxon peoples.[15]

As if God were only concerned about the Anglo-Saxon peoples. In his book, Tkach Jr. said church members used *The United States and Britain in Prophecy* as an *excuse* not to repent of racism. Quoting from a study paper on the subject, Tkach wrote in his book,

In the church, non-Anglo-Saxons sometimes found fellow Christians looking down on them simply because they were not "Israelites." To these people, being German, African-American, Hispanic, Asian, Ukrainian, Italian, Polish (or a member of any other ethnic group) was to be inferior. Perhaps as a form of psychological self-defense, a few of Eastern or Southern European descent would speculate that, perhaps due to Israel's wanderings, they were Israelite, not Gentile. It somehow seemed inferior to be 100 percent Gentile. Obviously, such views do not belong among God's people.[16]

How sad. We had racism in the church all those years—and all because of Mr. Armstrong's literature.

Yet, one of Mr. Armstrong's final acts as pastor general in the wcg was to appoint, as his successor, a Gentile man of Russian descent whose parents were both born in Czechoslovakia.

And On It Goes

Feazell wrote, "Armstrong had complete authority doctrinally and administratively. Disloyalty among ministers was dealt with by firing and expulsion from the church fellowship."[17] He described Mr. Armstrong as a harsh dictator. And yet, when you look at how the wcg's transformation was brought about, it could not have happened without authoritarian rule from the Tkaches *forcing* their new religion down our throats—or else forcing us out of the Worldwide Church of God. Tkach Jr. (and his father before him) has driven out nearly 75 percent of the church's membership, including even his own sister and brother-in-law.

Ralph Helge threatened my sister with jail time in 1989 because she retrieved a partial list of wcg ministers from a garbage can. No authoritative threats there! The night Joe Jr. fired Gerald Flurry on the spot, my father pleaded with Tkach to at least discuss the items in question with a group of 15 ministers or so who were also dissatisfied with the church's direction. He wouldn't even consider the request.

And my father wasn't the only minister who was mistreated. As David Hulme wrote in his resignation letter to Tkach Sr., "Upwards of 170 ministers are alienated, some terminated *under questionable circumstances.*"[18]

Feazell continued in the preface, "Based on Armstrong's interpretation of biblical passages, wcg members were taught that use of prescription drugs and most forms of surgery constituted a lack of faith in God's power to heal."[19] Yet another classic example of doublespeak. Notice what Tkach Jr. wrote to a member who was leaving the WCG in 1990: "Actually, if you carefully read the latter portion of his [Mr. Armstrong's] own booklet on healing, it will become clear that he was acknowledging that there is much good that doctors can do."[20] Indeed, Mr. Armstrong wrote, "[I]t is true that today most doctors prescribe medicines that are NOT poisons but rather are designed to help nature do its own healing."[21]

Today, of course, their story portrays Mr. Armstrong's teaching as dangerous and fanatical.

The preface concluded with this statement: "The material below is copyrighted and may not be reproduced in any form without this entire preface and without written permission from the Worldwide Church of God."[22]

Thus, as Matthew Morgan said in his rejection letter, due to the "additional benefit" of the WCG's e-publishing offer to help fulfill PCG's "alleged" *spiritual* needs, we could now direct prospective members, who might know nothing about Herbert Armstrong, to download a copy of *Mystery of the Ages* (at a cost of $25) with a 1,500-word preface denouncing the author as a self-absorbed, racially bigoted, religiously biased, uneducated hack who taught heretical doctrines and bizarre prophecies while wielding dictatorial control over the Worldwide Church of God.

TWENTY-TWO

OFFENSIVE WARFARE

*"The way we look at it, this preface gives us much
greater opportunities in the upcoming depositions and trial.
I believe this is the only way we can win."*

— GERALD FLURRY
Letter to legal team, *June 11, 2002*

L IKE Tkach Jr.'s "Christian duty" footnote in *Transformed by
Truth,* Feazell's preface backfired. For one, it showed how
phony the e-publishing scheme really was. They weren't about
to produce Mr. Armstrong's literature unless it was introduced by
Feazell's remarks. And there is no way we would have ever directed
prospective members to download that filth. Though we knew it
all along, the preface fully revealed just how interested they were
in "helping" fulfill our spiritual needs. The whole e-publishing
sham, as it turns out, was just another way for them to trash Mr.
Armstrong's legacy.

But the preface's impact on our legal arguments was minor
compared to the way it impacted *us.* I won't say it surprised us—
not after witnessing Tkachism's destructive assault on the church
the previous 16 years. But it did serve as a jolting reminder of what
we were fighting against: people who HATE *everything* Herbert W.
Armstrong stood for. We couldn't reason with them. We couldn't
deal with them—all we could do was fight.

So from that point forward, everything in the lawsuit would turn on Feazell's preface—at least, as far as we were concerned. My father wrote to our legal team on June 11, 2002,

> The preface to the wcg e-publishing sham is the opportunity we have been waiting for. Ever since Judge Letts was involved, I feel like we haven't been able to thoroughly get across what really happened in our church.
>
> This preface has opened up a tremendous opportunity to do that again. I feel like we can now go on the offensive as never before with an even bigger goal in mind (rfra, writing a book, etc.). I strongly believe that our answer to the preface is going to make them feel the heat. ...
>
> Perhaps we lost the appellate court decision because the wcg made a few comments labeling us a cult. ... The preface allows us to answer the *cult* attack. But it gives us a greater opportunity. We can now expose them for what they really are—a cult and much worse. At the same time, I believe we can help the judge and jury to understand the pcg's true motives.
>
> They say a battle is 50 percent won when you go on the offensive. The way we look at it, this preface gives us much greater opportunities in the upcoming depositions and trial. I believe this is the only way we can win.[1]

Over the next two months, our attorneys probably heard the word "preface" so often, they might have thought we were a broken record. Of course, they still had to accumulate evidence to support all of our legal arguments, insofar as copyright law is concerned. But since the wcg now wanted to insert Armstrong-bashing into the case, we insisted on telling the behind-the-scenes story, whether during a deposition, before a judge or jury, or within court documents. In fact, as you can see from the letter above, the preface is what prompted the whole idea for this book. The case had now gotten much bigger than just fighting for the right to distribute Mr. Armstrong's literature. Now we had to obtain the literature—and EXPOSE THEM in the process.

Turning Point

Even though we were technically going into the damages trial as the "loser" (with respect to *Mystery of the Ages*), my father believed something dramatic would happen, whether in court or out, that would eventually turn the tide in our favor. "If God is with us," he said, "we will win this. If He's been with us, He still is with us—that is, if we keep the faith."

Judge Snyder was hoping for a mid-October 2002 trial, which meant discovery and depositions needed to be completed by the end of the summer. As we geared up for a busy summer, my dad instructed his entire staff at Edmond to make the court case their top priority. More than a dozen people involved themselves in gathering information and helping to prepare for the depositions of the WCG's key witnesses—Joseph Tkach, Michael Feazell, Ron Kelly, Ralph Helge and Bernard Schnippert, as well as a few others. My father relieved Dennis Leap and me from some of our youth camp obligations that summer so we could devote more time to researching for depositions. PCG ministers Gary Rethford and Tim Thompson were also instrumental in digging up information for our lawyers.

This was a real turning point. In 1998, the bulk of deposition preparation was left to our attorneys, although Dennis and his wife made sure they were supplied with church documents and literature. We also offered a lot of feedback during conferences we had before depositions. But, for the most part, the lawyers were responsible for doing most of the research and drawing up the questions.

In 2002, the lawyers still did all that, *it's just that we did too*—only coming at it from the *preface* angle. If Tkach's fellows wanted to talk about Mr. Armstrong's heavy-handed approach to governance, then Tkach Jr. and Feazell were going to be asked about the legacy of Tkachism—how it forced people to go along or else FORCED THEM OUT OF THE CHURCH. If they wanted to bring up how Mr. Armstrong supposedly "hooked" people into his system of beliefs, then they would have to testify about all the lies Tkachism told in order to lull unsuspecting members to sleep so they wouldn't lose their tithes. If they wanted to bring up Mr. Armstrong's lack of "study" and "seminary training," then we were going to ask them about Tkach Sr.'s academic and theological credentials. If they wanted to talk about how burdensome it was in the church under Mr. Armstrong, then they were sure to hear about Tkachism's heavy legacy. And if they wanted to bring up Mr. Armstrong's "extravagant" lifestyle, then we would ask, *Well what did Tkachism do with its billions?*

So as we got ready for the 2002 depositions, our attorneys prepared *their* questions and documents and *we prepared ours.* Then, in a status conference before the depositions, we worked to blend the two together.

JOSEPH TKACH JR.

In the Tkach Jr. deposition on Friday, August 23, 2002, Mark Helm wasted little time in setting off explosives. Fifteen minutes into the deposition, Allan Browne instructed Tkach not to answer on account of Mark's "harassing and oppressive" questioning. Thirty minutes after that, he threatened to leave unless Mark lowered his voice!

Mark began by reviewing the December 4, 1998, Advisory Council of Elders minutes—where the WCG officially explained its position on discontinued literature and how it had plans to use the material again. In the case of *Mystery* being discarded, the WCG minutes explain, "As a consequence, an ecclesiastical determination was made that MOA and other such works be retired from circulation and not be distributed *until appropriate revisions could be effectuated,* compatible with the Bible."[2]

Now that the WCG intended to e-publish these works, Mark wondered if the preface counted as an "appropriate revision." After Tkach said "no," Mark then asked if the ecclesiastical determination had changed. Tkach indicated that they hadn't changed their decision, but that they felt comfortable enough e-publishing the literature as long as it had a preface to provide background. Since the WCG had made statements throughout the lawsuit that they would have considered licensing the works, Mark was trying to pin Tkach down to see if the terms for the hypothetical licensing meant the literature had to be prefaced by derogatory remarks about Mr. Armstrong. He also exposed the degree to which the wcg wanted to control the literature if a licensing agreement ever happened.

Later, he got Mr. Tkach to talk about Gerald Flurry. Tkach said he thought my father was mentally unbalanced, that he taught heresy, approved of lying and was engaged in unethical conduct. Mark then asked if Tkach's personal views toward Mr. Flurry might factor into any decision considering the pcg as a possible licensee. *It was brilliant.* Tkach answered, "I think the key here is that in developing a license agreement, we would be in a position to police or control that by the terms we dictated in the license agreement."[3] That's exactly the point. Assuming Tkach ever licensed the literature to a mentally deranged, heretical liar, he would only do so if the wcg maintained "control" and was able to "police" our actions. In that scenario, what would prevent him from then pulling the plug on the license agreement after litigation ended?

Later in his deposition, Tkach Jr. complained that we had misrepresented his "authorial intent" in saying he had a "Christian duty" to keep *Mystery of the Ages* out of print.[4] When asked what he meant by "out of print," Tkach said he was "expressing a feeling, but not a course of action."[5] Of course, with that kind of reasoning, you can back away from practically any hard-and-fast position. But the facts prove that their whole reason for filing suit in the first place was to prevent us from distributing *Mystery of the Ages*—to ACT on their Christian duty. In his book, Tkach Jr. also made this statement about another one of Mr. Armstrong's works: "... don't bother writing for a copy of *The United States and Britain in Prophecy.* You won't get it from us."[6] Was that just a feeling or do the fruits prove that they acted on that conviction? Tkach wrote, "Today we reject what is well known as 'Armstrongism,' that is, adherence to the teachings of Herbert W. Armstrong ...."[7] Feeling or action?

BOTH SIDES OF HIS MOUTH

Four times during his deposition, Tkach Jr. accused Mr. Armstrong of speaking out of "both sides of his mouth"—particularly with respect to his role as an *apostle*. At times, Tkach explained, Mr. Armstrong seemed to think he was right up there, on par with the apostles of the first century. Yet on other occasions, he apparently made statements relegating his apostleship to something less than first-century-like. But as we have already seen in this volume, it is Joseph Tkach Jr.—not Mr. Armstrong—who spoke from both sides of his mouth.

In his 1997 book, Tkach Jr. wrote, "Over two or three decades he claimed rank on a par with the first-century apostles"[8]—a very definitive commentary on Mr. Armstrong's views. *Two or three decades!* But on March 16, 1992, in a letter the wcg turned over in discovery, Tkach Jr. wrote, "It is good to remember, however, that Mr. Armstrong's role was not synonymous with the original 12 apostles." Later, he wrote, "Mr. Armstrong *never* claimed his writings were equivalent to Scripture."[9]

We reminded Tkach Jr. about what his father said two days after Mr. Armstrong died—that he was "confident that the same policies, doctrines and everything else which [Mr. Armstrong] taught would be preserved and carried out."[10] We asked if this comment contradicted what his father said about the "deathbed repentance"—that Mr. Armstrong commissioned Tkach Sr. to make the very changes in doctrine that had been made between 1986 and 1991 (a list of changes so extensive, you will recall, that he wanted a tape recorder so he could remember all of them). Tkach Jr. responded, under oath, by saying "no"—there is no contradiction.[11]

We asked him about this statement from his book: "It is said that power corrupts and absolute power corrupts absolutely. Mr. Armstrong may have never wielded absolute power in our church, but by that same token, there weren't many who would challenge him on an issue."[12] Tkach defended the statement this way: "The audience for this book was not only church members …. They were counter-cult ministries who viewed Mr. Armstrong in this way. And I'm explaining for the historical record that that was inaccurate for them to view him that way."[13] So the comment was actually intended to *defend* the manner in which Mr. Armstrong led the church!

Earlier in the deposition, Tkach described the manner in which Mr. Armstrong would sometimes deal with subordinates. "When he would correct people at times, he would ask, *Do you believe I'm an apostle? Do you believe I'm an apostle just like Peter and Paul are apos-*

tles? And the person would be generally trembling and responding in the affirmative."[14] He then described an incident where Mr. Armstrong called Tkach Sr. about a Bible study given in Pasadena. According to Tkach Jr., Mr. Armstrong "was very angry and yelled at my dad for about 40 minutes."[15] Yet at the same time, what he wrote in *Transformed by Truth* about Mr. Armstrong's governing style was supposedly a *defense* of the church's founder.

We reminded Tkach about the changes in government he promised in his 1997 book and got him to admit that nothing had changed in the five years since the book was released. He still retained all the absolute powers he is quick to condemn Mr. Armstrong for.

When asked about his description of the PCG in his book—that we are a "militant church of God"—he explained that we would "confront" their members and tell them if they didn't accept *Malachi's Message,* "they were going to burn in hell ...."[16] He said that "numerous people were confronted that way in restaurants and grocery stores."[17]

When we asked him earlier about whether or not he thought the PCG was a cult, he responded, "Unquestionably."[18] He went on to explain that there are two types of cults—theological and sociological. "Theological cults would be the ones that misrepresent history and Scripture but aren't necessarily pathological in nature. And then you have sociological cults, groups that are dangerous, David Koresh, Jim Jones, Heaven's Gate."[19] At least we only made it onto his list of theological cults. But "we're concerned," he went on to say, "that [the PCG] may be crossing the line into the sociological realm."[20]

For clarification, Mark asked, "So you have concerns that the Philadelphia Church of God may be a cult in the sense that it is dangerous, sociopathic?"

"Certainly," Tkach answered.[21]

Yet they wanted, all along, to license Mr. Armstrong's literature to us as a "benefit" to our work.

Talk about speaking from both sides of your mouth.

We also made sure to compare Mr. Armstrong's academic background with Tkach Sr.'s, which made the younger Tkach very uncomfortable.

MICHAEL FEAZELL

Since he was primarily responsible for authoring the preface, we were quite anxious to depose Mike Feazell. At our Edmond offices, our employees combed through Feazell's book and other writings of his, as well as documents that were written about him.

We assembled at the Los Angeles offices of Munger, Tolles and Olson for his deposition on Wednesday, July 24, 2002. Early on, Mark Helm quoted from Feazell's book, where he spoke of the church's transformation.

> One by one these core values shriveled and fell from the WCG tree. As they did, leaders and members became increasingly unsettled, fearful, and frustrated. "How are we different anymore?" "Where is all this leading?" "What will be changed next?" they asked.
>
> The church these people had come into had *slowly ceased to exist*.[22]

Any time we found statements by WCG officials describing the WCG today as being completely different from what it once was, we made note of them. If the *old* church no longer existed, why should the *new* church be allowed to keep others from continuing to distribute the traditional teachings?

When Mark asked him about his comparison of life in the Worldwide under Mr. Armstrong to a rape victim, which we discussed in chapter 1, Feazell tried to brush it aside as a "figurative expression."[23] Mark pressed further. "But by using the figurative term ... 'raped,' that is a feeling of the highest order, correct? It's not a casual feeling of unpleasantness, it's—it's a very serious feeling that you're trying to describe here; isn't that right?"

Feazell's lawyer tried to intervene repeatedly for his client by interrupting Mark. But Mark ignored him and insisted that Feazell answer the question. "Is rape a terrible crime?" Mark asked. Feazell's attorney asked Mark to calm down, but he refused. "No ... he is trying to walk away from what's clearly stated here, and acting as though ... 'spiritually and emotionally raped' ... [is like] a typo in a memo."[24]

After Feazell wouldn't answer, Mark came at the subject from another angle: "When you said you had been spiritually and emotionally raped, were the feelings that you experienced akin to having had a terrible crime committed against you?"[25] Feazell said *no*, repeating that he only used the term in a figurative sense.

"So when you figuratively used the term *rape*, it's not a terrible thing?" Mark followed.[26] It was as heated as we had ever seen Mark during a deposition. It made Feazell noticeably uncomfortable.

Later, Feazell said he believed the PCG is a cult "at least in the sense of its submission to the authority of one individual and his personal interpretation of the religious views of the organization ...."[27] In his book, he wrote about how Mr. Armstrong's authority had brought the church to a virtual "standstill administratively."[28] He said "decisions of any significance could not be made without" Mr. Armstrong's approval.[29] So at the deposition, we pointed Feazell to other statements in his book that talk about the authority Tkach Sr. inherited from Mr. Armstrong: that Tkach would not have been able to transform the church "without the unfettered hierarchical authority delegated to him by Armstrong"[30]; that the changes would have never happened unless Tkach had "total authority." We then asked about Tkach Jr.'s supposed plans to dismantle the authoritarian approach to governance in the church—and how that was one of his first goals after becoming pastor general in 1995. But as of 2002, when we asked Feazell if the younger Tkach had the same powers that Mr. Armstrong did, he responded, "[T]hat may well be true."[31]

On page 107 of his book, Feazell wrote, "In the Worldwide Church of God, however, we found ourselves in the no-win situation of having to change the core values. The changes we were forced to make devastated the very sense of identity of our church and its members."[32] Since the Tkaches had "total authority" to change the church's "core values," we wanted to remind Feazell that they forced their transformation on the ministers and members of the Worldwide Church of God. In response to that charge, Feazell testified, "The Church no more forced ... itself ... on the ministers after the changes than it did before the changes."[33] To which Mark brilliantly responded,

But after the changes took place, these were ministers who had joined a church [that] had different doctrines and were now being told: *Either teach the new doctrines or hit the road.* That is different from the ministers under Mr. Armstrong, isn't it, who joined the church knowing what the doctrines were and believing in them?[34]

Feazell couldn't see how that was different at all.

RON KELLY

Since Ron Kelly is mentioned in *Transformed by Truth* as having heard Mr. Armstrong supposedly say "I am Elijah," we were anxious to hear what he had to say under oath. Not surprisingly, Mr. Kelly could not remember where or when he heard Mr. Armstrong say that. We then showed Mr. Kelly the letter Tkach Jr. wrote to Mr. Leap in April 1990, where Tkach insisted that the Elijah prophecies had been fulfilled *by the work of the church* and that Mr. Armstrong NEVER claimed to be the exclusive fulfillment of them. We asked Mr. Kelly if he made his "I am Elijah" comment before or after Tkach wrote the letter to Mr. Leap. He said it "would have been made much later than this letter, which was April of 1990."[35] But Mr. Armstrong died in 1986. And in *Transformed by Truth*, Tkach Jr. indicates that Kelly came to him *after he heard* Mr. Armstrong say "I am Elijah."[36] It wouldn't make sense for Kelly to go to Tkach Jr. "much later" than April 1990 about a comment he heard Mr. Armstrong make. But that's the illogical chronology Kelly had to go with during his deposition, otherwise he would have been forced to admit that Tkach Jr. spoke from both sides of his mouth.

Ron Kelly went to Ambassador College in 1956 and went into the ministry after he graduated in 1960. He became the first dean of students at Ambassador College in Big Sandy in 1964. After Big Sandy closed in 1977, Mr. Kelly transferred to Pasadena and soon after settled into the field ministry as a pastor serving in Colorado. He returned to Big Sandy briefly after the campus opened in 1981. In 1982, he moved back to headquarters in Pasadena to fill a position in the editorial department. Two years after Mr. Armstrong died, Mr. Tkach appointed him to manage the editorial department. In 1991, Mr. Kelly transferred to Church Administration, where he directed pastoral development. In 1998, he became the church's controller in the finance and planning department. That was the position he held when we deposed him August 1, 2002.

In our preparations for Mr. Kelly's deposition, several articles and messages of his stood out because of his long history in the church. One document was particularly interesting. It was a sermon transcript the church produced in 1987—a year after Mr. Armstrong died. He built the sermon, titled "Principles of Living," around lessons he learned from Mr. Armstrong. He said, "Twenty-nine years ago, I began to sit at the feet of Mr. Armstrong and listen to what he had to say."[37] Later, he said, "I would especially like to bring out those points and principles that I feel Mr. Armstrong was *uniquely* able to instruct us in."[38] In his deposition, Kelly acknowledged that he had learned from Mr. Armstrong, but that today he wouldn't use the word *uniquely*. "I look at things from a more mature point of view," Kelly said. "I realize Mr. Armstrong had wonderful things to teach. They weren't always unique to him."[39]

Mr. Kelly then highlighted several of Mr. Armstrong's teachings that he now considers burdensome. Of course, he didn't think that way before embracing Tkachism—and we reminded him of that. "Mr. Armstrong taught me how to love my wife," he said in that 1987 sermon. "I told him so, and I hope it pleased him to realize that what he taught did work."[40]

Here is how he once described life for his children in the wcg:

My children have been reared all their lives with a knowledge of God's festivals. Now that some are grown, many of their fondest memories are of keeping the holy days. We have saved for trips to England and Australia. By observing the holy days with God's people, we have traveled as a family throughout most of the United States and Canada. ... We have grown each year in spiritual understanding and have profited from the education of travel.

No one can ever tell me keeping God's feasts is a yoke of bondage and a burden.[41]

Those memories have seemingly faded from view, along with the practical, biblically based way of living Mr. Armstrong taught and recorded in huge stacks of written works.

In March of 2005, someone contacted me anonymously about a bound collection of almost all the wcg's periodical literature, including the *Plain Truth, Good News, Tomorrow's World* and *Youth* magazines, between 1934 and 2004. The collection also included a complete set of the 58-lesson Bible correspondence course, produced during the 1960s. The individual wanted $10,000 for all the magazines and another $500 for leather-bound volumes of all Mr. Armstrong's books, including *Mystery of the Ages*.

My father thought the collection would be a great addition to our college library. So we made a lower offer and ended up settling on $5,000 for everything. We didn't know who to make the check payable to until about a week before we arranged to pick up the materials.

As it turns out, the anonymous seller was the same man who, because of Mr. Armstrong's teachings, learned how to really love his wife.

RALPH HELGE

Perhaps the most significant material we uncovered in preparing for Ralph Helge's deposition was the role he played in defending the wcg against the state of California in 1979. As head of the church's legal department, he fought right on the front lines against dissident ministers who wanted to wrest control of the church away from Mr. Armstrong. Speaking before church members inside Ambassador Auditorium on January 13, 1979, Helge asked, "Now what's really behind the scenes of this lawsuit? ... I'll tell you what it is. It's a few dissidents that want to take power and change the doctrines of the church of God. They don't like the way it's being run. And they don't like the doctrines."[42] That comment could just as easily describe our lawsuit with the Worldwide Church of God 18 years later, except this time the ones who wanted to take over power and change the doctrines were on the *inside*. And the tragedy is, Ralph Helge had joined the dissidents who wanted to take over and change the doctrines Mr. Armstrong had established.

Helge continued in his 1979 message with another comment that probably tens of thousands today would make about Tkachism: "We've got certain rules and we've got doctrines. If you like them, tremendous. And if you don't, or I don't (I'll point to myself), then I'll go to the church that teaches doctrines I do like. But I don't come in here and try to change the way Mr. Armstrong has set the doctrines"[43]—which is exactly what the Tkaches did. They didn't like the doctrines, changed them, and then FORCED everyone out who wouldn't go along.

When we reminded Helge about these statements in his 2002 deposition, he said it was different in 1979 because the dissidents attacked "from the outside."[44] But even in that case, those dissidents were *originally* on the INSIDE before Mr. Armstrong disfellowshiped them for attempting to liberalize church doctrine. In any event, a takeover attempt from the outside is not in any way worse than an inside job, spearheaded by a Judas-like betrayal.

Later in 1979, again while speaking at church services in Pasadena, Helge said, "You talk about contempt. You talk about utter contempt. Here a man [Herbert Armstrong] works all his life in the might and power of God to raise up churches, and here some pip-squeak dissident is going to control Mr. Armstrong and the church."[45] Talk about a self-fulfilling prophecy. Nineteen years later, Helge testified under oath that Mr. Armstrong was employed *by* the church, that the board had *control* over Mr. Armstrong's work, and the authority, if necessary, to FIRE him.

HELGE'S LATE CAREER MOVE

During the deposition, Helge said he had been told by the WCG he would soon retire and be replaced by Bernie Schnippert. It sounded like his final job assignment would be this lawsuit. Mark Helm asked him about the e-publishing project and how that got started. Helge said he got the idea sometime in 2001 while reading a magazine over lunch. "I just started to read it and it just clicked, hey, this is something to investigate."[46]

In looking at the timeline, however, the decision to e-publish appears to have been much more calculated than Helge indicated. On February 13, 2001, Mark Helm informed WCG attorneys that we intended to amend our counterclaim to allege that it would be futile for us to seek the WCG's permission to reprint Mr. Armstrong's works. We wanted to add this to our brief because the Ninth Circuit, even in ruling against us, did leave the door open slightly for us to possibly rely on the Religious Freedom Restoration Act. And for RFRA to be added to our counterclaim, we had to show how futile it would have been to obtain a license for the works.

On February 16, 2001, Ralph Helge contacted Zondervan Publishing for its evaluation on "the licensing fee or sales price for copyrighted literature owned by the church."[47] This means that just *three days* after we told them about the futility amendment, *they started contacting publishers about the procedures and fees for licensing their literature.* It was yet another made-for-litigation ploy.

Later during the summer is when they stated in court filings that they would have considered all along to license the works to us. Around this time is when the e-publishing idea "clicked" with Ralph Helge. At the deposition, Mark asked if there was anyone else at the WCG involved in the e-publishing project. "Not to my knowledge," Helge responded.[48] Later, after we asked who was in charge of coordinating promotion for the sale of Mr. Armstrong's books over the Internet, Helge answered, "I'm the man."[49]

So here was an elderly man on the verge of retirement, who had worked in the WCG's *legal* department for most of his adult life, given charge of the church's new e-publishing "department," established solely in order to undermine our futility claim and to "prove" they had never intended to suppress Mr. Armstrong's works at all.

It's pathetic, I know. But at the same time, it's fascinating history because it shows how much we had acquired in fighting for the truth—even after losing at the Ninth Circuit. As much as they hated the idea, *they knew* that to prevail on the merits in court, they HAD to convince a judge that they were still using Mr. Armstrong's material. So they lied about an annotated project and won at the Ninth Circuit. And in order to defeat our counterclaim, their in-house *attorney* established a new branch in the church's PUBLISHING department, even on the eve of his retirement.

These are supposedly religious men—and yet willing to do or say just about *anything* as long as it helped them win in court.

At the same time, look at what we forced them to do by simply confronting them. At the beginning of the case, remember, Tkach Jr. arrogantly asserted that the reason they filed this suit was to "block the republication of *Mystery of the Ages*." Their *duty* as Christians was to keep this book out of print because they believed "Mr. Armstrong's doctrinal errors are better left out of circulation." Two years later, even though it was a lie, they talked about using Mr. Armstrong's material again. Two years after that, they inquired about licensing and followed that up by making Mr. Armstrong's literature available on demand through e-publishing. True, the literature had to be prefaced by Feazell's attack, which we weren't about to accept. But still, *they were forced to do things they never would have dreamed of doing at the start,* simply because we were willing to fight for Mr. Armstrong's legacy.

My father's faithful determination was beginning to wear them down.

BERNARD SCHNIPPERT

As the wcg's director of finance and planning, Bernie Schnippert made some interesting comments about the relationship between the church's income and its distribution of literature. With Mr. Armstrong, Schnippert said, distributing free literature was designed to hook people into a well-orchestrated fundraising scheme. "If you're going to move someone to your state of mind, you begin at a place you think will interest them and you take them where you want them to go. ... The progression of topics is a type of psychology."[50] Later, he said, "Mr. Armstrong's books, when given, tend to create donations. ... [W]e discontinued *Mystery of the Ages* in spite of the fact that we knew it was, to be crass, a money-maker."[51]

Quite a difference from the party line in 1989—that they discontinued the book *because of* its expense.

Schnippert also elaborated on the wcg's new approach under Tkachism—charging subscription fees for church literature instead of distributing it freely. He said, "[W]hen you give free literature and the person is told they must tithe, in the end you've taken more money out of them in some ways less honestly than if you just charged them in the first place."[52] Of course, as Schnippert well knows, no one ever forced people to voluntarily give donations to the WCG. But that's certainly the way they love to portray Mr. Armstrong's followers—mindless dupes brainwashed into giving money to—OF ALL THINGS—a church!

Tkachism's approach, of course—even though it triggered a precipitous decline in church membership and donations—is much more *honest,* in Schnippert's view. They charged people up front for *new* literature and retired the flawed material so as to "not use it disingenuously" to make money when they "didn't believe it."[53] Yet now that they were in the midst of a legal struggle over the "flawed" stuff, they had no problem disingenuously making money off Mr. Armstrong's literature, *so long as the e-publishing scheme helped them win the case.* Schnippert said they could now justify profiting from Mr. Armstrong's works so long as the writings contained a "disclaimer that plainly tells everyone that we don't agree with it."[54] So he not only revealed the rank hypocrisy behind their supposedly courageous move to retire money-makers in 1989, he admitted that they WOULD NOT make Mr. Armstrong's writings available without a derogatory preface attached. This was another huge admission for us.

Later, in discussing the preface, Schnippert said they worded it as carefully as possible in order "to be respectful of Mr. Armstrong and anyone who were to read it."[55] So Mark went through several statements from the preface, giving Schnippert an opportunity to explain what he meant by "respectful." We asked him if he thought using phrases like "personal bias" and "advertising hook" were complimentary toward Mr. Armstrong. "Do you believe that Mr. Armstrong's views were the result of a personal bias?" Mark asked.[56]

WCG attorney Miles Feldman objected to the question and asked how Schnippert's personal views were relevant to the case. But *they were the ones trying to inject this preface into the litigation,* we maintained.

A lengthy exchange then followed with Miles threatening to call the court magistrate to settle the dispute and Mark complaining that Miles was wasting time. "This is a serious matter," Miles said, raising his voice. "And if you're going to accuse me of bad faith, I'm suggesting right now let's get the magistrate on the phone and we'll get to the bottom of this."[57]

After Miles cooled off, Mark turned to Schnippert:

> Suppose that the wcg literature had a preface which said that the doctrines of that church under Joseph Tkach Jr. were biblically unsound, he was an uneducated dictator with crackpot ideas, that his views were of interest only as a historical curiosity. ... Do you think that would be an effective marketing tool for your literature?"[58]

Miles went ballistic.

But this was all *their* doing. *They* were the ones who introduced the preface and then insisted it be attached to every publication they supposedly offered as a "benefit" to us. *They* were the ones who made the preface CENTRAL to the case. So we took them to task on the preface and exposed the fact that they were guilty of the very things they accused Mr. Armstrong of. And when called upon to answer for their self-righteous hypocrisy, they ran for cover like cowards, hiding behind their lawyer's objections: *Inappropriate! Argumentative! Irrelevant! Invasion of privacy!*

But we weren't about to let them off the hook.

One might think both sides in this battle were being driven further apart in the summer of 2002—hardened by the grueling deposition warfare that took place over the course of two months. And from what we saw on the surface, wcg officials were getting angrier and more defiant by the day.

But on the inside, they were deeply conflicted. *They had the copyrights to Mr. Armstrong's literature* and they burned with anger at the thought of our little church—their nemesis—obtaining rights to distribute these works, especially after we tried to "steal" them.

On the other hand, they did not want to be exposed.

The wcg's preface turned out to be a tremendous opportunity for us. Our forceful response to it, my father said at the beginning of the summer, was the only way we could win.

And he was right.

TWENTY-THREE

© PHILADELPHIA CHURCH OF GOD

"We are pleased to announce that the Worldwide Church of God ... has reached a successful conclusion in its lawsuit against the Philadelphia Church of God."

— RALPH HELGE
Worldwide News, *April 2003*

AT the height of the depositions in August 2002, Ralph Helge wrote to Bob Ardis in an effort to give "accurate information" about the court case. Ardis, a minister disfellowshiped from the PCG in 1997, copied Helge's letter and sent it to his entire mailing list, comprised mostly of PCG members.

In the letter, Mr. Helge accused Gerald Flurry of "pirating" *Mystery of the Ages*, of misinforming and misleading PCG members, of disobeying and disregarding the laws of the land, of using nearly every trick in the book to disrupt the legal process, among other things. He explained how we initially won at the district court level. Judge Letts said we had a right to distribute *Mystery* because, in Helge's own words, "WCG was *not publishing it at the time,* and because it was allegedly central to PCG's religion ...."[1]

Exactly! If there is one thing the WCG learned during the lawsuit, it's that they *could not use their copyrights to suppress Mr. Armstrong's written works.* For all their screaming at the outset of the case—we were "stealing"; we "broke the law"—it turns out that they were the ones misapplying the copyright law. That's what Helge indirectly admitted to Ardis. We won the first round, he said, only because they were not publishing *Mystery of the Ages* "at the time." In fact, they had a "Christian duty" not to. But once they realized they couldn't use a copyright to suppress written works, they concocted a plan to publish them.

Helge told Ardis that the three-judge panel at the Ninth Circuit reversed Judge Letts's ruling. He failed to mention why—because they developed "plans" to publish—in the form of an annotated version.

Helge then made this astonishing comment:

> ... Mr. Flurry has made representations to the PCG members, giving the misimpression that there is still the possibility in the case that the court is going to award PCG the right to pirate the MOA. This is simply, again, misinformation. The case has been finally decided and concluded regarding MOA, and Mr. Flurry, out of sheer desperation, has exhausted all legal remedies available to him. Any attempt of PCG to acquire any court ordered right to print the MOA is over, done, finished. Legally there is NO PLACE ELSE FOR HIM TO GO ON THIS ISSUE. I don't know how else I can say it. PCG's only "right" is to stand before the bar of justice and have damages assessed against them and attorney's fees for the wrong that it has committed.[2]

In quick response, our lead attorney drafted a letter to Helge on September 18, saying, "Any competent lawyer knows that these statements are undeniably false, and you in particular know that they are. It is beyond any dispute that the Ninth Circuit's September 2000 decision did not constitute a final judgment."[3]

Even at my own deposition in 2002, WCG attorney Allan Browne wanted me to acknowledge that we lost the court case and were therefore found guilty of breaking the law. "[A]re you of the understanding that the Ninth Circuit Court of Appeals held that, in terms of *Mystery of the Ages*, we, the Worldwide Church of God, are entitled to damages?"⁴ I told him I understood that, but that it was a decision that could be appealed. "Well, are you aware that your counsel filed a petition … in the United States Supreme Court on that issue and that it was turned down …?" he asked.

> Flurry: Right. And I'm also aware that we have the right to do that yet again.
> Browne: Well, after the damages trial is held, is that what you mean?
> Flurry: Yes.
> Browne: Okay.
> Flurry: Is that not true?
> Browne: Well, I'm not answering questions here today, you are.
> Mark Helm: He knows it is true. So he won't answer.⁵

It was as if they expected us to lay down our weapons and surrender after one setback. The damages trial hadn't even started yet. And we certainly intended to appeal after that. On top of that, the counterclaim had not yet been decided at the district level, let alone the court of appeals or at the Supreme Court.

Yet, in the summer of 2002, Ralph Helge concluded that we had "exhausted *all* legal remedies"—that there was nowhere else for us to go. I think the underlying message in Helge's attempt to misinform was this: *Why won't these guys just give up?* He just wanted all of this to be over, and he boiled over at the fact that we intended to fight them—to take advantage of every possible legal option at our disposal. To Helge, exercising all *our* options was some kind of technical maneuvering intended to thwart the judicial process. He obviously felt much different about exercising all legal options if it benefited *them*, even if it was dubious and dishonest—like when they dismissed their lawsuit in California three weeks after filing in early 1997 because Judge Letts wouldn't grant their request for a temporary restraining order, hoping a lawsuit filed in Oklahoma would render better results. Or after they realized they were losing at the district level and floated the idea that they would publish an annotated *Mystery of the Ages*—a technical maneuver intended to thwart the judicial process. And later, when the e-publishing scheme was established—not by WCG's publishing department or Plain Truth Ministries or ANYTHING having to do with literature, but *by Ralph Helge's legal department,* and for the admitted purpose of undermining our argument that Mr. Armstrong's works were unavailable.

All of this, spearheaded by a man who then accused *us* of thwarting the judicial process.

TELEVISION CUTS

Just days before Helge's letter landed in the mailboxes of many PCG members, my dad called for an Advisory Council of Elders meeting at our headquarters facility in Edmond on September 11. During this meeting with leading ministers of the church, he announced that we would be cutting all of our television stations, except for the cable channel WGN, because of the court case. He said that we were now in the heat of the battle and that our time, energies and finances needed to flow in that direction. He reassured the ministry that if we had the faith of the Prophet Habakkuk, God would eventually give us Mr. Armstrong's material.

While the decision to cut television costs certainly helped increase the work's cash flow, it wasn't made for that reason alone. As our television audience had grown through the years, we were being contacted by an increasing number of respondents who knew very little or nothing about Herbert Armstrong—let alone his teachings. Without Mr. Armstrong's literature, we felt these new contacts could not be spiritually nurtured until we had a breakthrough in the court case. It is difficult to grasp the full depth of our own literature without the foundational teachings of Mr. Armstrong. The idea was, *let's win the court battle first, and then concentrate on taking our message to the largest audience possible.* My father also admonished us to educate our members as to why we were involved in this legal battle. He said, "Maybe God wants to teach the whole church how vital these works are." To win this battle, every member had to do his part.

A week and a half later, PCG members from all over the world convened at various locations to celebrate our annual fall festival—

the Feast of Tabernacles. During the Feast, my dad delivered two messages that were broadcast live, via satellite, to most of the PCG's worldwide membership. In his first message, on September 22, he said he didn't think he would ever give a more important message because of what was happening in our work. He went on to discuss the meaning of the court case—saying it was a test for us, but that if we had faith, God would revive this work and give us that litera-ture somehow—some way. To obtain those works, though, he said we had to be willing to fight to the end—willing to do whatever God required of us.

He concluded the sermon by quoting from Helge's letter to Bob Ardis. Regarding Helge's comment that we had "pirated" Mr. Armstrong's works, my dad said it was WCG leaders who had in fact pirated an ENTIRE CHURCH.[6]

In his second live sermon, on September 27, my dad explained that one reason this trial might be dragging on is because God wants us to EXPOSE the WCG. He told the membership that we intended to press forward, fully intent on exposing them every step of the way.

At the end of the sermon, he announced the TV cuts he had made at the September 11 meeting. He told the membership that our message to the world could not be truly effective until we acquired the right to publish Mr. Armstrong's works. "We must go all out in this court case," he said.[7]

ABOUT FACE

Two weeks after our fall festival ended, on October 14 (the trial had been pushed back to early December), events took yet another dramatic turn: The WCG offered to sell us *Mystery of the Ages* for $4 million. It left us in a state of shock. We thought the price was far too high for just one book, but still, that WCG now wanted to sell it outright—with no restrictive license—was unbelievable.

Why—after all the rhetoric about annotation and e-publishing, after Morgan's ridicule of our March offer to license, after Helge's scathing editorial about PCG's hopeless position ("the case has been finally decided and concluded"; "legally there is no place else for [the PCG] to go"; "PCG's only 'right' is to stand before the bar of justice and have damages assessed against them and attorney's fees for the wrong that it has committed")—would WCG now *ask us* to settle?

This breakthrough was HUGE.

We felt like we had finally worn them down. Our first thought was to get *all* the works—*Mystery of the Ages* and the 18 we were seeking in the counterclaim. Our second thought was about finances. At the time, we only had about $1 million cash on hand, in reserve.

So on Monday, October 21, we offered the WCG $825,000 for *all* the copyrights and first right of refusal to buy any other Armstrong literature they might later sell. They were insulted by the offer and said if we heard laughter coming from Pasadena that night, we would know why. But we were now convinced they didn't want to go to trial with this. They feared the negative publicity it would bring. It was clear they wanted to cut and run and were hoping to get as much as possible from us in return.

They came back with a $3.5 million offer to grant us perpetual licenses for *all* 19 works. On the one hand, we were ecstatic because they dropped from $4 million for *Mystery* to $3.5 million for *everything* we wanted. But instead of selling them outright, they would be licensed. We were understandably wary of any settlement offer that allowed the WCG to interfere with our plans. But they assured us that we would have control over the literature and that the licenses would be permanent. In researching the matter further, we discovered that a perpetual license was far better than anything we could have obtained from the courts—even if we fought to the end and won in the Supreme Court. In that scenario, the Court would have simply ruled that what we did between 1997 and 2000—copying and distributing Mr. Armstrong's literature—was NOT a violation of the copyright law. But it would not have granted us a perpetual license.

About the only thing we couldn't do with a license is sell the works to someone else, which we wouldn't do anyway. But still, we wouldn't *own* the works. And for as hard as we fought, anything other than "© Philadelphia Church of God" inside the front cover of those books just didn't seem right. We also didn't like the idea of any lingering association with the WCG after a six-year lawsuit.

We bumped our original offer up to $950,000, with the same requests—all 19 copyrights and first right of refusal on anything else.

HELGE LASHES OUT AGAIN

Meanwhile, Ralph Helge wouldn't stop spouting off. The *Journal*, a newspaper reporting on the news of WCG and its many splinter groups, interviewed Helge on October 29. The article that was published in the October 31 issue was loaded with Helgeisms: "In various court rulings over the years, the WCG's arguments … have *overwhelmingly* prevailed" and WCG "seeks to recover costs for attorneys' fees plus damages from the PCG for *illegally* printing *Mystery.*"[8]

Helge informed the *Journal* that the WCG was now electronically publishing the very works we were seeking in this case. Even the *Journal* expressed skepticism about the sincerity of such a move, wondering if it was simply a strategy employed to undermine the PCG's position. "Mr. Helge insists the church's real motive is to make the works of Mr. Armstrong available to the public and that removing the PCG's legal claim that these works are unavailable is of only secondary importance."[9]

To admit that removing our legal claim was at least of "secondary importance" was astounding. They never hinted at this in the court proceedings. They made it seem like a genuine attempt to serve the needs of our members. But going back to Helge's assessment of the lawsuit, why would the WCG *even need* to make the works available if we were in such an indefensible position? Hadn't the courts been ruling "overwhelmingly" in WCG's favor? Were we not left with just one option in this litigation—standing before the bar of justice to have damages assessed against us for our "unlawful" and "illegal" distribution of *Mystery?*

Helge concluded his interview with another personal attack against my father. "Mr. Helge predicted that, whenever the final court hearing adjourns and the PCG is still not allowed to print Mr. Armstrong's books, 'I'll bet he says this is a famine of hearing the Word, that Satan did this ….'"[10]

He said that two weeks *after* the WCG offered to sell us *Mystery of the Ages*.

Meanwhile, my dad had called for a church-wide fast within the PCG. Members were asked to beseech God for special deliverance in this struggle. He scheduled the fast for the fourth weekend of November.

DENIED SUMMARY JUDGMENT AGAIN

The WCG lowered its settlement offer to $3.1 million, but insisted that the figure was much too low for any discussion about selling the copyrights. Their offer was for perpetual licenses only and we would have to print a disclaimer on the literature saying, "Used by permission of the Worldwide Church of God." There's no way we would have ever agreed to that.

We bumped our offer to $1.5 million—again, for all the copyrights and first right of refusal on anything else they might sell.

Meanwhile, preparations for the December trial had to move forward. In the *Journal* article, Helge had indicated that if the November 6 summary judgment hearing came out in favor of WCG, then the next step would undoubtedly be a "trial to determine attorneys' fees and damages the PCG would have to pay the WCG." [11]

But at the hearing, Judge Snyder again denied their motion for summary judgment on the grounds of the Religious Freedom Restoration Act.

Even though they were now e-publishing the works we wanted, the judge said they were "charging too much" for *Mystery of the Ages*. Our attorney pointed out that "although the Ninth Circuit did say that having to ask for a license and presumably having to pay for it couldn't be a substantial burden, they didn't say that the Worldwide Church could set the price wherever they wanted." [12]

"And in fact," the judge added, "they implicitly suggest that it *has to be available* on a *reasonable* basis." [13]

It was yet another sharp blow to the WCG's already wobbly legal position. Judge Snyder set the next hearing for November 25, when she would consider the arguments of both sides to exclude evidence at trial.

JUNK SCIENCE

While formulating a defense against our counterclaim, the WCG also had to prove how badly they had been "damaged" by our distribution of *Mystery*—a book we gave away FOR FREE; one that the WCG had distributed for free during Mr. Armstrong's life, and now had a "Christian duty" to keep out of print. The bulk of evidence in this regard fell on the shoulders of a "forensic economist" named John Crissey, who had worked as an expert in numerous cases for Allan Browne's law firm. According to Crissey's September 18, 2002, preliminary expert report, WCG had been denied "profits" totaling $3.84 million—$4.3 million with interest—by our distribution of nearly 100,000 copies of *Mystery*. He also calculated the *future* "losses" of WCG to be $3.3 million. All totaled, WCG would be seeking $7.63 million in damages at trial—just for *Mystery of the Ages*.[14] (They would also be seeking millions of dollars in attorneys' fees.)

Crissey based his findings on the fact that *Mystery* recipients gave more money than non-recipients of the book—never mind the fact that *Mystery* recipients might be more inclined to agree with the PCG's overall message and work. What Crissey ignored was that pre-1997 data showed that *Mystery* recipients had *already* been giving at a higher rate long before PCG even started distributing the book! He ignored this data (which we supplied him) because it completely contradicted his "expert" analysis. Many of our own members and their children were the first ones to request copies of *Mystery* once we began distribution. These people were already "pre-disposed" to giving more—they were already tithing members of the church!

In PCG's motion to dismiss Crissey's report, Mark Helm argued that the court should not admit Crissey's testimony, calling it bogus, fatally flawed and defective junk science, among other things.

Judge Snyder agreed. She wrote in her tentative order, a few days after a November 25 hearing, "[T]he methodology employed by Mr. Crissey has not been shown to be sufficiently reliable to allow it to be presented to the trier of fact, and therefore his quantitative estimate of the amount of contributions that are attributable to distribution of MOA is not admissible."[15]

Thus, on the eve of the damages trial, the WCG was faced with the prospect of not having any real evidence to show how much they were "damaged" by our *Mystery* distribution. Of course, they had much difficulty with this argument long before Crissey came along.

When we started distributing the work in 1997, we absorbed all the printing and mailing costs, and then gave it away free of charge. Under any circumstances, it would be difficult to show how this was some sort of moneymaking scheme for PCG. But for WCG to then claim that our free distribution was actually stealing "profits" from them is the height of hypocrisy. Aside from the unfathomable logic of the idea to begin with, why would they now seek "profits" from a book they had been ridiculing for years and had vowed to keep out of circulation? Bernie Schnippert, after all, testified that "as a matter of scruples," they determined long ago not to disingenuously profit from material they "didn't believe."[16]

THE CULT "EXPERT"

Besides John Crissey, the WCG relied on other biased "experts" like Ruth Tucker, the self-proclaimed authority on "cultic movements." Of course, when we brought up Tkachism's personal beliefs, like during the Schnippert deposition, the WCG legal team would blow a gasket. But when they brought up *our* personal beliefs and tried to make us look like a dangerous cult, to them it was completely relevant to the merits of the case.

Tucker's report was a boring rehash of what Tkachism had been saying all along. *Mr. Armstrong was a dictator with bizarre teachings; Mystery of the Ages was a huge money-making scheme; the Tkaches courageously transformed the church; Gerald Flurry thinks he's above the law,* and so on.

Tucker said our claim that Mr. Armstrong wanted every prospective member to read *Mystery of the Ages* before baptism had "absolutely no merit at all,"[17] even though the requirement was clearly stated in the *Pastor General's Report* in 1986. Relying instead on page 26 of *Transformed by Truth,* Tucker said Mr. Armstrong's baptismal requirements were, if anything, "lax." She also said "there is no evidence that the PCG ever had a baptismal prerequisite" for reading *Mystery,* even though we had stated the policy verbally and in print numerous times between 1989 and 1996.[18]

On the point of government, Tucker said Mr. Armstrong "was an authoritarian leader. His personality and leadership style dominated the WCG for five decades ...."[19] In an article she wrote for *Christianity Today* in 1996, she characterized the WCG as a "classic case study of an authoritarian cult."[20] Mr. Armstrong, she wrote, "held tight reins over his diverse empire. His authority was unquestioned by most church members ...."[21]

So at her deposition, we asked if she believed Mr. Tkach Sr. had inherited the same degree of control from Mr. Armstrong in 1986. She confidently said NO,[22] even though Feazell and Schnippert had both said the opposite earlier at their depositions. We told Tucker about how Tkach Sr. designated himself as an apostle in 1986 and about Tkach Jr.'s empty promises to modify the church's form of governance—and she started backpedaling: "I'm not an expert in the area of church government."[23] But mention *Herbert Armstrong* or *Gerald Flurry* and she immediately becomes one.

Tucker wrote, "Former members of the PCG have told how Mr. Flurry's words were often presented as the very words of God."[24] We asked about the identity of these "former members," but she couldn't remember which *website* she got it from. She assured us that "there are a number of sites that have postings from former members of the Philadelphia Church of God."[25] She did not, however, personally contact any current or former members of the PCG, nor any PCG officials, while preparing her "expert" testimony about our church.

We asked her if there was anything about the establishment of the PCG that she would characterize as positive. "Not that I can think of," she responded.[26] "... I've never heard or seen literature that would indicate that the Philadelphia Church of God was particularly looking to assess its views against scripture."[27] That is incredible. She finds *nothing* positive about the PCG—*nothing biblical* about our doctrines. She just knows.

Regarding our supporters, she said the people attracted to Mr. Armstrong's teachings are book readers. "They might not be terribly sophisticated thinkers, but they were certainly people that read books ...."[28] That's how she characterizes hundreds of thousands of members who joined the WCG over the course of Mr. Armstrong's ministry and millions more who read his literature and donated to his work—*they're all simple-minded.*

Far from being hired for her expert testimony, Ruth Tucker was brought in because she is pre-programmed to heap praise on Tkachism no matter what. Her intimate relationship with the Tkaches goes way back. In 1988—two years after Mr. Armstrong died—Michael Snyder, the WCG's assistant public relations director, contacted her about the doctrinal reforms taking place in the WCG. He wanted her to have the most up-to-date information for a book she was writing about cults. In 1991, Tucker invited Snyder's boss, David Hulme, to speak at the Trinity Evangelical Divinity School about the progress the WCG had made in accepting the trinity doctrine. In 1996, the WCG returned the favor and invited Tucker to speak at its ministerial conferences. "Dr. Tucker was excited about our reforms and encouraged us in every way she could," Tkach Jr. wrote in 1997. "We consider her a gift from God."[29]

GUTTING THEIR CASE

Judging by Ruth Tucker's expert report, Mike Feazell's preface and questions we were asked during our depositions, the WCG clearly intended to label us as a cult in court. They wanted to show how we were supposedly a racially bigoted, misogynistic fringe group, led by a self-proclaimed dictator.

But in her tentative order after the November 25 hearing, Judge Snyder said she would not allow the trial to turn into an "attack on Flurry" because it would "distract the jury from the issues at trial" and "unfairly prejudice PCG." Later, the court concluded that the "WCG should not be permitted to describe specific religious tenets— either its own, or PCG's—regarding racial issues because such evidence will be unfairly prejudicial and will confuse the issues at trial."[30] In explaining why they discontinued *Mystery,* the judge said she would allow WCG to say that it considered its message to be "no longer *socially* acceptable." But so far as the judge was concerned, they couldn't even use the word "race."[31]

Another huge breakthrough for us. Added to the ruling on

Crissey, we felt the tentative order would pretty much gut the WCG's case for damages. Not only were they unable to prove damages, now they couldn't sling mud. Added to that, they still had to tackle our counterclaim, not to mention subject themselves to a rigorous PCG defense dead set on exposing their lies and deceit.

SEALING THE DEAL

The damages trial had now been pushed back to March 4, allowing both sides more time to argue over what evidence would be allowed at trial. At a December 18 hearing, as a follow-up to her tentative order, the judge said she wasn't inclined to change her tentative ruling.

Two days after that hearing, the WCG seemed all the more eager to settle, lowering its licensing offer to a $3 million bottom line. Sensing desperation on their part, my dad was inclined to be patient. On December 24, we put together a $2.5 million package offer for all the copyrights to the 19 works involved in the litigation.

We didn't hear back from WCG, despite their insistence to get things done quickly, until after their executives returned from their Christmas/New Year's holiday celebration.

On Tuesday, January 7, the WCG came down to $2.8 million for perpetual licenses, but with these added concessions: The copyright notice, agreed upon by both sides before finalizing the deal, would say something like "© Publishing Inc.," but we would not have to print any disclaimers under the copyright.

But buying the copyrights altogether, at a price range this "low," was not possible, they told us. Their offer intrigued us: no disclaimer and a copyright notice that was at least inoffensive. For the most part, that's what we had at the beginning of our distribution in 1997. We printed the works without a disclaimer and a notice that read "© Herbert W. Armstrong."

In weighing their offer, we took a step back and considered our ultimate objective at the outset of our distribution of Mr. Armstrong's works. It was to keep the WCG from destroying those writings forever by making them freely available to all who valued them. With that in mind, we began to see a scenario in which we actually could live with a license.

After weighing our options for several days, we reached a final decision on Monday, January 13, 2003: $2.65 million for the WCG to "grant PCG a worldwide, nonexclusive, perpetual, irrevocable, fully paid-up, non-royalty-bearing license" to all 19 works. Under the agreement, the copyright notice would read "© Herbert W. Armstrong."

The next day, to our utter amazement and shock, the WCG asked us to submit an alternative offer for buying the copyrights outright. Thus, by the end of the 14th, we had two final offers on the table— one for licenses and one for full copyright ownership. We offered $2.65 million for perpetual licenses and $3 million to buy everything outright.

On Thursday morning, January 16—*17 years to the day after Herbert W. Armstrong's death*—the WCG agreed to sell us *all* the copyrights for $3 million. Apart from contributions from our insurance carrier, the total cost to the PCG was an even $2 million. With about $1 million on hand, we planned to finance the other $1 million.

Later that day, Mark Helm and the WCG's attorney conference-called Judge Snyder to tell her that both sides had agreed to terms of settlement. Thus, for all intents and purposes, six years of litigation ended the afternoon of January 16, 2003.

WCG's "Successful" Conclusion

After settlement, Ralph Helge wrote to the members of the WCG, "We are pleased to announce that the Worldwide Church of God ... has reached a successful conclusion in its lawsuit against the Philadelphia Church of God."[32] This is how he spun the negotiation process: "During the last year or so, PCG made different offers to license or purchase some or all of the literary works in question, and thereby settle the litigation. As the church did not consider that the amounts offered were sufficient, the offers were rejected. But then PCG made a substantial offer of $3 million to purchase 19 of the literary works written by Mr. Armstrong, and settle the litigation."

That version of the story, as is customary with Tkachism, leaves out all the essential facts. But it didn't matter to us. *We knew that* deep in his heart of hearts, *Helge knew* who came out victorious in this case.

Think about it.

Their publicly stated goal, from the very beginning of the battle, was to keep Mr. Armstrong's teachings out of circulation. Joe Jr. had to eat those words.

They told the court early on that they had suffered irreparable harm by our "unlawful" action because in distributing *Mystery of the Ages,* we were "perpetuating beliefs no longer followed by Worldwide Church." They *loathed* the thought of Mr. Armstrong's teachings resurfacing.

The WCG owned the copyrights, Greg Albrecht said in 1997, and they "DO NOT ALLOW OTHERS to publish our former teachings and doctrines for a *variety* of reasons."[33] Flurry *understood,* they told the court in 1999, that the WCG "refused" requests to reprint *Mystery of the Ages.* This was common knowledge. *They* refused to make Mr. Armstrong's works available—and they wouldn't allow OTHERS to do it either.

After Judge Letts ruled that we could rightfully distribute *Mystery of the Ages,* Helge called the judgment an "erroneous view of the law" and said our reprinting was "in violation of both the commandment of God and the copyright law of the United States."[34]

They brought up the annotated plan in an attempt to overturn Judge Letts's decision. After that happened at the Ninth Circuit, Helge said we only had "certain limited rights."[35] But for all practical purposes, he continued, the Ninth Circuit's decision "would seem to be final in all material respects." That, as it turns out, was wishful thinking.

Then, in April 2001, Tkach Jr. told *Christianity Today* that if the Supreme Court refused to hear our appeal, "WCG lawyers will go after several overseas websites that post the complete text of *Mystery of the Ages.*"[36] Intimidating words!

After the Supreme Court decided it would not hear our appeal, Ralph Helge's assistant, Earle Reese, incorrectly asserted, "This is the end of the PCG's ability to appeal to a higher court."[37]

After that, the WCG worked to make the literature available

through print on demand. Not because they wanted to—they *had* to. But they still had the upper hand, they were convinced, because all the literature downloaded would include a nasty preface. Yet this turned out to be yet another stronghold position they gave up on.

Then, when asked about the likelihood of licensing Mr. Armstrong's works to a potentially dangerous sociopath like my father, Joseph Tkach Jr. testified to this: The WCG had to be in a position where it could "police or control" the literature if there was to ever be a settlement in terms of licensing. More words they would have to eat.

And what about Helge's letter to Bob Ardis, where he portrayed my father as a stiff-necked rebel attempting to thwart the legal process? We were completely out of options, he said. We were staggering along, acting on sheer desperation, but with no place to go, except before the bar of justice to be judged guilty and sentenced to pay up to the Worldwide Church of God. Of course, none of that ever happened either.

What did happen is this: They sold us a storehouse of literature for an amount of money that, by our estimate, barely covered their legal costs, if even that. They retrieved no "profits" or "damages" from us. All their "overwhelming" victories in court were conditioned on them making Mr. Armstrong's works available. And in the end, they were exactly where they started before the case, money-wise, but having forfeited ownership of all 19 copyrights.

ETHICAL QUESTIONS

Writing in *Christianity Today* after the lawsuit settled, Marshall Allen said, "At one point, the WCG said it was fighting the countersuit because it didn't want to see the heretical works republished."[38] But the church had since reversed its course, he wrote. Allen quoted Reginald Killingley, a former WCG pastor, as saying, "They're willing, in effect, to support what they condemn—to permit the perpetuation and promotion of heresy for the sake of money."

The article sent shock waves through the WCG, even prompting a response in the *Worldwide News*. The *last thing* the WCG wanted from this whole ordeal was for their friends in the evangelical community to turn on them. *Christianity Today* had long been a staunch supporter of Tkachism.

In its coverage of the lawsuit in 2001, the magazine summarized the case this way: "[T]he Ninth Circuit Court of Appeals ruled on a 2-1 vote that Armstrong legally willed his copyright of *Mystery of the Ages* to the WCG, which could restrict its distribution. The court majority said that despite the WCG action to suppress the book, PCG could not claim fair use in reprinting the entire book. Because they now believe *Mystery of the Ages* is 'riddled with error,' WCG officials say they feel a Christian duty to withhold the book."[39] Believing many of the same doctrines Tkachism accepted, *Christianity Today* had no problem reporting on what they viewed as the WCG's attempt to "withhold the book." They didn't want the book in circulation either!

So when the WCG granted us unrestricted ownership of all the copyrights, you can see why they were disturbed by the WCG's about-face.

The WCG surrender also bothered another Tkachism advocate, Philip Arnn. Writing for *Watchman Expositor* in 1993, Arnn said, "The current doctrinal revisions being brought about by the efforts of Joseph Tkach and his team are to be applauded as extraordinary in light of their spiritual benefits to the church membership."[40] But their decision to sell the copyrights 10 years later, according to Arnn, raised ethical questions about the WCG. "These are heretical doctrines that are destructive to the eternal life of anyone who comes under their influence," Arnn said. "To have profited from the release of the copyrights is a matter that I would think [would be] very troubling to the conscience."[41]

Even the WCG's hometown newspaper, the *Pasadena Star-News*, called into question the church's ethical standing. "The settlement ... allows Armstrong's followers in the Philadelphia Church of God to reproduce the books. ... Present Pastor General Joseph Tkach Jr., however, once wrote that it was their 'Christian duty' to keep the book out of print 'because we believe Mr. Armstrong's doctrinal errors are better left out of circulation.'"[42] The lawsuit had finally ended. It had been six years since Tkach Jr. wrote his book.

And here he was *still* getting pummeled for the "Christian duty" statement—and from a newspaper in his own backyard!

According to the *Star-News*, Bernie Schnippert said it would have been financially "imprudent" for them not to accept the settlement offer. "We came to an end where we received a considerable sum of money and the other party received a number of works that are out of date and inaccurate according to most of the Christian world," said Schnippert.[43]

Just nine months earlier, we listened to Schnippert testify smugly that Tkachism had supposedly taken the moral high ground by *not* milking revenue from teachings they didn't believe in—which is precisely what they did in the end.

TO THE VICTOR GO THE SPOILS

Contrast the WCG's sellout with what the Philadelphia Church of God obtained in this struggle. Our ONE GOAL at the outset, stated clearly in all our literature, was to make *Mystery of the Ages* available to a wide audience. In the end—something we could not have imagined in our wildest dreams before the case—we OWNED *Mystery of the Ages,* as well as SIX OTHER BOOKS by Mr. Armstrong, *11 booklets* and a 58-LESSON Bible correspondence course.

On top of the literature, we obtained access to thousands of internal documents through discovery—letters, reports, bulletins, interoffice memos, board minutes, e-mails, interviews, books, magazines, newspapers, sermons, announcements, transcripts, financial disclosures, contracts, surveys, spreadsheets and statistics. We obtained multiple thousands of pages of sworn testimony in affidavits, declarations and depositions. There was six years' worth of court documents that we and the WCG had filed—briefs, rebuttals, motions, opposition motions, petitions, claims and counterclaims. Add to that all the documents filed by the judicial branch— courtroom transcripts, orders, tentative orders, summary judgments, injunctions, opinions and dissenting opinions.

Without these documents, it would not have been possible to write *this* book. And without this book, we could not have exposed Tkachism's deceptive agenda nearly to the extent that we now have.

Besides *Raising the Ruins,* we had the opportunity to expose their lies during litigation—before judges, magistrates, attorneys, clerks, law students, reporters—even the general public. This case, after all, did attract national attention, including a feature story on the front page of the *Wall Street Journal.*

Then there were the depositions—particularly those during the summer of 2002. What an opportunity for a little "peanut shell" supposedly going nowhere. After the Tkaches absolutely wrecked the church we loved, we found ourselves in the enviable position of making them, under oath, ANSWER FOR ALL THEY HAD DONE.

For their predisposed hatred for Mr. Armstrong and their slanderous assassination of his character.

For all the lies they told to the membership.

For the ministers they bullied or fired.

The selfish will they FORCED upon an unsuspecting flock.

For the reputations they destroyed.

The marriages and families they split apart.

For the work, the property, the publications and programs they either sold off or discontinued.

For their inept mismanagement of all the money and resources they inherited.

And for their self-righteous ARROGANCE. A *Christian* duty to keep Mr. Armstrong's doctrines "out of circulation"? I mean, really, who do they think they are?

They hated answering for all this. And the fact that WE were in the same room, giving our attorneys suggestions and input along the way, made it that much more awkward and upsetting for them. In fact, at the very first deposition we had in the case, in the summer of 1998, their attorney objected to the fact that we had three PCG representatives in attendance—my father, Dennis Leap and me.

They wanted to strip away all the *historical* intrigue—the PASSIONATE spiritual and emotional involvement we had invested in this case, in this *way of life* under Mr. Armstrong. They knew we were righteously indignant—even angry—about what Tkachism had done. They knew we would intensely fight for our spiritual livelihood—so they didn't want us around. They wanted this battle to be fought between lawyers only—and over what they considered to be purely a legal matter involving the Copyright Act and "stolen" property. But we insisted on being there for all of it. And we were. All three of us attended every major deposition—sometimes we even brought a fourth representative from our church. And besides the first hearing with Judge Letts, we attended every major hearing after that, even though it meant frequent flights between Oklahoma and California.

If they couldn't prevent our attendance, they worked to prevent us from saying anything about the lawsuit. Early on, they designated just about *everything* as confidential. They didn't want their story going public which, in itself, is a story. We, on the other hand, wanted complete transparency, which is why we later moved to have the confidentiality seal removed. I'm not saying we weren't nervous when they deposed us. *But we had nothing to hide.* Our position was clear from the start. *Yes, we printed Mr. Armstrong's works— and we firmly believe, before God and the authorities of our land, that it was lawful.* Besides that, we looked upon being deposed as if we were testifying on behalf of Herbert W. Armstrong's legacy. What an honor.

There were many other moments we were proud of during our six-year struggle: The miraculous start to the case, when Judge Letts whipped the wcg into a tailspin, essentially saying, "I think you are going to lose." Then at the Ninth Circuit, even though we lost, to appear in court a few blocks from the Pasadena headquarters *Mr. Armstrong built*—it was a privileged opportunity I'll never, ever forget. I'm proud of the fact that we submitted a petition to the United States Supreme Court, even though it didn't hear the case.

Besides all the proud moments, there were the many profound lessons we learned: the unwavering faith of my father; the willingness to stand up and fight for a worthy cause and the abundant fruit that came from that; how we must go on the offensive to overcome evil—like printing *Mystery of the Ages* irrespective of what they might do, or filing the counterclaim, or kicking off the ad campaign, or our response to the preface.

These all were powerful lessons I will never forget. What an education. I think of the many sermons and articles our struggle has *already* inspired—and now this book.

None of this would have happened without the lawsuit.

Honestly, I find it difficult to pinpoint *anything* negative about the litigation. Naturally, no one wants to be sued, but even in the midst of the litigation, our work prospered. *Four* out of the six years, we were able to freely distribute *Mystery of the Ages* to 100,000 recipients. For two years during the lawsuit, we freely distributed five other works by Mr. Armstrong.

Even looking at it financially, it was a blessing. Jesus likened the kingdom of God to a pearl of great price. Upon finding that "pearl," it says in Matthew 13, the merchant went and sold *everything* he had to obtain it. In Matthew 19, Jesus told a rich man who wanted to inherit the spiritual riches of God's Kingdom that he had to be willing to give up EVERYTHING of *physical* value.

Over the course of six years, including the $2 million we were responsible for at settlement, we spent about $5 million on this lawsuit—*less than one tenth of our total income during this same period.*

And considering what we obtained in return—it's by far the best money we've ever spent.

TWENTY-FOUR
VICTORY PROPHESIED

*"I prophesy to you that, one way or the other, God will
provide a way for us to mail that book again."*

— GERALD FLURRY
Trumpet, *March-April 2001*

RUTH Tucker says we don't base our beliefs on Scripture, but
it was actually the Bible that served as our guide throughout
the entirety of this struggle. Our God-given commission,
grounded in Scripture, is what prompted my father to print *Mystery
of the Ages* in the first place. Then, after the WCG attacked, my father
relied on *Scripture* to establish the framework for our legal strategy:
OFFENSIVE WARFARE. And after every setback, he turned to *God's word*
for encouragement.

"I'm not discouraged—I'm not depressed," my father told PCG
members a few days after the Ninth Circuit ruled against us on
September 18, 2000. "I want to fight more than ever. I asked the
lawyers to fight as if our lives depended on it, but to really fight it
with a positive attitude—realizing that God is with us." [1]

Soon after the decision at the appellate level, our attorneys petitioned for a rehearing. We submitted a brief to all 27
judges at the Ninth Circuit, hoping one of them would move
to have our case submitted before an 11-judge panel. No one
responded.

"It's not over yet," my father insisted. "We're going to win this thing in the end. We absolutely know that."

While waiting to hear if the Supreme Court would accept our case, my dad made this amazing statement in the March-April 2001 *Trumpet*: "We are in a court battle over Herbert W. Armstrong's book *Mystery of the Ages*. The big issue is, *who owns the copyright?* ... Now there has been an injunction issued. We have had to stop printing and mailing *Mystery of the Ages* (and all of Mr. Armstrong's writings).

"We have appealed to the U.S. Supreme Court. There is less than a 1 percent chance of our getting into the Supreme Court, but I believe we will. I prophesy to you that, *one way or the other*, God will provide a way for us to mail that book again."[2]

A few weeks after that appeared in print, on April 2, the Supreme Court declined to hear our petition without comment as to why. On the surface, things had gone from bad to worse.

Yet everything my dad kept saying assured PCG members that things would eventually take a turn for the better. That's because, in relying on the sure word of *Bible prophecy,* he knew what the lawsuit's outcome would be *even before it ended.*

In *The Royal Book of Revelation,* published about the same time the Supreme Court decided not to hear our case, he wrote,

> Should we deliver *Mystery of the Ages*? I tell you WE MUST DELIVER IT! When the Bible talks about prophesying again, that primarily means the *same* prophecy—again. God is talking about a message that has been prophesied before. WE MUST PROPHESY AGAIN, BECAUSE WE HAVEN'T YET REACHED THE LARGEST AUDIENCE POSSIBLE WITH *MYSTERY OF THE AGES*. THE JOB IS STILL INCOMPLETE.
>
> God won't allow anybody to stop this message until that work is done. The injunction is only a temporary delay![3]

He based his strong statements on certain prophecies in Revelation 10, where God said the "mystery of God" had to be "finished" before Christ returned (see Revelation 10:7, 11). This is why, he went on to say, the PCG has been commissioned to get *Mystery of the Ages* to the world. "But for this temporary injunction,

HERBERT W. ARMSTRONG
1892-1986
Founder and pastor general of the Worldwide Church of God,
author of Mystery of the Ages

Herbert W. Armstrong works at his first office on the Ambassador College campus in what later became part of the college library. The work started small, but it grew to have worldwide impact. The Plain Truth *magazine had a peak circulation of 8.4 million—nearly as much as* Time *and* Newsweek *combined.*

Ambassador College was known for its elegance and beauty. At left, the Loma D. Armstrong Academic Center and Italian Gardens. Above, the Hall of Administration.

Completed in 1974, Ambassador Auditorium was the crown jewel of the Ambassador College campus and Worldwide Church of God headquarters. Acclaimed as the "Carnegie Hall of the West," it hosted performances by hundreds of great artists including Joan Sutherland, Vladimir Horowitz, Luciano Pavarotti and Arthur Rubinstein. After Mr. Armstrong died, the concert series was canceled and the auditorium sold.

In one of his last public appearances, Mr. Armstrong presents Mystery of the Ages *to students at Ambassador College. A summary of his life's work, the book was declared to be heresy by his successors and shelved only 2½ years after his death.*

A pioneer in religious broadcasting, Herbert W. Armstrong was heard by millions on radio and television for over 50 years. At its peak, his program, the World Tomorrow, *was the most viewed religious program in the United States. It was canceled in 1994.*

Mr. Armstrong traveled in the church's Gulfstream II aircraft, visiting heads of state, dignitaries and church areas around the world. At his death, letters of condolence were sent to the WCG by heads of state from all over the globe, including one from U.S. President Ronald Reagan, who said, "You can take pride in his legacy."

Highly honored and praised as an "unofficial ambassador for world peace," Mr. Armstrong met with leaders and audiences in more than 70 countries—including the king and queen of Thailand, pictured above.

Mr. Armstrong meets with President Hosni Mubarak of Egypt. Mubarak's predecessor, Anwar Sadat, was a close friend of Mr. Armstrong.

Mr. Armstrong visits with first lady Nancy Reagan and China's Little Ambassadors of Shanghai. The Chinese performers' trip to the U.S., sponsored by the Ambassador International Cultural Foundation, included tours of Ambassador College and the White House.

The first PCG headquarters building in Edmond, Oklahoma.

Left: PCG Pastor General Gerald Flurry packs envelopes with the first printing of
Malachi's Message *in a church member's home. Right: PCG members answer phone*
calls in response to the Key of David *television program in the first call center.*

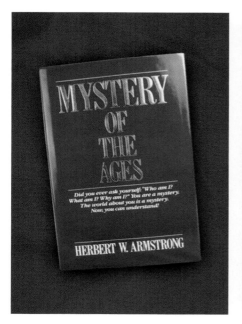

On January 4, 1997, Gerald Flurry announced that the PCG would begin reprinting Mr. Armstrong's last work, Mystery of the Ages. The WCG sued for copyright infringement, saying it was their "Christian duty" to keep the book out of print.

PCG representatives meet with attorneys to discuss court strategy. From left: Kelly Klaus, Dennis Leap, Mark Helm, Gerald Flurry, Stephen Flurry and Craig Winters. The PCG counter-sued the WCG for rights to 18 other works. The WCG eventually agreed to abandon their "Christian duty" to keep Mystery of the Ages out of print, and sold the copyrights to it and the 18 other works to the PCG.

Counterclockwise from top: Gerald Flurry speaks in the John Amos Field House, under construction. Inside of the gymnasium under construction. Author Stephen Flurry teaches a class during the second year of the college. With a golden shovel, Gerald Flurry officially breaks ground on the new building project.

College students sit beside a lushly landscaped koi pond outside the John Amos Field House. Herbert W. Armstrong College seeks to replicate the beauty and standard that was set at Ambassador College.

Students study outside a dormitory.

*Artist's rendering of the proposed new auditorium, future home of the
Armstrong International Cultural Foundation concert series.*

*The John Amos Field House is the location for many college activities. It is
currently the venue for performances hosted by the Armstrong International
Cultural Foundation and the Young Ambassadors.*

The Young Ambassadors, patterned after the WCG group of the same name, perform at schools, parades and more. Here, they pose after filming a video for a film to be played for Church members at festival sites around the world.

The Berlin Philharmonic Wind Quintet performs in the John Amos Field House. The PCG hosts several concerts each year in the tradition of Mr. Armstrong's performing arts series.

Broadcasting to a potential worldwide audience of over 400 million people on over 180 stations, Gerald Flurry discusses world events in the light of Bible prophecy on the weekly Key of David television program.

German   French   Italian   Spanish

Students and volunteers in the Mail Processing Center help package some of the 4 million-plus pieces of literature the church mails each year. On the opposite page is a sampling of the magazines and literature produced and distributed by the PCG, including some of Mr. Armstrong's works the PCG successfully fought the WCG for the rights to print.

Over one million pieces of literature are stored in the church's Mail Processing Center warehouse. Literature is freely distributed worldwide to all who request it.

The Hall of Administration of the Philadelphia Church of God

Mystery of the Ages is going out again. Understanding this really puts things into a greatly reduced time frame," he wrote.

He didn't know all the answers with respect to HOW God would do it—only that God would do it!

PROPHECY GETS MORE SPECIFIC

In the May 31, 2001, issue of the *Journal,* Bill Stough wrote,

> The director of the Worldwide Church of God's legal department says that if the Philadelphia Church of God wants to publish and distribute WCG-copyrighted publications it should negotiate directly with the Worldwide Church of God.[4]

So far as we know, this was the WCG's first indication that they might annul their "Christian duty" doctrine. And in reading between the lines, Helge was indirectly admitting, *There are no plans to annotate or make Mr. Armstrong's works available in their original form, so go ahead and make us an offer.* Reality had set in. They knew they had to, in some form, make Mr. Armstrong's works available to the public.

Later that year, in September 2001, we produced another book, titled *Who Is "That Prophet"?* My dad wrote on page 86,

> I believe we will not lose the court case. Yes, our chances of winning are small. But that only makes greater odds for God. He is like the Supreme Court in that He only takes certain cases. But He usually takes them when you've already gone into the fiery furnace! *Mystery of the Ages* was an open door for us. God has put it on hold temporarily. BUT ISAIAH 22:22 SAYS THAT WHEN ELIAKIM OPENS A DOOR, NONE CAN SHUT IT. WE MUST HAVE FAITH IN THAT.[5]

Whereas Revelation 10 (as expounded on in *The Royal Book of Revelation*) revealed that the message in *Mystery of the Ages* would, in fact, go out again, the prophecies discussed in *That Prophet* indicated more. Isaiah 22 says that someone in this end time would come as a type of Eliakim. Notice what verse 24 says regarding this man: "And they shall hang upon him all the glory of his father's house, the offspring and the issue, all *vessels of small quantity*, from the *vessels* of cups, even to all the *vessels* of flagons."[6]

Anciently, these vessels were the tools needed to perform the temple services. My dad explained that today, "These must refer to all of our books and booklets. All the glory hangs on Eliakim—ALL THE REVELATION FROM MR. ARMSTRONG ...."[7]

This was the first indication we had that God wanted more for us than just the right to copy and distribute Mr. Armstrong's works. *He wanted us to own them!*

E-PUBLISHING—MORE REVELATION

Around this time is when Helge devised the e-publishing scheme. Initially, they wanted us to absorb the costs of the project. In November 2001, however, they told us they would move forward with the e-publishing venture, at their own cost, in order to undermine our argument that it would be futile to request a license.

That same month, we produced yet another book, *The God Family Vision*. In it, my dad wrote, "*Mystery of the Ages* DOESN'T BELONG to the Worldwide Church of God. It is the knowledge of God!"[8]

On pages 132-135 of that book, my dad discussed how the Worldwide Church of God had sold its spiritual birthright, comparing that church to Esau. He wrote, "If you sell your birthright for all the wealth in the world today, it's still just a bowl of soup!"[9] And that's what the WCG had been doing for a number of years—selling off valuable gifts given to Mr. Armstrong, fine furniture, youth campsites and facilities, festival sites, college campuses. They were even trying to sell their headquarters facilities in Pasadena, including the church's crown jewel—Ambassador Auditorium.

But would they also sell off Mr. Armstrong's writings? Up to that time, they had only suggested licenses—and very restrictive ones at that.

HABAKKUK REVEALED THE OUTCOME

As 2002 wore on, though the damages trial had yet to begin and the counterclaim was unresolved, Bible prophecy indicated the lawsuit was quickly winding down. My dad wrote a lengthy article in our September-October issue of *Royal Vision*. The title speaks for itself: "Habakkuk Reveals the Outcome of Our Court Case." Regarding Habakkuk 3:2, he wrote,

> THE PCG HAS NEVER NEEDED *REVIVING* EXCEPT IN THE COURT CASE. This is a prophecy about God reviving us. So we need to prepare for a spectacular end! Yes—WE ARE GOING TO GET MR. ARMSTRONG'S WRITINGS. ... I believe that God will *have* to give us Mr. Armstrong's writings. I state that in faith, and I strongly believe He will if we have the faith we need.[10]

Once again, he based such strong statements on what was revealed in Scripture. Notice Habakkuk 1:1-2: "The burden which Habakkuk the prophet did see. O Lord, how long shall I cry, and thou wilt not hear! even cry out unto thee of violence, and thou wilt not save!" There was a temple crisis in Habakkuk's day—a type of what the PCG has endured in this end time.

Verse 3 reads, "Why dost thou shew me iniquity, and cause me to behold grievance? for spoiling and violence are before me: and there are that raise up *strife* and *contention*." The original Hebrew words for *strife* and *contention* indicate that this is referring to a LEGAL STRUGGLE.

And notice, God's faithful people in Habakkuk's day didn't fare well in court. "Therefore the law is slacked, and judgment doth never go forth: for the wicked doth compass about the righteous; therefore wrong judgment proceedeth" (verse 4). Again, notice the legal language—*law, judgment, wrong judgment*. The Hebrew word for *judgment,* according to *Strong's Exhaustive Concordance,* means "a verdict (favorable or unfavorable) pronounced judicially, especially a sentence or formal decree ...." The *Anchor Bible* says, "[T]he juridical language of verse 4 is unmistakable ... it could be describing corruption in the courts."

Habakkuk's reference to a wrong judgment, or verdict, is especially interesting in light of our court battle. There is no mention of a right judgment to correct the wrong. It just abruptly moves into this most inspiring verse: "Behold ye among the heathen, and regard, and wonder marvelously: for I will work a work in your days, which ye will not believe, though it be told you" (verse 5). My dad wrote,

> God says He will raise up a work that people will hear about but won't believe—and this is in the context of the court battle. I believe this has already been fulfilled in general, but is God also saying there will be a specific fulfillment related to the court case, a specific miracle, that will fill God's people with wonder? A miracle that will remove the *injustices* and *destruction?* Do we have the faith to believe?
>
> I believe we will see something dramatic on the scene VERY SOON! I can't read these verses any other way. This is in the context of a *revival,* and a *court battle,* and God says a DOUBLE WONDER IS COMING.[11]

Later in the article, my dad wrote, "If God reveals Habakkuk, then it follows that He is going to revive this work *soon* if we walk by faith. ... We must continue. If so, WE CANNOT LOSE. God will revive His work."[12]

A GENERAL AND SPECIFIC FULFILLMENT

This specific understanding of Habakkuk in that issue of *Royal Vision* set the tone for my dad's messages at the Feast of Tabernacles in September 2002. On September 22, he compared two verses in Daniel. In Daniel 8:11, it says that in this end time, Satan will *take away* the "daily"—meaning God's truth (see verse 12). My dad explained that this was a direct reference to Mr. ARMSTRONG'S LITERATURE and how it had been cast to the ground in this end time because of the court case.

Then, in comparing that passage with Daniel 12:11, we read that God (not Satan) takes away the "daily" just before the Great Tribulation begins. Elsewhere in Scripture, this is referred to as the *famine of the word* (see Amos 8:11).

The point is this: For the daily to be taken away now (by Satan) and then again just before the Great Tribulation (by God), it PROVED, my dad said in September 2002, that we would somehow take the daily (in this case, represented by Mr. Armstrong's literature) to the world again before Christ returns.

A week later, on September 28, my dad expounded on Revelation 10:11: "And he said unto me, Thou must prophesy again before many peoples, and nations, and tongues, and kings." In *The Royal Book of Revelation* he had explained the general meaning of the verse: that we were to prophesy *again*, the way Mr. Armstrong did before he died. Yet look at this verse in all its specific detail, he told the PCG membership. "Prophesy again implies that it was stopped. Then God says 'prophesy again.' But we must fight our way through it and *see how God delivers us.*"[13]

AND THEN—"DOUBLE WONDER"

Less than three weeks later, on October 14, the Worldwide Church of God made an offer they had not made throughout the six years of litigation and, in fact, had vowed in 1997 *never* to make. They asked if we would be interested in BUYING *Mystery of the Ages.* Later, they not only slashed the asking price, they tacked on the other 18 works we were seeking in our counterclaim!

Everything we had been fighting for was now ours. No one but God could have predicted such an incredible outcome for the Philadelphia Church of God. Yet given these numerous specific prophecies, that is exactly what He had done.

ANSWERING THE CRITICS

In the *Journal* story quoted earlier, the author asked Helge if he was aware of the prophecy Gerald Flurry made in the March-April 2001 *Trumpet*—that "one way or the other, God will provide a way for us to mail that book again." Helge responded this way: "[Mr. Flurry] won't want his prophecy to fail, so what he is probably really doing is pronouncing ahead of time what he is actually planning on doing. Hence his words are really nothing more than a self-fulfilling prophecy."[14]

Think about that for a moment. The Ninth Circuit had ruled against us eight months earlier. There had been an injunction served against us. And we had just heard that the Supreme Court chose not to hear our petition. The WCG had WON THE LAWSUIT over *Mystery* at the appellate level and would receive damages from us at trial! Yet Helge told the *Journal* that my father's comment, "God will provide a way for us to mail that book again," was a self-fulfilling prophecy?

It's as if Helge knew, even then, that we would somehow get these works. And when we did, he wanted everyone to know that it wouldn't be because God said so, but because of a self-fulfilling prophecy of Gerald Flurry!

But how in the world could Gerald Flurry have "planned" for the case to end up the way it did? Wasn't it Helge who said our only "right" was to "stand before the bar of justice and have damages assessed against" us? How could my dad have known the WCG would completely reverse its course and willingly give up everything?

After settlement, Helge misrepresented the facts entirely, suggesting that we were the ones who initiated offers to settle— offers that were repeatedly "rejected." In actuality, long before there were ever *any* negotiations, the WCG board of directors met and *decided they wanted out of this lawsuit.* They knew they were trapped. They were afraid of being exposed. And they knew that the longer they litigated, the more material we would have to expose them. This is why, on October 14, they offered to sell *Mystery of the Ages* on the condition that we drop our counterclaim.

WE REJECTED this initial offer, and many others to follow, just as sure as WCG rejected a number of our *counter*offers. What's more, even after both sides had agreed to the principal terms of settlement on January 16, 2003, contractual negotiations were nearly derailed when the WCG insisted that we either give back or destroy all the documents we had accumulated in this case from the WCG.

We told them this was a DEAL BREAKER for us. Besides obtaining the 19 works, we believed God wanted us to write a book about the lawsuit as well, which made the discovery documents an indispensable piece of any settlement agreement.

On February 27, 2003, my dad told Dennis Leap and me that he was getting his "second wind" and was prepared to go back to court if WCG insisted on that clause in the contract. We were actually prepared to GIVE UP MR. ARMSTRONG'S WORKS and go back to court *if the WCG insisted on retrieving all their documents.* Halting negotiations at the 11th hour, insisting we call the judge to resume litigation—as my dad did—are not the acts of one pressured to make a deal. They are not the acts of one desperately trying to bring about a self-fulfilling prophecy.

Four days after we called the whole thing off, Helge wrote to tell us that WCG had reconsidered and, "in the spirit of Christian cooperation," had agreed to delete the paragraph requiring destruction of court documents from the contract.[15]

In light of what Helge said in the months that led up to October 14, it makes sense that he would spin the settlement discussions the way he did. All along, he had made no secret of the fact that he felt WCG was in the driver's seat—that PCG was in a totally indefensible position, faced with the prospect of not getting Mr. Armstrong's literature and paying out multiple millions of dollars.

In their "ideal" position, the only way the WCG would even talk to us was if *we* approached them with an offer they couldn't refuse. But that's *not* how it happened. It was *the WCG,* despite their spin, that was pressured to make a deal in order to get out of this lawsuit.

My father, on the other hand, had prophesied from the start that—one way or another—we would be able to distribute Mr. Armstrong's literature.

In the end, that's exactly what happened.

TWENTY-FIVE
RAISING
THE RUINS

"[A]nd I will raise up his ruins, and I will build it as in the days of old."

— AMOS 9:11

AFTER work on June 29, 2000, I picked up my wife and newborn daughter at home and we drove about seven miles north in Edmond before pulling off the road onto an open field. The sun was setting—we have beautiful sunsets in Oklahoma—and since it was June, it wasn't too hot yet. We got out of our car and walked across the field. I was holding our baby girl, and everything was calm and peaceful.

Not long after we arrived, a few other cars full of people pulled up and did the same thing—slowly driving through grass before parking and getting out. It reminded me of *Field of Dreams*— a movie about a farmer who built a beautiful baseball field and people from miles around showed up just to see it.

We didn't have that many people show up—there were about 25 of us. And there was no baseball field. In fact, there was nothing! I mean, there was a certain natural beauty to the place—especially because of a small, spring-fed pond surrounded by clusters of trees—but most of it was just an open field with wild grass that had grown up to about knee level.

There were no roads.

No real entrance onto the property.

No buildings.

Nothing.

And yet, there we were—25 of us—wandering around, sipping champagne. We were fellowshiping. We were laughing. We were envisioning the future.

Shortly after we visited that field, my father wrote in the *Trumpet,* "I plan to start a small college in 2001, perhaps 2002. In June, the Philadelphia Church of God purchased 38 acres of land with a beautiful three-acre lake."[1]

That was quite an announcement! In our church newspaper, it had been mentioned that this 38 acres might also be the site for a future *television studio,* an *office building,* an *auditorium* and a *youth camp.* And—on top of that, a new college! That's a lot to squeeze on 38 acres, especially when a small lake and shoreline cover seven or eight of those acres. My father continued,

> At our college, we will teach our young people to open their minds to all truth and "prove all things." … [O]ur aim will be to provide students with a well-rounded, liberal arts education. We plan to have strong classes in history, journalism, music, nutrition, computers, television production, speech and leadership.[2]

He wrote this just *two weeks* after buying a field. Later in the article, he wrote,

> We will have a class on news analysis, where students will be taught the true meaning behind world news. They will see how world news is fulfilling Bible prophecy. Their Bibles will come alive as they never imagined!
>
> We also have the capacity to teach accounting, agriculture, English, Spanish and some other basic classes.[3]

We hadn't broken ground on a single building. There were no administrators. There were no departments, no teachers and no students. Even more astounding was that just a few weeks after my father wrote that article, the church purchased another field of 120 acres!

Without a doubt, our college and new headquarters facility had to begin first as a *vision.*

DAY OF SMALL THINGS

In the Old Testament, God commissioned his servant Zerubbabel to lead a band of captive Jews from Babylon to Jerusalem in order to build a temple.[4] In Zechariah 4:6, God said to Zerubbabel, "Not by might, nor by power, but by my spirit." In other words, for Zerubbabel to successfully complete his task—even in the face of numerous obstacles and strong enemy resistance—he needed *God's power.* Unless *God* built the house through His human instruments, all their labor would have been in vain.[5]

So God started His rebuilding work in Jerusalem, which had become a desolate wasteland during its Babylonian captivity, through this small remnant of Jews. "For who hath despised the day of small things?" God asked in Zechariah 4:10. Zerubbabel's enemies were critical of his work because of how small it started.

Mr. Armstrong's critics also found fault with the way the Worldwide Church of God began. His God-given commission to preach the gospel to the world started in 1933 on a small 100-watt radio station in Eugene, Oregon. He began publishing the *Plain Truth* magazine the following year; the inaugural issue, mimeographed by hand, went to 234 recipients. Everything seemed so small and insignificant *at the beginning.* But it was all by DESIGN.

"When the great God, Creator and Ruler of the vast universe, does something by Himself," Mr. Armstrong wrote,

> He demonstrates His supreme power by doing it in a stupendous, awe-inspiring manner. But when it is actually God who is doing something through humans, it must start the smallest. Like the grain of mustard seed, the smallest of herbs, which grows to become the largest, God's works through humans must start the smallest, but they grow, and grow, and grow, until they become the biggest![6]

Though his work started from practically *nothing,* Mr. Armstrong walked by faith. He had no scholarly training, no corporate funding, and yet, thanks to the blessings of God, over a period of decades he raised up a highly successful, globe-encompassing work. When God builds something through people, He starts small, because He never wants us to forget that *He is the one who provides the increase.*

"Had Ambassador College started big," Mr. Armstrong continued,

> with several hundred or a few thousand students, a great campus filled with large college buildings—an administration building, classroom buildings, laboratories, music conservatory, large ornate auditorium, gymnasium, a fine quarter-mile track and football field, a large library building with 500,000 volumes, dormitories, dining halls—everything complete, then I could certainly have no faith in accepting it as God's college.[7]

That wasn't how Ambassador College developed at all. It began as a modest institution, almost comically tiny.

A MAN OF VISION

On November 27, 1946, Mr. Armstrong located what seemed to be a suitable building for the school, though it was somewhat run-down. Within weeks of the purchase, Mr. Armstrong produced a special edition of the *Plain Truth* magazine, January-February 1947, announcing the exciting news: "This year, September 22, our own new school, Ambassador College, will swing open its doors to students!"[8]

If something like this seemed unlikely in 2000 after we bought those 38 acres, how much more so in 1947, considering the limited help and experience Mr. Armstrong had at his disposal? He wasn't raising ruins that had been built before—he was starting from scratch! Mr. Armstrong continued,

> Ambassador is to be a general liberal arts institution—not a Bible school, ministers' college, or theological seminary. It will

fit students for all walks of life, offering a general and practical basic education, with unusual advantages for special technical courses, as well as a thorough, sound, complete Bible course. ... There is no other college like Ambassador.[9]

No other college like Ambassador? THERE WAS NO AMBASSADOR at that point. All the church had was a run-down building in Pasadena. And besides Mr. Armstrong, there was no faculty. No students had even applied.

But why was Mr. Armstrong so confident his vision of Ambassador College would turn into reality?

Because he had faith in the POWER of God!

Here is how Mr. Armstrong described this college which, as he wrote, did not yet exist: "It is, in a sense, a revolutionary new-type college—*different* from those of today's world—a forward-looking, progressive institution built on soundest principles, having highest goals and objectives, yet employing the best of proved methods of administration, and maintaining highest academic standards."[10] How CLEAR the concept was in Mr. Armstrong's mind. He continued,

> The vision of this new and *different* college, and its imperative urgent need, came like a revelation straight from God last spring. At first the idea seemed impossible, for us—almost fantastic.
>
> But the Eternal our God is a miracle-working God who promises to supply every need. And literally, God has performed a miracle! When one knows the facts and circumstances, that cannot be doubted. Events have happened swiftly! Amazing developments occurred unexpectedly. The vision has become a definite reality. The opening of Ambassador College next September is assured.[11]

What an example of faithful reliance on God—and of *vision*.

In that same article, Mr. Armstrong described the vast difference between an Ambassador education as compared to what any other college had to offer. Instead of teaching students how to make a living, Ambassador's focus would be on *how to live*—on developing godly character.

Modern education, he wrote, wastes precious years on "nonconsequential details and impractical and untrue theories, instead of teaching young men and women the basic knowledge of life—what life is, why we are here, where we are going, and *how to live* successfully, usefully, happily, joyfully!"[12]

Ambassador was to be the solution to the evils of modern education. Its curriculum would be different from all other colleges. He wanted to offer general education courses in science, math, music and physical health. But the spiritual instruction on how to live would underpin all of it.

Mr. Armstrong also had a crystal-clear vision of social life at Ambassador. He said it would be "directed not toward just 'fun' alone, or worldly pleasures, but toward personality and character-development, the acquisition of that portion of culture which includes the graces of politeness, courtesy, kindness, gentleness, self-restraint, selflessness."[13]

This great visionary was in his 50s when he wrote this, and he had never been to college himself. Even more remarkable is how this 1947 article perfectly describes Ambassador College during the 1980s—*more than 30 years later*. The Ambassador College that existed at the time of Mr. Armstrong's death in 1986 truly was the product of a vision that started in the smallest of ways—in one man's mind.

THE REMNANT AND THE RUINS

Amos 9:11 says, "In that day will I raise up the tabernacle of David that is fallen, and close up the breaches thereof; and I will raise up his ruins, and I will build it as in the days of old." Even in the early days of the PCG, my father said this scripture was a prophecy that the work built by Herbert W. Armstrong would be turned to ruins—and that we would then raise it back up. God wanted to replicate the way things were done "in the days of old."

Verse 12 continues, "That they may possess the remnant of Edom, and of all the heathen, which are called by my name, saith the Lord that doeth this." As my father has taught, *Edom* and the *heathen* refer to those who have forsaken God's truth in this end time. God says those who raise up the ruins will take possession of the remnant, or surviving portion, of Edom. That remnant, my father wrote in 2001, "must include *Mystery of the Ages* and Mr. Armstrong's other books and booklets."[14]

That has now happened. God gave us those books and booklets.

In Amos 9, God says possessing those many books and booklets *coincides directly* with the work of *raising the ruins that were built before Mr. Armstrong died!* Of course, as with everything God builds through human beings, it started incredibly small. There were no visible manifestations of construction and building when we started printing Mr. Armstrong's literature in late 1996.

But God did plant a *seed* in one man's mind.

We received our first copy of *Mystery of the Ages* from the printer on December 20, 1996. My father announced the new phase to our members on January 4, 1997. During this same time period, the Worldwide Church of God entered its final phase of destroying Mr. Armstrong's legacy.

When Mr. Tkach decided to pursue accreditation for Ambassador College in 1988, it set off a chain reaction that had a massive impact on the college and the work of the church. They broke ground on a new administration building in Big Sandy the same day my father was fired—December 7, 1989. The following year, Tkachism closed the campus in Pasadena and consolidated all college resources in Big Sandy. They intended to move *all* headquarters operations to Big Sandy. They built nine new buildings on the Texas campus in 1990 *alone*—including the Hall of Administration, Ambassador Hall and student residence halls.

On June 25, 1994, Tkachism finally obtained accreditation for the college. Upon receiving the news, Tkach Sr. decided to change the name of the college to Ambassador University, saying it was a "more appropriate description of the range and diversity of programs" the institution had to offer.[15] By 1996, the sprawling campus had become a virtual self-contained city. There were more than 50 buildings encompassing 730,000 square feet—administrative buildings, multi-purpose centers, a gymnasium, classrooms and lecture halls, dormitories, a huge convention center and 25 single-family homes. The campus center was surrounded by 2,000 acres of farmland and timberland. There were two beautiful lakes, a campground, on-site water and waste treatment plants and an airstrip with a hangar to accommodate corporate jets.

Yet, on December 29, 1996, just two and a half years after being accredited—and *nine days* after we received that first reprinted copy of *Mystery of the Ages*—Ambassador's board of regents shocked the surrounding community, as well as its own church membership, by announcing that the college would abruptly and permanently close after the spring semester ended in May 1997. Exactly 50 years after Mr. Armstrong established the school to support the church's worldwide mission, Ambassador College had been completely ruined.

Yet, even in the midst of this desolation, *God planted a seed.*

THE VISION EXPANDS

Big Sandy's demise in 1997 set off another chain reaction—one that had a massive impact on *our* work.

Two months after the college's final graduation in May, our news bureau chief, Ron Fraser, toured the facilities in Big Sandy on a fact-finding mission for my father. "I was informed," Mr. Fraser wrote soon after his visit, "that the wcg would seek to sell the whole campus intact."[16] He explained that if the campus didn't sell after 12 months, the wcg would consider breaking up the property to sell off parcels. This piqued my father's interest.

In September of 1997, Grubb and Ellis, a real estate agency in Dallas, listed the property with an asking price of $32 million, which was reasonable, considering how much money the wcg had invested into it. At the same time, however, the property was uniquely designed to service the church's needs during the days of Mr. Armstrong, and it was situated in a remote location in the middle of East Texas. We didn't think there would be too many interested buyers—not at that price.

Apparently, the wcg didn't think there would be either. After the property was listed, one of our members in Dallas obtained additional information from a broker who had contacts at Grubb and Ellis. He said that while it was listed at $32 million, the fire-sale figure floating within real estate circles was $6.5 million. That figure *really* piqued my dad's interest.

By early 1998, the campus was still on the market. Meanwhile, my father's vision for our work had expanded. To reach the largest audience possible with Mr. Armstrong's books and booklets, he believed we needed the same kind of facilities Mr. Armstrong used for his work—we needed to resurrect those desolate ruins. At the time, it seemed like the best way to accomplish this was by breathing life into a dead campus that had been built specifically for the needs we had.

My father wanted more information before taking such a bold step for a small work that was already entangled in litigation over *Mystery of the Ages*. So I sifted through all the church writings I could find about Big Sandy. Having attended there for a semester in 1989, I was somewhat familiar with the environs and its facilities. I found a couple of articles I thought my dad would be interested in and then wrote to him on April 18, 1998. I said,

> If God should provide us with Big Sandy and all the buildings on that campus, I cannot see Him doing so unless He has huge plans for this work and plans for resurrecting the now-defunct Ambassador College. If you read those articles I included in this packet, you will notice two things that happened quickly after AC started in the 1960s [in Big Sandy]: 1) The work began to grow phenomenally and fast. 2) They began to reap much fruit in the way of qualified personnel and leadership after just two or three years.[17]

I went on to explain how we needed student labor in order to produce more literature, process more mail, answer more calls and correspond with more prospective members. I drew up a proposed course load for an incoming freshman class of an estimated 24 students. I totaled the number of hours those students could work part-time and explained how this work force would impact the day-to-day operations of the work. "In short," I concluded, "the opportunities Big Sandy would open up for us, this work and for God's children are truly limitless."[18]

The following month is when we made our anonymous offer of $5 million for the Big Sandy property.

What we didn't fully realize at the time is that when God begins a work through human beings—even a work of resurrecting what has been ruined—it MUST start the smallest! God didn't want us to make a big splash with a ready-made infrastructure like Big Sandy.

He did, however, want us to THINK big! So He used Big Sandy's demise to help focus my father's thoughts on acreage and facilities—administrative buildings, multi-purpose centers, a gymnasium, classrooms, lecture halls, dormitories, a convention center, faculty homes and an airstrip. But God didn't want us to obtain all those facilities with one single transaction.

We had to start from scratch.

RAISING UP THE COLLEGE

By the time we purchased those 38 acres in 2000, my father's vision had become crystal clear. We had to raise up *everything* the Tkaches ruined. And so we began in earnest, as soon as the contract was signed, to set up meetings with land developers, building contractors and landscape architects.

Tim Thompson, who negotiated the land purchase for the church, said, "In a couple of years, you won't recognize this place. Five years and it will be a paradise."[19] We were thinking big.

Ten weeks after the purchase, on September 8, my father officially broke ground on the new property in a ceremony attended by our headquarters staff and their families. My father said the land belonged to God and that He had an intense interest in the building program. He reminded us of the many prophecies in Scripture that describe the worldwide rebuilding to take place after Jesus Christ returns to this Earth. Ours was the first of many ground-breaking ceremonies to occur in the World Tomorrow and beyond, he said.

One week after we broke ground on the 38 acres, we signed the deed on the *additional 120 acres* adjacent to our original plot. It was mostly pasture land that the previous owner originally wanted to develop into an upscale neighborhood for airplane owners. He had already developed a small, unpaved airstrip on the property. But his development plans changed and he instead decided to sell the property. Commenting on the fact that the 120 acres had an airstrip, my father said later in a sermon, "We know what Mr. Armstrong has done in the past …. And I think maybe that gives you some idea of what God is planning in the future. … [M]aybe God wants me to fly around, and others of the ministers, to get to people more quickly and do the work even faster than we have done it."[20]

So as of Friday, September 15, 2000, we had 158 acres ready for developing. "Think about what could happen in a few years," my father told our members. "I think God is kind of hurling the [158] acres out there to say, all right, now, here's the vision. There's something really wonderful going to happen in the near future. … [A]mazing developments are going to occur right before our eyes."[21]

Three days after we acquired the additional property, on Monday, September 18, 2000, the Ninth Circuit filed its opinion on our case, ruling in favor of the Worldwide Church of God. Distribution of *Mystery of the Ages* would have to stop and yet, here we were about to embark on a huge building and development program so we might reach the largest audience possible *with Mr. Armstrong's literature.*

My father knew God had opened the door for us to build, so he wasn't about to let the Ninth Circuit discourage us. The *same week* we received the bad news from the Ninth Circuit, we broke ground on a 22,400-square-foot multipurpose center complete with a gymnasium, a raised stage at one end for church services and musical performances, a second-floor sound booth overlooking the gym, locker rooms for men and women, a commercial kitchen, dining hall and several offices scattered throughout the facility. For a church as small as ours, having dumped hundreds of thousands of dollars into a court case we just lost, as well as land we just bought, this was a HUGE undertaking.

As we pressed forward with construction through the winter months, we waited for the judge's injunction that would prevent us from mailing out Mr. Armstrong's literature. At the same time, my father waited as long as possible before deciding on whether to start

the college in the fall of 2001 or to wait until 2002. I wrote to my
dad in January of 2001,

> In reading from Mr. Armstrong's experiences, you do imme-
> diately think about starting things smaller—the mustard seed
> beginning, just like the *Trumpet* and *The Key of David* started.
> Do you suppose starting the college this fall, with a smaller
> class and fewer courses offered, would be better than waiting
> until 2002? It seems like by fall of 2002 that the land would be
> much better developed, more buildings would be in place and
> we'd be able to accept more students—all of that would kind of
> go against the "mustard seed" beginning.[22]

My father was leaning toward the smaller start in 2001. But
even with a small beginning, it had to be done right. He wondered
if our headquarters staff would have enough time to develop the
highest quality courses in theology and the liberal arts, and if
the time commitment to do so could be justified for such a small
freshman class.

By the end of January 2001, the court-ordered injunction was
filed and we stopped mailing Mr. Armstrong's literature. Two weeks
later, my dad gave the school, named Imperial College, a green light
for fall classes later that year. We announced it to the membership
on February 17. After he made the decision, my father admonished
those of us who would be teaching at the school, saying that "if
the college is done right, it can stir and motivate the entire church
to get more and more behind the work."[23] He reminded us that
we're not here just to start a college, but that the college would be
established to support the work's worldwide mission and to facilitate faster growth.

On February 24, my father then told the church membership
that there is "no money in the budget for the college," but that we
are in a time of "no more delay" and must move forward.[24]

On April 2, more bad news on the lawsuit front—the Supreme
Court rejected our petition. As we prepared for the damages trial in
court, out on the land we rushed to complete the field house before
the start of classes in August. That summer, we moved two mobile

homes on campus to temporarily serve as student residences. We accepted 10 full-time students, including two married students, who would live just off campus.

At orientation on Thursday, August 30, my father kicked off our first school year by explaining why God raised up Imperial College. Though off to a mustard-seed beginning, he said, the college would eventually grow to be the biggest, until finally established world-wide after Christ's return. On Tuesday, September 4, a full slate of classes began. The field house was not yet complete, so the students had to commute to our Waterwood offices each day for the first three weeks of classes. After classes and work at headquarters, they returned to the two trailers on the 158 acres.

What an exciting time that was for us. It was all so reminis-cent of the way Ambassador started. "Would you really say it was a college that finally swung open its door to students the eighth of October, 1947?" Mr. Armstrong asked in his autobiography.

> There were only four students! There were no dormitories—
> no place for students to be in residence on the original little
> "campus" of one and three-quarter acres. We had some books
> and encyclopedias on shelves in the one room that served as
> music room, assembly room, library, study room and lounge—
> but no real college library. There was no gymnasium, no track
> or athletic field.[25]

Few people would have considered Imperial a legitimate college in 2001. But it has since enjoyed abundant growth—and at a much faster rate than Ambassador experienced in its early years. In 2002, we constructed two duplexes for use as student residences, one of which had a classroom built in between. The two structures, big enough to house 24 students, enabled us to accept 14 more students in 2002. With all the students moving into the duplexes that year, we converted both mobile homes into faculty housing, including one for my family. We also added an outdoor sports complex that summer—including a fenced-in softball diamond, a soccer field and a small two-story structure providing storage for athletic equipment and a classroom on the second floor.

In 2003, we completed construction on two faculty homes. We also finished work on a new swimming pool and bath house, located behind the field house. During our youth camp that summer, we received news from U.S. Immigration that the college had been certified and could begin accepting international applicants. Within weeks, after being accepted at the last minute, we had five new international students on campus. That September, in the tradition of Mr. Armstrong's world-renowned concert series, the Philadelphia Foundation hosted the internationally acclaimed Canadian Brass in the field house. Later that year, in November, the church purchased an additional 10 acres, adjacent to the western edge of the campus. The acreage included a home, which was immediately purchased by another headquarters ministerial family, and a steel barn and fenced corral.

The following year, in 2004, we finished two more faculty homes, which meant five headquarters families were now living on campus—a total of 22 people, counting children. We also completed work on a new 5,000-square-foot men's dormitory, with enough living space to house 22 students. The additional space enabled us to accept our biggest freshman class yet—23 students coming from five countries. It doubled the size of our student body to 46—14 of whom were from nations outside the United States. We were just beginning our fourth year and we had 46 students representing eight countries.

In July of that year, we purchased two items auctioned off by the Worldwide Church of God in Pasadena. With one of our representatives on hand at the auction, and several of us listening in on speakerphone in Edmond, we purchased a 9-foot Steinway concert grand piano and two 7-foot-tall candelabra, all from Ambassador Auditorium. The piano was one of three Steinways the wcg used for its concert series. The candelabra were made of crystal used by the late Shah of Iran for the 2,500th anniversary of the Persian Empire in 1971, then later acquired by the wcg and placed in the lobby of the auditorium.

In 2005, the college's Choral Union gave its first-ever public performance, together with members of the Oklahoma City Philharmonic Orchestra and professional soloists. On April

10, the 49-member chorus, 28-piece Baroque orchestra and four soloists packed the field house stage to perform Handel's *Messiah*.

In the fall, we began our fifth year at the college—our first with a full four-year load of courses offered. We accepted 18 students, upping the student body size to 54. And with every student working for the church part-time, student labor was beginning to really flex its muscle. As our chief financial officer, Andrew Locher, explained,

> Part of each student's education comes through the work-study program, which places them in responsible positions in nearly all departments of church operations. The church in turn benefits from quality labor at a very reasonable cost. Altogether, the students combine to equal 25 full-time employees—at a fraction of the cost! The students are rewarded by earning their way through college and graduating without financial obligation to the church. This is truly a win-win situation conceived by Mr. Armstrong for Ambassador College.[26]

Yet another program we had raised from the ruins.

Later in 2005, we changed the name of our school to "Herbert W. Armstrong College." Imperial College *of London* had wanted us to make the change years earlier, so as to avoid any confusion over the name. So we proposed various ways to use "Imperial," but in a way that would make the name distinctly different, like "Imperial College of Edmond." After our litigation ended with the WCG, however, we considered going in a completely different direction. Herbert W. Armstrong College was a name we almost used when we started the college in 2001, but since we were then embroiled in a lawsuit over Mr. Armstrong's literature, we didn't think it would be wise to use his name for our college as well. But by the end of 2005, after winning all that literature, and with our first crop of seniors months away from graduating—changing the name to Herbert W. Armstrong College seemed like a perfect ending to the story of our legal struggle—and what a fitting tribute to Mr. Armstrong's legacy.

GROWTH OF THE WORK

In his autobiography, Mr. Armstrong repeatedly said the growth of the work "directly paralleled" the development of the college. He said, "Without the college, the work of thundering Christ's gospel around the whole world could not have been possible. It could never have gone around the world. It was the development of the college in Pasadena that made possible the growth of the whole gospel work!"[27] The same has been true with our work as we raise up the ruins.

After obtaining all the literature in March of 2003, we saw an immediate need for a multi-purpose facility where we could store huge quantities of literature and process mail. We also wanted to update and expand our TV studio in anticipation of offering Mr. Armstrong's literature on *The Key of David*. In a matter of months, we completed plans for a 17,400 square-foot Mail Processing Center. Today, the building anchors the northeast corner of the church's property and can be seen from nearly anywhere on campus. Two thirds of the structure is an enclosed warehouse for all our literature, stored on double-pallet storage racks. Adjacent to the warehouse, under the same roof, are the centers for processing mail and answering calls for the TV program. There are also six offices for MPC employees. Above the offices, there is a 2,400 square-foot mezzanine, soundproofed and enclosed for our state-of-the-art television studio and editing equipment.

In the spring of 2004, a year after the victory, we began the piecemeal process of moving our headquarters staff from the Waterwood complex out to the 168 acres, beginning with those assigned to work at the MPC. We also unveiled plans for a two-story, 22,825 square-foot Hall of Administration to serve as our new headquarters.

Later that year, after we acquired the piano and candelabra from the WCG auction, my father took the purchase as God's signal for us to begin thinking about building an auditorium in the tradition of Ambassador. It would be smaller and less expensive than Ambassador Auditorium, but a beautiful centerpiece on the campus landscape nonetheless. "I do believe ... that with God giving us these beautiful furnishings right out of the house of God

[Ambassador Auditorium], that He does want us to build an auditorium," he said just three months before we were scheduled to begin construction on the $3.7 million Hall of Administration.[28] My dad said that because of the urgency of time, we might have to consider building our facilities, not successively, but perhaps concurrently.

In October 2004, during the same week we broke ground on the Hall of Administration, the *Pasadena Star-News* revealed the WCG's plan to move its headquarters operations *off* the Ambassador College campus in Pasadena and onto the "smaller, less expensive trappings of an industrial building" in Glendora, California.[29] Even as Tkachism prepared for its last ruinous act, selling off the formerly great Pasadena headquarters, God showed His mighty hand by raising the ruins in Edmond—*and during the very same week*.

In the summer of 2005, with construction on the Hall of Administration in full swing, we broke ground on a $2 million college building that would provide housing for 34 more students downstairs and serve as an academic center upstairs. Thus, we had two huge structures going up concurrently on campus in 2005, just as my father had indicated might happen.

Meanwhile, the work of the church was experiencing explosive growth. The year the lawsuit ended, *The Key of David* aired weekly on just one station: WGN. In March of 2005, two years later, we were on 92 television stations around the world. And with all of Mr. Armstrong's works printed except his autobiography, we were churning out an average of 45,000 pieces of mail per month (not counting any of our magazines). Perhaps the biggest step forward in 2005, as far as literature is concerned, came in January when we started updating and revising Mr. Armstrong's Bible correspondence course. By the time 2005 ended, we had sent out twice as much mail as in 2004 and had received 50 percent more phone calls from the TV program than we had the year before.

In January 2006, exactly 20 years after Mr. Armstrong's death, all that was left from the PCG operations at the old Waterwood complex moved into the new Hall of Administration. Herbert W. Armstrong College and the church's headquarters were now completely joined together.

The new administration building—rising 41 feet above the mostly residential countryside—instantly doubled the PCG's executive office space and made for a tremendous upgrade in quality. Ron Fraser said, "Mr. Armstrong knew that by lifting the tone and quality of environment to the highest possible standard, humans would be inspired to lift themselves to meet that standard."[30]

The 40-office building has several open spaces for numerous cubicles as well as an elegant and spacious library on the ground floor which wraps around the central staircase. Commenting on the building's breathtaking beauty, my father told members, "Shouldn't the most wonderful message people could ever hear ... come out of a building like that—something that is worthy of God?"[31] As with every other structure on campus, the *building itself* is a message— a testament to our work of raising Mr. Armstrong's ruins. God has raised the ruins so we might give a powerful warning to this dying world.

Our First Graduates

Of course, we will always have our critics. Mr. Armstrong certainly had his share. In 1951, after Mr. Armstrong had labored for four years to get the college off and running, there were some, even in the Worldwide Church of God, who could not see the vision Mr. Armstrong had for the college and the work. Mr. Armstrong wrote,

> When God first started Ambassador College, many brethren and co-workers lacked faith. They couldn't see God's hand in it. Some felt your pastor's duty was solely to preach the gospel to the world—not realizing that one man alone can't do it all!
>
> They had forgotten that Jesus, Peter and Paul surrounded themselves with specially God-called men whom they trained to assist them in their great mission.
>
> Some said, "Why, there isn't time! It will be four years before the first students graduate, and even then they will still be just youths without maturity or actual experience." ...
>
> But there was, and still is, enough time—though there is not a day to lose. The end of this age can't come until this very

gospel of the kingdom has been preached and published in all the world as a witness to all nations (Matt. 24:3, 14).[32]

This had been his lifelong approach: preach God's message to the largest audience possible while surrounding himself with specially called individuals he could train in order for the work to expand further. Mr. Armstrong went on to explain how Ambassador's first graduates were already having a strong impact on the work after only four years.

The same has been true of our work. We had 13 seniors graduate from Herbert W. Armstrong College in May 2006. And from that group, nine were hired by the church. Three of them were given positions in Editorial, two in Mail Processing, and one each in the business office, Information Technology, the call center and college administration. With only 66 full-time employees working at headquarters, that nine of them are AC graduates is remarkable when you consider that we have only had one senior class to this point.

And even as the college facilitates a more expansive work, we continue upgrading and expanding the college itself. With the completion of the new dormitory/academic center in July 2006, we doubled our classroom space and have enough accommodations on campus for about 90 students. So we have room for growth—and we will certainly need it.

Viewer response to *The Key of David* in 2006 increased by 45 percent over 2005. And with more people being exposed to our literature, it follows that more have requested contact with our ministers. In 2006, ministerial visit requests jumped 80 percent over the previous year.

We also re-launched the personal appearance campaigns in 2006 (our first series occurred in the late 1990s). *Public lectures, radio and television broadcasts* and *printed matter* were all part of Mr. Armstrong's "three-point" plan—the strategy he employed for preaching the gospel message to the largest audience possible. It was yet another of the ruins we have been able to raise up. In describing the initiative to our members on May 6, 2006, my father called it a "new phase" for our work. He explained how Christ's commission in Matthew 10:23 was actually intended for the Philadelphia Church of God and that we wouldn't be able to cover all the "cities of Israel" before the return of Jesus Christ. In the first phase of the campaign, from July to September, my father visited Philadelphia, Chicago, Los Angeles, Houston, Dallas, New York and Portland.

During this same time period, our architects put the finishing touches on the drawings for the $15 million, 800-seat auditorium we intend to build and dedicate to our great God. We hope to break ground on God's house in 2007.

THE ROAD AHEAD

As I look out my window across campus from my second-floor office in the Hall of Administration, I sit here in absolute awe of WHAT GOD HAS DONE. To think that all of this started 16 years ago with a Worldwide Church of God minister who was fired and excommunicated, offered no severance pay or pension and then laughed to scorn within the circle of Tkachism for simply believing and teaching what he had always been taught.

That's what God had to work with at the start of raising these ruins—*that,* AND FAITH.

Even today, in viewing what God has raised up *already* through a relatively small church with a modest annual income of $14 million or so, the numbers just don't add up. Yet the work keeps growing and prospering as more doors swing open for us to finish our commission.

Mr. Armstrong introduced one of his books by writing, "No story of fiction ever was so strange, so fascinating, so absorbing, so packed with interest and suspense, as this gripping story ...."[33] That's the way I feel about our story. It's so strange it seems almost unbelievable. And yet, what a fascinating and incredible ride this has been. But we still have a long way to go.

Herbert W. Armstrong died with his mind on reaching the largest audience possible with a message—a commission the Tkaches were dead-set against. They stopped the work and ruined everything God had given Mr. Armstrong *for* the work.

Then God raised it right back up. He began with a small,

faith-filled ministry intent on delivering the exact same message Mr. Armstrong did. A few people responded to that message and devoted their lives to support that work. Later, God amplified the message with many of the same tools Mr. Armstrong had used so effectively—radio and television programs, magazines, books and booklets. And when the fledgling work of the Philadelphia Church of God plateaued, God raised up a college to train additional personnel for service in the work—to make it possible for the work to have a worldwide impact. At the same time, God dramatically increased the size of our facilities for doing the work.

Now God has granted us ownership of all that literature.

It's as if everything to this point has happened to prepare us for what's ahead—to make reaching the "largest audience possible," *possible*. In many ways, to paraphrase the conclusion in *Mystery of the Ages*, it feels like the story is just beginning.

AFTERWORD

"Buy the truth, and sell it not …."

— PROVERBS 23:23

HY did we do it? Why bog down in six grueling years of spiritual trench warfare? Why spend $5 million in legal fees and settlement costs for books and booklets we're going to give away free?

The best answer to that question is, read it for yourself.

With the exception of Mr. Armstrong's *Autobiography,* everything we fought for and now own the copyrights to—7 books, 11 booklets and a monthly correspondence course—we now furnish to anyone who asks for it.

Mystery of the Ages is the capstone of Mr. Armstrong's life-long work. In it, he sought to summarize and make plain all the Bible's major truths in one volume, supplying the reader with "the thread of the Bible." He wrote it to be very accessible to the reader completely unacquainted with his teachings, which is why he marketed it to bookstores and libraries. Ask us for a free copy to see what was at the heart of the wcg v. pcg battle. What did Joseph Tkach believe was his "Christian duty" to keep out of your hands? Why did we so fervently disagree? Read it for yourself.

The Incredible Human Potential, which focuses on the transcendent destiny of humankind, is one of Mr. Armstrong's most inspiring works. It explains the overview of God's master plan for humans, answering our deepest questions about why we are here.

The Missing Dimension in Sex is a treasure trove of practical, Bible-based knowledge regarding marriage, family, dating and sex. A companion book we also own is Mr. Armstrong's *Why Marriage— Soon Obsolete?*

Mr. Armstrong considered the message contained in *The United States and Britain in Prophecy* to be the "strongest proof" of God's existence and the inspiration of the Holy Bible. Written during the 1930s, this book probably did more to help build the Worldwide Church of God under Mr. Armstrong than anything else he ever published. During his lifetime, more than 6 million people had obtained copies. The foundational history and prophecy it covers is more urgently needed today than ever before.

The Wonderful World Tomorrow draws on numerous biblical passages to vividly describe what human civilization will be like during the 1,000-year reign of Jesus Christ, now just ahead of us. This is the vision that kept Mr. Armstrong's focus on the future. It's why he was such a positive, joy-filled, forward thinker!

We could go on. Other booklets by Mr. Armstrong that we will eagerly send you at no charge include: *Does God Exist?*, *The Proof of the Bible*, *Who or What Is the Prophetic Beast?*, *The Plain Truth About Healing*, *What Science Can't Discover About the Human Mind*, *The Seven Laws of Success*, *What Is Faith?*, *Just What Do You Mean … Born Again?*, *Which Day Is the Christian Sabbath?* and *Pagan Holidays or God's Holy Days—Which?*

On top of all that, the 58-lesson correspondence course we won the rights to publish has become the basis for an updated course: *The Herbert W. Armstrong College Bible Correspondence Course.* Monthly lessons help you to find your way around the Bible proving basic doctrines and learning vital lessons in Christian living.

Finally, I encourage you to request a free copy of another book that is central to the story you have just read. It is the manuscript that got my father fired and excommunicated from the WCG. It is the book that launched the Philadelphia Church of God. It is the agonized cry of the betrayed—and the call to remembrance of the faithful. It is the trumpet alarm we blasted to every minister and member of the wcg we possibly could: *Malachi's Message to God's Church Today.* Those who, after reading *Raising the Ruins,* take the time to read *Malachi's Message* will discover that everything I have described—the casting down of Mr. Armstrong's teachings, the lies that supplanted them, the treachery of the men who drove the transformation, the breakaway of a remnant holding fast to the truths once delivered—was foretold in Scripture, just as the court battle itself was. Chapter 24 of this book gave you a look at the biblical basis for the faith that propelled us forward in our legal struggle; *Malachi's Message* will give you an understanding of how God foresaw what would happen to His church in our day, and how He prophesied it in the Bible. Having read the details of what actually happened in the wcg, you will be amazed at how vividly descriptive and thorough the Bible's prophecies of these events are. *Malachi's Message* contains the scriptural indictment of the wcg's betrayal of Mr. Armstrong—the truth that angered Joseph Tkach Jr. enough to summarily fire my father and later accuse him of trending toward "sociopathic cult" status. Read it for yourself.

Some few have criticized us for *paying money* for Mr. Armstrong's literature. They question why we would give even *one dollar* to an organization we so fervently disagree with. But giving up "mammon" for the truth of God did not violate our faith one bit. To the contrary, God's word says, "Buy the truth, and sell it not" (Proverbs 23:23). It is the Worldwide Church of God that ought to be ashamed that they "sold" the truth. Like Esau, they gave up their spiritual inheritance for what amounts to a bowl of soup.

You simply cannot affix a monetary value to spiritual truth. That is why Mr. Armstrong always gave away his literature for free. He did also offer his major works for sale in bookstores, but only to reach a larger audience with that material. However he went about it, Mr. Armstrong's mission was ALWAYS about *giving* the word of God—and to *as many people* as possible. As President Reagan remarked in 1986, Mr. Armstrong wanted to *share* that way of life with his community and throughout the nation—and the world, we would add. He genuinely wanted everyone else to have what he had been given. As his ministry grew, he invested every available resource the church had right back into the work so that the MESSAGE could be freely distributed to the largest audience possible.

That's who he was. That's what he did. And now that you know the truth about his legacy, we hope you'll take a closer look at what we fought for in court for six years—for the MESSAGE Herbert W. Armstrong proclaimed.

That is why we did it—that is why we fought. And that is why, even after six years of litigation and spending millions of dollars, we will always make Mr. Armstrong's literature available for free.

All you have to do is ask for it.

And then, read it for yourself.

CONTACT INFORMATION

To reach the Philadelphia Church of God to order literature or to request a visit from one of our ministers:

Visit us online: www.pcog.org

In North America, call us toll-free: 1-800-772-8577

MAILING ADDRESSES WORLDWIDE

United States: Philadelphia Church of God, P.O. Box 3700, Edmond, OK 73083

Canada: Philadelphia Church of God, P.O. Box 315, Milton, ON L9T 4Y9

Caribbean: Philadelphia Church of God, P.O. Box 2237, Chaguanas, Trinidad, W.I.

Britain, Europe, Middle East, India and Sri Lanka: Philadelphia Church of God, P.O. Box 9000, Daventry NN11 5TA, England

Africa: Philadelphia Church of God, P.O. Box 2969, Durbanville 7551, South Africa

Australia and the Pacific Isles: Philadelphia Church of God, P.O. Box 6626, Upper Mount Gravatt, QLD 4122, Australia

New Zealand: Philadelphia Church of God, P.O. Box 38-424, Howick, Auckland 1730

Philippines: Philadelphia Church of God, P.O. Box 1372, Q.C. Central Post Office, Quezon City, Metro Manila 1100

Latin America: Philadelphia Church of God, Attn: Spanish Department, P.O. Box 3700, Edmond, OK 73083 United States

NOTES

FOREWORD

1. Joseph Tkach, *Transformed by Truth* (Sisters, OR: Multnomah Publishers, 1997), 203.
2. Declaration of Ralph Helge at 3, *Worldwide Church of God v. Philadelphia Church of God*, No. CV-97-5306-CAS (C.D. Cal. dismissed April 14, 2003).

CHAPTER 1: ABSOLUTE POWER

1. *Pastor General's Report*, May 24, 1985, 1.
2. John Dart, *Los Angeles Times*, September 28, 1985, part 2, 4. 80,000 of these were baptized members.
3. The 210,000 figure included 80,000 co-workers and 130,000 donors. Co-workers were those who made donations to the church at least twice during a six-month period (*Pastor General's Report*, June 7, 1985, page 9). The *Pastor General's Report*, April 18, 1986, reported that there were 91,937 co-workers, but that 11,903 had been added the first three months of 1986 (page 11). Since Mr. Armstrong died on January 16 of that year,

I did not count the ones added those first three months. Thus, at the time of his death, there were approximately 80,000 co-workers. Added to those figures, there were 130,000 donors (ibid.). Donors are defined in the March 15, 1985, *Pastor General's Report* as "those who send a donation once or twice in a year" (page 3). The April 18 issue reported that there were 148,328 donors, but that 15,889 had been added the first three months of 1986. Since Mr. Armstrong died on January 16 of that year, I did not count the ones added those first three months. Thus, at the time of his death, there were approximately 130,000 donors.

4. *Pastor General's Report*, May 24, 1985, 1.
5. According to the August 28, 1989, *Worldwide News*, the church's income for 1987 amounted to $192,081,000 (page 7). Using that established figure, we then calculated the published percentage increases in reverse. According to *The Worldwide News*, income in 1987 increased by 5.5 percent over 1986 (July 11, 1988, page 3), which means the income in 1986 would have been approximately $182 million. This figure, according to *The Worldwide News* (May 11, 1987, page 3), was 11.2 percent above 1985, which means revenue for 1985 would have been approximately $163.7 million.
6. Richard N. Ostling, "Power, Glory—and Politics; Right-wing preachers dominate the dial," *Time Magazine*, February 17, 1986, 62; "Speaker Says Slide to Liberalism is Costing Methodists Members," *Washington Post*, July 12, 1986, D10. The *Time* article identified Falwell's annual income at $100 million, while the *Post* reported Graham's revenues to be $55.3 million.
7. Richard N. Ostling, "Power, Glory—and Politics; Right-wing preachers dominate the dial," *Time Magazine*, February 17, 1986, 62. The annual income for these preachers during the mid-1980s breaks down like this: Swaggart, $140 million; Roberts, $120 million; Bakker, $100 million; Falwell, $100 million. The article did not include an exact figure for Robert Schuller, but noted that his annual TV budget was $37 million and that he spent "an additional $5.7 million on non-TV operations."
8. "World Tomorrow: No. 1," *The Worldwide News*, August 19, 1985, 1.
9. "1985: year of media expansion," *The Worldwide News*, January 27, 1986, 7.
10. Richard Rice, "MPC records greatest harvest," *The Worldwide News*, January 27, 1986, 7.
11. Paul Richter, "End of the Paternalistic Era," *Los Angeles Times*, January 31, 1986, part 4, 1.
12. "1 in every 633 receives the *Plain Truth* magazine," *The Worldwide News*, May 13, 1985, 5.
13. Richard Rice, "MPC records greatest harvest," *The Worldwide News*, January 27, 1986, 7.
14. Paul Richter, "End of the Paternalistic Era," *Los Angeles Times*, January 31, 1986, part 4, 1; Alison Rogers and Karen Kraner, *Adweek*, November 18, 1985. *Time's* circulation was 5.9 million and *Newsweek's* was 3 million—totalling 8.9 million. *The Plain Truth* and *The Good News*, by comparison, totaled 9.23 million.
15. "Update," *The Worldwide News*, December 16, 1985, 8.

16. Richard Rice, "AC Bible course passes three decades of printing," *The Worldwide News*, January 7, 1985, 1.
17. Ibid.
18. Herbert W. Armstrong, Co-worker letter, January 1986, 2.
19. Richard Rice, *Pastor General's Report*, June 7, 1985, 8.
20. Richard Rice, *Pastor General's Report*, June 24, 1987, 12.
21. Richard Rice, *Pastor General's Report*, August 2, 1985, 5.
22. Richard Rice, "MPC records greatest harvest," *The Worldwide News*, January 27, 1986, 7.
23. Ibid.
24. Herbert W. Armstrong, Co-worker letter, November 25, 1985, 1.
25. "Update," *The Worldwide News*, December 30, 1985, 8. "This is the largest number of books to be distributed in such a short time period."
26. Joseph Tkach, *Transformed by Truth* (Sisters, OR: Multnomah Publishers, 1997), 105.
27. *The Journal*, Church of God Timeline: 1996-2004. Available at http://www.thejournal.org/archives/cgtimln4.html.
28. Gary Scott, "Auditorium preserved," *Pasadena Star-News*, May 14, 2004.
29. Joseph Tkach, *Transformed by Truth* (Sisters, OR: Multnomah Publishers, 1997), 184.
30. Ibid., 185.
31. J. Michael Feazell, *The Liberation of the Worldwide Church of God* (Grand Rapids, MI: Zondervan Publishing House, 2001), 43-44.
32. Ibid., 27.
33. Ibid., 23.
34. Ibid., 45.
35. Ibid.
36. Deposition of J. Michael Feazell at 236-37, *Worldwide Church of God v. Philadelphia Church of God*, No. CV-97-5306-CAS (C.D. Cal. dismissed April 14, 2003).
37. J. Michael Feazell, *The Liberation of the Worldwide Church of God* (Grand Rapids, MI: Zondervan Publishing House, 2001), 45.
38. Joseph Tkach, *Transformed by Truth* (Sisters, OR: Multnomah Publishers, 1997), 98.
39. Ibid., 186.
40. Worldwide Church of God, Intended preface to the e-publishing works, 2002, 2.
41. Deposition of J. Michael Feazell at 230, *Worldwide Church of God v. Philadelphia Church of God*, No. CV-97-5306-CAS (C.D. Cal. dismissed April 14, 2003).
42. *Id.* at 225.
43. J. Michael Feazell, *The Liberation of the Worldwide Church of God* (Grand Rapids, MI: Zondervan Publishing House, 2001), 146.
44. Ibid., 114, 45.
45. Ibid., 146.
46. Ibid., 112.

47. Ibid., 120.
48. Ibid., 120-21.
49. Deposition of Joseph Tkach at 451, *Worldwide Church of God v. Philadelphia Church of God*, No. CV-97-5306-CAS (C.D. Cal. dismissed April 14, 2003).
50. Ronald Kelly, "Planning under way for new financial model," *The Worldwide News*, June 2004, 24.

CHAPTER 2: LEGACIES

1. Joseph Tkach, *Transformed by Truth* (Sisters, OR: Multnomah Publishers, 1997), 143.
2. Ibid., 71.
3. J. Michael Feazell, *The Liberation of the Worldwide Church of God* (Grand Rapids, MI: Zondervan Publishing House, 2001), 146.
4. Joseph Tkach, "Forgive Us Our Trespasses," *The Plain Truth*, March/April 1996, 1.
5. Ibid., 26.
6. "Book charts church's reformation," *The Worldwide News*, June 24, 1997, 3.
7. Joseph W. Tkach Jr., "A Church Reborn," *Christian Research Journal*, Winter 1996.
8. Joseph Tkach, *Transformed by Truth* (Sisters, OR: Multnomah Publishers, 1997), front matter.
9. "Book charts church's reformation," *The Worldwide News*, June 24, 1997, 3.
10. Ibid.
11. Greg Albrecht, "Updates from Plain Truth Ministries," *The Worldwide News*, January 27, 1998, 13.
12. Personal interview with Multnomah representative, December 29, 2005.
13. J. Michael Feazell, *The Liberation of the Worldwide Church of God* (Grand Rapids, MI: Zondervan Publishing House, 2001), front matter.
14. Ibid.
15. "Zondervan publishes book by Michael Feazell," *The Worldwide News*, July 2001, 3.
16. Deposition of J. Michael Feazell at 39-40, *Worldwide Church of God v. Philadelphia Church of God*, No. CV-97-5306-CAS (C.D. Cal. dismissed April 14, 2003).
17. Personal interview with Zondervan representative, December 29, 2005.
18. Joseph W. Tkach, "He Remembered You," *The Plain Truth*, November/December 1986, 1.
19. Herbert W. Armstrong, Co-worker letter, February 25, 1985, 2.
20. Herbert W. Armstrong, *Mystery of the Ages* (New York: Dodd, Mead & Company, 1985), xii.
21. Joseph Tkach, *Transformed by Truth* (Sisters, OR: Multnomah Publishers, 1997), 12.
22. Ibid., 103-04.
23. Joseph W. Tkach Jr., Letter to Dennis Leap, April 20, 1990, 1.

24. Joseph W. Tkach, "Personal," *The Worldwide News*, May 21, 1990, 6.
25. Joseph Tkach Jr., "A Church Reborn," *Christian Research Journal*, Winter 1996.
26. "Journal reviews book by HWA," *The Worldwide News*, November 18, 1985, 1.
27. "Update," *The Worldwide News*, December 2, 1985, 8.
28. *Pastor General's Report*, December 6, 1985, 7.
29. "Update," *The Worldwide News*, December 30, 1985, 8.
30. Richard Rice, *Pastor General's Report*, December 20, 1985, 7.
31. Declaration of Roger Lippross at 2, *Worldwide Church of God v. Philadelphia Church of God*, No. CV-97-5306-JSL (C.D. Cal. April 20, 1999).
32. *Pasadena Star-News*, January 17, 1986.
33. Joseph Tkach, "Forgive Us Our Trespasses," *The Plain Truth*, March/April 1996, 1.
34. Joseph Tkach Jr., "A Church Reborn," *Christian Research Journal*, Winter 1996.
35. "Friends Remember Mr. Armstrong," *The Good News*, May 1986, 15.
36. Ibid., 16.
37. "Dignitaries, leaders share loss of pastor general," *The Worldwide News*, February 10, 1986, 12.
38. "Friends Remember Mr. Armstrong," *The Good News*, May 1986, 18.
39. Joseph Tkach, "Forgive Us Our Trespasses," *The Plain Truth*, March/April 1996, 1.
40. "Friends Remember Mr. Armstrong," *The Good News*, May 1986, 15, 17.
41. "Dignitaries, leaders share loss of pastor general," *The Worldwide News*, February 10, 1986, 1.
42. "Milestones in Church's work," *The Worldwide News*, February 24, 1986, 5.
43. "Friends Remember Mr. Armstrong," *The Good News*, May 1986, 15.
44. Herbert W. Armstrong, *Mystery of the Ages* (New York: Dodd, Mead & Company, 1985), 23-24.
45. Ibid., viii.
46. Stephen Flurry, "The Other Side of the Story," *The Philadelphia Trumpet*, April 1997, 1.
47. Deposition of Joseph Tkach at 78, *Worldwide Church of God v. Philadelphia Church of God*, No. CV-97-5306-JSL (C.D. Cal. April 20, 1999).
48. Denise Hamilton and Daniel Cariaga, "Ambassador concert hall to close in May," *Los Angeles Times*, January 28, 1995, A1.
49. Diane Haithman, "Hall needs a rescuer," *Los Angeles Times*, December 20, 2002, part 5, 2.
50. "Church sells lower portion of Ambassador Campus," *The Worldwide News*, June 2004.
51. Herbert W. Armstrong, "Recent history of the Philadelphia Era of the Worldwide Church of God," *The Worldwide News*, June 24, 1985, special edition, 3.
52. Stanley Rader, *Against the Gates of Hell* (New York: Everest House, 1980), 86.
53. Ibid., 138-39.
54. Ibid., 86.

55. Larry Omasta, "HWA 'a natural communicator,' says director of Media Services," *The Worldwide News*, February 10, 1986, 4.

56. Norman A. Smith, "Evangelist remembers early broadcasts," *The Worldwide News*, February 10, 1986, 4.

57. Dexter H. Faulkner, "Editor in chief lives on through training of staff," *The Worldwide News*, February 10, 1986, 5.

58. Ellis La Ravia, "Foundation helped HWA deliver Gospel," *The Worldwide News*, February 10, 1986, 5.

59. Roderick C. Meredith, "HWA's hallmarks: involvement and drive," *The Worldwide News*, February 10, 1986, 8.

60. Leroy Neff, "HWA's favorite subject: the work of God," *The Worldwide News*, February 10, 1986, 9.

61. Frank Brown, "Mr. Armstrong's clarity of vision helped inspire Church's growth," *The Worldwide News*, February 10, 1986, 10.

62. Joseph W. Tkach, "God's will was 'the joy of his life,' says pastor general about HWA," *The Worldwide News*, February 10, 1986, 3.

63. Joseph W. Tkach, Lecture to staff, Pasadena CA, January 16, 1986.

64. Joseph W. Tkach, Closing prayer at funeral service of Herbert W. Armstrong, Pasadena CA, January 19, 1986.

65. Worldwide Church of God, "Transformed by Christ: A Brief History of the Worldwide Church of God." Available at http://www.wcg.org/lit/aboutus/history.htm.

CHAPTER 3: THE SELF-APPOINTED APOSTLE

1. Herbert W. Armstrong, "Christ now moves to put God's government back on the track," *The Good News*, September 1979, 28.

2. Herbert W. Armstrong, "Recent history of the Philadelphia Era of the Worldwide Church of God," *The Worldwide News*, June 24, 1985, special edition, 4.

3. Ibid.

4. Deposition of Ralph Helge at 149-50, *Worldwide Church of God v. Philadelphia Church of God*, No. CV-97-5306-JSL (C.D. Cal. April 20, 1999).

5. Personal interview with Aaron Dean, November 22, 2005.

6. Herbert W. Armstrong, Letter to Roderick C. Meredith, March 14, 1980.

7. Personal interview with Aaron Dean, November 22, 2005.

8. Ibid. Mr. Dean said that since Mr. Meredith had obviously been ruled out, the other candidates pretty much were the other men on the council— ministers like Leroy Neff, Herman Hoeh—even himself.

9. Ibid.

10. Ibid.

11. Deposition of Ralph Helge at 140, *Worldwide Church of God v. Philadelphia Church of God*, No. CV-97-5306-JSL (C.D. Cal. April, 1999).

12. *Id*. at 136.

13. Herbert W. Armstrong, Co-worker letter, January 10, 1986, 1.

14. Personal interview with Aaron Dean, November 22, 2005.

15. "Worldwide Church of God Founder Names Successor," *Associated Press*, January 15, 1986.
16. Herbert W. Armstrong, Co-worker letter, December 9, 1985, 1.
17. Ibid.
18. Deposition of Ralph Helge at 141, *Worldwide Church of God v. Philadelphia Church of God*, No. CV-97-5306-JSL (C.D. Cal. April 20, 1999).
19. Joseph W. Tkach, Co-worker letter, part 2, January 16, 1986, 1.
20. Aaron Dean, Sermon, March 24, 1996.
21. Larry R. Salyer, *Pastor General's Report*, December 2, 1986, 4.
22. Ibid.
23. "Update," *The Worldwide News*, January 26, 1987, 8.
24. "Spirit is catalyst of unity, says apostle in Pasadena," *The Worldwide News*, February 9, 1987, 1; Jeff E. Zhorne, "Christ's apostle 'deeply inspired' by trip to Jordan, Egypt, Israel," *The Worldwide News*, March 9, 1987, 1.
25. Herbert W. Armstrong, "The 19-Year Cycles—What Happened January 7—What My Commission Is!" *Tomorrow's World*, February 1972, 1.
26. Herbert W. Armstrong, "Six More Ministers Now Ordained," *The Good News,* February-March 1955, 7.
27. Acts 8:18-19.
28. Personal interview with Aaron Dean, November 22, 2005.
29. Ibid.

Chapter 4: Credentials
1. Personal interview with Aaron Dean, November 22, 2005.
2. Jeff Zhorne and Michael Snyder, "The Passing of the Baton," *The Worldwide News*, January 27, 1986, 3.
3. Personal interview with Gerald Flurry, January 9, 2006.
4. "Passing the Baton," *The Good News*, May 1986, 13.
5. Jeff Zhorne and Michael Snyder, "The Passing of the Baton," *The Worldwide News*, January 27, 1986, 3.
6. Joseph Tkach, *Transformed by Truth* (Sisters, OR: Multnomah Publishers, 1997), 81.
7. Personal interview with Gerald Flurry January 9, 2006.
8. Personal interview with Roderick C. Meredith, January 9, 2006.
9. Ibid.
10. Ibid.
11. Personal Correspondence Department L168, 1989.
12. Jeff Zhorne, "Milestones in the life of Joseph W. Tkach," *The Worldwide News*, December 5, 1995, 5.
13. Joseph Tkach, *Transformed by Truth* (Sisters, OR: Multnomah Publishers, 1997), 79.
14. Joseph W. Tkach, "A Boy from the Inner City," *The Plain Truth*, June 1986, 1.
15. Jeff Zhorne, "Milestones in the life of Joseph W. Tkach," *The Worldwide News*, December 5, 1995, 5.

16. Joseph W. Tkach, "Personal," *The Worldwide News*, January 26, 1987, 1.
17. Jeff Zhorne and Michael Snyder, "The Passing of the Baton," *The Worldwide News*, January 27, 1986, 3.
18. Based on a review of school archives by degreechk.com.
19. Worldwide Church of God, Intended preface to the e-publishing works, 2002, 1.
20. J. Michael Feazell, *The Liberation of the Worldwide Church of God* (Grand Rapids, MI: Zondervan, 2001), 24.
21. Ibid., 25.
22. Joseph Tkach, *Transformed by Truth* (Sisters, OR: Multnomah Publishers, 1997), 12.
23. Personal interview with Aaron Dean, November 22, 2005.
24. Joseph Tkach, *Transformed by Truth* (Sisters, OR: Multnomah Publishers, 1997), 83.
25. Personal interview with Roderick C. Meredith, January 9, 2006.
26. Deposition of Joseph Tkach at 380, *Worldwide Church of God v. Philadelphia Church of God*, No. CV-97-5306-CAS (C.D. Cal. dismissed April 14, 2003).
27. *Id.*
28. *Id.*
29. Herbert W. Armstrong, *Autobiography of Herbert W. Armstrong*, Vol. 1 (Pasadena, CA: Worldwide Church of God, 1986), 305.
30. Ibid.
31. Herbert W. Armstrong, *Mystery of the Ages* (New York: Dodd, Mead & Company, 1985), 280.
32. Deposition of Joseph Tkach at 380, *Worldwide Church of God v. Philadelphia Church of God, Inc.*, No. CV-97-5306-CAS (C.D. Cal. dismissed April 14, 2003).
33. *Id.* at 381-382.
34. Joseph Tkach, *Transformed by Truth* (Sisters, OR: Multnomah Publishers, 1997), 35.
35. Ibid., 89. The WCG's Personal Correspondence Department made this same point in a letter dated December 8, 1994, written by a WCG official: "From an ethical point of view, it is well-known by our critics, and we must face the fact, that Mr. Armstrong did not originate this teaching (that the tribes of Israel went to the British Isles)." Actually, Mr. Armstrong never made the claim that everything he wrote in *The United States and Britain in Prophecy* originated with him. Mr. Armstrong wrote, "*Very few,* indeed, have ever noticed that the promises to Abraham were twofold" (page 29). Later, he wrote, "*Few,* indeed, are the clergymen, theologians, or professed Bible scholars who know that [the fact that many prophecies about Israel do not refer to the Jews] today. Many refuse to know it!" (page 43). Repeatedly, he stressed that *only a few* have understood.
36. Herbert W. Armstrong, Bible study, Pasadena CA, July 19, 1980.
37. Ibid.

38. J. H. Allen, *Judah's Sceptre and Joseph's Birthright* (Merrimac, MA: Destiny Publishers, 1917), 13.

39. Herbert W. Armstrong, *The United States and Britain in Prophecy* (Worldwide Church of God, 1980), ix.

40. In chapter 9 of the third section, for example, Allen discusses the impossibility of America and Britain ever being conquered militarily. Then, in the last chapter of the book, "The Coming Exodus," he reveals his total ignorance regarding Israel's biblically prophesied captivity at the hands of the modern-day Assyrians.

41. Joseph Tkach, *Transformed by Truth* (Sisters, OR: Multnomah Publishers, 1997), 66.

42. Ibid.

43. Ibid., 66-67.

44. Deposition of J. Michael Feazell at 20-21, *Worldwide Church of God v. Philadelphia Church of God*, No. CV-97-5306 CAS (C.D. Cal. dismissed April 14, 2003).

45. Personal interview with Roderick C. Meredith, January 9, 2006.

46. J. Michael Feazell, *The Liberation of the Worldwide Church of God* (Grand Rapids, MI: Zondervan, 2001), 138.

47. Joseph Tkach, *Transformed by Truth* (Sisters, OR: Multnomah Publishers, 1997), 83.

48. Worldwide Church of God, "Transformed by Christ: A Brief History of the Worldwide Church of God." Available at http://www.wcg.org/lit/aboutus/history.htm.

CHAPTER 5: TKACH'S FELLOWS

1. Personal interview with Aaron Dean, November 22, 2005.

2. Personal interview with Bob Herrington, November 18, 2005.

3. Joseph W. Tkach, *Pastor General's Report*, September 29, 1987, 1.

4. Edward Glancy, "Ambassador considers addition of more majors," *The Portfolio*, December 28, 1973, 1.

5. Herbert W. Armstrong, Co-worker letter, September 25, 1978, 4.

6. Herbert W. Armstrong, Co-worker letter, June 28, 1978, 6.

7. Ibid., 7.

8. Ibid., 8.

9. Herbert W. Armstrong, "Recent History of the Philadelphia Era of the Worldwide Church of God," *The Worldwide News*, June 24, 1985, special edition, 3-4.

CHAPTER 6: FINGERPRINTS

1. Joseph Tkach, *Transformed by Truth* (Sisters, OR: Multnomah Publishers, 1997), 84.

2. Ibid., 21.

3. Herbert W. Armstrong, *Mystery of the Ages* (New York: Dodd, Mead & Company, 1985), 251.

4. Joseph W. Tkach, "God restored these 18 truths: How thankful are you for them?" *The Worldwide News*, August 25, 1986, 5.

5. Basil Wolverton, *The Bible Story*, Vol. 1 (Radio Church of God, 1961), viii-ix.

6. Ibid., 52.

7. Ibid., 53.

8. Herbert W. Armstrong, *The Plain Truth About Christmas* (Ambassador College Press, 1970), 10-11.

9. On page 7 of *The Plain Truth About Christmas*, Mr. Armstrong asked, "But if we got Christmas from the Roman Catholics, and they got it from paganism, where did the pagans get it? Where, when, and what was its real origin?" As Mr. Armstrong went on to explain, the church had taught for decades that these pagan customs originated in ancient Babylon, beginning with Nimrod and his wife Semiramis soon after the Flood.

Not true, according to a discovery made by wcg scholars a year after Mr. Armstrong died. "It started in ancient Egypt in the days of King Osiris and Queen Isis, about 3000 B.C. Yes, it stems from roots whose beginning was *long before the Flood!*" (*Pastor General's Report*, February 10, 1987, page 7).

To say that it came from King Osiris and Queen Isis *before* the Flood is to completely disassociate these two from Nimrod and Semiramis. Mr. Armstrong always taught that Nimrod and King Osiris were one and the same. Likewise for Semiramis and Isis.

This is how the wcg explained the change to its ministers: "It should be carefully noted that these editings take account of the error of Alexander Hislop in *The Two Babylons* in which he confused Nimrod, in the second generation after the Flood, with Osiris ... who lived around 3000 B.C., before the Flood" (ibid.). What's interesting about this explanation is that neither Hislop nor his book are even mentioned in *The Plain Truth About Christmas*. Yet, Mr. Armstrong and Ambassador College graduates did draw upon this source, as well as many others, when researching the earliest beginnings of man's civilization after the Flood. Now, all writing based on Hislop's point that Osiris and Isis are the Egyptian equivalent of Nimrod and Semiramis would have to be changed.

"Theses or dissertations that were based on references to Hislop's *The Two Babylons* need to have this erroneous assumption corrected as well. Note also that Isis is not Semiramis, a claim by Hislop that EVERY HISTORIAN would correctly reject as false" (ibid., page 8). According to Tkachism, Hislop was WAY off!

Joe Tkach Jr. later referred to *The Two Babylons* as an "anti-Catholic polemic." He said, "Most scholars would not spend time and effort to demolish the conclusions of a polemic work with a narrow reading audience. Since, however, Alexander Hislop's work has been rather widely circulated by certain religious groups [like the Worldwide Church of God, for instance], we should take note of its basic flaw. It has absolutely no chronological framework to support the author's conclusions" (*Pastor General's Report*, January 31, 1989, page 5). Poor, ignorant Alexander Hislop.

In *Mystery of the Ages*, chapter 4 is titled "Mystery of Civilization." In that chapter, Mr. Armstrong referred to Alexander Hislop and his work on two occasions. Discrediting Alexander Hislop proved to be yet another way for Tkachism to take an indirect swipe at *Mystery of the Ages*.

Incidentally, Hislop's scholarship stands up quite well against Tkach's criticisms. His book *The Two Babylons* (first published in 1853) references more than 260 sources, including Gibbon's *Decline and Fall*, Adam's *Roman Antiquities*, Begg's *Handbook of Popery*, Kennedy's *Ancient and Hindoo Mythology*, Potter's *Greek Antiquities*, and Stanley's *History of Philosophy*. Hislop meticulously cited all his proof.

10. Keith Stump, *The History of Europe and the Church* (Worldwide Church of God, 1984), 42.

11. Herbert W. Armstrong, *United States and Britain in Prophecy* (Worldwide Church of God, 1980), 93.

12. Ibid., 147.

13. Ibid., 143-44.

14. *Pastor General's Report*, November 15, 1985, 6.

15. Genesis 10:6 says that Cush was a son of Ham. According to *Easton's Bible Dictionary*, as well as numerous other Bible helps, the Hebrew word Cush means *black*. Cush is often translated into English as Ethiopia. See the Moffatt translation for Genesis 10:6.

16. Herbert W. Armstrong, Co-worker letter, December 9, 1985, 1-2.

17. Richard Ames, *Pastor General's Report*, December 27, 1985, 5.

18. Aaron K. Dean, "Education: What does God expect?" *The Worldwide News*, December 30, 1985, 1.

19. Ken Tate, "Pastor general addresses 4,600 during trip to Big Sandy campus," *The Worldwide News*, March 24, 1986, 1.

20. "Texas campus to remain open, says chancellor in college forum," *The Worldwide News*, April 21, 1986, 1.

21. Joseph W. Tkach, *Pastor General's Report*, March 21, 1986, 1.

22. Joseph W. Tkach, *Pastor General's Report*, April 18, 1986, 2.

23. "Texas campus to remain open, says chancellor in college forum," *The Worldwide News*, April 21, 1986, 1.

24. Herbert W. Armstrong, "The 19-Year Time Cycles—What Happened January 7—What My Commission Is!" *Tomorrow's World*, February 1972, 32.

25. Herbert W. Armstrong, Co-worker letter, September 17, 1982, 1.

26. Herbert W. Armstrong, Sermon, Pasadena CA, December 17, 1983.

27. Herbert W. Armstrong, *The Plain Truth About Healing* (Worldwide Church of God, 1979), 53.

28. Joseph W. Tkach, Sermon, Pasadena CA, January 18, 1986.

29. John 6:44.

30. Herbert W. Armstrong, "Congress of leading ministers hears defined and reemphasized spiritual organization of church," *The Worldwide News*, March 6, 1981, 5.

31. Joseph W. Tkach, Sermon, Pasadena CA, January 18, 1986.
32. Joseph W. Tkach, *Pastor General's Report*, January 24, 1986, 2.
33. Herbert W. Armstrong, Co-worker letter, September 12, 1985, 1.
34. Herbert W. Armstrong, *Mystery of the Ages* (New York: Dodd, Mead & Company, 1985), 289.
35. Ibid., 290.
36. Ibid., 290-91.
37. Ibid., 291.
38. Larry R. Salyer, *Pastor General's Report*, December 16, 1986, 8.
39. Ibid., 9.
40. Herbert W. Armstrong, *The Incredible Human Potential* (Herbert W. Armstrong, 1978), 5.
41. Herbert W. Armstrong, *What Do You Mean—"The Unpardonable Sin"?* (Pasadena, CA: Ambassador College Press, 1972), 8-9.
42. Larry R. Salyer, *Pastor General's Report*, December 30, 1986, 11.
43. To understand the significance of this change, we need some context. Mr. Armstrong taught that human beings are wholly physical—made from the dust of the ground (Genesis 2:7). God, on the other hand, is entirely spirit (John 4:24). And yet, it says in Genesis 1:26, man was created in God's image and likeness. God's purpose, as revealed from the beginning, was to make mankind into God kind. Our incredible human potential is to be born into the family of God by a literal spirit birth, as described in John 3:3-6.

But how would this be brought about? How would God take an entirely physical creation and make it spirit? How would He bridge the gap between Himself and man? By creating physical man with a *spiritual attribute* called the "spirit in man" (Job 32:8). Besides giving man the power of intellect, putting us on a plane far superior to animals, this human spirit makes possible the transition of mortal man into spirit being in God's Kingdom.

Of and by itself, the human spirit gives man a godly type mind, because it enables us to think and reason within the scope of physical, material things. But it is incomplete without another spirit—the Spirit of God. God gives His Spirit, as a gift, to those who repent of their sins, accept the sacrifice of Jesus Christ and are baptized. That's when God's Spirit combines with our spirit, making us the begotten children of God (Romans 8:16). The actual birth occurs when we are resurrected to spirit life at Jesus Christ's return.

That leads us to one other vital purpose for the human spirit. "The spirit that is in every human acts as a mold. It preserves the human's memory, his character, his form and shape," Mr. Armstrong wrote on page 85 of *The Incredible Human Potential*. This "sculptor's mold" is what God, as the Master Potter (Isaiah 64:8), uses when He gives us our spirit bodies at the resurrection.

On page 71 of the book, referring to the human spirit, Mr. Armstrong wrote, "It is that nonphysical component in the human brain that *does not exist in the brain of animals*. It is the ingredient that makes possible the transition from human to divine, *without changing* matter into spirit, at the time of resurrection." These two sentences were combined as one in the 1986 version: "It is that nonphysical component in the human brain that is the ingredient that makes possible the transition from human to divine, *from* matter into spirit, at the time of resurrection."

First, notice they left out the fact that this nonphysical component does not exist in animals. (They made a similar edit in *Never Before Understood—Why Humanity Cannot Solve Its Evils* where Mr. Armstrong said "man has mind, while animal has *only* brain with instinct." They edited the word "only" out so as to leave the subject "open to future growth in understanding," Larry Salyer wrote in the *Pastor General's Report* (January 27, 1987)—presumably, in case their scholars later discovered a spiritual dimension to the animal brain.) Second, "without changing matter into spirit" was changed to "from matter into spirit," which gives the passage an entirely different meaning. Now, instead of the Sculptor using *the mold* to create our spirit bodies, He instead uses *the clay*—changing it into spirit.

44. Larry R. Salyer, *Pastor General's Report*, December 16, 1986, 10.
45. Herbert W. Armstrong, *Mystery of the Ages* (New York: Dodd, Mead & Company, 1985), 50.
46. Larry R. Salyer, *Pastor General's Report*, December 30, 1986, 12.
47. K. J. Stavrinides, "Does elohim refer to a family of divine beings?" *The Worldwide News*, August 3, 1993, 4.
48. David Hulme, Letter of resignation to Joseph Tkach, April 17, 1995, 6.
49. Joseph Tkach, *Transformed by Truth* (Sister, OR: Multnomah Publishers, 1997), 69-70.
50. Ibid.

CHAPTER 7: RIDDLED WITH ERROR

1. Deposition of Joseph Tkach at 155, *Worldwide Church of God v. Philadelphia Church of God*, No. CV-97-5306-JSL (C.D. Cal. April 20, 1999).
2. *Id.*
3. Herbert W. Armstrong, *United States and Britain in Prophecy* (Worldwide Church of God, 1980), 64.
4. Ibid., 65.
5. Ibid., 43.
6. Larry R. Salyer, *Pastor General's Report*, February 10, 1987, 9.
7. Mr. Armstrong NEVER said Jews were not Israelites—BUT MOST ISRAELITES ARE NOT JEWS. Furthermore, when the Bible speaks of these peoples as nations—and this fact is critical to understanding prophetic events— "Israel" refers to the United States and Britain (and to a lesser degree, the nations of northwest Europe), whereas "Judah" refers to the people who reside in the land *mistakenly* called "Israel" today. Again, this is the whole point of Mr. Armstrong's book! But it couldn't survive the editor's knife *in 1986* because it had become a "source of criticism." During Mr.

Armstrong's ministry, more than 6 million people requested *The United States and Britain in Prophecy*. It was the most popular piece of literature Mr. Armstrong ever produced. Yet, within months of Mr. Armstrong's death, Tkach's editors lopped off the book's central point.

8. Larry R. Salyer, *Pastor General's Report*, February 10, 1987, 9.

9. Mr. Armstrong explained in *The United States and Britain in Prophecy* that, because of ancient Israel's rebellion, God withheld their birthright promises, made unconditionally to Abraham, for a period of 2,520 years. In Israel's case, the 2,520-year withholding, using Mr. Armstrong's dates, means that God would then bestow the birthright blessings on the descendants of Israel from 1800 to 1803—the latter date being when the United States purchased the Louisiana Territory. Isolating Israel's captivity date to 721 B.C., however, limits the end of the prophesied withholding to 1800. A slight difference, yes, but one that de-emphasizes the prophetic significance of the Louisiana Purchase.

    The hazy date regarding Judah's captivity is much more significant from a prophetic standpoint. Using the dates Mr. Armstrong researched, Judah's 2,520-year punishment would have ended in 1917—which is the year the British took control of Palestine. While Mr. Armstrong does not refer to this specific prophecy in *The United States and Britain in Prophecy*, he does allude to another prophecy regarding Turkey and how God prophesied that they would have to give up the land of Palestine, which they did in 1917. Tkach's editors left this entire section of the book ("Prophecy for Turkey") out of the 1986 version.

    Mr. Armstrong thoroughly explained the 2,520-year curse on Judah in *The Bible—Superstition or Authority? ... and Can You Prove It?*—a booklet he wrote just after finishing *Mystery of the Ages* in 1985. In fact, Mr. Armstrong wanted the booklet sent to all those who requested *Mystery of the Ages*. He said it could even be the opening chapter of the book in future editions.

10. *Pastor General's Report*, August 18, 1987, 10.

11. Joseph Tkach, *Transformed by Truth* (Sisters, OR: Multnomah Publishers, 1997), 130.

12. "Anglo-Israelism" and "British Israelism," incidentally, are terms Mr. Armstrong never used. Some groups who DO foster racial prejudice use these terms. And certainly, Tkach Jr. and fanatical "cult watchers" throw these terms around to "foster rebuke" against people they deem to be racist. Mr. Armstrong was NOT racist—nor did he foster racial prejudice. He taught the Bible's interpretation of the modern identity of nations as well as why those nations—*all* of them, whether Israelite or gentile—are headed for disaster unless we repent.

13. Joseph Tkach, *Transformed by Truth* (Sisters, OR: Multnomah Publishers, 1997), 131.

14. Herbert W. Armstrong, Co-worker letter, August 14, 1978, 11.

15. Joseph W. Tkach, "As Passover Approaches ... New Understanding of the Meaning of Christ's Broken Body and the Church's Teaching on Healing," *The Worldwide News*, March 23, 1987, 1.

16. Herbert W. Armstrong, *The Plain Truth About Healing* (Worldwide Church of God, 1979), 66, 58.
17. Ibid., 65.
18. Ibid., 58.
19. Psalm 103:3; Isaiah 53:5; Matthew 8:17; 1 Peter 2:24.
20. Luke 22:14-20; 1 Corinthians 11:23-30.
21. Romans 7:14.
22. Romans 6:23.
23. Joseph W. Tkach, "As Passover Approaches ... New Understanding of the Meaning of Christ's Broken Body and the Church's Teaching on Healing," *The Worldwide News,* March 23, 1987, 1.
24. Worldwide Church of God, "Healing," *Systematic Theology Project,* 1978, 7.
25. Joseph Tkach, *Transformed by Truth* (Sisters, OR: Multnomah Publishers, 1997), 144.
26. Joseph W. Tkach, *Pastor General's Report,* March 18, 1987, 14.
27. Personal Correspondence Department L028, July 1987, 2.
28. Joseph W. Tkach, *Pastor General's Report,* February 9, 1988, 2.
29. Ibid., 3.
30. Ibid.
31. Ibid., 2.
32. Herbert W. Armstrong, *Mystery of the Ages* (New York: Dodd, Mead & Company, 1985), 291.
33. Ibid., 348.
34. Ibid., 9.
35. Ibid., 51-56.
36. Ibid., 149-56.
37. Ibid., 183.
38. Richard Rice, *Pastor General's Report,* September 15, 1987, 17.
39. Dexter H. Faulkner, *Pastor General's Report,* December 15, 1987, 7.

CHAPTER 8: DISCARD

1. Deposition of Joseph Tkach at 101-02, *Worldwide Church of God v. Philadelphia Church of God,* No. CV-97-5306-JSL (C.D. Cal. April 20, 1999).
2. "Update," *The Worldwide News,* December 21, 1987, 8.
3. "Update," *The Worldwide News,* March 14, 1988, 8.
4. Dexter Faulkner, Interoffice memo to Joseph Tkach, April 18, 1988.
5. Literature Coordination Report 5, May 13, 1988, 1.
6. Literature Coordination Report 6, May 20, 1988, 1.
7. Literature Coordination Report 8, June 2, 1988, 1-2.
8. Declaration of Roger Lippross at 3, *Worldwide Church of God v. Philadelphia Church of God,* No. CV-97-5306-JSL (C.D. Cal. April 20, 1999).
9. Deposition of Joseph Tkach at 101, *Worldwide Church of God v. Philadelphia Church of God,* No. CV-97-5306-JSL (C.D. April 20, 1999).

10. *Id.* at 112.

11. Literature Coordination Report 8, June 2, 1988, 2.

12. Mail Processing Center Procedures 553, June 30, 1988, 2.

13. Literature Coordination Report 14, July 14, 1988, 1.

14. Deposition of Joseph Tkach at 113, *Worldwide Church of God v. Philadelphia Church of God*, No. CV-97-5306-JSL (C.D. April 20, 1999).

15. *Id.* at 114.

16. Joseph W. Tkach, *Pastor General's Report*, July 19, 1988, 1.

17. Herbert W. Armstrong, *Autobiography of Herbert W. Armstrong,* Vol. 1 (Pasadena, CA: Worldwide Church of God, 1986), 295.

18. On page 170 of *Mystery of the Ages*, Mr. Armstrong wrote, "*Everything* God has done, since the creation of the first humans, has been another progressive step in God's overall supreme purpose!" The phrase "first human[s]," by the way, appears nine times in *Mystery*, in reference to either Adam or Adam and Eve.

    On page 75, Mr. Armstrong explained that Genesis 1 (except for the first verse) actually describes a *re*-creation of the Earth's surface, not the original creation. "What is described from verse 2 on, in the supposed creation chapter of the Bible, did occur, according to the Bible, approximately 6,000 years ago. But that could have been millions or trillions of years after the actual creation of the earth described in verse 1!" He offers further explanation about Genesis 1:1-2 on page 99.

    These teachings all rest on the foundation of another critical doctrine explained in Mr. Armstrong's book: "God set apart a *7,000-year period* to complete his original supreme purpose of reproducing himself through man. It was a masterminded master plan for working out the purpose here below" (page 143). Once scholars suggested that "modern forms of human life may have existed long before 4,000 B.C.," as the Personal Correspondence Department later explained, it all but obliterated God's 7,000-year master plan as taught by Mr. Armstrong.

19. Joseph W. Tkach, *Pastor General's Report*, August 2, 1988, 1.

20. Ibid.

21. Herbert W. Armstrong, *Mystery of the Ages* (New York: Dodd, Mead & Company, 1985), 265-70.

22. Herbert W. Armstrong, Co-worker letter, December 9, 1985, 1.

23. Herbert W. Armstrong, *Mystery of the Ages* (New York: Dodd, Mead & Company, 1985), 1.

24. Ibid., 25.

25. Ibid., 140. On this page, Mr. Armstrong wrote, "Jesus Christ, through the Church, built three colleges—two in the United States and one in England. The three campuses, in material beauty, have mutually excelled each other, as a high character physical setting for the development of God's righteous character in students. The beauty of godly character in these students has excelled the physical beauty of the campuses.... These campuses are an example of what mankind should have done, and a modest foretaste of the beauty that will blossom forth over the whole earth after Christ and

his saints in his kingdom are ruling the earth in the wonderful world tomorrow."

26. Joseph W. Tkach, *Pastor General's Report*, November 22, 1988, 1.
27. Ibid.

CHAPTER 9: INCIDENTAL POINTS

1. Literature Coordination Report 21, December 2, 1988, 1.
2. Literature Coordination Report 5, May 13, 1988, 1.
3. Literature Coordination Report 21, December 2, 1988, 1.
4. Ibid.
5. Ibid.
6. Mail Processing Center Procedures 566, December 22, 1988, 1.
7. Ibid., 4.
8. Larry R. Salyer, *Pastor General's Report,* January 31, 1989, 4; Joseph W. Tkach, "Personal," *The Worldwide News,* February 20, 1989, 1.
9. *Pastor General's Report*, December 19, 1989, 6.
10. Joseph W. Tkach, *Pastor General's Report*, January 3, 1989, 1.
11. Ibid.
12. Matthew 17:11.
13. Matthew 17:13.
14. Joseph W. Tkach, *Pastor General's Report*, January 17, 1989, 1.
15. Ibid.
16. Herbert W. Armstrong, *Mystery of the Ages* (New York: Dodd, Mead & Company, 1985), 131.
17. Larry R. Salyer, *Pastor General's Report*, January 31, 1989, 3-4.
18. Ibid., 4.
19. Deposition of Joseph Tkach at 127, *Worldwide Church of God v. Philadelphia Church of God*, No. CV-97-5306-JSL (C.D. Cal. April 20, 1999).
20. Dexter Faulkner, Interoffice memo to Joseph Tkach, April 18, 1988.
21. Deposition of Joseph Tkach at 127, *Worldwide Church of God v. Philadelphia Church of God*, No. CV-97-5306-JSL (C.D. Cal. April 20, 1999).
22. *Id*. at 128.
23. Joseph W. Tkach, *Pastor General's Report*, April 19, 1985, 1.
24. Herbert W. Armstrong, Co-worker letter, September 12, 1985, 1.
25. "Literature editors meet to form literature core," *The Worldwide News*, June 13, 1988, 1.
26. "Update," *The Worldwide News*, December 21, 1987, 8.
27. Ibid.
28. Literature Coordination Report 21, December 2, 1988, 1-2.
29. Ibid., 2.
30. "Literature editors meet to form literature core," *The Worldwide News*, June 13, 1988, 1.
31. Declaration of Roger Lippross at 2, *Worldwide Church of God v. Philadelphia Church of God*, No. CV-97-5306-JSL (C.D. Cal. April 20, 1999).

32. Richard Rice, *Pastor General's Report*, June 24, 1987, 12.

33. Richard Rice, *Pastor General's Report*, July 8, 1986, 11.

34. Larry R. Salyer, *Pastor General's Report*, January 31, 1989, 4.

35. Herbert W. Armstrong, *Mystery of the Ages* (New York: Dodd, Mead & Company, 1985), 94.

36. Larry R. Salyer, *Pastor General's Report*, January 31, 1989, 4.

37. Ibid.

38. Joseph W. Tkach, *Pastor General's Report*, February 14, 1989, 1.

39. Ibid.

40. Ibid.

41. Ibid., 2.

42. Ibid.

43. Ibid., 1.

44. *Pastor General's Report*, September 19, 1989, 3.

45. Paul Kroll, E-mail to Aluko Michaels, June 30, 2003.

CHAPTER 10: THE AGENDA

1.   Joseph Tkach, *Transformed by Truth* (Sisters, OR: Multnomah Publishers, 1997), 23.

2.   Ibid., 67.

3.   Joseph W. Tkach, Sermon, Pasadena CA, April 30, 1994.

4.   Joseph W. Tkach, Commencement exercises at Ambassador College, May 20, 1994.

5.   Joseph W. Tkach, "The true Church: what and where is it?" *The Worldwide News*, May 17, 1994, 7.

6.   Joseph W. Tkach, Sermon, Pasadena CA, November 12, 1994.

7.   Joseph W. Tkach, Sermon, Washington DC, December, 1994.

8.   David Hulme, Resignation letter to Joseph Tkach, April 17, 1995, 1.

9.   Ibid., 6.

10. Joseph W. Tkach Jr., Letter to Dennis Leap, April 20, 1990, 1.

11. Ibid., 3.

12. Ibid., 2.

13. Joseph W. Tkach, *Pastor General's Report*, June 7, 1985, 2.

14. Joseph W. Tkach, "God restored these 18 truths: How thankful are you for them?" *The Worldwide News*, August 25, 1986, 5.

15. Joseph W. Tkach, *Pastor General's Report*, February 9, 1988, 3.

16. Joseph W. Tkach Jr., Letter to Dennis Leap, April 20, 1990, 3-4.

17. Herbert W. Armstrong, Co-worker letter, March 19, 1981, 5-6.

18. David G. Hunsberger, "What the Church teaches about Malachi and his message," *The Worldwide News*, June 24, 1991, 4.

19. Ibid.

20. Ibid.

21. Joseph Tkach, *Transformed by Truth* (Sisters, OR: Multnomah Publishers, 1997), 181.

22. Ibid., 182.
23. Ibid.
24. Ibid., 182-83.
25. Joseph Tkach Jr., Letter to Donald Wheatley, former member of the Worldwide Church of God, October 10, 1994, 1.
26. Joseph Tkach Jr., Interview with Pat Robertson for *The 700 Club*, March 6, 1998.
27. Herbert W. Armstrong, *Mystery of the Ages*, (New York: Dodd, Mead & Company, 1985), 51.
28. Herbert W. Armstrong, *The Missing Dimension in Sex* (Worldwide Church of God, 1981), 29.
29. Philip Stevens, "Who Was Jesus' Father?" *The Good News*, November-December, 1990, 10.
30. Michael A. Snyder, Letter to Craig Branch, March 5, 1991, 2.
31. Michael A. Snyder, Phone interview with Watchman Fellowship, April 12, 1991.
32. K. J. Stavrinides, *Reviews You Can Use*, January/February 1991.
33. David Hulme, Presentation to Trinity Evangelical Divinity School, 1991.
34. Joseph W. Tkach, "How Do You React to Change?" *The Worldwide News*, July 22, 1991, 4.
35. Ibid.
36. Ibid.
37. Joseph Tkach Jr., Letter to Glen Myers, November 12, 1991, 5-6.
38. Joseph W. Tkach, "Personal," *The Worldwide News*, December 23, 1991, 1.
39. *God Is …* (Worldwide Church of God, 1992), 15, 41.
40. Joseph W. Tkach, *The Worldwide News*, August 25, 1992.
41. Joseph W. Tkach, "Personal," *The Worldwide News*, August 3, 1993, 3, 6.
42. Joseph W. Tkach, "Personal," *The Worldwide News*, August 17, 1993, 7.
43. Joseph Tkach Jr., Letter to a former member of the Worldwide Church of God, March 16, 1992, 5. The individual's name was redacted from the letter.
44. Ibid.
45. Joseph Tkach, *Transformed by Truth* (Sisters, OR: Multnomah Publishers, 1997), 137.
46. Ibid., 138.
47. Joseph Tkach Jr., Letter to a former member of the Worldwide Church of God, March 16, 1992, 5. The individual's name was redacted from the letter.
48. Joseph Tkach, *Transformed by Truth* (Sisters, OR: Multnomah Publishers, 1997), 96.
49. Ibid., 16.
50. Ibid., 19.
51. Ibid., 24.
52. Joseph Tkach Jr., Letter to a former member of the Worldwide Church of God, March 16, 1992, 8. The individual's name was redacted from the letter.

53. Joseph Tkach, *Transformed by Truth* (Sisters, OR: Multnomah Publishers, 1997), 119.
54. Ibid., 126.
55. Ibid., 21.
56. Ibid., 52-53.
57. Ibid., 54.

CHAPTER 11: DEATHBED REPENTANCE

1.   Joseph W. Tkach, "Personal," *The Worldwide News*, May 21, 1990, 6.
2.   Ibid.
3.   Joseph W. Tkach, Co-worker letter, part 2, January 16, 1986, 2.
4.   Joseph W. Tkach, "He Remembered You," *The Plain Truth*, November/ December 1986, 1.
5.   Ibid., 1, 4.
6.   Joseph W. Tkach, "Personal," *The Worldwide News*, May 21, 1990, 6.
7.   Joseph Tkach Jr., Letter to Glen Myers, November 12, 1991, 2.
8.   Joseph W. Tkach, Video to be played in all church areas, November, 1992.
9.   Ibid.
10. Ibid.
11. Worldwide Church of God, "Behind the Work," Fall Festival Film, 1985.
12. Herbert W. Armstrong, Co-worker letter, September 12, 1985, 1.
13. Herbert W. Armstrong, Co-worker letter, November 25, 1985, 1.
14. Joseph W. Tkach Jr., Letter to Dennis Leap, April 20, 1990, 1.
15. Worldwide Church of God, "Behind the Work," Fall Festival Film, 1985.
16. Herbert W. Armstrong, Letter to *Mystery of the Ages* recipients, 1985.
17. Joseph Tkach Jr., Letter to a former member of the Worldwide Church of God, September 26, 1990, 1. The individual's name was redacted from the letter.
18. David G. Hunsberger, "What the Church teaches about Malachi and his message," *The Worldwide News*, June 24, 1991, 6.
19. Joseph Tkach Jr., Letter to a former member of the Worldwide Church of God, March 16, 1992, 4. The individual's name was redacted from the letter.
20. Joseph Tkach Jr., Letter to a former member of the Worldwide Church of God, September 14, 1994, 5. The individual's name was redacted from the letter.
21. Ibid., 5.
22. Joseph Tkach, *Transformed by Truth* (Sisters, OR: Multnomah Publishers, 1997), 126.
23. Ibid., 184.
24. Ibid.
25. Ibid., 107.
26. Joseph Tkach Jr., Letter to a former member of the Worldwide Church of

God, March 16, 1992, 3. The individual's name was redacted from the letter.

27. David G. Hunsberger, "What the Church teaches about Malachi and his message," *The Worldwide News*, June 24, 1991, 6.

28. Worldwide Church of God, "Behind the Work," Fall Festival Film, 1985.

29. Joseph Tkach Jr., Letter to a former member of the Worldwide Church of God, March 16, 1992, 3. The individual's name was redacted from the letter.

30. "Herbert W. Armstrong Tribute," *The World Tomorrow* television program, January 26, 1986.

31. Joseph Tkach, *Transformed by Truth* (Sisters, OR: Multnomah Publishers, 1997), 184-85.

32. Herbert W. Armstrong, Co-worker letter, September 12, 1985, 1.

33. Herbert W. Armstrong, *Mystery of the Ages* (New York: Dodd, Mead & Company, 1985), xii.

34. Joseph Tkach, "Forgive Us Our Trespasses," *The Plain Truth*, March/April 1996, 1, 26.

35. *Transformed by Truth* advertisement, *The Plain Truth*, July/August 1997, inside cover.

36. Joseph W. Tkach, "Local churches to benefit from evangelical associations," *The Worldwide News*, February 18, 1997, 1.

CHAPTER 12: STEWARDSHIP

1. Joseph Tkach, *Transformed by Truth* (Sisters, OR: Multnomah Publishers, 1997), 165.

2. Ibid., 182.

3. Ibid., 184.

4. Ibid., 186.

5. Ibid.

6. Ibid., 188.

7. Ibid.

8. Ibid., 72.

9. Joseph W. Tkach, *Pastor General's Report*, December 16, 1986, 3.

10. Ibid.

11. Ibid., 1.

12. Herbert W. Armstrong, Co-worker letter, May 16, 1985, 2.

13. Joseph W. Tkach, *Pastor General's Report*, December 16, 1986, 3-4.

14. Joseph W. Tkach, *Pastor General's Report*, December 30, 1986, 3.

15. Joseph W. Tkach, *Pastor General's Report*, December 16, 1986, 3.

16. *Pastor General's Report*, November 17, 1987, 13.

17. *The Worldwide News*, May 11, 1987, 3. The Treasurer's Office report notes that the 1986 audit reported a 11.2 percent increase over 1985, though it did not give the actual income figures. But based on the 1985 income of $163.7 million, which we established in chapter 1, an 11.2 percent increase means the 1986 income was just over $182 million.

18. Larry R. Salyer, *Pastor General's Report*, May 26, 1987, 5.

19. *The Plain Truth*, May 1987, table of contents.
20. *The Plain Truth*, June 1987, table of contents.
21. Joseph W. Tkach, *Pastor General's Report*, June 24, 1987, 1.
22. Joseph W. Tkach, *Pastor General's Report*, December 1, 1987, 1.
23. Gerald Waterhouse, Sermon, Tallahassee FL, January 25, 1992.
24. Joseph W. Tkach, *Pastor General's Report*, January 26, 1988, 1.
25. Worldwide Audited Financial Report, *The Worldwide News*, August 28, 1989, 7.
26. Jeff E. Zhorne, "Look for ways to improve, says Mr. Tkach at conference," *The Worldwide News*, July 11, 1988, 1.
27. Worldwide Audited Financial Report, *The Worldwide News*, August 28, 1989, 7.
28. Leroy Neff, "Report from the Treasurer's Office," *The Worldwide News*, January 9, 1989, 3.
29. *Pastor General's Report*, February 28, 1989, 8.
30. Joseph W. Tkach, *Pastor General's Report*, January 3, 1989, 1.
31. Joseph W. Tkach, "Personal," *The Worldwide News*, January 23, 1989, 8.
32. Joseph W. Tkach, "Personal," *The Worldwide News*, January 4, 1988, 1.
33. Joseph W. Tkach, *Pastor General's Report*, October 25, 1988, 4.
34. Jeff E. Zhorne, "Mr. Tkach travels to Pacific regions, Asia," *The Worldwide News*, January 18, 1988, 1.
35. Ibid., 3.
36. Aaron Dean, *The Worldwide News*, March 18, 1985, 1, 3.
37. Jeff E. Zhorne, "Mr. Tkach attends gala event, meets Washington brethren," *The Worldwide News*, December 26, 1988, 1.
38. Joseph W. Tkach, "Personal," *The Worldwide News*, April 17, 1989, 1, 4.
39. Joseph W. Tkach, "Personal," *The Worldwide News*, May 8, 1989, 1, 7.
40. Joseph W. Tkach, Co-worker letter, May 25, 1989.
41. Joseph W. Tkach, "Personal," *The Worldwide News*, September 11, 1989, 1.
42. Ibid., 3.
43. Worldwide Audited Financial Report, *The Worldwide News*, September 2, 1991, 6.
44. Joseph W. Tkach, "Personal," *The Worldwide News*, January 22, 1990, 1.
45. Bill Palmer, "Telecast takes top spot, airs on better stations," *The Worldwide News*, March 19, 1990, 6.
46. David Hulme, "1985: year of media expansion," *The Worldwide News*, January 27, 1986, 7.
47. Joseph W. Tkach, Co-worker letter, July 26, 1990.
48. Joseph W. Tkach, "Personal," *The Worldwide News*, June 19, 1989, 1.
49. Joseph W. Tkach, Co-worker letter, September 25, 1990.
50. Herbert W. Armstrong, *Autobiography of Herbert W. Armstrong*, Vol. 2 (Pasadena, CA: Worldwide Church of God, 1987), 268.
51. Joseph W. Tkach, "Personal," *The Worldwide News*, January 14, 1991, 11.
52. *The Good News*, January/February 1990, table of contents.
53. Joseph W. Tkach, "Personal," *The Worldwide News*, January 14, 1991, 11.
54. Joseph W. Tkach, *Pastor General's Report*, August 18, 1987, 2.

55. Joseph W. Tkach, "Personal," *The Worldwide News*, September 19, 1988, 1.
56. Worldwide Audited Financial Report, *The Worldwide News*, September 2, 1991, 6.
57. Worldwide Audited Financial Report, *The Worldwide News*, July 28, 1992, 7.
58. Worldwide Audited Financial Report, *The Worldwide News*, September 2, 1991, 6.
59. Ibid.
60. Joseph W. Tkach, *Pastor General's Report*, March 27, 1990, 2.
61. Worldwide Audited Financial Report, *The Worldwide News*, August 28, 1989, 7.
62. Worldwide Audited Financial Report, *The Worldwide News*, September 2, 1991, 6.
63. Philippians 3:8.
64. Joseph Tkach, *Transformed by Truth* (Sisters, OR: Multnomah Publishers, 1997), 72.
65. Income for 1981 was reported in the February 5, 1982, *Pastor General's Report*, page 3. The 1982 and 1983 figures appear in the Worldwide Audited Financial Report, published in *The Worldwide News*, June 4, 1984, page 6. The next published audit we found was from 1987, when the WCG had a total income of $192 million (*The Worldwide News*, August 28, 1989, page 7). See note 5 from chapter 1 to see how we calculated WCG income for 1985 and 1986. And since the income for 1985 ($163.7 million) was 10.8 percent above 1984 (*Worldwide News*, June 16, 1986, page 3), then total revenue in 1984 was about $147.8 million.
66. See note 5 for chapter 1 to see how we calculated total income for 1986. For all four years after 1986, the WCG published its audited financial information in the *Worldwide News*. *For 1987*, see August 28, 1989, page 7. *For 1988*, see July 16, 1990, page 3. *For 1989*, see September 2, 1991, page 6. *And for 1990*, see July 28, 1992, page 7.
67. Joseph Tkach, *Transformed by Truth* (Sisters, OR: Multnomah Publishers, 1997), 71.
68. *For 1991 income figures*, see *Worldwide News*, July 6, 1993, page 7. *For 1992 and 1993*, see *Worldwide News*, June 28, 1994, page 7. *For 1994*, Tkach Jr. wrote in *Transformed by Truth* that it was $164.6 million (page 72). He also indicated that income for 1995, after "The Sermon," dropped to $103.4 million. This last figure, however, contradicts what was reported in *The Worldwide News* just before the release of Tkach's book. The February 18, 1997, issue reported that income in 1995 was about $20 million less than 1994. This would have put the 1995 income at around $145 million. I decided to use the figure from Tkach's book.
69. Worldwide Audited Financial Report, *The Worldwide News*, August 28, 1989, 7.
70. Joseph Tkach, "Member donations fund discretionary assistance ministry," *The Worldwide News*, March 2003, 6.
71. Ibid.
72. Ronald Kelly, "April donations continue positive," *The Worldwide News*, June 2004, 24.

73. Herbert W. Armstrong, Co-worker letter, May 15, 1979, 1.
74. Herbert W. Armstrong, *Autobiography of Herbert W. Armstrong*, Vol. 2 (Pasadena, CA: Worldwide Church of God, 1987), 591.
75. Philippians 1:23.
76. Herbert W. Armstrong, "Recent History of the Philadelphia Era of the Worldwide Church of God," *The Worldwide News*, June 24, 1985, special edition, 4.
77. Herbert W. Armstrong, Co-worker letter, March 29, 1971, 3.
78. Herbert W. Armstrong, *Autobiography of Herbert W. Armstrong*, Vol. 1 (Pasadena, CA: Worldwide Church of God, 1986), 43.
79. Herbert W. Armstrong, "Where This Breakdown of Family Life Is Taking Us!" *The Good News*, February 1979, 1.
80. Herbert W. Armstrong, Co-worker letter, November 25, 1985, 1.
81. Joseph Tkach, "He Remembered You," *The Plain Truth*, November/December 1986, 1.
82. Herbert W. Armstrong, "Congress of leading ministers hears defined and reemphasized spiritual organization of church," *The Worldwide News*, March 6, 1981, 12.
83. Herbert W. Armstrong, Co-worker letter, September 29, 1968, 5.
84. "The Autobiography of Herbert W. Armstrong," *The Plain Truth*, November 1957, 17.
85. Last will and testament of Herbert W. Armstrong, January 12, 1986.
86. Ibid.
87. Ibid.
88. Matthew 10:37.
89. Mark 3:33-34.
90. John 9:4.
91. Matthew 22:37.
92. Acts 20:35.
93. Herbert W. Armstrong, "Recent history of the Philadelphia Era of the Worldwide Church of God," *The Worldwide News*, June 24, 1985, special edition, 4.
94. Ibid.

CHAPTER 13: BREAKING GROUND

1. Michael A. Snyder, "Pastor general conducts services for 5,130 on Sabbath, Holy Day," *The Worldwide News*, June 30, 1986, 1.
2. Revelation 3:15.
3. Revelation 3:17.
4. Herman L. Hoeh, *A True History of the True Church* (Radio Church of God, 1959), 31.
5. Herbert W. Armstrong, "What God Never Did—Never Will—Allow to Happen," *The Good News*, August 1979, 27.
6. Joseph W. Tkach, *Pastor General's Report*, February 14, 1989, 1.
7. Joseph W. Tkach, *Pastor General's Report*, December 19, 1989, 2.

8. Ibid., 2-3.
9. Ibid., 3.

CHAPTER 14: FIRST SIP OF A BITTER CUP

1. Deposition of Joseph Tkach at 145, *Worldwide Church of God v. Philadelphia Church of God*, No. CV-97-5306-JSL (C.D. Cal. April 20, 1999).
2. Joseph Tkach Jr., Disfellowship notice for Gerald Flurry, December 8, 1989.
3. Deposition of Joseph Tkach at 146, *Worldwide Church of God v. Philadelphia Church of God*, No. CV-97-5306-JSL (C.D. Cal. April 20, 1999).
4. *Id.* at 151-52.
5. *Id.* at 156-57.
6. Arnold Clauson, Interoffice memo to Joseph Tkach Jr., December 14, 1989, 1.
7. Ibid., 2.
8. Ralph K. Helge, Letter to Gerald Flurry, December 7, 1989, 1-2.
9. Joseph Tkach Jr., Letter to Gerald Flurry, December 11, 1989.
10. Gerald Flurry, Letter to Ralph Helge, December 21, 1989, 1.
11. Joseph Tkach Jr., Letter to Gerald Flurry, January 23, 1990.
12. Gerald Flurry, Letter to Oklahoma City and Enid Brethren, January 11, 1990, 1-2.

CHAPTER 15: PEANUT SHELL

1. *Pastor General's Report*, December 19, 1989, 6.
2. *Pastor General's Report*, January 30, 1990, 4.
3. Joseph W. Tkach, *Pastor General's Report*, November 14, 1990, 1.
4. Ibid., 2
5. Joseph W. Tkach, *Pastor General's Report*, December 11, 1990, 1.
6. Ibid., 2
7. Dean Blackwell, Sermon, Columbus OH, May 4, 1991.
8. Ibid.
9. Ibid.
10. Ibid.
11. Herbert W. Armstrong, Co-worker letter, March 19, 1981, 1.
12. Dean Blackwell, Sermon, Columbus OH, May 4, 1991.
13. Joseph W. Tkach, "Personal," *The Worldwide News*, June 24, 1991, 5.
14. David G. Hunsberger, "What the Church teaches about Malachi and his message," *The Worldwide News*, June 24, 1991, 4.
15. Ibid.
16. Gerald Waterhouse, Sermon, Tallahasee FL, January 25, 1992.
17. Matthew 16:18.
18. Hebrews 13:5, New King James version.
19. Joseph W. Tkach, Closing prayer at funeral service of Herbert W. Armstrong, Pasadena CA, January 19, 1986.

20. J. Michael Feazell, *The Liberation of the Worldwide Church of God* (Grand Rapids, MI: Zondervan, 2001), 109.

CHAPTER 16: "LARGEST AUDIENCE POSSIBLE"

1. Herbert W. Armstrong, Co-worker letter, February 25, 1985, 1-2.
2. Ibid., 2.
3. Herbert W. Armstrong, *Mystery of the Ages* (New York: Dodd, Mead & Company, 1985), 5.
4. Joseph W. Tkach, *Pastor General's Report*, April 19, 1985, 1.
5. Richard Rice, *Pastor General's Report*, April 19, 1985, 6.
6. Joseph W. Tkach, *Pastor General's Report*, June 7, 1985, 2.
7. Herbert W. Armstrong, Presentation of *Mystery of the Ages* to the sophomore class, Ambassador College, September 9, 1985.
8. Herbert W. Armstrong, *Mystery of the Ages* (New York: Dodd, Mead & Company, 1985), xi.
9. *Pastor General's Report*, July 22, 1986, 3.
10. Gerald Flurry, *Malachi's Message* (Philadelphia Church of God, 1990), 24.
11. Dennis Leap, Ministerial Conference lecture, Edmond OK, May 31, 1994.
12. Gerald Flurry, *Philadelphia Ministers' Report*, February 9, 1996, 1.
13. Michael A. Snyder, "Mystery of the Ages completed; printing begins in U.S. facilities," *The Worldwide News*, August 5, 1985, 1.
14. Ibid.
15. *Mystery of the Ages* advertisement, *The Wall Street Journal*, March 18, 1997, 3.
16. Worldwide Church of God, "Behind the Work," Fall Festival Film, 1985.
17. Herbert W. Armstrong, Co-worker letter, September 12, 1985, 1.
18. Joseph W. Tkach, Co-worker letter, part 2, January 16, 1986, 2.
19. Joseph W. Tkach, "He Remembered You," *The Plain Truth*, November/December 1986, 1.
20. Ibid., 1, 4.
21. Herbert W. Armstrong, Presentation of *Mystery of the Ages* to the sophomore class, Ambassador College, September 9, 1985.
22. *Mystery of the Ages* advertisement, *The Philadelphia Trumpet*, January 1997, back cover.
23. Gerald Flurry, Sermon, Edmond OK, January 4, 1997.
24. Ibid.
25. Gerald Flurry, "The Largest Audience Possible," *The Philadelphia Trumpet*, February 1997, front cover, 1-2.
26. Ibid, 2.

CHAPTER 17: BATTLE LINES DRAWN

1. Ralph K. Helge, Letter to Gerald Flurry, January 21, 1997.
2. Complaint for Damages and Injunctive Relief Against Copyright

Infringement and Related Claims, and for Unjust Enrichment at 4, *Worldwide Church of God v. Philadelphia Church of God*, No. CV-97-875-JSL (C.D. Cal. April 20, 1999).

3. Benjamin Scheibe, Letter to Philadelphia Church of God, February 11, 1997, 1.
4. Terry Moyer, Letter to Benjamin D. Scheibe, February 12, 1997.
5. Application for TRO Transcript of Proceedings at 4, *Worldwide Church of God v. Philadelphia Church of God*, No. CV-97-875-JSL (C.D. Cal. recorded February 18, 1997).
6. *Id.* at 5.
7. *Id.* at 22.
8. *Id.* at 12.
9. *Id.* at 22.
10. Complaint for Damages and Injunctive Relief Against Copyright Infringement and Related Claims, and for Unjust Enrichment at 2, *Worldwide Church of God v. Philadelphia Church of God*, No. CV-97-875-JSL (C.D. Cal. April 20, 1999)
11. Deposition of Ralph Helge at 23-24, 30, 44-45, *Worldwide Church of God v. Philadelphia Church of God*, No. CV-97-5306-JSL (C.D. Cal. April 20, 1999).
12. Herbert W. Armstrong, "Congress of leading ministers hears defined and reemphasized spiritual organization of church," *The Worldwide News*, March 6, 1981, 8.
13. Ibid.
14. Deposition of Ralph Helge at 104, *Worldwide Church of God v. Philadelphia Church of God*, No. CV-97-5306-JSL (C.D. Cal. April 20, 1999).
15. *Id.* at 109.
16. *Id.* at 120.
17. *Id.* at 125.
18. Joseph Tkach, *Transformed by Truth* (Sisters, OR: Multnomah Publishers, 1997), 184-85.
19. Motion for Preliminary Injunction For Copyright Infringement and Brief in Support at 3, *Worldwide Church of God v. Philadelphia Church of God*, No. CIV-97-0299 M (W.D. Okla. filed March 24, 1997).
20. *Id.* at 6.
21. *Id.*
22. *Mystery of the Ages* advertisement, *Los Angeles Times*, March 18, 1997, 14.
23. Ibid.
24. Joseph Tkach, *Transformed by Truth* (Sisters, OR: Multnomah Publishers, 1997), 203.

CHAPTER 18: ROUND ONE: PCG

1. *Ex Parte* Application of Defendant Philadelphia Church of God To Transfer Venue at 1, *Worldwide Church of God v. Philadelphia Church of God*, No. CIV-97-0299-M (W.D. Okla. filed March 24, 1997).
2. Worldwide Church of God, Inc.'s Brief in Opposition to Defendant's

Application to Transfer Venue at 1, *Worldwide Church of God v. Philadelphia Church of God*, No. CIV-97-0299-M (W.D. Okla. filed March 24, 1997).

3. Answer and Counterclaim of Defendant Philadelphia Church of God at 9, *Worldwide Church of God v. Philadelphia Church of God*, No. CIV-97-0299-M (W.D. Okla. filed March 24, 1997).

4. Plaintiff's Motion to Dismiss and Supporting Brief at 4, *Worldwide Church of God v. Philadelphia Church of God*, No. CIV-97-0299-M (W.D. Okla. filed March 24, 1997).

5. Worldwide Church of God, Minutes of the Board of Directors, April 2, 1997, 5.

6. Stephen Flurry, "Lying Words," *The Philadelphia Trumpet*, November 1997, 20.

7. Greg Albrecht, E-mail to Ronnie Tallie, July 7, 1997.

8. Notice of Motion and Motion of Plaintiff Worldwide Church of God for Partial Summary Judgment at 7, *Worldwide Church of God v. Philadelphia Church of God*, No. CV-97-5306-JSL (C.D. April 20, 1999).

9. *Id.* at 21.

10. 17 U.S.C. § 107.

11. Deposition of Joseph Tkach at 22, *Worldwide Church of God v. Philadelphia Church of God*, No. CV-97-5306-JSL (C.D. Cal. April 20, 1999).

12. *Id.* at 28.

13. *Id.* at 30-31.

14. Deposition of Gregory Albrecht at 114, *Worldwide Church of God v. Philadelphia Church of God*, No. CV-97-5306-JSL (C.D. Cal. April 20, 1999).

15. Deposition of Joseph Tkach at 48, *Worldwide Church of God v. Philadelphia Church of God*, No. CV-97-5306-JSL (C.D. Cal. April 20, 1999).

16. Worldwide Church of God, Minutes of the Advisory Council of Elders of the Church of God an Unincorporated Association, December 4, 1998, 5.

17. Joseph Tkach, *Transformed by Truth* (Sisters, OR: Multnomah Publishers, 1997), 22.

18. Ibid., 15-16, 22.

19. Ruth Tucker, "From the Fringe to the Fold," *Christianity Today*, July 15, 1996, 27.

20. Worldwide Church of God, Minutes of the Advisory Council of Elders of the Church of God an Unincorporated Association, December 4, 1998, 5.

21. Joseph Tkach, *Transformed by Truth* (Sisters, OR: Multnomah Publishers, 1997), 98.

22. Worldwide Church of God, Minutes of the Advisory Council of Elders of the Church of God an Unincorporated Association, December 4, 1998, 7-8.

23. Motion for Preliminary Injunction at 4-5, *Worldwide Church of God v. Philadelphia Church of God*, No. CV-97-5306-JSL (C.D. Cal. April 20, 1999).

24. *Id.* at 8.

25. *Id.*

26. Order and Judgment Denying Plaintiff's Motion for Partial Summary Judgment and Motion for Preliminary Injunction and Granting

Defendant's Motion for Summary Adjudication at 2, *Worldwide Church of God v. Philadelphia Church of God*, No. CV-97-5306-JSL (C.D. Cal. April 20, 1999).

27. Gerald Flurry, Sermon, Edmond OK, February 13, 1999.

28. Gerald Flurry, "Victory in Court!" *The Philadelphia Trumpet*, March/April 1999, 1.

CHAPTER 19: ROUND TWO: WCG

1. Deposition of Ralph Helge at 30, *Worldwide Church of God v. Philadelphia Church of God*, No. CV-97-5306-JSL (C.D. Cal. April 20, 1999).

2. Appellant's Opening Brief at 6, 22, *Worldwide Church of God v. Philadelphia Church of God*, 227 F.3d 1110 (9th Cir. 2000) (nos. 99-55850, 99-55934, 99-56005).

3. *Id*. at 43.

4. *Id*.

5. Appellee's Answering Brief at 7, 39-40, *Worldwide Church of God v. Philadelphia Church of God*, 227 F.3d 1110 (9th Cir. 2000) (nos. 99-55850, 99-55934, 99-56005).

6. *Id*. at 26.

7. *Id*. at 33.

8. Partial Transcript of Oral Arguments on Dec. 6, 1999, *Worldwide Church of God v. Philadelphia Church of God*, 227 F.3d 1110 (9th Cir. 2000) (No. 99-55850).

9. Literature Coordination Report 21, December 2, 1988, 1.

10. Joseph W. Tkach, *Pastor General's Report*, February 14, 1989, 1.

11. Worldwide Church of God, Minutes of the Advisory Council of Elders of the Church of God an Unincorporated Association, December 4, 1998, 7.

12. Joseph Tkach, *Transformed by Truth* (Sisters, OR: Multnomah Publishers, 1997), 203.

13. Matthew 7:20.

14. Partial Transcript of Oral Arguments on Dec. 6, 1999, *Worldwide Church of God v. Philadelphia Church of God*, 227 F.3d 1110 (9th Cir. 2000) (No. 99-55850).

15. *Id*.

16. *Id*.

17. *Id*.

18. *Id*.

19. *Id*.

20. Colossians 1:26.

21. *Worldwide Church of God v. Philadelphia Church of God*, 227 F.3d 1110, 1113 (9th Cir. 2000) *cert. denied*, 532 U.S. 958 (2001).

22. Appellant's Opening Brief at 7, *Worldwide Church of God v. Philadelphia Church of God*, Inc., 227 F.3d 1110 (9th Cir. 2000) (nos. 99-55850, 99-55934, 99-56005).

23. *Worldwide Church of God, v. Philadelphia Church of God*, 227 F.3d 1110, 1118 (9th Cir. 2000) *cert. denied*, 532 U.S. 958 (2001).
24. *Id.*
25. *Id.* at 1118-19.
26. Matthew 23:23.
27. *Worldwide Church of God, v. Philadelphia Church of God*, 227 F.3d 1110, 1119 (9th Cir. 2000) *cert. denied*, 532 U.S. 958 (2001).
28. *Id.* at 1122.
29. *Worldwide Church of God, v. Philadelphia Church of God*, 227 F.3d 1110, 1122 (9th Cir. 2000) (Brunetti, C. J., dissenting) *cert. denied*, 532 U.S. 958 (2001).
30. *Id.* at 1124.
31. *Id.* at 1124-1125.
32. Gerald Flurry, Sermon, Edmond OK, September 23, 2000.
33. Ibid.
34. Ralph K. Helge, "Court rules in favor of WCG in copyright infringement case," *The Worldwide News*, October 2000.
35. Ralph K. Helge, "Court denies PCG plea in copyright case," *The Worldwide News*, December 2000.
36. Ibid.
37. Ibid.
38. To be heard again, at least one judge had to step forward and call for a vote among all 27. If that happened, 14 of the 27 judges (a simple majority) must then vote in favor of hearing the case again. Assuming it got that far, an 11-judge panel would then be selected randomly from among the 27 to hear the case again. From there, a majority ruling would overturn the decision.
39. Gerald Flurry, sermon, Edmond OK, September 23, 2000.
40. Ibid.

CHAPTER 20: COUNTERCLAIM TO THE RESCUE

1. "Our Christian Duty," *The Philadelphia Trumpet*, November 2000, front cover, 5.
2. *The United States and Britain in Prophecy* advertisement, *The Philadelphia Trumpet*, January 2001, 14-15.
3. *The Missing Dimension in Sex* advertisement, *The Philadelphia Trumpet*, February 2001, 14-15.
4. Bill Stough, "Mystery of the Ages: WCG and PCG settle after six years of bitter battle over HWA book," *The Journal*, March 31, 2003, 1.
5. Bill Stough, "WSJ Reporter says suit story one of a kind," *The Journal*, February 28, 2001.
6. Jess Bravin, "Bad Tithings: Sect Disavows Tenets, And Woe to Him Who Printeth Them Anyway," *The Wall Street Journal*, February 21, 2001, A1.
7. Bill Stough, "The Wall Street Journal gives WCG-PCG Mystery of the Ages story wide front-page play," *The Journal*, February 28, 2001.

8. "Pastor General comments on Wall Street Journal article," *The Worldwide News*, April 2001.
9. Bill Stough, "The Wall Street Journal gives WCG-PCG Mystery of the Ages story wide front-page play," *The Journal*, February 28, 2001.
10. *The Harvard Law Review,* April 2001, 1807.
11. Ibid., 1810-11.
12. Ibid., 1810.
13. *Worldwide Church of God v. Philadelphia Church of God* at 26, 532 U.S. 958 (2001).
14. Deposition of Gregory Albrecht at 169, *Worldwide Church of God v. Philadelphia Church of God*, No. CV-97-5306-JSL (C.D. Cal. April 20, 1999).
15. Greg Albrecht, E-mail to Ronnie Tallie, July 7, 1997.
16. Worldwide Church of God, Minutes of the Board of Directors, June 19, 2001.
17. Matthew H. Morgan, Letter to Gerald Flurry, October 19, 2001, 1.
18. Ibid., 1-2.
19. Allan Browne, Letter to Mark Helm, October 31, 2001.
20. Order at 19, *Worldwide Church of God v. Philadelphia Church of God*, No. CV-97-5306-CAS (C.D. Cal. entered Nov. 15, 2001).

CHAPTER 21: THE INFAMOUS PREFACE
1. Gerald Flurry, Letter to Matthew H. Morgan, March 14, 2002, 2.
2. Ibid.
3. Matthew H. Morgan, Letter to Gerald Flurry, April 8, 2002, 1.
4. Ibid, 2.
5. Gerald Flurry, Sermon, Edmond OK, April 6, 2002.
6. Dennis Leap, "Continuing to Fight," *The Philadelphia Trumpet*, February 2002, 27.
7. Matthew H. Morgan, Letter to Gerald Flurry, April 8, 2002, 2.
8. Worldwide Church of God, Intended preface to the e-publishing works, 2002, 1.
9. Ibid.
10. Ibid.
11. 2 Corinthians 4:4.
12. Revelation 12:9.
13. 1 Timothy 2:4; 2 Peter 3:9.
14. John 3:16.
15. Worldwide Church of God, Intended preface to the e-publishing works, 2002, 3.
16. Joseph Tkach, *Transformed by Truth* (Sisters, OR: Multnomah Publishers, 1997), 130-31.
17. Worldwide Church of God, Intended preface to the e-publishing works, 2002, 3.
18. David Hulme, Letter of resignation to Joseph Tkach, April 17, 1995, 5.

19. Worldwide Church of God, Intended preface to the e-publishing works, 2002, 2.
20. Joseph Tkach Jr., Letter to a former member of the Worldwide Church of God, June 29, 1990. The individual's name was redacted from the letter.
21. Herbert W. Armstrong, *The Plain Truth About Healing* (Worldwide Church of God, 1979), 65.
22. Worldwide Church of God, Intended preface to the e-publishing works, 2002, 3.

CHAPTER 22: OFFENSIVE WARFARE

1. Gerald Flurry, Letter to PCG lawyers, June 11, 2002.
2. Worldwide Church of God, Minutes of The Advisory Council of Elders of the Church of God an Unincorporated Association, December 4, 1998, 6-7.
3. Deposition of Joseph Tkach at 320, *Worldwide Church of God v. Philadelphia Church of God*, No. CV-97-5306-CAS (C.D. Cal. dismissed April 14, 2003).
4. *Id.* at 337.
5. *Id.* at 338.
6. Joseph Tkach, *Transformed by Truth* (Sisters, OR: Multnomah Publishers, 1997), 121.
7. Ibid., 98.
8. Ibid., 183.
9. Joseph Tkach Jr., Letter to a former member of the Worldwide Church of God, March 16, 1992, 1. The individual's name was redacted from the letter.
10. Joseph Tkach, Sermon, Pasadena CA, January 18, 1986.
11. Deposition of Joseph Tkach at 418, *Worldwide Church of God v. Philadelphia Church of God*, No. CV-97-5306-CAS (C.D. Cal. dismissed April 14, 2003).
12. Joseph Tkach, *Transformed by Truth* (Sisters, OR: Multnomah Publishers, 1997), 184.
13. Deposition of Joseph Tkach at 453-54, *Worldwide Church of God v. Philadelphia Church of God*, No. CV-97-5306-CAS (C.D. Cal. dismissed April 14, 2003).
14. *Id.* at 408.
15. *Id.* at 409.
16. *Id.* at 475-76.
17. *Id.* at 476.
18. *Id.* at 321.
19. *Id.* at 322.
20. *Id.*
21. *Id.* at 323.
22. J. Michael Feazell, *The Liberation of the Worldwide Church of God* (Grand Rapids, MI: Zondervan Publishing House, 2001), 108-09.

23. Deposition of J. Michael Feazell at 72, *Worldwide Church of God v. Philadelphia Church of God*, No. CV-97-5306-CAS (C.D. Cal. dismissed April 14, 2003).

24. *Id.* at 75.

25. *Id.* at 76-77.

26. *Id.* at 77.

27. *Id.* at 96.

28. J. Michael Feazell, *The Liberation of the Worldwide Church of God* (Grand Rapids, MI: Zondervan Publishing House, 2001), 43.

29. Ibid., 42.

30. Ibid., 45.

31. Deposition of J. Michael Feazell at 236-37, *Worldwide Church of God v. Philadelphia Church of God*, No. CV-97-5306-CAS (C.D. Cal. dismissed April 14, 2003).

32. J. Michael Feazell, *The Liberation of the Worldwide Church of God* (Grand Rapids, MI: Zondervan Publishing House, 2001), 107.

33. Deposition of J. Michael Feazell at 230, *Worldwide Church of God v. Philadelphia Church of God*, No. CV-97-5306-CAS (C.D. Cal. dismissed April 14, 2003).

34. *Id.*

35. Deposition of Ron Kelly at 130, *Worldwide Church of God v. Philadelphia Church of God*, No. CV-97-5306-CAS (C.D. Cal. dismissed April 14, 2003).

36. Joseph Tkach, *Transformed by Truth* (Sisters, OR: Multnomah Publishers, 1997), 182-83.

37. Ron Kelly, "Principles of Living," Sermon Scripts S85-33, 1987, 1.

38. Ibid., 2.

39. Deposition of Ron Kelly at 191, *Worldwide Church of God v. Philadelphia Church of God*, No. CV-97-5306-CAS (C.D. Cal. dismissed April 14, 2003).

40. Ron Kelly, "Principles of Living" Sermon Scripts S85-33, 1987, 38.

41. Ronald D. Kelly, "Keeping God's Feasts Yesterday and Today," *The Good News*, September 1985, 14.

42. Ralph K. Helge, "Church faces massive crisis," *The Worldwide News*, January 15, 1979, 2.

43. Ibid.

44. Deposition of Ralph Helge at 271, *Worldwide Church of God v. Philadelphia Church of God*, No. CV-97-5306-CAS (C.D. Cal. dismissed April 14, 2003).

45. "Transcript of Mr. Helge's comments from Aug. 25," *The Worldwide News*, September 10, 1979, 8.

46. Deposition of Ralph Helge at 94, *Worldwide Church of God v. Philadelphia Church of God*, No. CV-97-5306-CAS (C.D. Cal. dismissed April 14, 2003).

47. Ralph K. Helge, Letter to Zondervan Publishing, February 16, 2001.

48. Deposition of Ralph Helge at 87, *Worldwide Church of God v. Philadelphia Church of God*, No. CV-97-5306-CAS (C.D. Cal. dismissed April 14, 2003).

49. *Id.* at 171.

50. Deposition of Bernard William Schnippert at 53, *Worldwide Church of God v. Philadelphia Church of God*, No. CV-97-5306-CAS (C.D. Cal. dismissed April 14, 2003).
51. *Id.* at 75.
52. *Id.* at 57.
53. *Id.* at 79.
54. *Id.* at 122.
55. *Id.* at 129-30.
56. *Id.* at 134.
57. *Id.* at 139.
58. *Id.* at 139-40.

CHAPTER 23: © PHILADELPHIA CHURCH OF GOD

1. Ralph K. Helge, Letter to Bob Ardis, August 13, 2002, 1.
2. Ibid.
3. Mark Helm, Letter to Ralph K. Helge, September 18, 2002.
4. Deposition of Stephen Flurry at 136, *Worldwide Church of God v. Philadelphia Church of God*, No. CV-97-5306-CAS (C.D. Cal. dismissed April 14, 2003).
5. *Id.* at 137.
6. Gerald Flurry, Feast of Tabernacles sermon, Edmond OK, September 22, 2002.
7. Gerald Flurry, Feast of Tabernacles sermon, Ogden UT, September 27, 2002.
8. Bill Stough, "WCG, to affirm its right, will reprint *Mystery* book," *The Journal*, October 31, 2002, 1.
9. Ibid., 17.
10. Ibid.
11. Ibid.
12. Transcript of Oral Arguments at 11, *Worldwide Church of God v. Philadelphia Church of God*, No. CV-97-5306-CAS (C.D. Cal. dismissed April 14, 2003).
13. *Id.* at 12.
14. Crissey Economic Damages Preliminary Report at 2, *Worldwide Church of God v. Philadelphia Church of God*, No. CV-97-5306-CAS, (C.D. Cal. dismissed April 14, 2003).
15. Tentative Minute Order at 19, *Worldwide Church of God v. Philadelphia Church of God*, No. CV-97-5306 CAS (C.D. Cal. filed November 27, 2002).
16. Deposition of Bernard William Schnippert at 79, *Worldwide Church of God v. Philadelphia Church of God*, No. CV-97-5306-CAS (C.D. Cal. dismissed April 14, 2003).
17. Tucker Expert Report at 22, *Worldwide Church of God v. Philadelphia Church of God*, No. CV-97-5306-CAS (C.D. Cal. dismissed April 14, 2003).
18. *Id.* at 22-23.
19. *Id.* at 9.

20. Ruth Tucker, "From the Fringe to the Fold," *Christianity Today*, July 15, 1996.
21. Ibid.
22. Deposition of Ruth Tucker at 38, *Worldwide Church of God v. Philadelphia Church of God*, No. CV-97-5306-CAS (C.D. Cal. dismissed April 14, 2003).
23. *Id.* at 42.
24. Tucker Expert Report at 22, *Worldwide Church of God v. Philadelphia Church of God*, No. CV-97-5306-JSL (C.D. Cal. dismissed April 14, 2003).
25. Deposition of Ruth Tucker at 169-70. *Worldwide Church of God v. Philadelphia Church of God*, No. CV-97-5306-CAS (C.D. Cal. dismissed April 14, 2003).
26. *Id.* at 81.
27. *Id.* at 80-81.
28. *Id.* at 125.
29. Joseph Tkach, *Transformed by Truth* (Sisters, OR: Multnomah Publishers, 1997), 50.
30. Tentative Minute Order at 24, 26, *Worldwide Church of God v. Philadelphia Church of God*, No. CV-97-5306-CAS (C.D. Cal. entered November 27, 2002).
31. *Id.*
32. Ralph K. Helge, "WCG litigation settled," *The Worldwide News*, April 2003, 16.
33. Greg Albrecht, E-mail to Ronnie Tallie, July 7, 1997.
34. Ralph K. Helge, "WCG to appeal copyright ruling," *The Worldwide News*, March 1999, 18.
35. Ralph K. Helge, "Court rules in favor of WCG in copyright infringement case," *The Worldwide News*, October 2000.
36. Mark A. Kellner, "Unfair Use Alleged," *Christianity Today*, April 23, 2001, 15.
37. Bill Stough, "U.S. Supreme Court denies Philadelphia Church of God's petition for hearing," *The Journal*, April 30, 2001.
38. Marshall Allen, "Church Sells Armstrong's Works," *Christianity Today*, June 2003, 23.
39. Mark A. Kellner, "Unfair Use Alleged," *Christianity Today*, April 23, 2001, 15.
40. Phillip Arnn, "Jesus and the Law," *Watchman Expositor*, Vol. 10, No. 7, 1993, 17.
41. Marshall Allen, "Church Sells Armstrong's Works," *Christianity Today*, June 2003, 23.
42. Marshall Allen, "Closing the book; Settlement reached over texts," *Pasadena Star-News*, March 26, 2003.
43. Ibid.

CHAPTER 24: "VICTORY PROPHESIED"

1. Gerald Flurry, Sermon, Edmond OK, September 23, 2000.
2. Gerald Flurry, "Our Appeal to the Supreme Court," *The Philadelphia Trumpet*, March/April 2001, 1.

3. Gerald Flurry, *Unveiled At Last: The Royal Book of Revelation* (Philadelphia Church of God, 2001), 35.
4. Bill Stough, "Court allows PCG more time in WCG legal wrangle," *The Journal*, May 31, 2001.
5. Gerald Flurry, *Who Is "That Prophet"?* (Philadelphia Church of God, 2001), 86.
6. Ibid., 88.
7. Ibid., 89.
8. Gerald Flurry, *The God Family Vision* (Philadelphia Church of God, 2001), 98.
9. Ibid., 134.
10. Gerald Flurry, "Habakkuk Reveals the Outcome of Our Court Case," *Royal Vision*, September/October 2002, 3.
11. Ibid., 5.
12. Ibid., 13.
13. Gerald Flurry, Feast of Tabernacles sermon, Ogden UT, September 28, 2002.
14. Bill Stough, "Court allows PCG more time in WCG legal wrangle," *The Journal*, May 31, 2001.
15. Ralph K. Helge, Letter to Philadelphia Church of God, March 3, 2003.

CHAPTER 25: RAISING THE RUINS

1. Gerald Flurry, "Education Filled With Hope," *The Philadelphia Trumpet*, August 2000, 1.
2. Ibid., 2.
3. Ibid.
4. Ezra 5:2.
5. Psalms 127:1.
6. Herbert W. Armstrong, *Autobiography of Herbert W. Armstrong*, Vol. 2 (Pasadena, CA: Worldwide Church of God, 1987), 231-32.
7. Ibid., 232.
8. Herbert W. Armstrong, "and now ... Our Own New College!" *The Plain Truth*, January/February 1947, 8.
9. Ibid., 9.
10. Ibid.
11. Ibid.
12. Ibid., 10.
13. Ibid., 13.
14. Gerald Flurry, *Who Is "That Prophet"?* (Philadelphia Church of God, 2001), 91.
15. Joseph W. Tkach, "SACS Accredits Ambassador!" *The Worldwide News*, June 28, 1994, 1.
16. Ron Fraser, Letter to Gerald Flurry, July 25, 1997.
17. Stephen Flurry, Letter to Gerald Flurry, April 18, 1998.
18. Ibid.
19. Joel Hilliker, "PCG Lands 38-Acre Deal," *The Philadelphia News*, July/August 2000, 4.

20. Gerald Flurry, Sermon, Edmond OK, September 23, 2000.
21. Ibid.
22. Stephen Flurry, Letter to Gerald Flurry, January 2001.
23. Gerald Flurry, Sermon, Edmond OK, February 17, 2001.
24. Gerald Flurry, Sermon, Edmond OK, February 24, 2000.
25. Herbert W. Armstrong, *Autobiography of Herbert W. Armstrong*, Vol. 2 (Pasadena, CA: Worldwide Church of God, 1987), 231.
26. Andrew Locher, "Treasurer's Report: expenditures, donations up," *The Philadelphia News*, September 2005, 1.
27. Herbert W. Armstrong, *Autobiography of Herbert W. Armstrong*, Vol. 2 (Pasadena, CA: Worldwide Church of God, 1987) 282.
28. Gerald Flurry, Sermon, Edmond OK, July 17, 2004.
29. Gary Scott, "Worldwide Church of God leaving Pasadena," *Pasadena Star-News*, October 25, 2004.
30. Michael Dattolo, "Headquarters Moves," *The Philadelphia News*, April 2006, 1.
31. Gerald Flurry, Sermon, Edmond OK, January 21, 2006.
32. Herbert W. Armstrong, "Here's Good News!" *The Good News*, April 1951, 1.
33. Herbert W. Armstrong, *United States and Britain in Prophecy* (Worldwide Church of God, 1980), 4.

INDEX

412   RAISING THE RUINS

identity of modern Assyria, 71-72,
94-95
identity of modern Babylon, 68-71,
94-95
identity of modern Ephraim and
Manasseh, 86-87
"lost century," 81
nature of God, *see trinity*
one true church, 139-140
theistic evolution, 101
trinity, 82, 133-138

Ending Your Financial Worries, 80

e-publishing, 284-285, 288-289, 294-295

Fair Use, 242, 247-248

Feazell, J. Michael, 43, 63, 65
ghost writing, 55-56, 58-59
preface to e-publishing works, 290-297
references to deposition, 7-8, 17,
302-303, 323
Tkach's personal assistant, 58-59

Flurry, Gerald
decision to print additional literature,
255-256
fired from WCG, 197-199, 206
getting "second wind," 342
last Feast sermon in WCG, 193
letter to Oklahoma and Enid brethren after being fired, 204-206
reaction to *Mystery of the Ages* being
discontinued, 187-188
sermons referred to, 224-225, 253,
271-272, 274, 289, 316-317,
335, 341, 353-354, 359-361
vision for 38 acres purchased, 346-347, 354-355
writing *Malachi's Message*, 188-191

Flurry, Stephen
initial reading of *Malachi's Message*,
190-191
job as tape librarian, 191
references to deposition, 314-315
transfer to Big Sandy, 187

government, 6-7, 10-11

Good News Magazine, 2, 18-19, 23, 136,
168, 177
discontinued, 4, 167
reduction in number of issues, 159-160

Gulfstream III, 162-164

Hanegraaff, Hank, 141-142

Harvard Law Review, 227-228

Helge, Ralph, 229
interview with *The Journal*, 319-320
letter he wrote to Bob Ardis, 313-315
references to 1998 depositions, 233-234
references to 2002 depositions, 306-308,
retirement, 307-308

Helm, Mark, 229, 232-233
"Gettysburg Address" before Ninth
Circuit, 260-262

Herbert W. Armstrong College, 355-359
first graduates, 363
renaming the college, 359

Herrington, Bob, 57-58

Hislop, Alexander, 118

Hulme, David,
resignation letter to Tkach, 83, 125-126, 293
discussions with Trinity Evangelical
Divinity School, 134-136

Imperial College, *see Herbert W.
Armstrong College*

Incredible Human Potential, 80-82, 95,
108, 120, 176, 255, 367-368

*Judah's Scepter and Joseph's Birthright, see
Allen, J.H.*

Kelly, Ronald, 64, 304-306
references to deposition, 303-305
comments on sale of property, 12